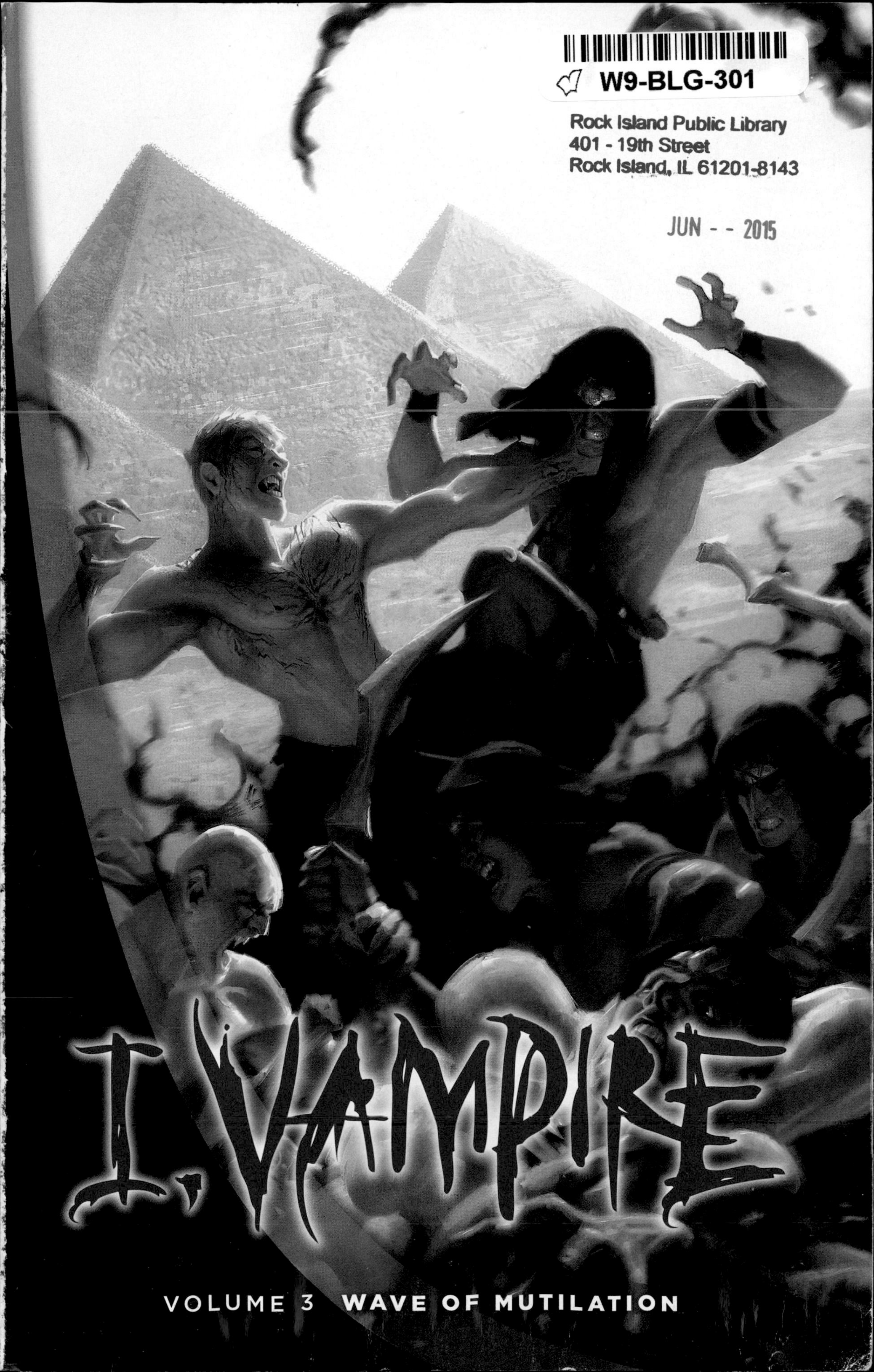
I, VAMPIRE
VOLUME 3 WAVE OF MUTILATION

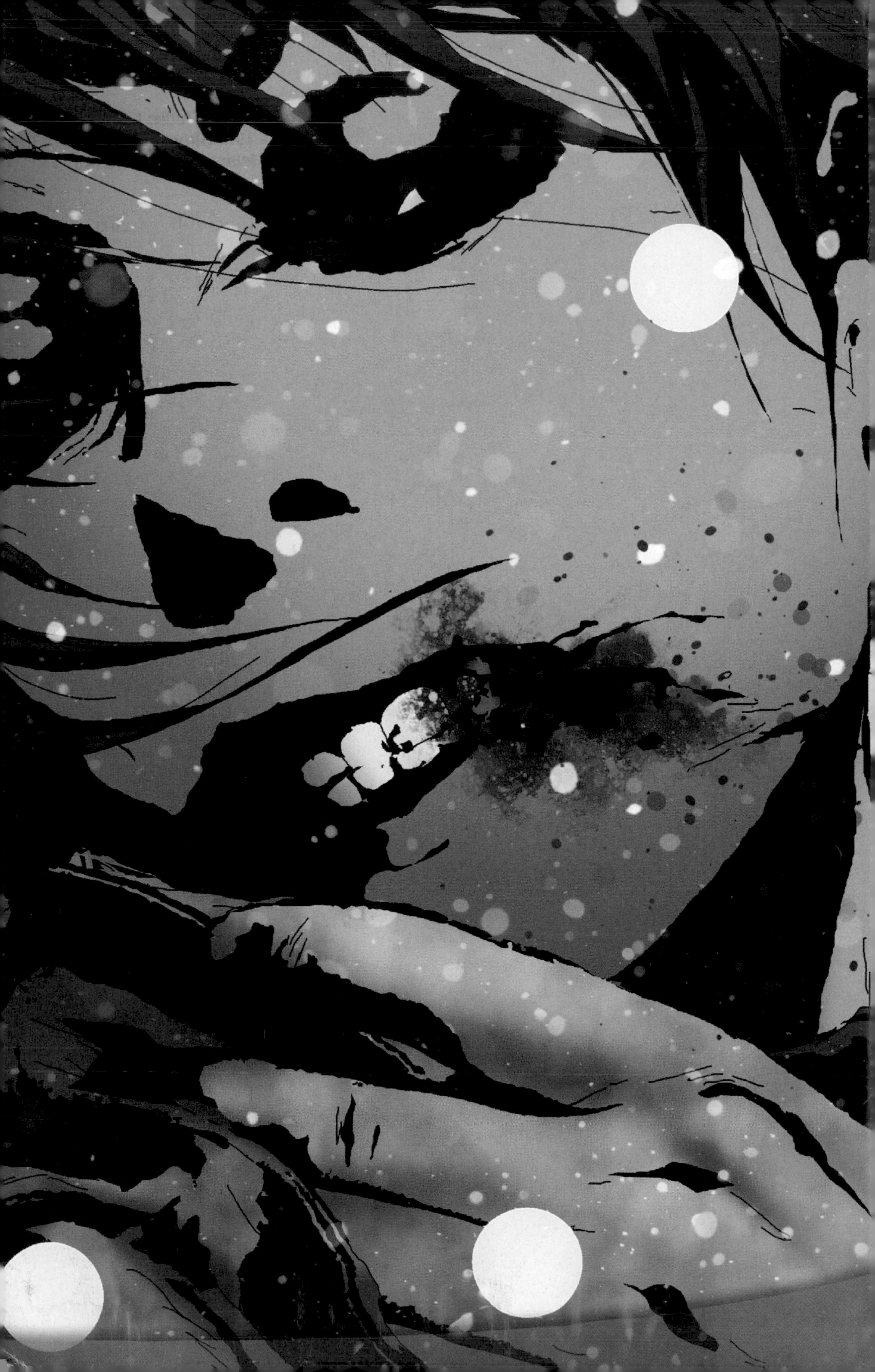

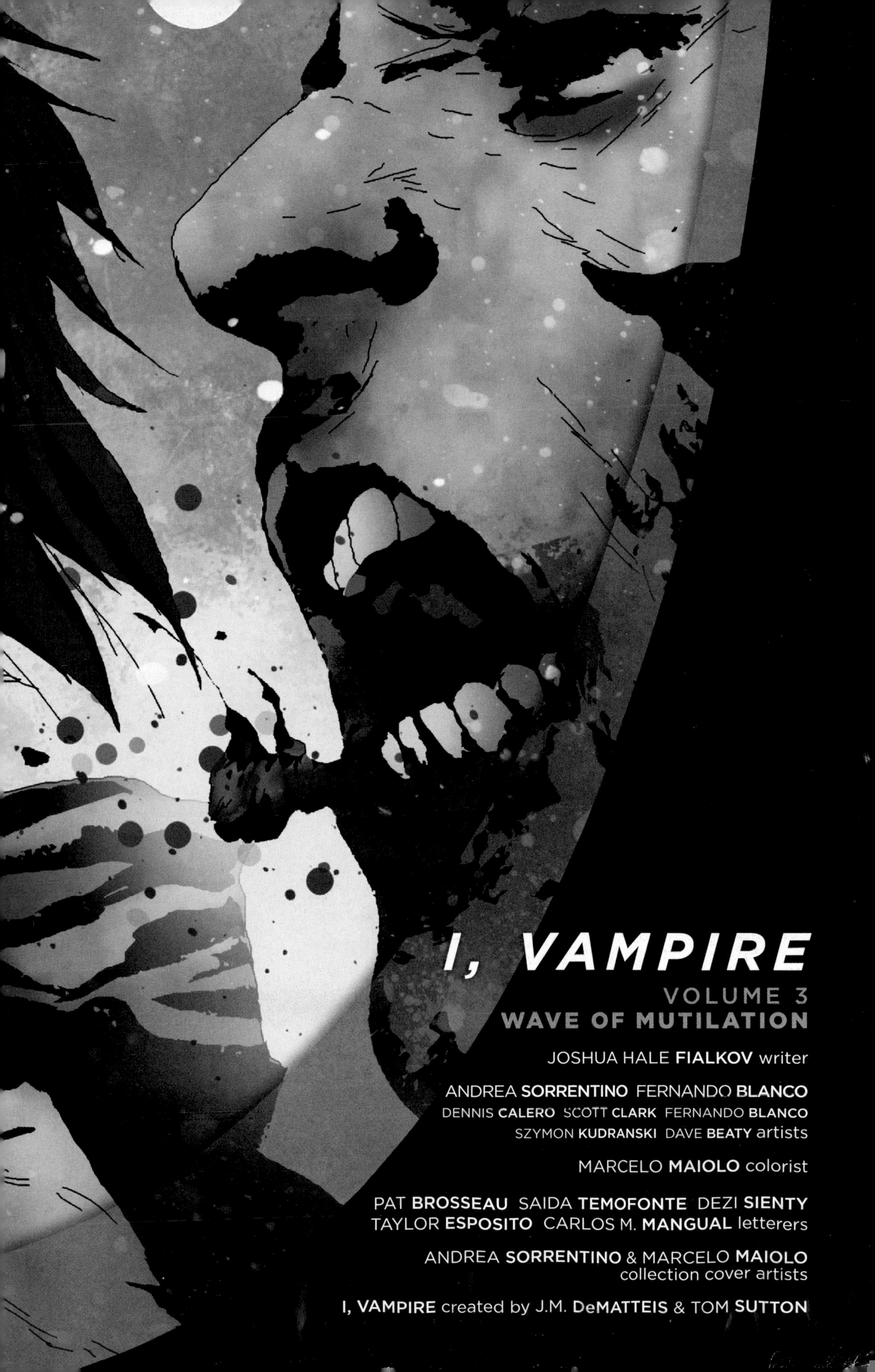

I, VAMPIRE

VOLUME 3
WAVE OF MUTILATION

JOSHUA HALE **FIALKOV** writer

ANDREA **SORRENTINO** FERNANDO **BLANCO**
DENNIS **CALERO** SCOTT **CLARK** FERNANDO **BLANCO**
SZYMON **KUDRANSKI** DAVE **BEATY** artists

MARCELO **MAIOLO** colorist

PAT **BROSSEAU** SAIDA **TEMOFONTE** DEZI **SIENTY**
TAYLOR **ESPOSITO** CARLOS M. **MANGUAL** letterers

ANDREA **SORRENTINO** & MARCELO **MAIOLO**
collection cover artists

I, VAMPIRE created by J.M. **DeMATTEIS** & TOM **SUTTON**

MATT IDELSON CHRIS CONROY Editors – Original Series ROWENA YOW Editor
ROBBIN BROSTERMAN Design Director – Books ROBBIE BIEDERMAN Publication Design

BOB HARRAS Senior VP – Editor-in-Chief, DC Comics

DIANE NELSON President DAN DIDIO and JIM LEE Co-Publishers GEOFF JOHNS Chief Creative Officer
JOHN ROOD Executive VP – Sales, Marketing and Business Development AMY GENKINS Senior VP – Business and Legal Affairs
NAIRI GARDINER Senior VP – Finance JEFF BOISON VP – Publishing Planning
ORRI CUNNINGHAM VP – Editorial Administration ALISON GILL Senior VP – Manufacturing and Operations
HANK KANALZ Senior VP – Vertigo and Integrated Publishing JAY KOGAN VP – Business and Legal Affairs, Publishing
JACK MAHAN VP – Business Affairs, Talent NICK NAPOLITANO VP – Manufacturing Administration
SUE POHJA VP – Book Sales COURTNEY SIMMONS Senior VP – Publicity BOB WAYNE Senior VP – Sales

I, VAMPIRE VOLUME 3: WAVE OF MUTILATION

Published by DC Comics. Cover and compilation Copyright © 2013 DC Comics. All Rights Reserved.

Originally published in single magazine form in I, VAMPIRE 0, 13-19 © 2012, 2013 DC Comics. All Rights Reserved.
All characters, their distinctive likenesses and related elements featured in this publication are trademarks of DC Comics.
The stories, characters and incidents featured in this publication are entirely fictional.
DC Comics does not read or accept unsolicited ideas, stories or artwork.

DC Comics, 1700 Broadway, New York, NY 10019
A Warner Bros. Entertainment Company.
Printed by RR Donnelley, Salem, VA, USA. 9/6/13. First Printing.

ISBN: 978-1-4012-4278-7

Library of Congress Cataloging-in-Publication Data

Fialkov, Joshua Hale, 1979- author.
I, Vampire. Volume 3, Wave of Mutilation / Joshua Hale Fialkov, Andrea Sorrentino.
pages cm
"Originally published in single magazine form as I, VAMPIRE 0, 13-19."
ISBN 978-1-4012-4278-7
I. Sorrentino, Andrea, illustrator. II. Title. III. Title: Wave of Mutilation.
PN6728.I23F55 2013
741.5'973—dc23
2013021254

SUSTAINABLE FORESTRY INITIATIVE
Certified Chain of Custody
At Least 20% Certified Forest Content
www.sfiprogram.org
SFI-01042
APPLIES TO TEXT STOCK ONLY

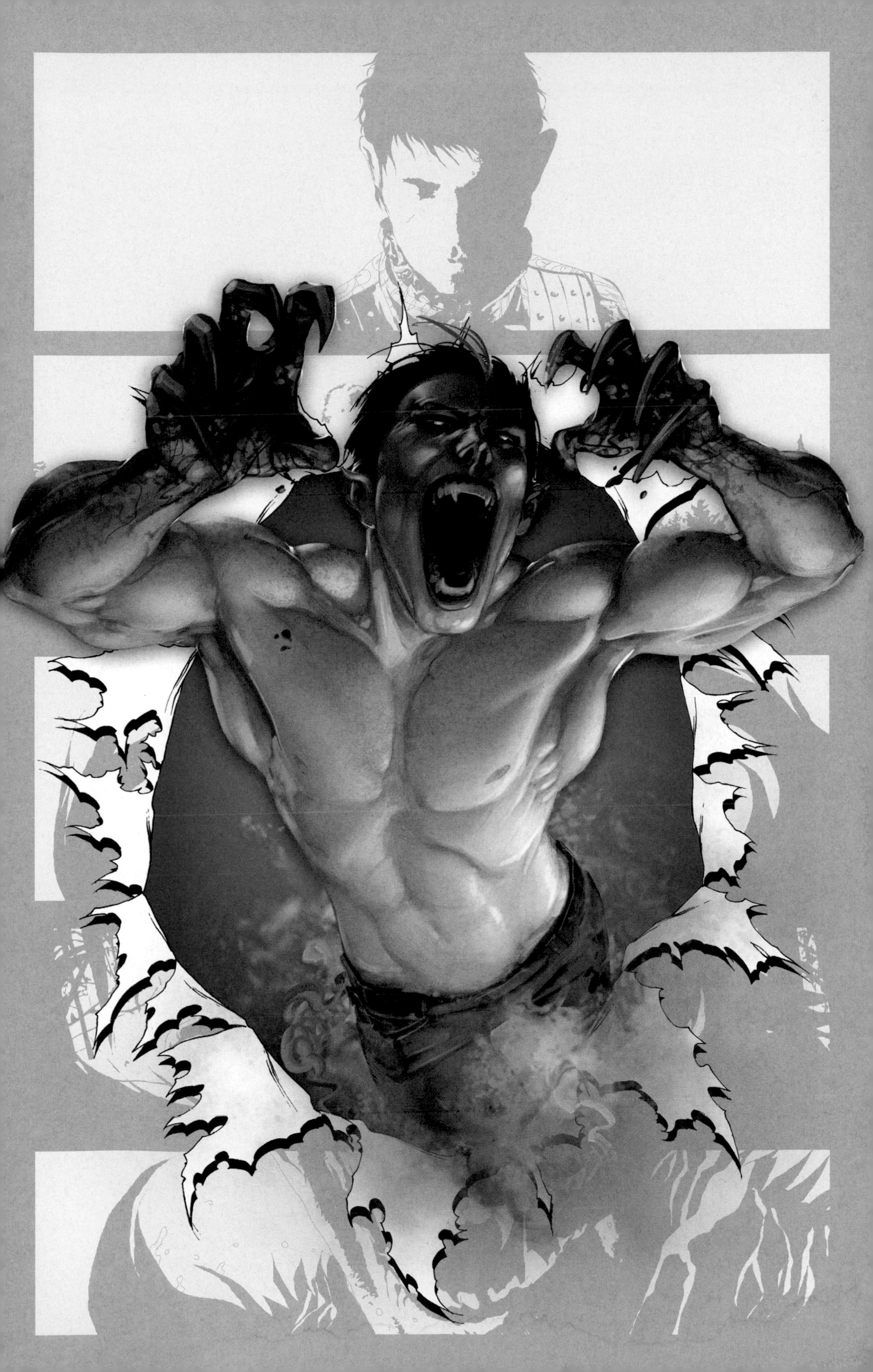

BREAK MY BODY

JOSHUA HALE FIALKOV writer ANDREA SORRENTINO artist cover art by CLAYTON CRAIN

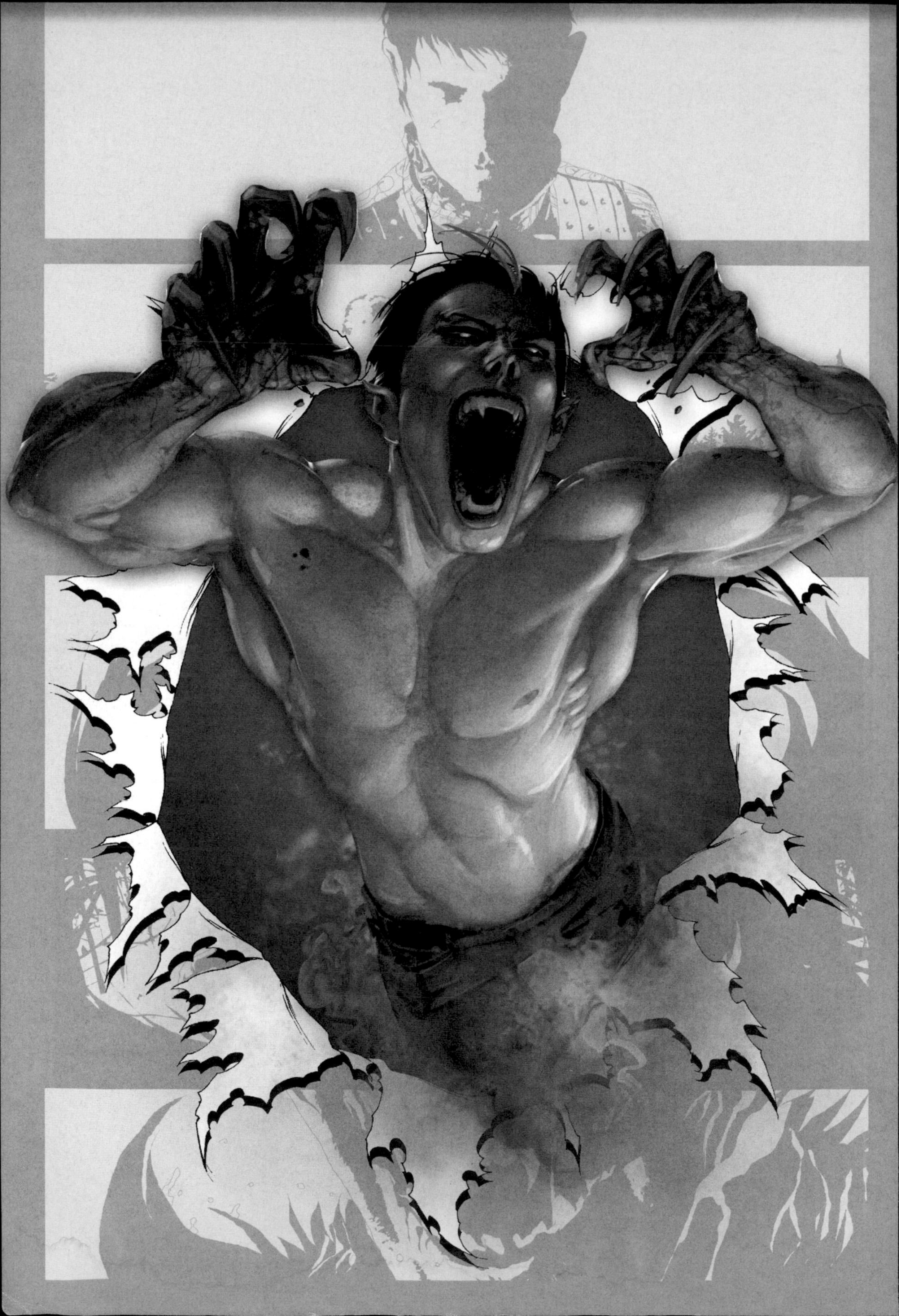

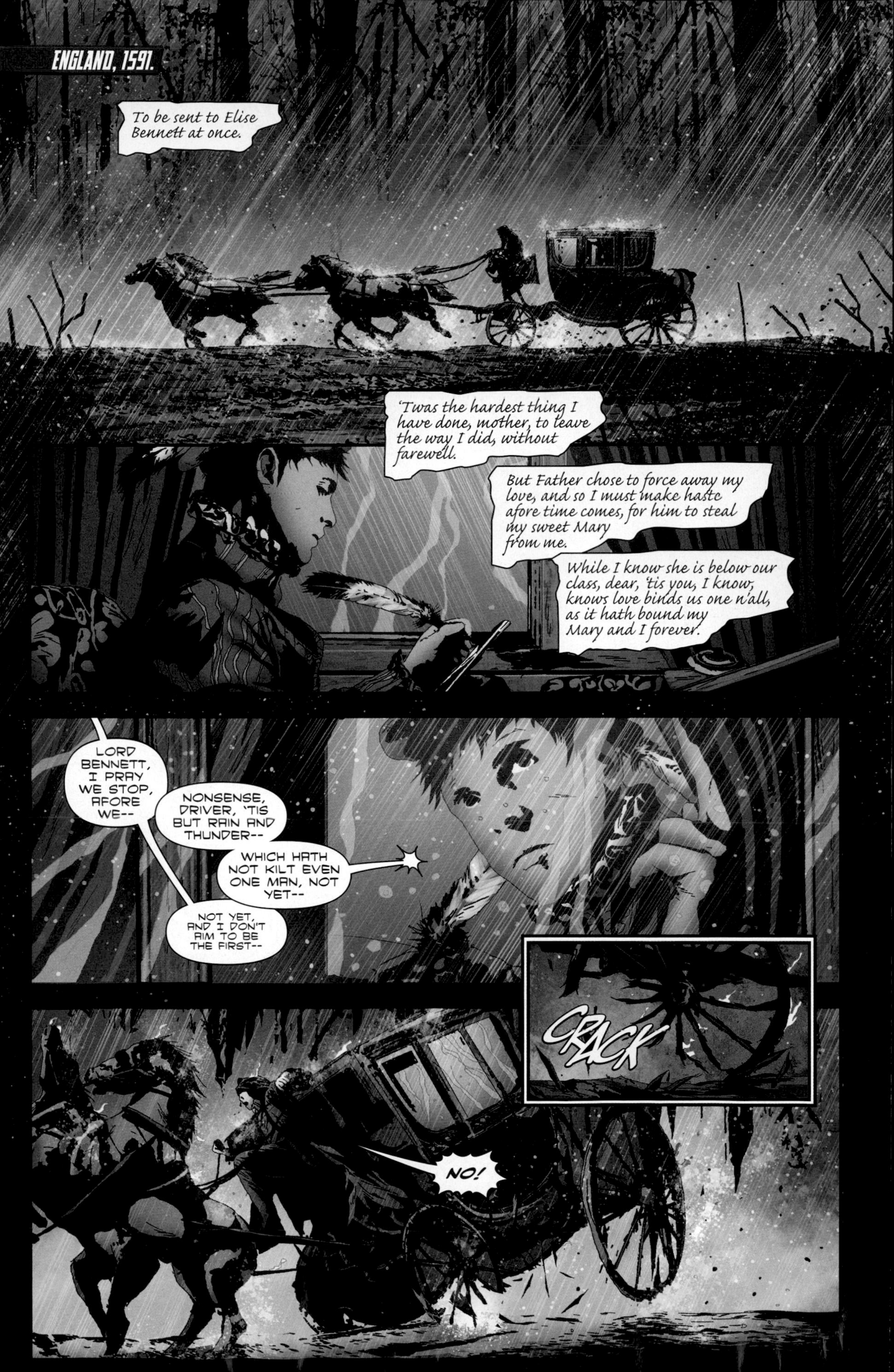
ENGLAND, 1591.
To be sent to Elise Bennett at once.
'Twas the hardest thing I have done, mother, to leave the way I did, without farewell.
But Father chose to force away my love, and so I must make haste afore time comes, for him to steal my sweet Mary from me.
While I know she is below our class, dear, 'tis you, I know, knows love binds us one n'all, as it hath bound my Mary and I forever.
LORD BENNETT, I PRAY WE STOP, AFORE WE--
NONSENSE, DRIVER, 'TIS BUT RAIN AND THUNDER--
WHICH HATH NOT KILT EVEN ONE MAN, NOT YET--
NOT YET, AND I DON'T AIM TO BE THE FIRST--
CRACK
NO!

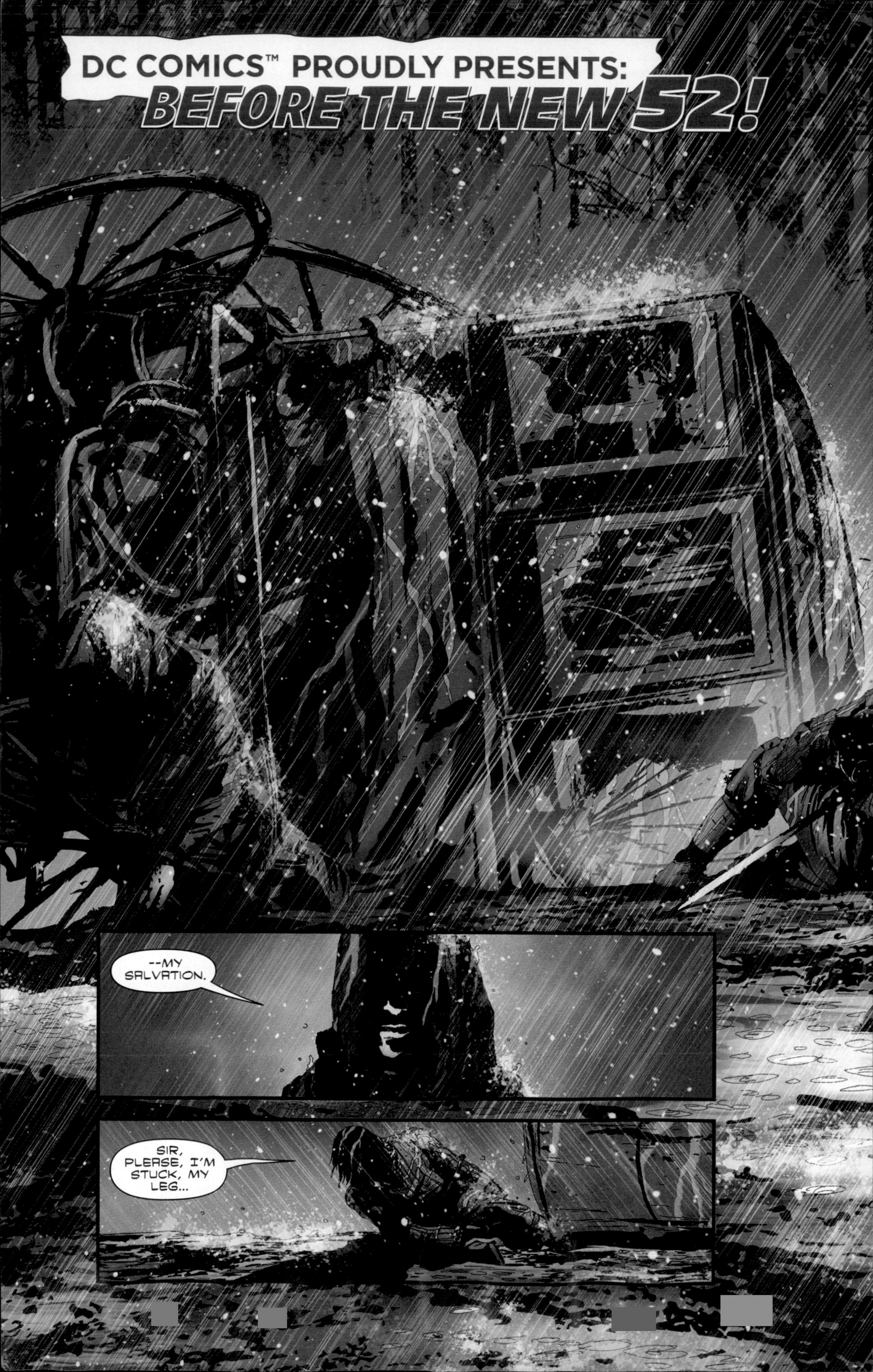
DC COMICS™ PROUDLY PRESENTS:
BEFORE THE NEW 52!
--MY SALVATION.
SIR, PLEASE, I'M STUCK, MY LEG...

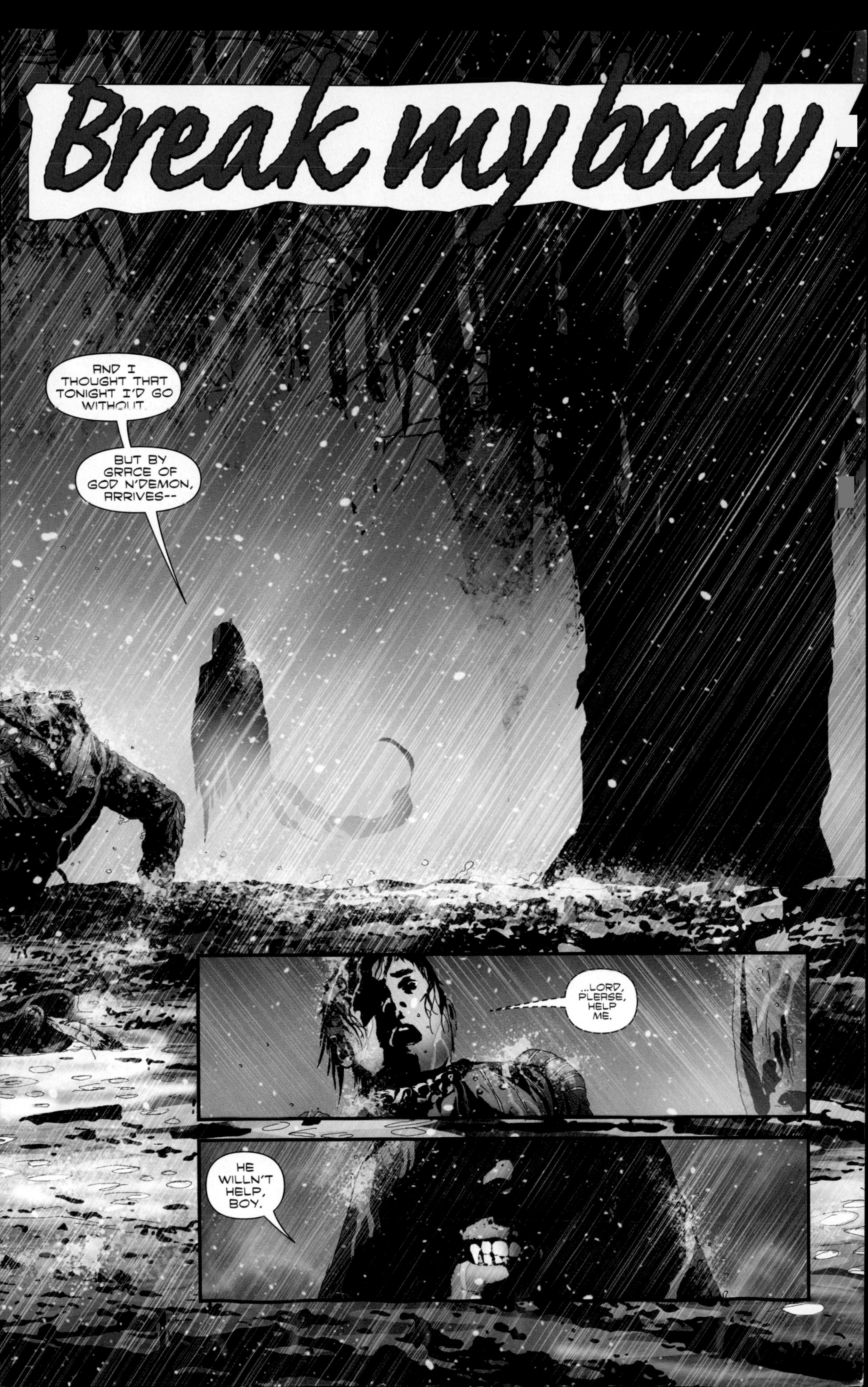
Break my body
AND I THOUGHT THAT TONIGHT I'D GO WITHOUT.
BUT BY GRACE OF GOD N'DEMON, ARRIVES--
...LORD, PLEASE, HELP ME.
HE WILLN'T HELP, BOY.

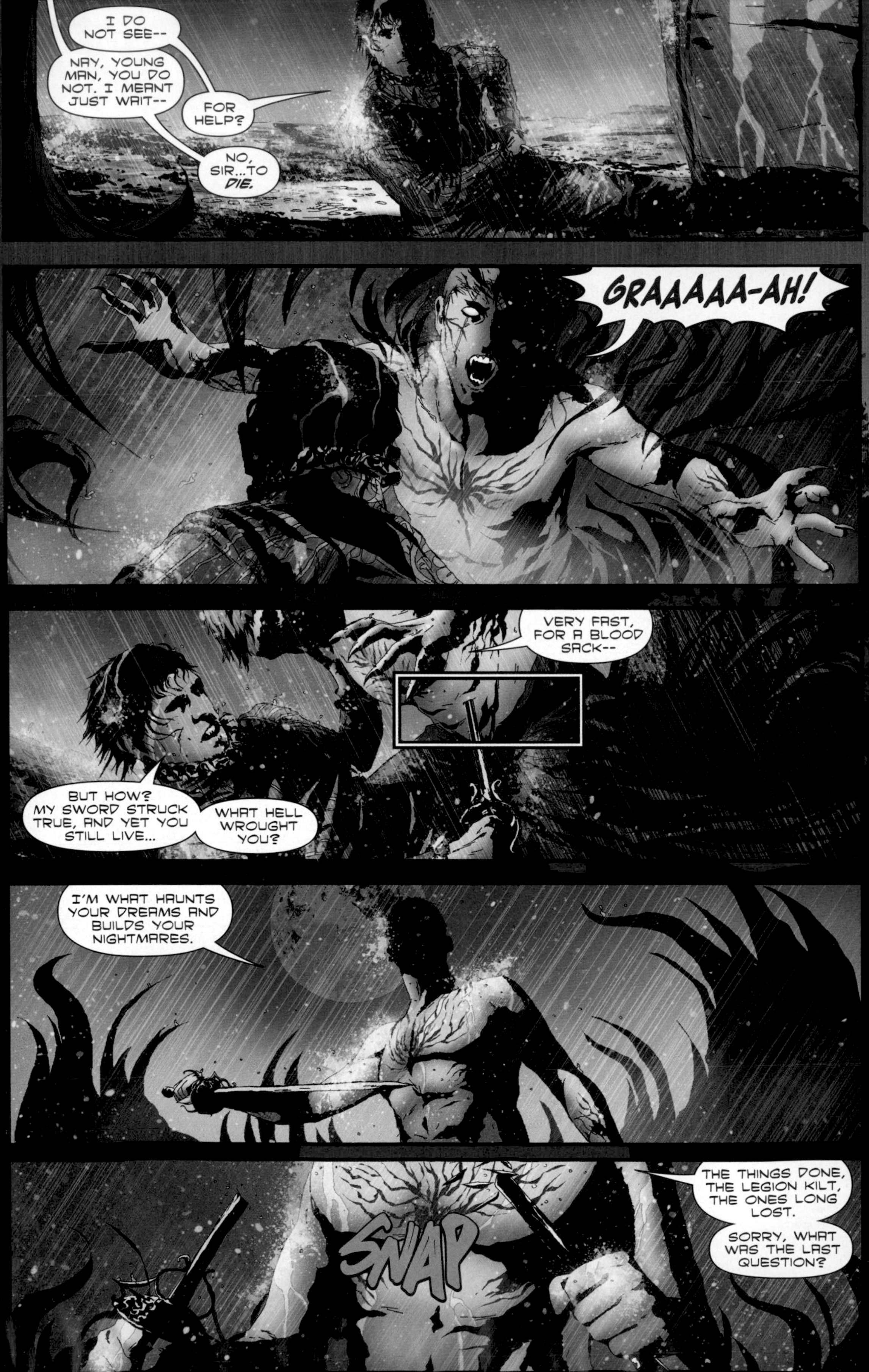
I DO NOT SEE--
NAY, YOUNG MAN, YOU DO NOT. I MEANT JUST WAIT--
FOR HELP?
NO, SIR...TO *DIE.*
GRAAAAA-AH!
VERY FAST, FOR A BLOOD SACK--
BUT HOW? MY SWORD STRUCK TRUE, AND YET YOU STILL LIVE...
WHAT HELL WROUGHT YOU?
I'M WHAT HAUNTS YOUR DREAMS AND BUILDS YOUR NIGHTMARES.
SNAP
THE THINGS DONE, THE LEGION KILT, THE ONES LONG LOST.
SORRY, WHAT WAS THE LAST QUESTION?

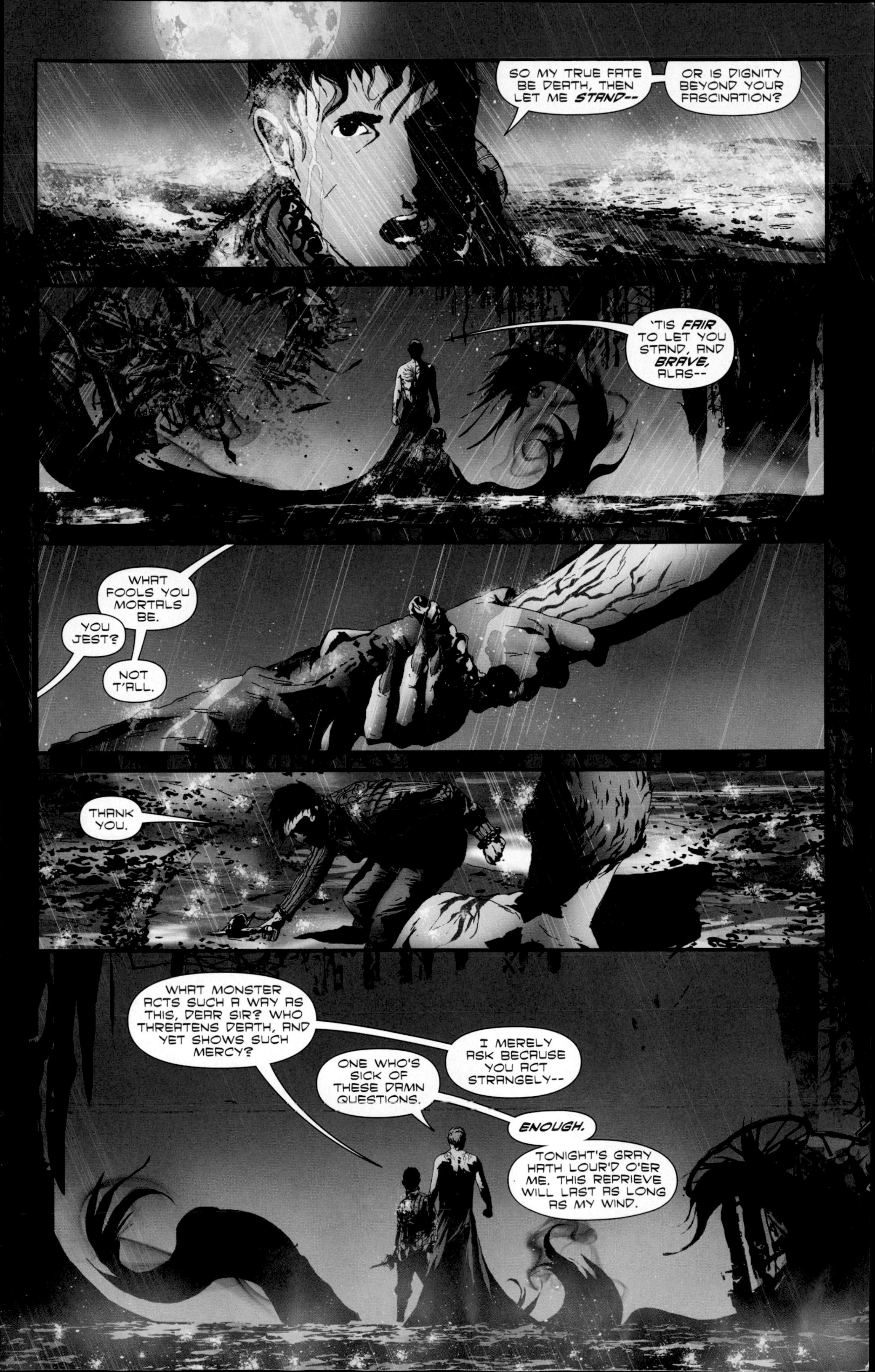
SO MY TRUE FATE BE DEATH, THEN LET ME STAND--
OR IS DIGNITY BEYOND YOUR FASCINATION?
'TIS FAIR TO LET YOU STAND, AND BRAVE, ALAS--
WHAT FOOLS YOU MORTALS BE.
YOU JEST?
NOT T'ALL.
THANK YOU.
WHAT MONSTER ACTS SUCH A WAY AS THIS, DEAR SIR? WHO THREATENS DEATH, AND YET SHOWS SUCH MERCY?
ONE WHO'S SICK OF THESE DAMN QUESTIONS.
I MERELY ASK BECAUSE YOU ACT STRANGELY--
ENOUGH.
TONIGHT'S GRAY HATH LOUR'D O'ER ME. THIS REPRIEVE WILL LAST AS LONG AS MY WIND.

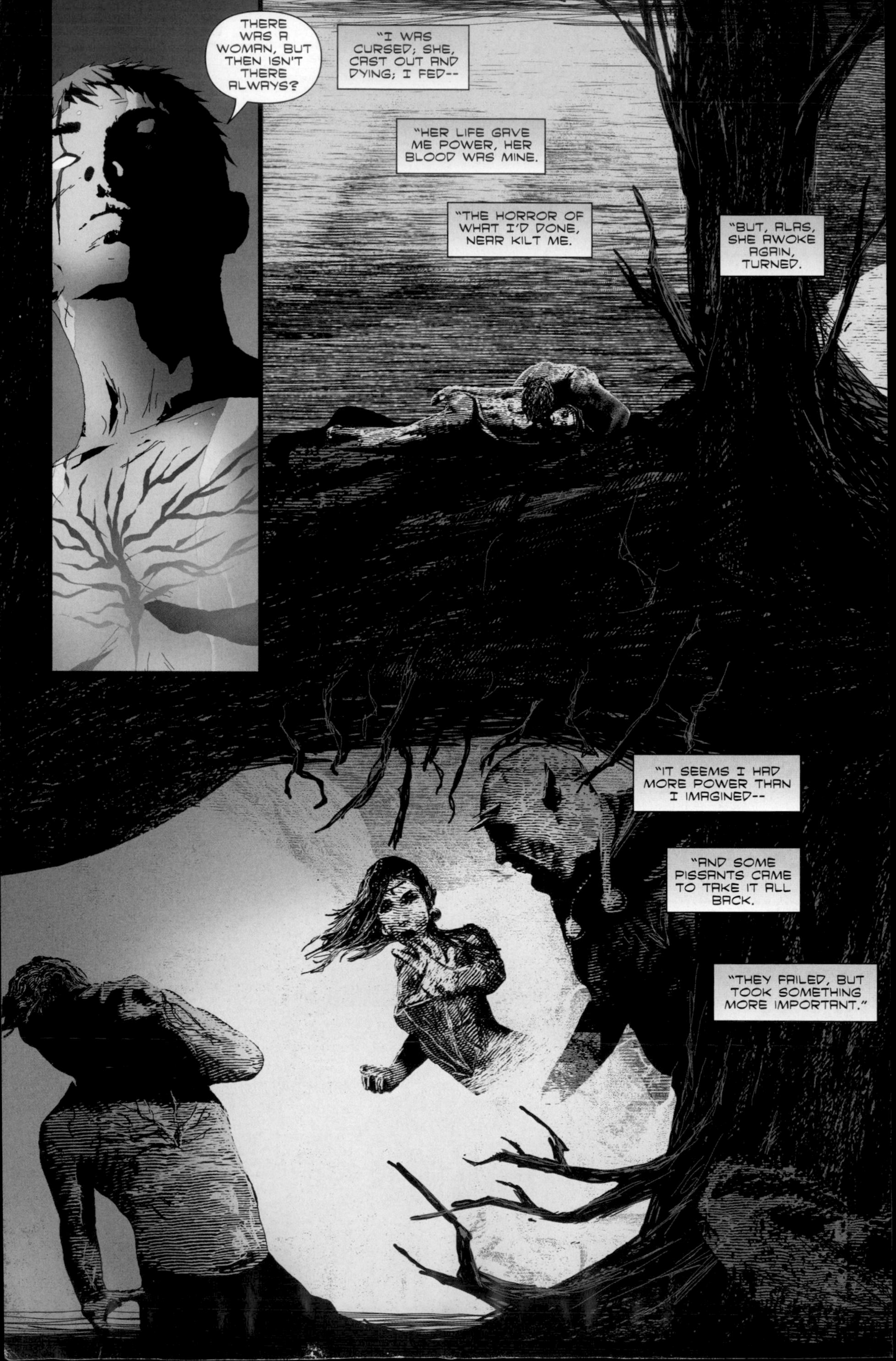
THERE WAS A WOMAN, BUT THEN ISN'T THERE ALWAYS?
"I WAS CURSED; SHE, CAST OUT AND DYING; I FED--
"HER LIFE GAVE ME POWER, HER BLOOD WAS MINE.
"THE HORROR OF WHAT I'D DONE, NEAR KILT ME.
"BUT, ALAS, SHE AWOKE AGAIN, TURNED.
"IT SEEMS I HAD MORE POWER THAN I IMAGINED--
"AND SOME PISSANTS CAME TO TAKE IT ALL BACK.
"THEY FAILED, BUT TOOK SOMETHING MORE IMPORTANT."

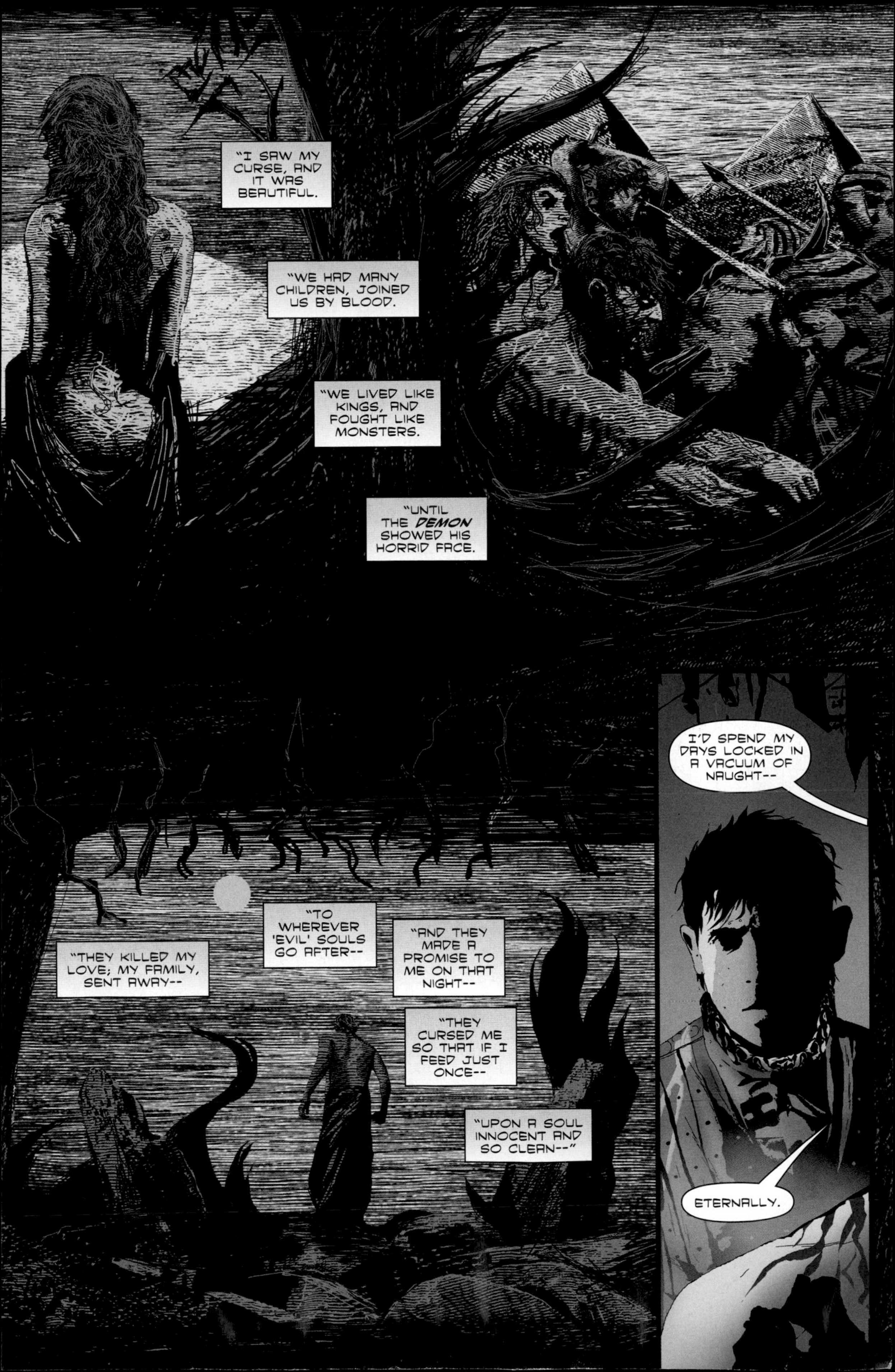
"I SAW MY CURSE, AND IT WAS BEAUTIFUL.
"WE HAD MANY CHILDREN, JOINED US BY BLOOD.
"WE LIVED LIKE KINGS, AND FOUGHT LIKE MONSTERS.
"UNTIL THE *DEMON* SHOWED HIS HORRID FACE.
"THEY KILLED MY LOVE; MY FAMILY, SENT AWAY--
"TO WHEREVER 'EVIL' SOULS GO AFTER--
"AND THEY MADE A PROMISE TO ME ON THAT NIGHT--
"THEY CURSED ME SO THAT IF I FEED JUST ONCE--
"UPON A SOUL INNOCENT AND SO CLEAN--"
I'D SPEND MY DAYS LOCKED IN A VACUUM OF NAUGHT--
ETERNALLY.

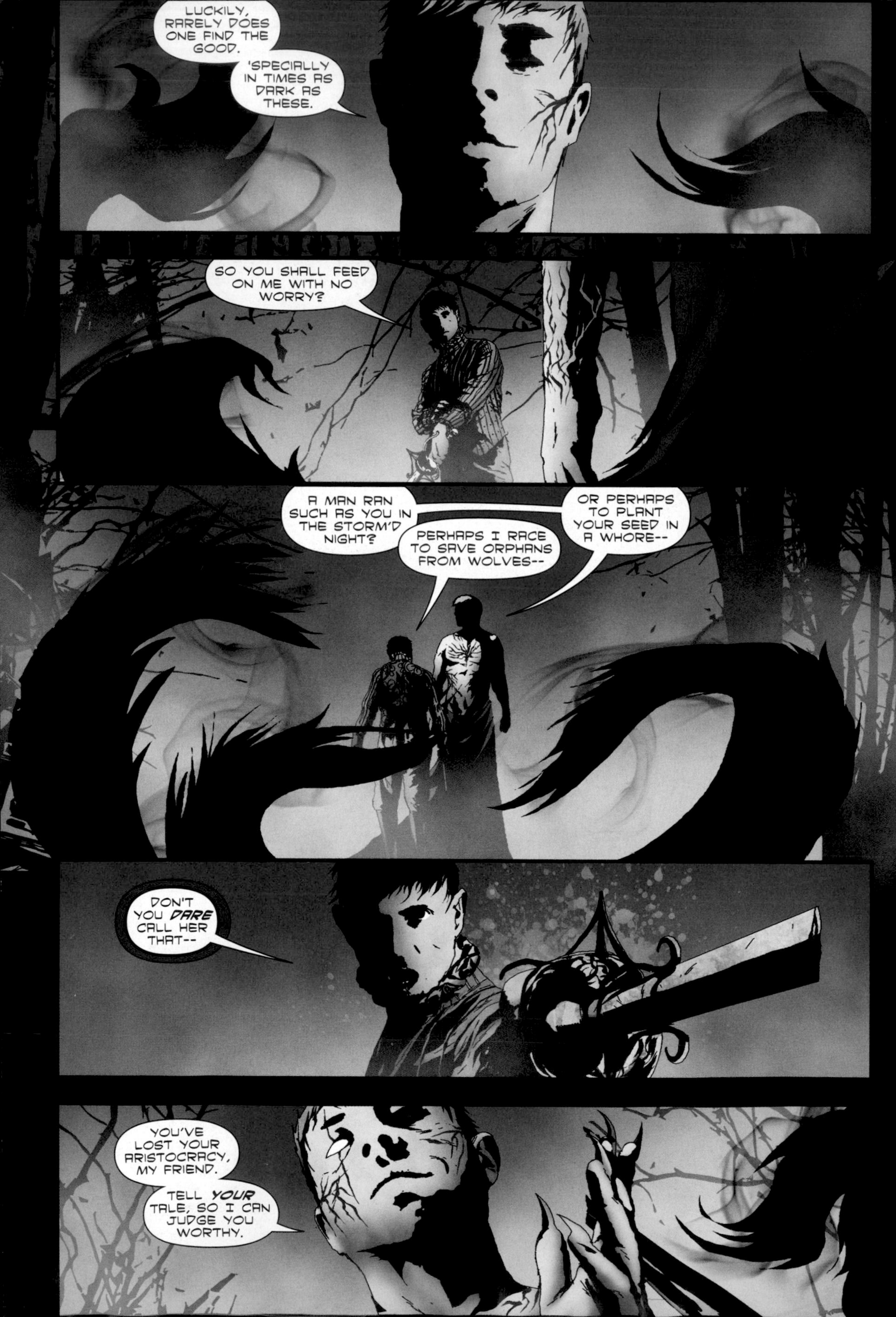
LUCKILY, RARELY DOES ONE FIND THE GOOD.
'SPECIALLY IN TIMES AS DARK AS THESE.
SO YOU SHALL FEED ON ME WITH NO WORRY?
A MAN RAN SUCH AS YOU IN THE STORM'D NIGHT?
PERHAPS I RACE TO SAVE ORPHANS FROM WOLVES--
OR PERHAPS TO PLANT YOUR SEED IN A WHORE--
DON'T YOU *DARE* CALL HER THAT--
YOU'VE LOST YOUR ARISTOCRACY, MY FRIEND.
TELL *YOUR* TALE, SO I CAN JUDGE YOU WORTHY.

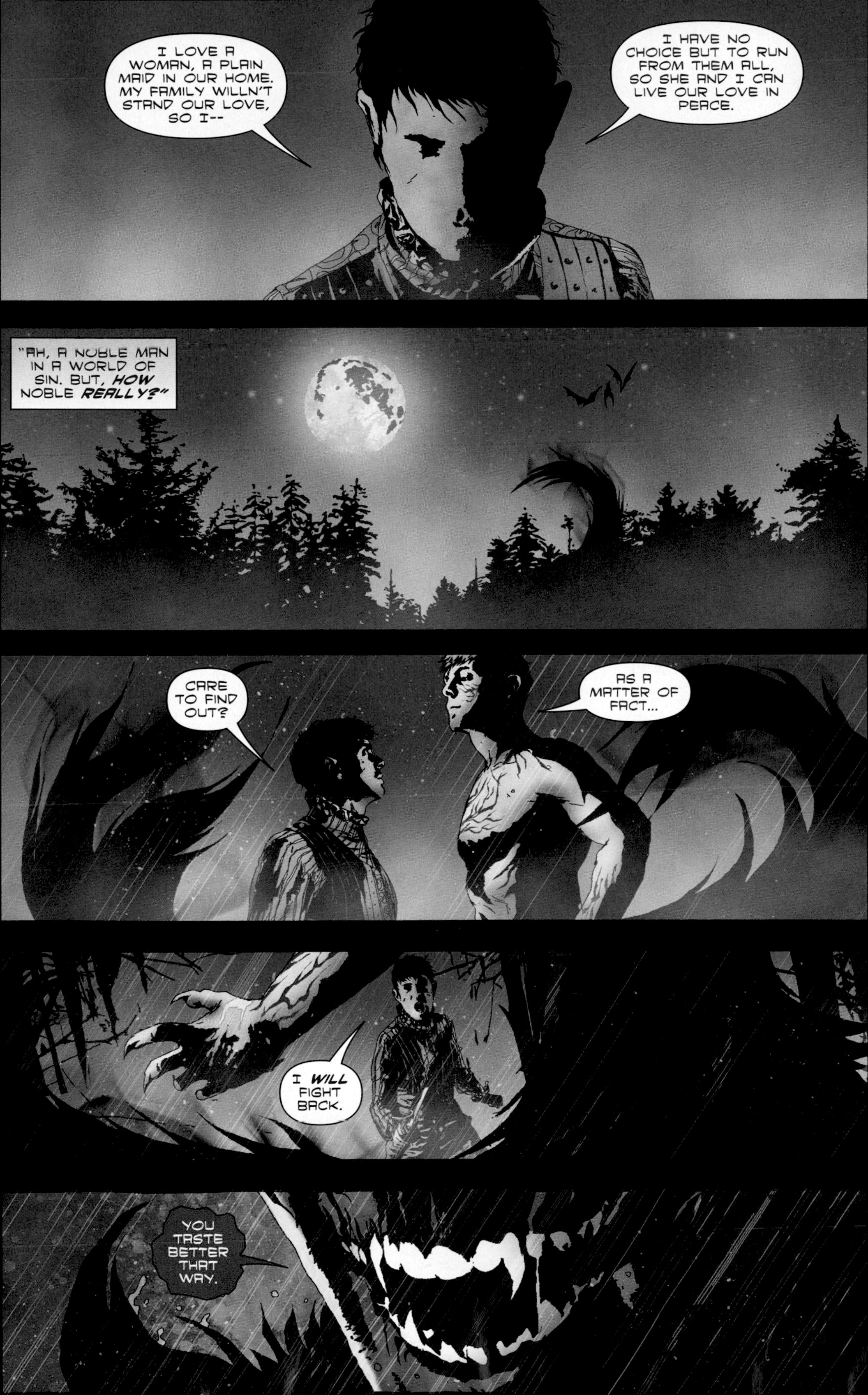
I LOVE A WOMAN, A PLAIN MAID IN OUR HOME. MY FAMILY WILLN'T STAND OUR LOVE, SO I--
I HAVE NO CHOICE BUT TO RUN FROM THEM ALL, SO SHE AND I CAN LIVE OUR LOVE IN PEACE.
"AH, A NOBLE MAN IN A WORLD OF SIN. BUT, *HOW* NOBLE *REALLY?*"
CARE TO FIND OUT?
AS A MATTER OF FACT...
I *WILL* FIGHT BACK.
YOU TASTE BETTER THAT WAY.

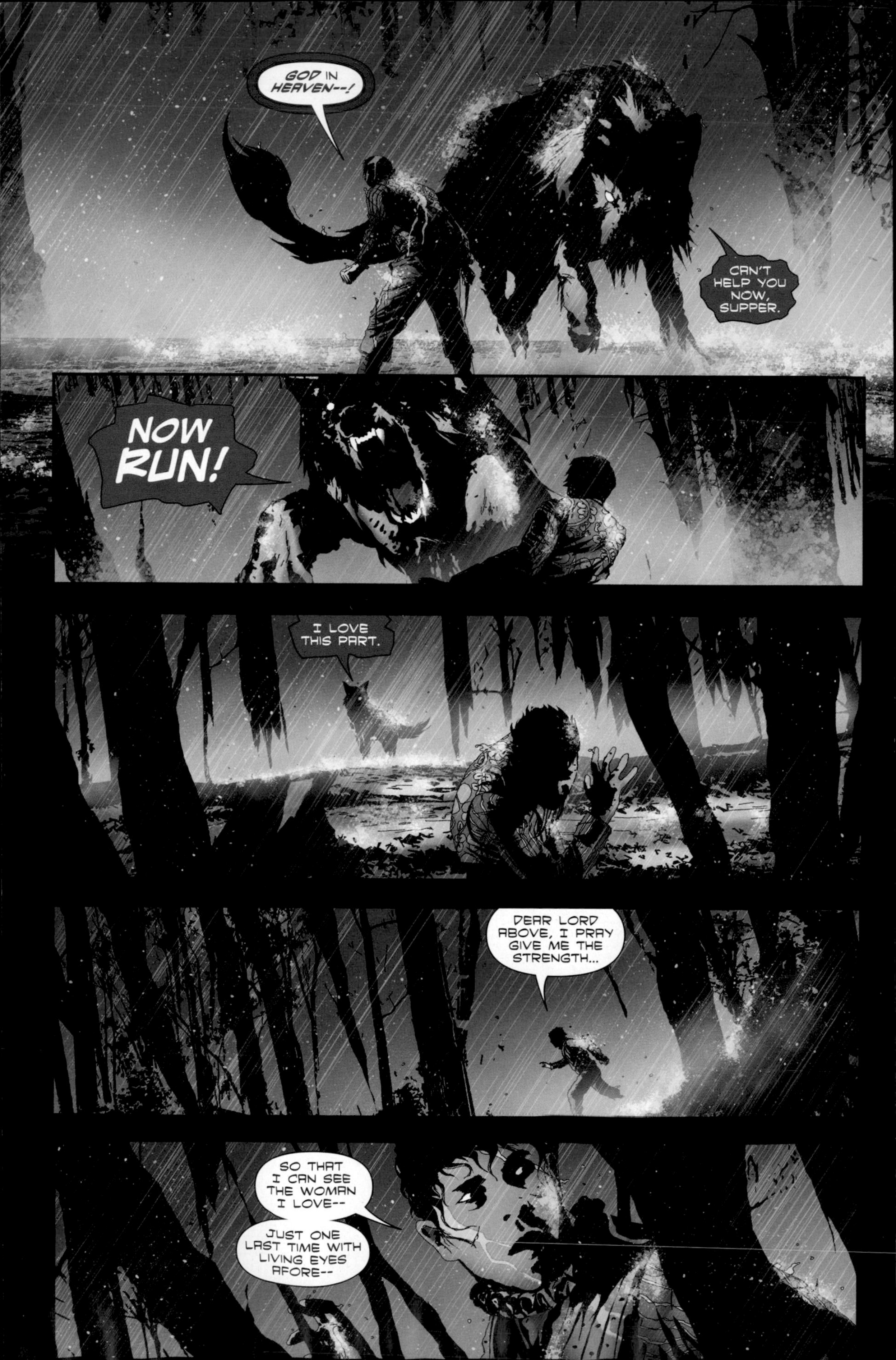
GOD IN HEAVEN--!
CAN'T HELP YOU NOW, SUPPER.
NOW RUN!
I LOVE THIS PART.
DEAR LORD ABOVE, I PRAY GIVE ME THE STRENGTH...
SO THAT I CAN SEE THE WOMAN I LOVE--
JUST ONE LAST TIME WITH LIVING EYES AFORE--

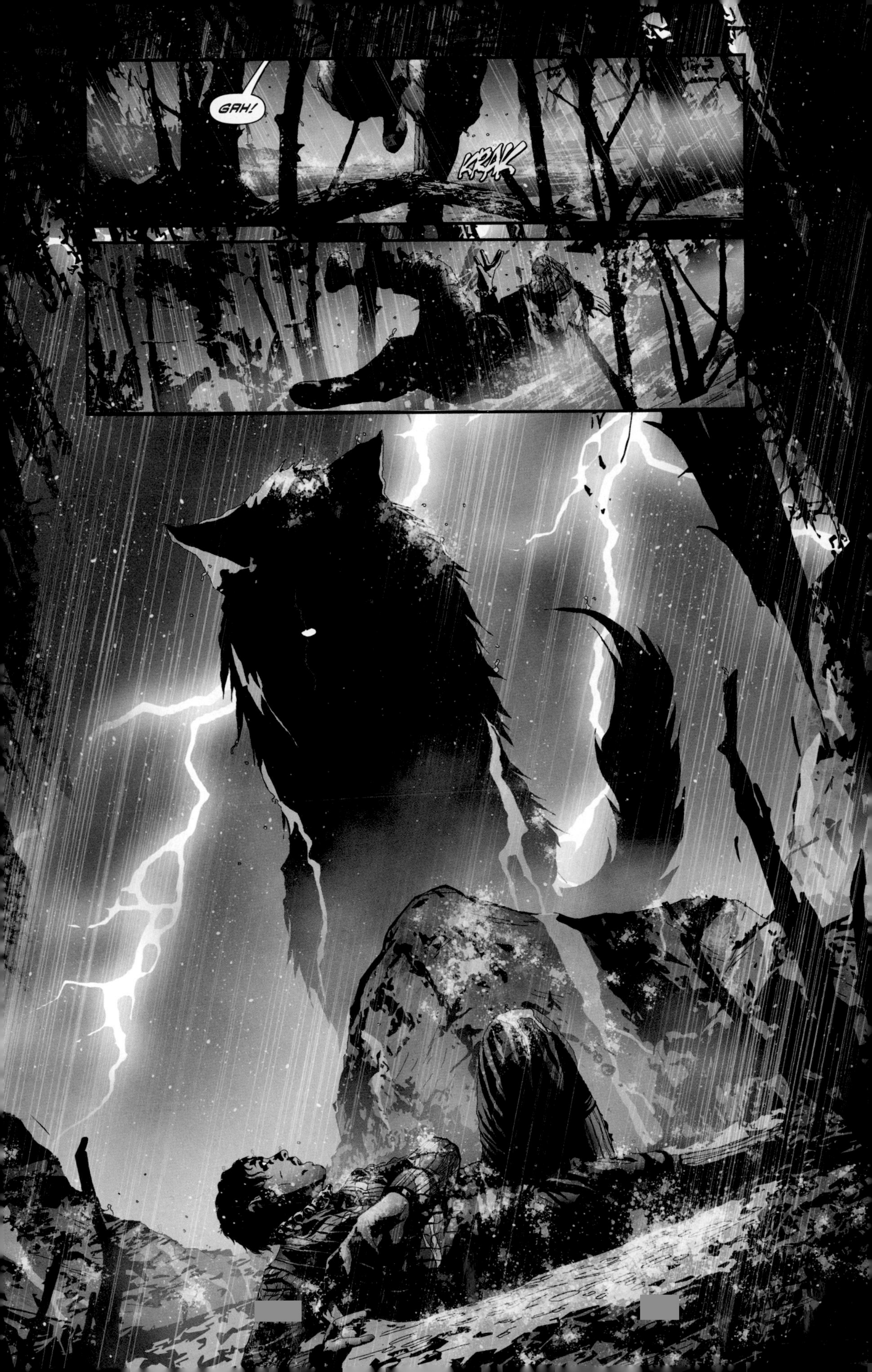
GRAH!
KRAK

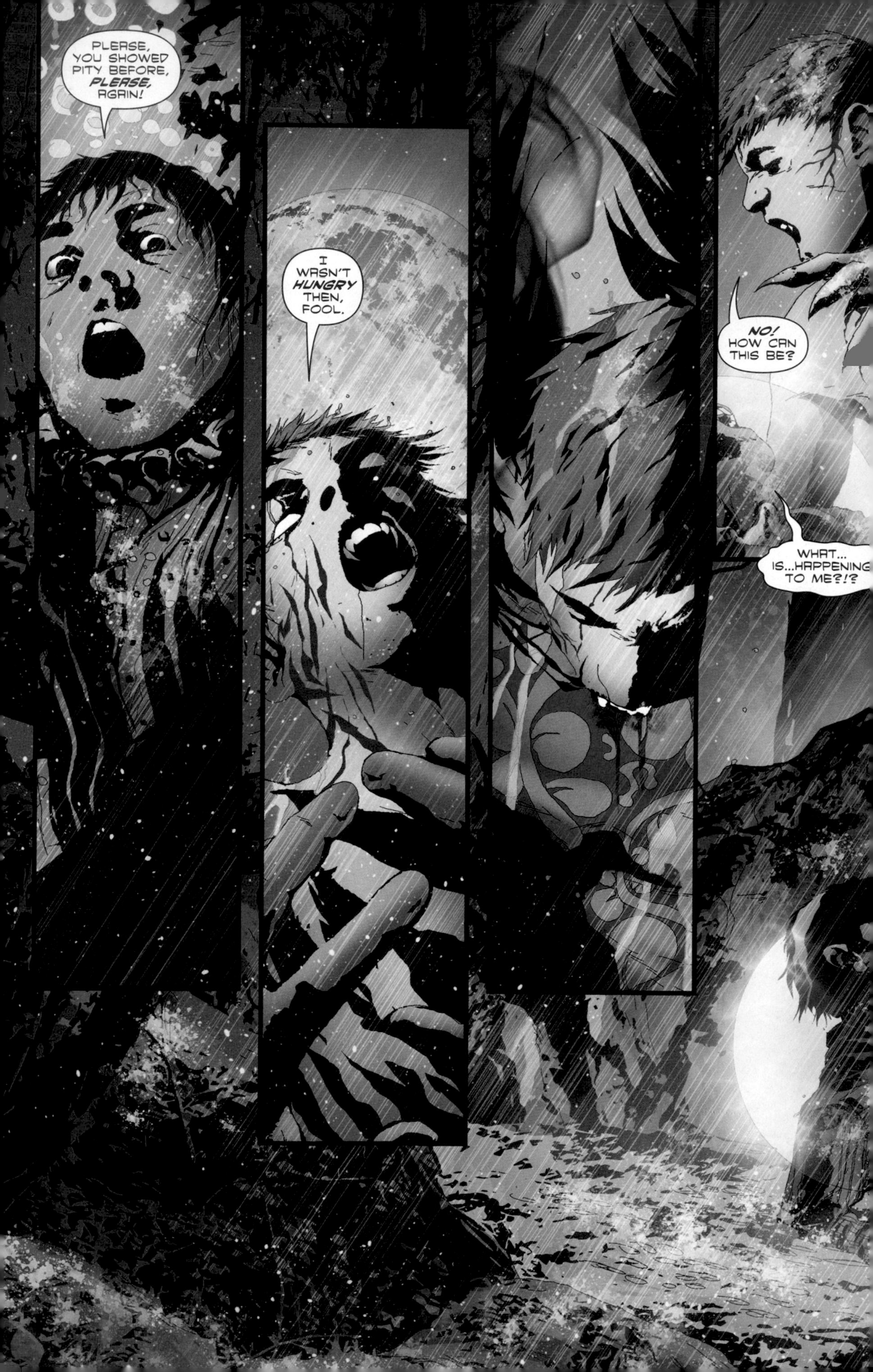
PLEASE, YOU SHOWED PITY BEFORE, *PLEASE,* AGAIN!
I WASN'T *HUNGRY* THEN, FOOL.
NO! HOW CAN THIS BE?
WHAT... IS...HAPPENING TO ME?!?

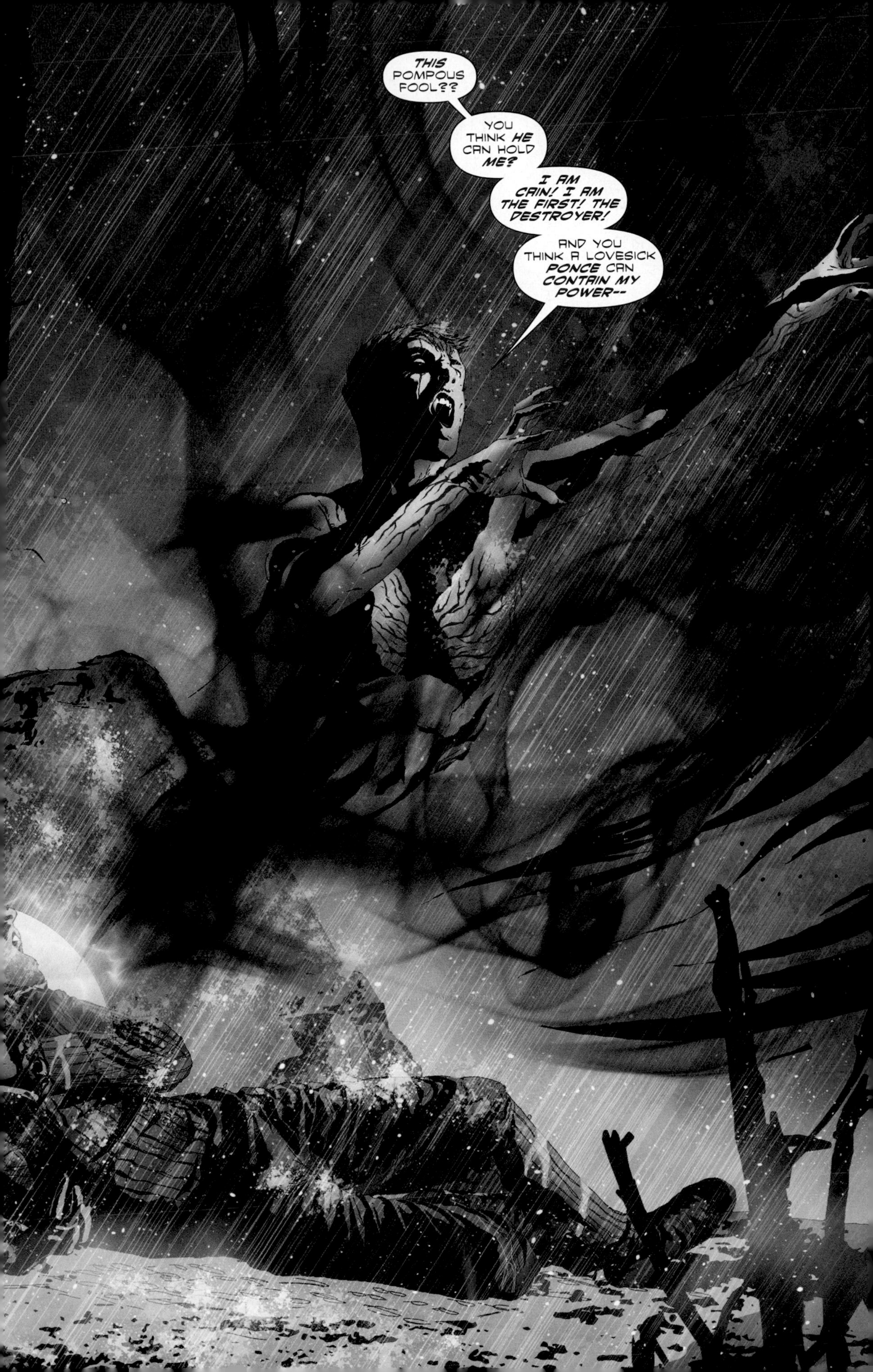
THIS POMPOUS FOOL??
YOU THINK HE CAN HOLD ME?
I AM CAIN! I AM THE FIRST! THE DESTROYER!
AND YOU THINK A LOVESICK PONCE CAN CONTAIN MY POWER--

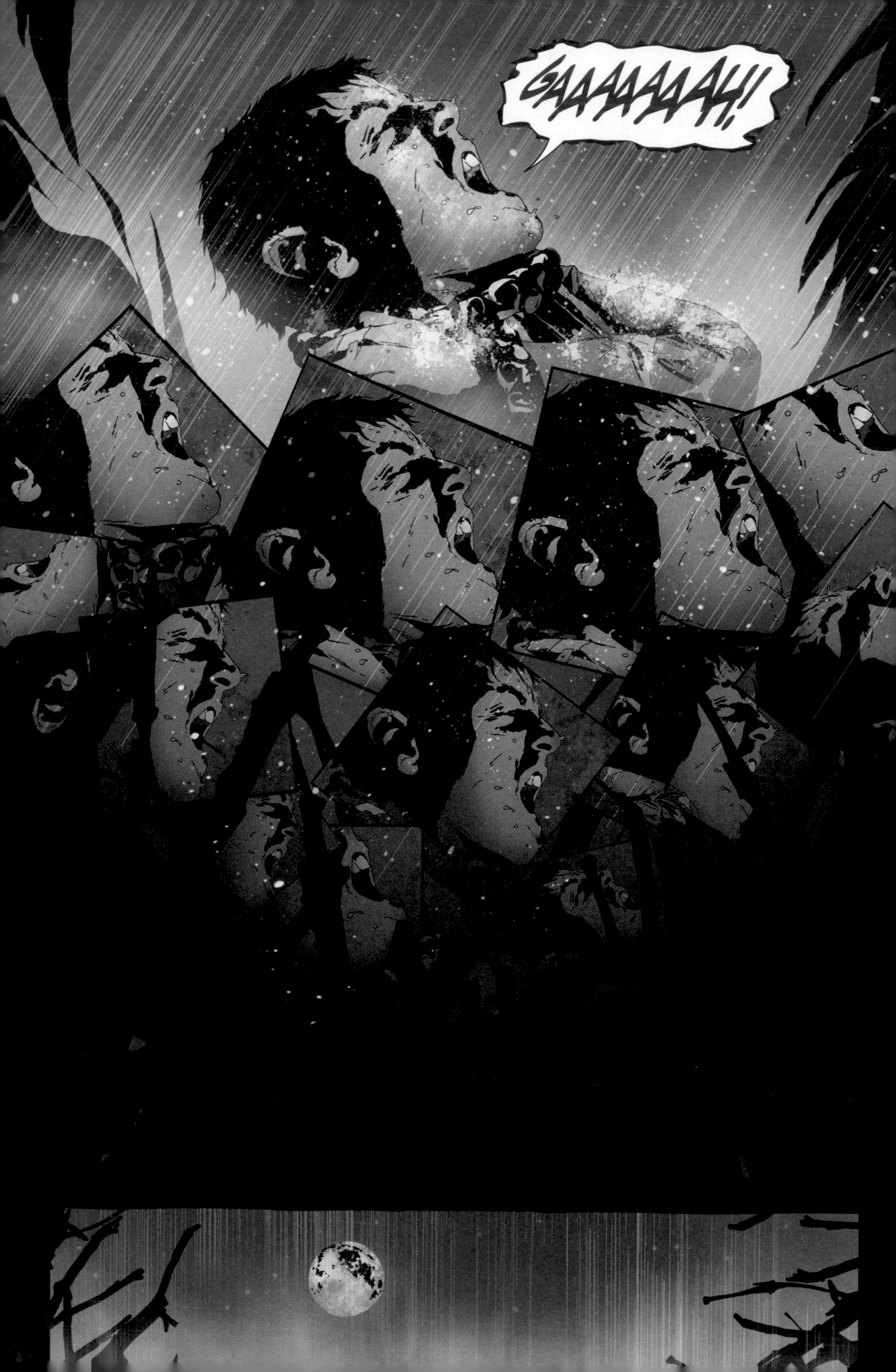
GAAAAAAAH!

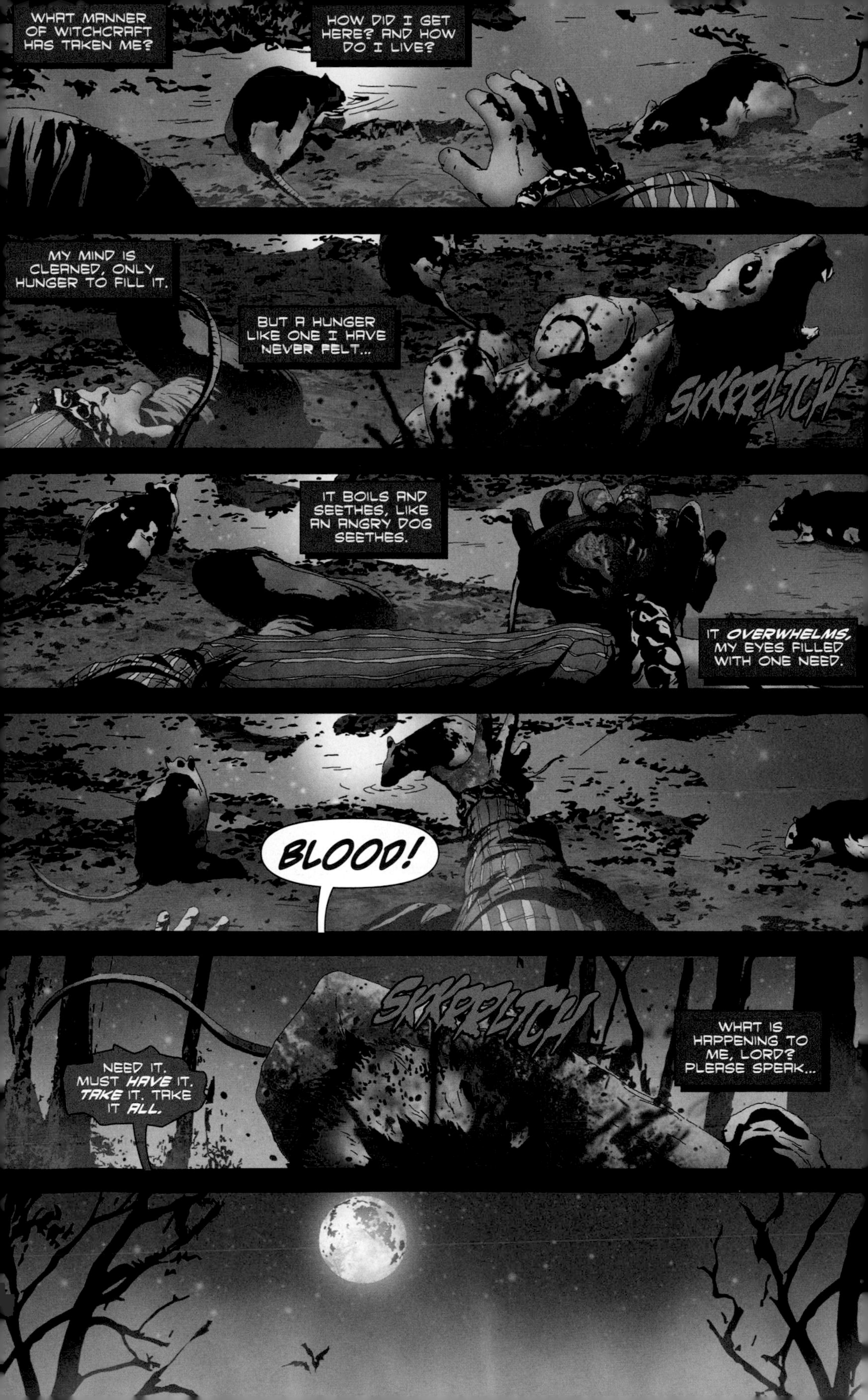
WHAT MANNER OF WITCHCRAFT HAS TAKEN ME?
HOW DID I GET HERE? AND HOW DO I LIVE?
MY MIND IS CLEANED, ONLY HUNGER TO FILL IT.
BUT A HUNGER LIKE ONE I HAVE NEVER FELT...
SKKRRLTCH
IT BOILS AND SEETHES, LIKE AN ANGRY DOG SEETHES.
IT OVERWHELMS, MY EYES FILLED WITH ONE NEED.
BLOOD!
SKKRRLTCH
NEED IT. MUST HAVE IT. TAKE IT. TAKE IT ALL.
WHAT IS HAPPENING TO ME, LORD? PLEASE SPEAK...

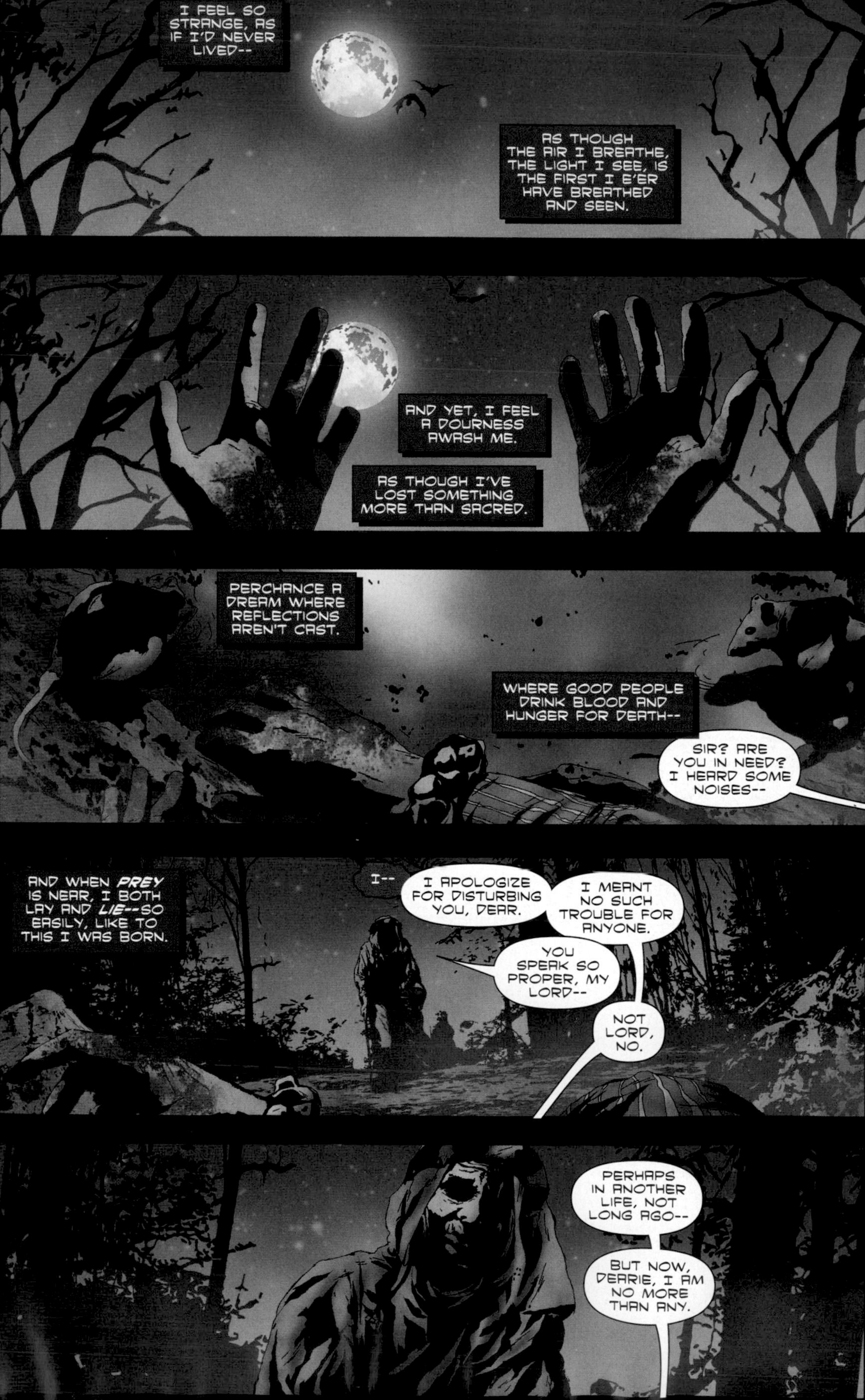
I FEEL SO STRANGE, AS IF I'D NEVER LIVED--
AS THOUGH THE AIR I BREATHE, THE LIGHT I SEE, IS THE FIRST I E'ER HAVE BREATHED AND SEEN.
AND YET, I FEEL A DOURNESS AWASH ME.
AS THOUGH I'VE LOST SOMETHING MORE THAN SACRED.
PERCHANCE A DREAM WHERE REFLECTIONS AREN'T CAST.
WHERE GOOD PEOPLE DRINK BLOOD AND HUNGER FOR DEATH--
SIR? ARE YOU IN NEED? I HEARD SOME NOISES--
AND WHEN *PREY* IS NEAR, I BOTH LAY AND *LIE*--SO EASILY, LIKE TO THIS I WAS BORN.
I--
I APOLOGIZE FOR DISTURBING YOU, DEAR.
I MEANT NO SUCH TROUBLE FOR ANYONE.
YOU SPEAK SO PROPER, MY LORD--
NOT LORD, NO.
PERHAPS IN ANOTHER LIFE, NOT LONG AGO--
BUT NOW, DEARIE, I AM NO MORE THAN ANY.

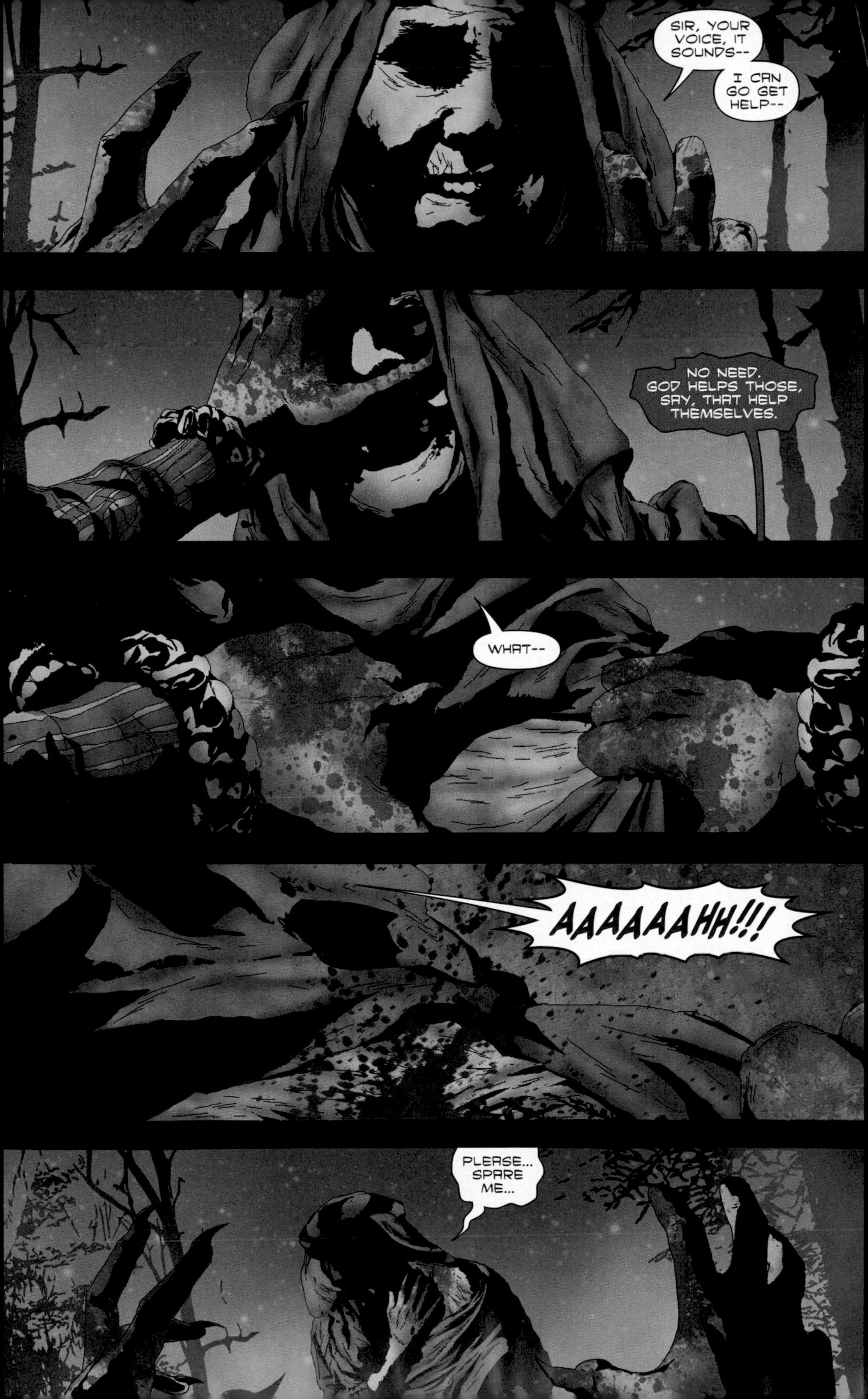
SIR, YOUR VOICE, IT SOUNDS--
I CAN GO GET HELP--
NO NEED. GOD HELPS THOSE, SAY, THAT HELP THEMSELVES.
WHAT--
AAAAAAHH!!!
PLEASE... SPARE ME...

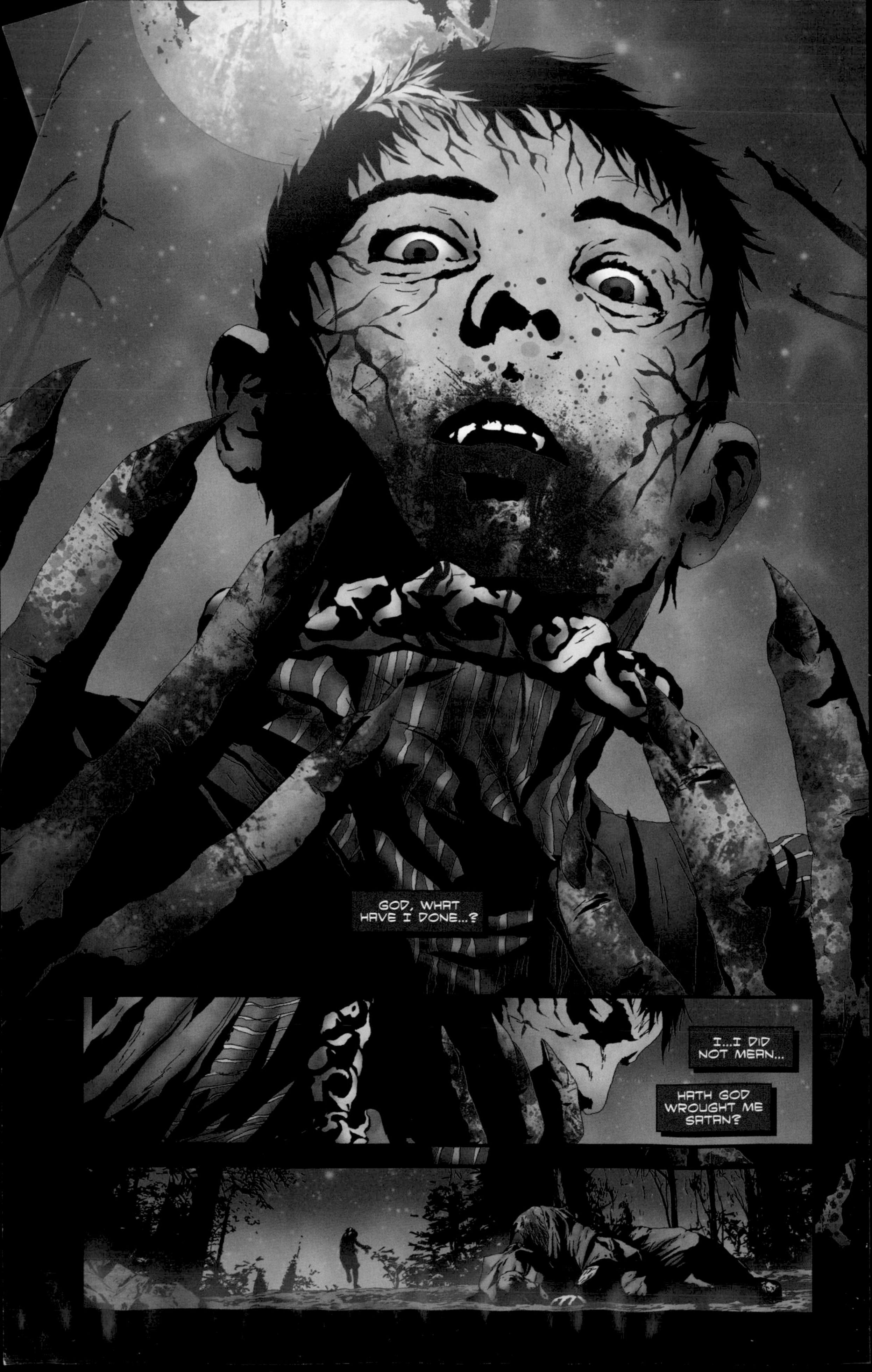
GOD, WHAT HAVE I DONE...?
I...I DID NOT MEAN...
HATH GOD WROUGHT ME SATAN?

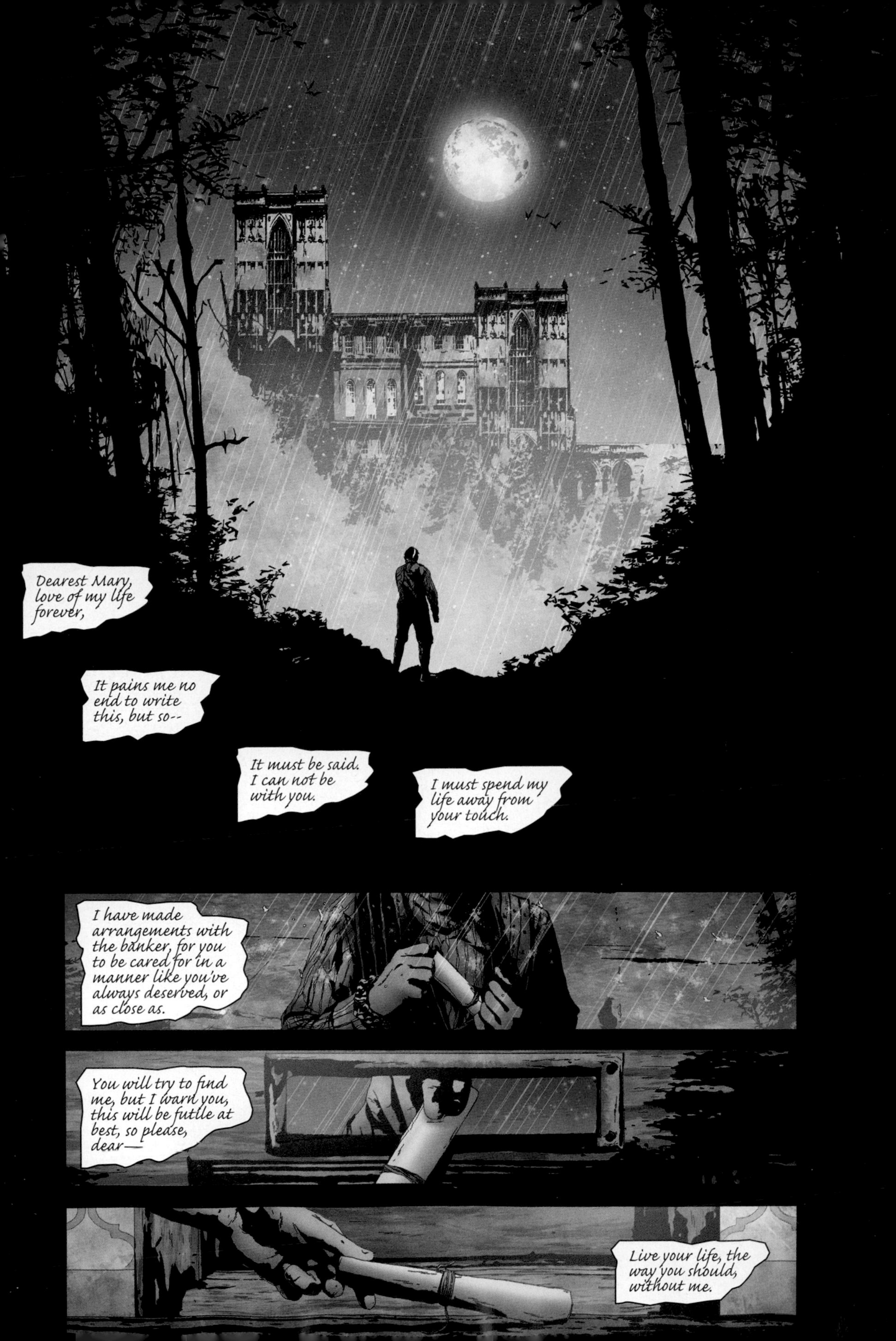
Dearest Mary, love of my life forever,
It pains me no end to write this, but so--
It must be said. I can not be with you.
I must spend my life away from your touch.
I have made arrangements with the banker, for you to be cared for in a manner like you've always deserved, or as close as.
You will try to find me, but I warn you, this will be futile at best, so please, dear—
Live your life, the way you should, without me.

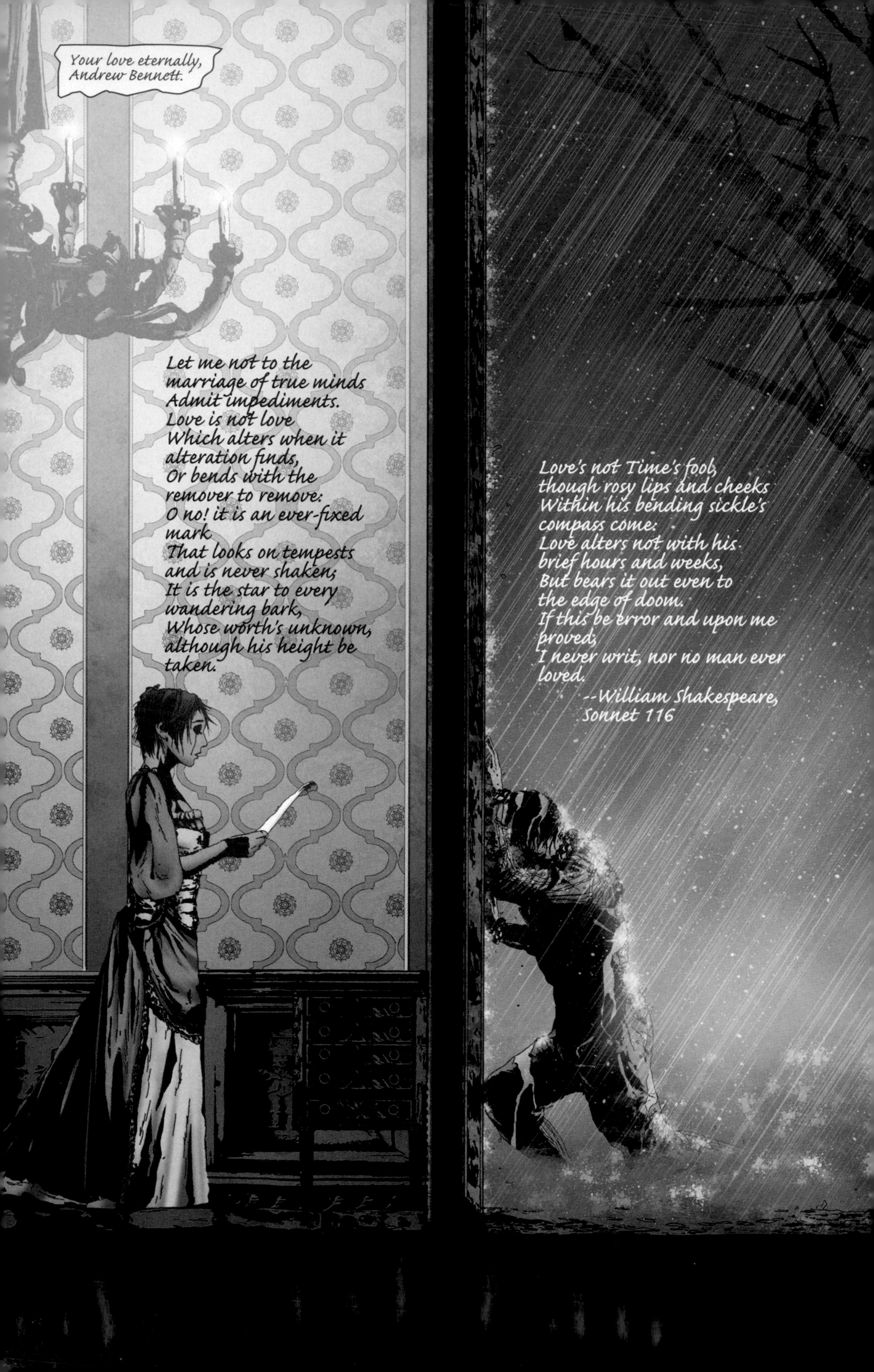
Your love eternally, Andrew Bennett.
Let me not to the marriage of true minds Admit impediments. Love is not love Which alters when it alteration finds, Or bends with the remover to remove: O no! it is an ever-fixed mark That looks on tempests and is never shaken; It is the star to every wandering bark, Whose worth's unknown, although his height be taken.
Love's not Time's fool, though rosy lips and cheeks Within his bending sickle's compass come: Love alters not with his brief hours and weeks, But bears it out even to the edge of doom. If this be error and upon me proved, I never writ, nor no man ever loved.
--William Shakespeare, Sonnet 116

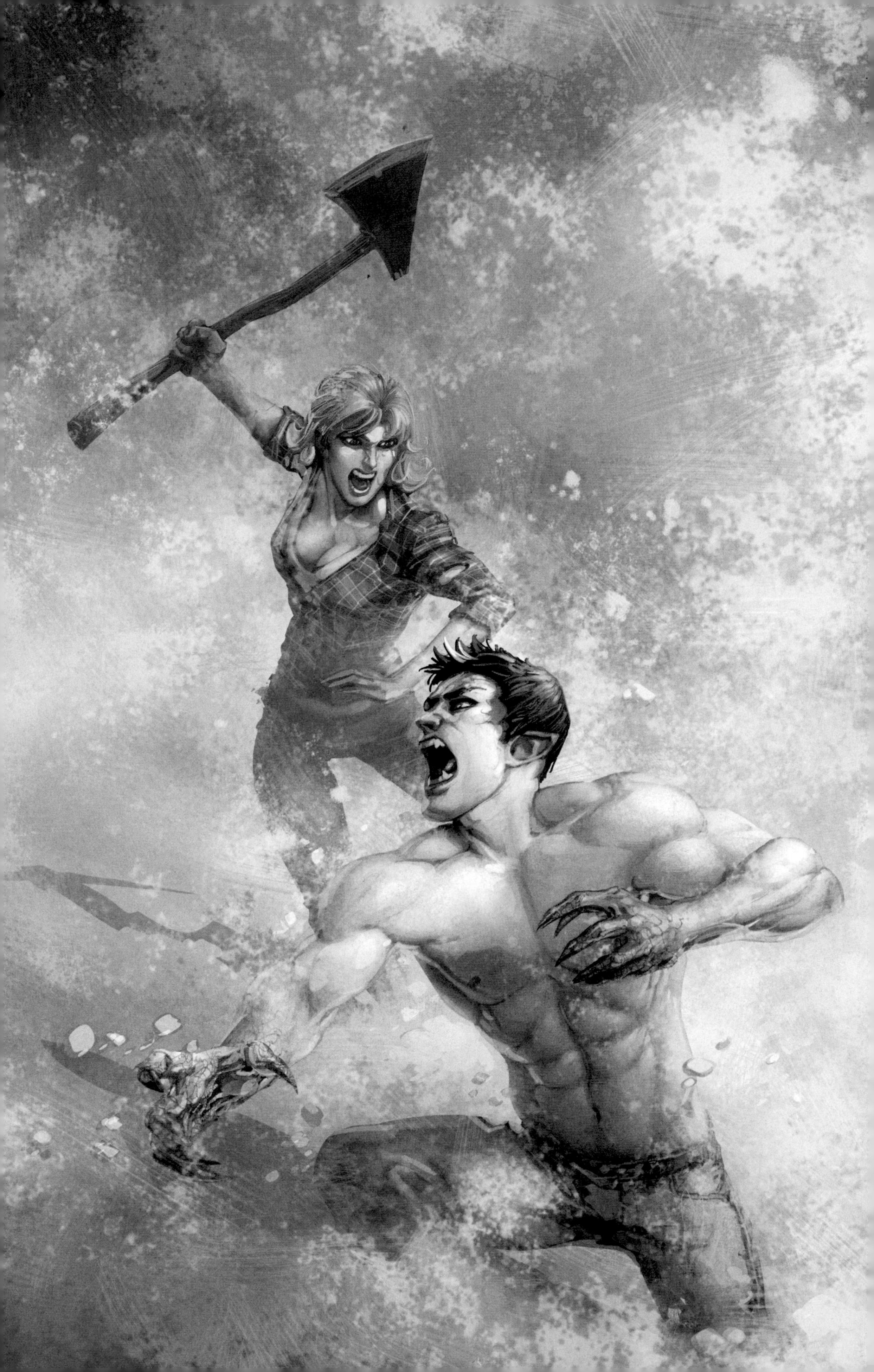

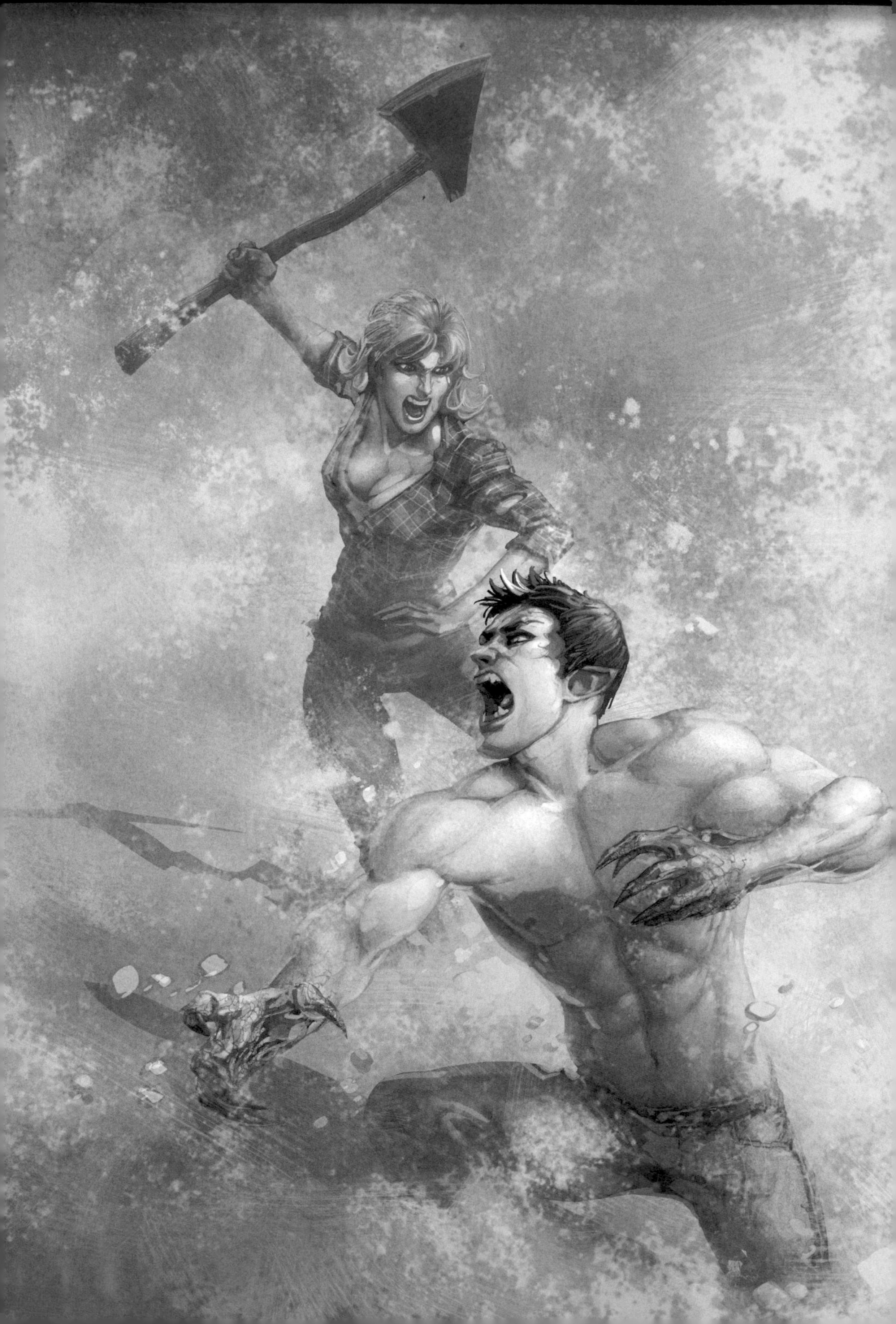

TWO MONTHS AGO, THE WORLD
AS MANY OF US KNEW IT ENDED.

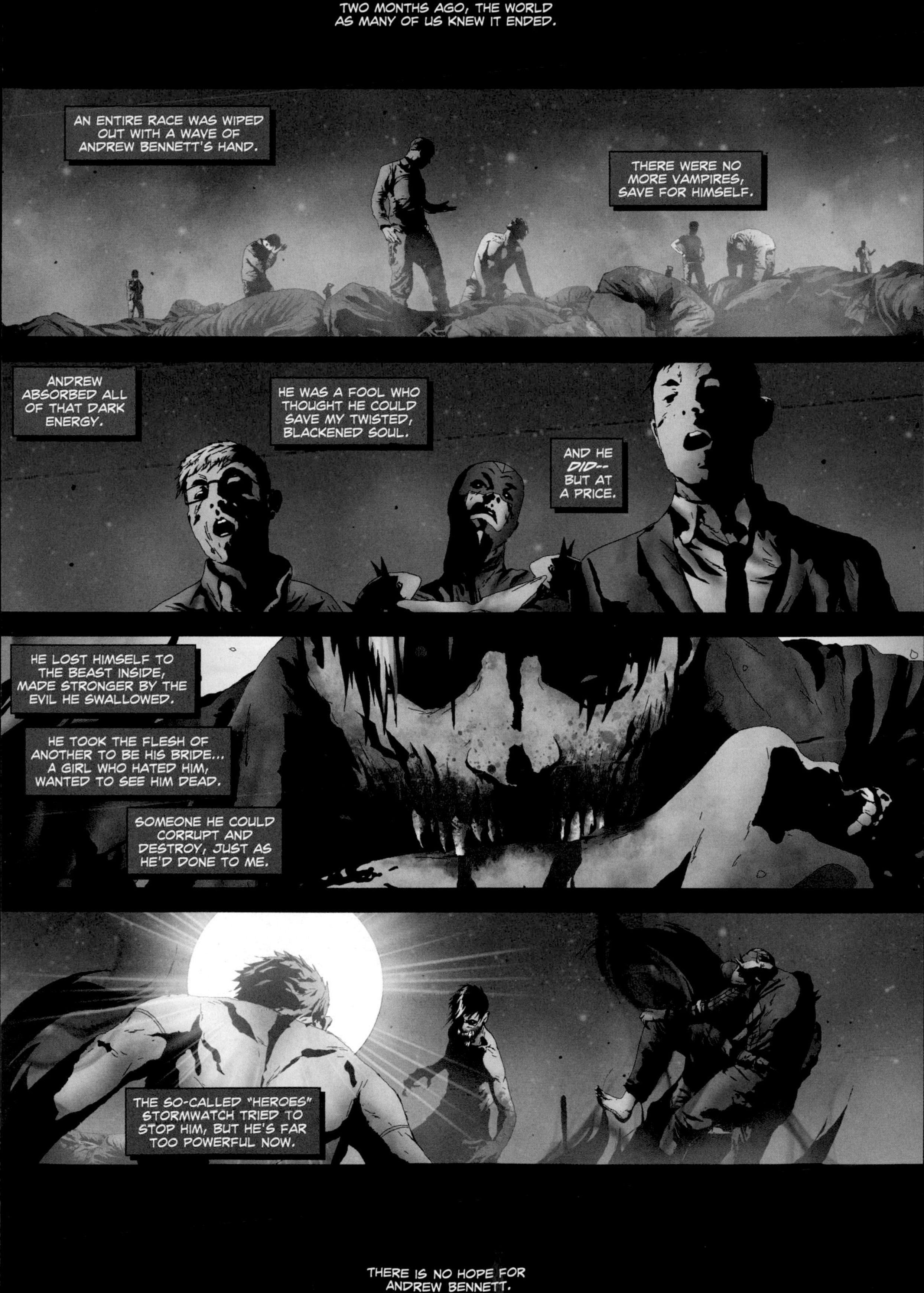
AN ENTIRE RACE WAS WIPED OUT WITH A WAVE OF ANDREW BENNETT'S HAND.
THERE WERE NO MORE VAMPIRES, SAVE FOR HIMSELF.
ANDREW ABSORBED ALL OF THAT DARK ENERGY.
HE WAS A FOOL WHO THOUGHT HE COULD SAVE MY TWISTED, BLACKENED SOUL.
AND HE *DID*-- BUT AT A PRICE.
HE LOST HIMSELF TO THE BEAST INSIDE, MADE STRONGER BY THE EVIL HE SWALLOWED.
HE TOOK THE FLESH OF ANOTHER TO BE HIS BRIDE... A GIRL WHO HATED HIM, WANTED TO SEE HIM DEAD.
SOMEONE HE COULD CORRUPT AND DESTROY, JUST AS HE'D DONE TO ME.
THE SO-CALLED "HEROES" STORMWATCH TRIED TO STOP HIM, BUT HE'S FAR TOO POWERFUL NOW.

THERE IS NO HOPE FOR
ANDREW BENNETT.

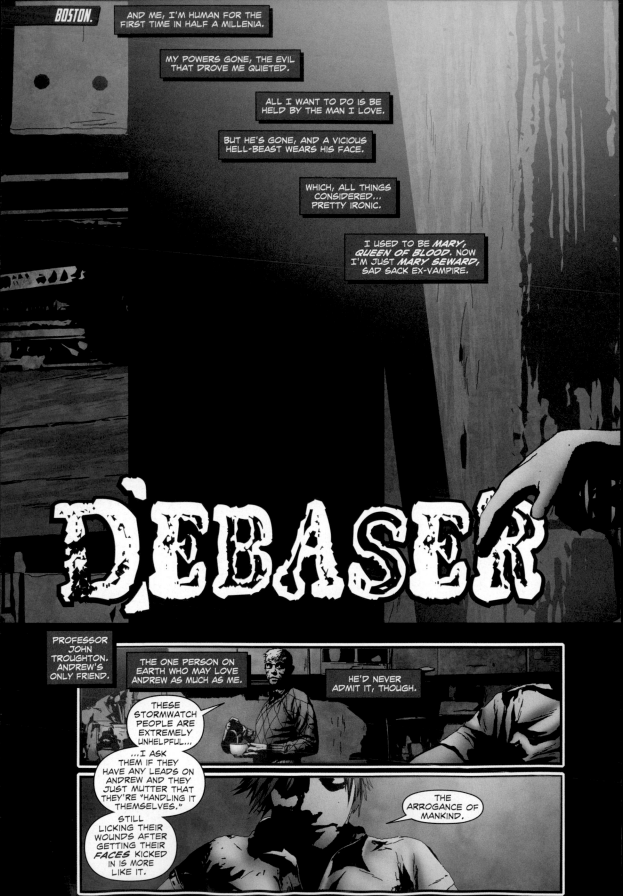

BOSTON.

AND ME, I'M HUMAN FOR THE FIRST TIME IN HALF A MILLENIA.

MY POWERS GONE, THE EVIL THAT DROVE ME QUIETED.

ALL I WANT TO DO IS BE HELD BY THE MAN I LOVE.

BUT HE'S GONE, AND A VICIOUS HELL-BEAST WEARS HIS FACE.

WHICH, ALL THINGS CONSIDERED... PRETTY IRONIC.

I USED TO BE *MARY, QUEEN OF BLOOD*. NOW I'M JUST *MARY SEWARD*, SAD SACK EX-VAMPIRE.

DEBASER

PROFESSOR JOHN TROUGHTON. ANDREW'S ONLY FRIEND.

THE ONE PERSON ON EARTH WHO MAY LOVE ANDREW AS MUCH AS ME.

HE'D NEVER ADMIT IT, THOUGH.

THESE STORMWATCH PEOPLE ARE EXTREMELY UNHELPFUL...

...I ASK THEM IF THEY HAVE ANY LEADS ON ANDREW AND THEY JUST MUTTER THAT THEY'RE "HANDLING IT THEMSELVES."

STILL LICKING THEIR WOUNDS AFTER GETTING THEIR *FACES* KICKED IN IS MORE LIKE IT.

THE ARROGANCE OF MANKIND.

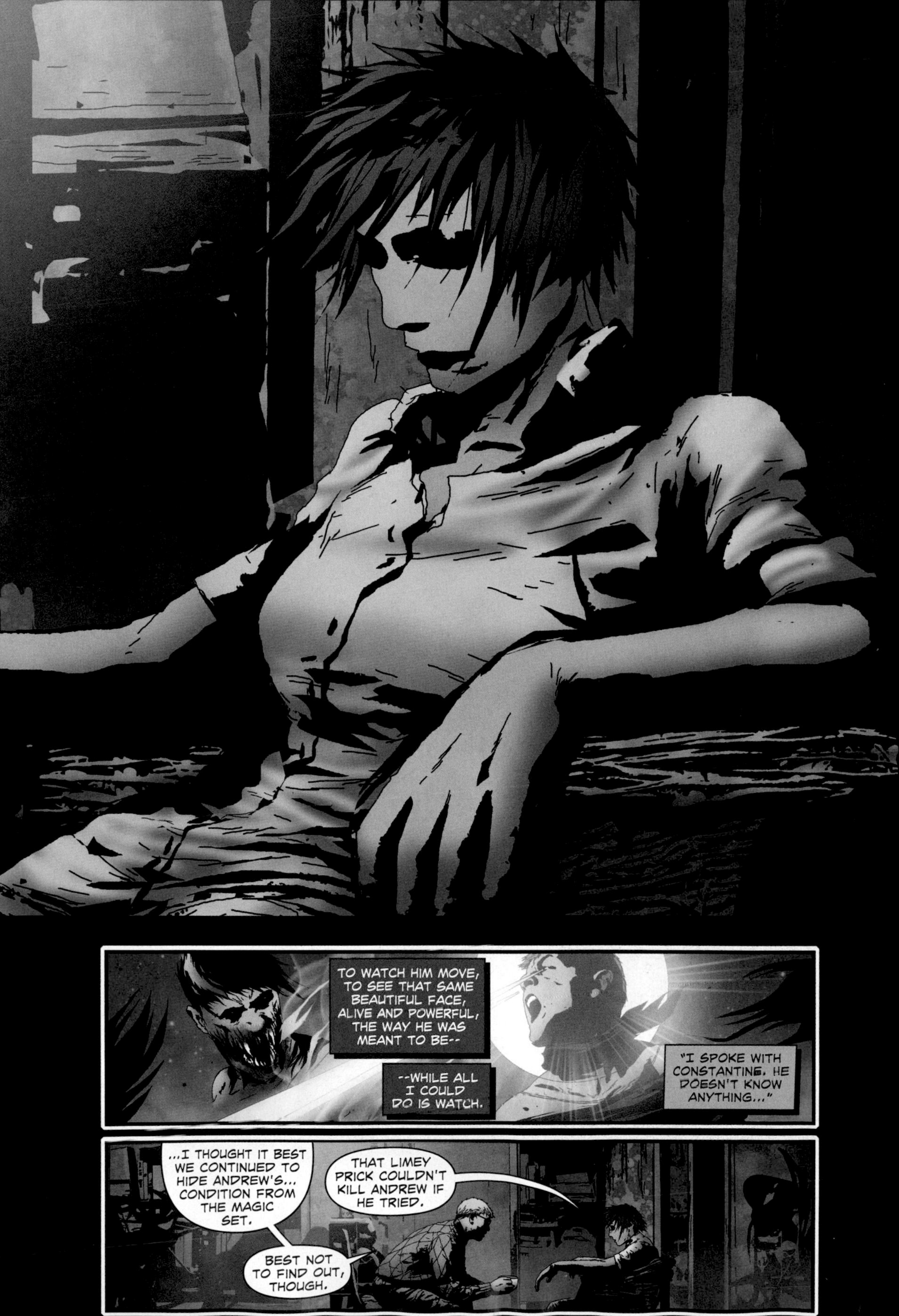
TO WATCH HIM MOVE, TO SEE THAT SAME BEAUTIFUL FACE, ALIVE AND POWERFUL, THE WAY HE WAS MEANT TO BE--
--WHILE ALL I COULD DO IS WATCH.
"I SPOKE WITH CONSTANTINE. HE DOESN'T KNOW ANYTHING..."
...I THOUGHT IT BEST WE CONTINUED TO HIDE ANDREW'S... CONDITION FROM THE MAGIC SET.
THAT LIMEY PRICK COULDN'T KILL ANDREW IF HE TRIED.
BEST NOT TO FIND OUT, THOUGH.

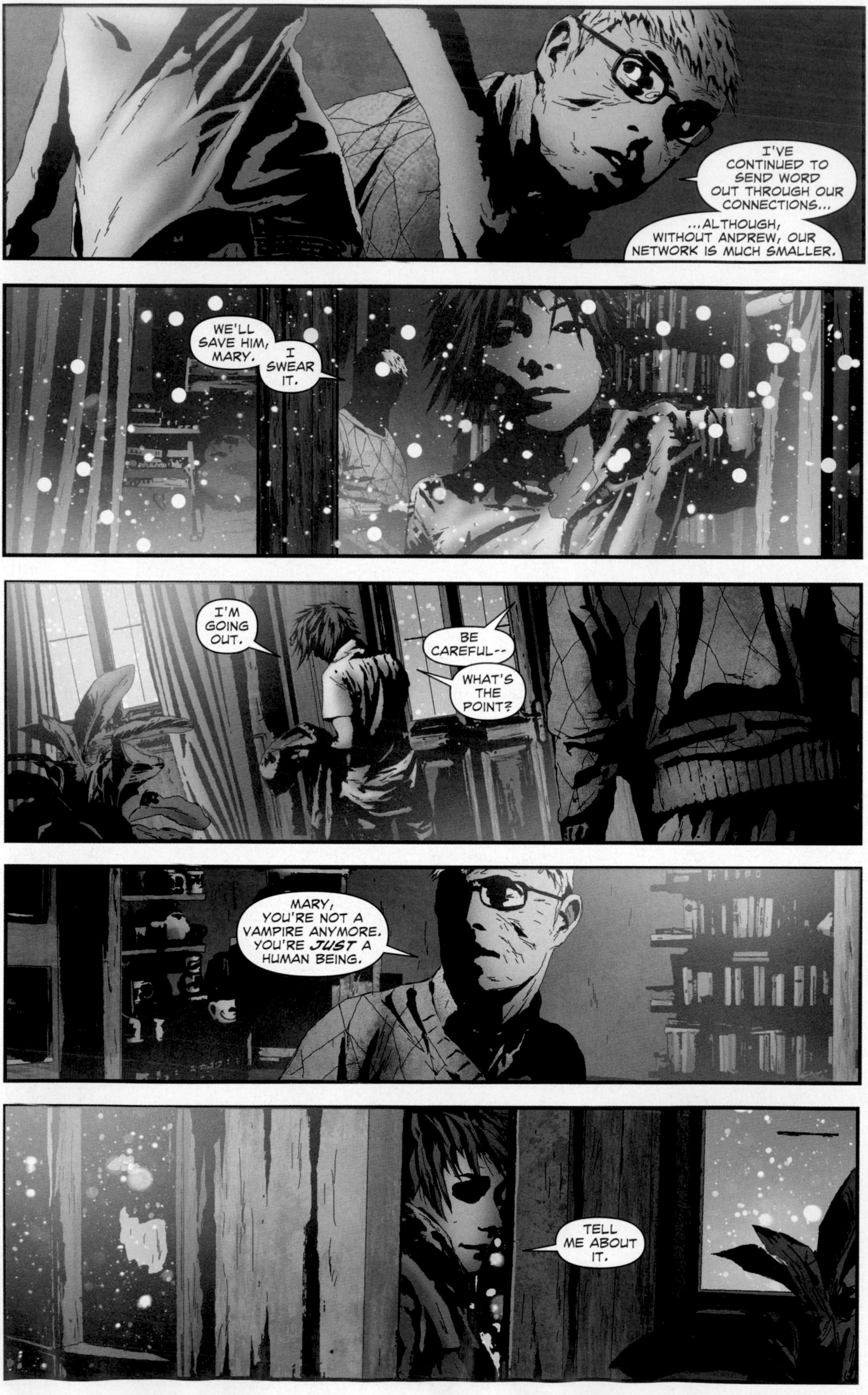
I'VE CONTINUED TO SEND WORD OUT THROUGH OUR CONNECTIONS...
...ALTHOUGH, WITHOUT ANDREW, OUR NETWORK IS MUCH SMALLER.
WE'LL SAVE HIM, MARY.
I SWEAR IT.
I'M GOING OUT.
BE CAREFUL--
WHAT'S THE POINT?
MARY, YOU'RE NOT A VAMPIRE ANYMORE. YOU'RE JUST A HUMAN BEING.
TELL ME ABOUT IT.

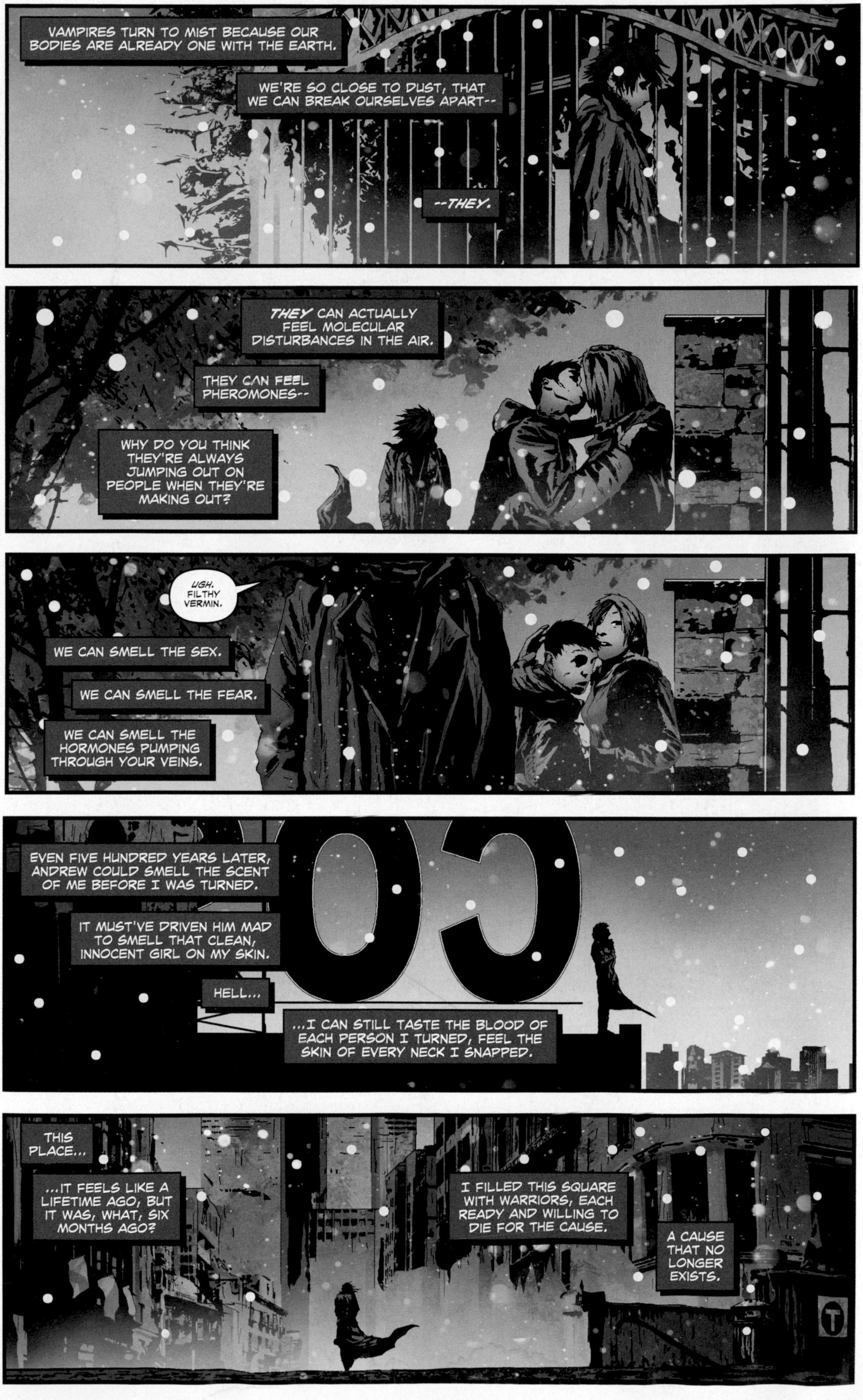
VAMPIRES TURN TO MIST BECAUSE OUR BODIES ARE ALREADY ONE WITH THE EARTH.
WE'RE SO CLOSE TO DUST, THAT WE CAN BREAK OURSELVES APART--
--THEY.
THEY CAN ACTUALLY FEEL MOLECULAR DISTURBANCES IN THE AIR.
THEY CAN FEEL PHEROMONES--
WHY DO YOU THINK THEY'RE ALWAYS JUMPING OUT ON PEOPLE WHEN THEY'RE MAKING OUT?
UGH. FILTHY VERMIN.
WE CAN SMELL THE SEX.
WE CAN SMELL THE FEAR.
WE CAN SMELL THE HORMONES PUMPING THROUGH YOUR VEINS.
EVEN FIVE HUNDRED YEARS LATER, ANDREW COULD SMELL THE SCENT OF ME BEFORE I WAS TURNED.
IT MUST'VE DRIVEN HIM MAD TO SMELL THAT CLEAN, INNOCENT GIRL ON MY SKIN.
HELL...
...I CAN STILL TASTE THE BLOOD OF EACH PERSON I TURNED, FEEL THE SKIN OF EVERY NECK I SNAPPED.
THIS PLACE...
...IT FEELS LIKE A LIFETIME AGO, BUT IT WAS, WHAT, SIX MONTHS AGO?
I FILLED THIS SQUARE WITH WARRIORS, EACH READY AND WILLING TO DIE FOR THE CAUSE.
A CAUSE THAT NO LONGER EXISTS.

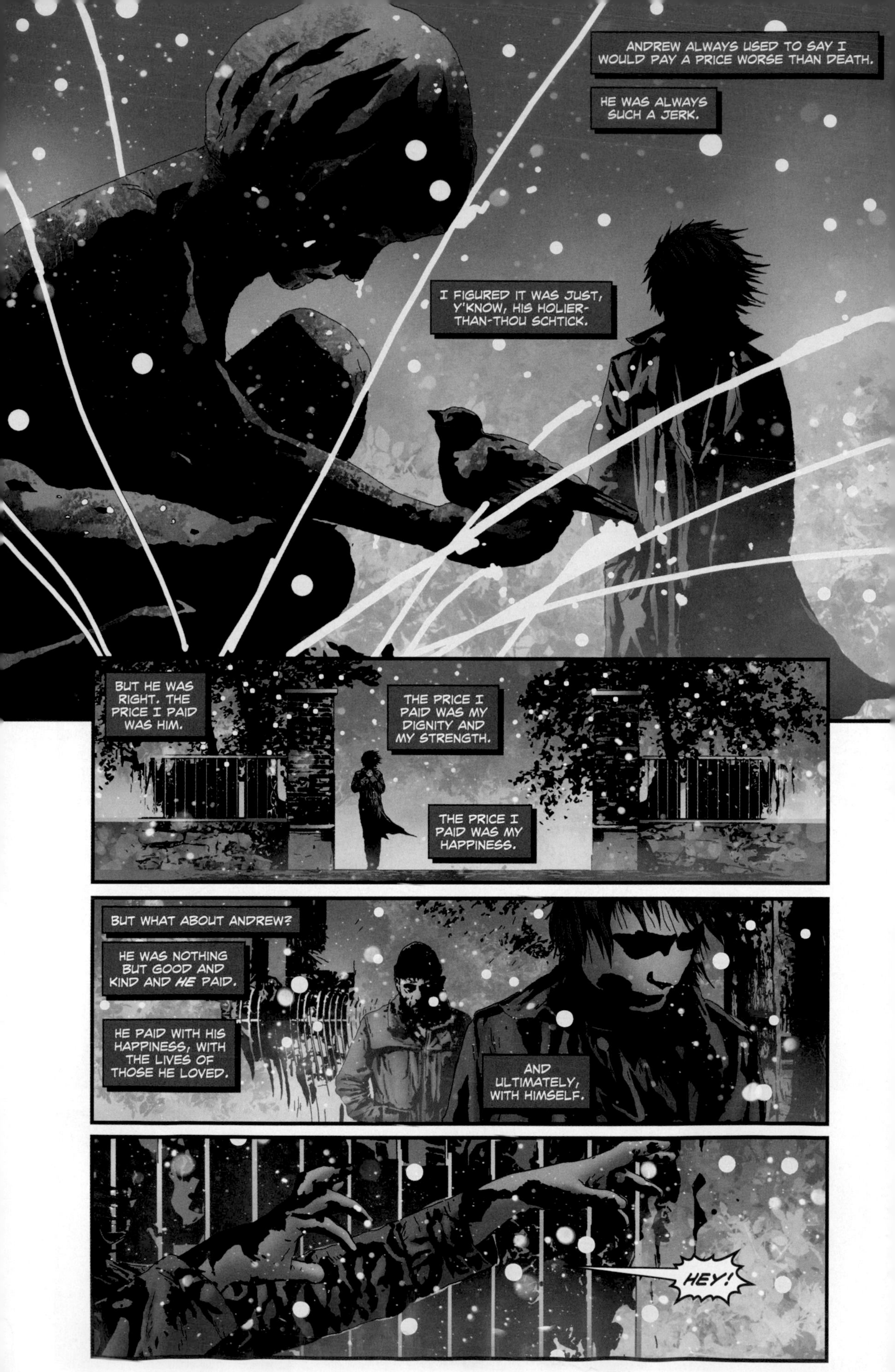
ANDREW ALWAYS USED TO SAY I WOULD PAY A PRICE WORSE THAN DEATH.
HE WAS ALWAYS SUCH A JERK.
I FIGURED IT WAS JUST, Y'KNOW, HIS HOLIER-THAN-THOU SCHTICK.
BUT HE WAS RIGHT. THE PRICE I PAID WAS HIM.
THE PRICE I PAID WAS MY DIGNITY AND MY STRENGTH.
THE PRICE I PAID WAS MY HAPPINESS.
BUT WHAT ABOUT ANDREW?
HE WAS NOTHING BUT GOOD AND KIND AND *HE* PAID.
HE PAID WITH HIS HAPPINESS, WITH THE LIVES OF THOSE HE LOVED.
AND ULTIMATELY, WITH HIMSELF.
HEY!

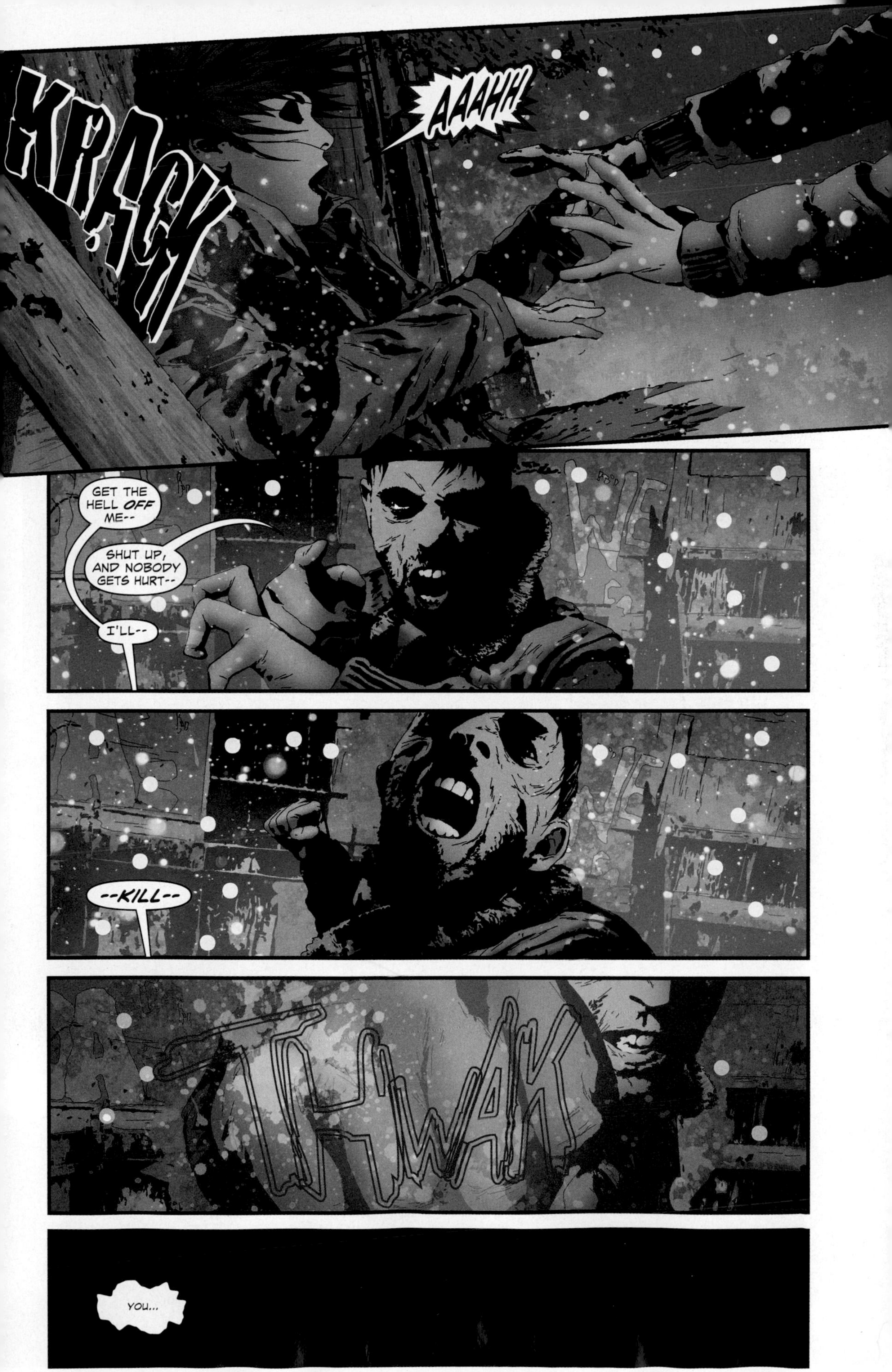
KRACK
AAAHH!
GET THE HELL OFF ME--
SHUT UP, AND NOBODY GETS HURT--
I'LL--
--KILL--
THWAK
YOU...

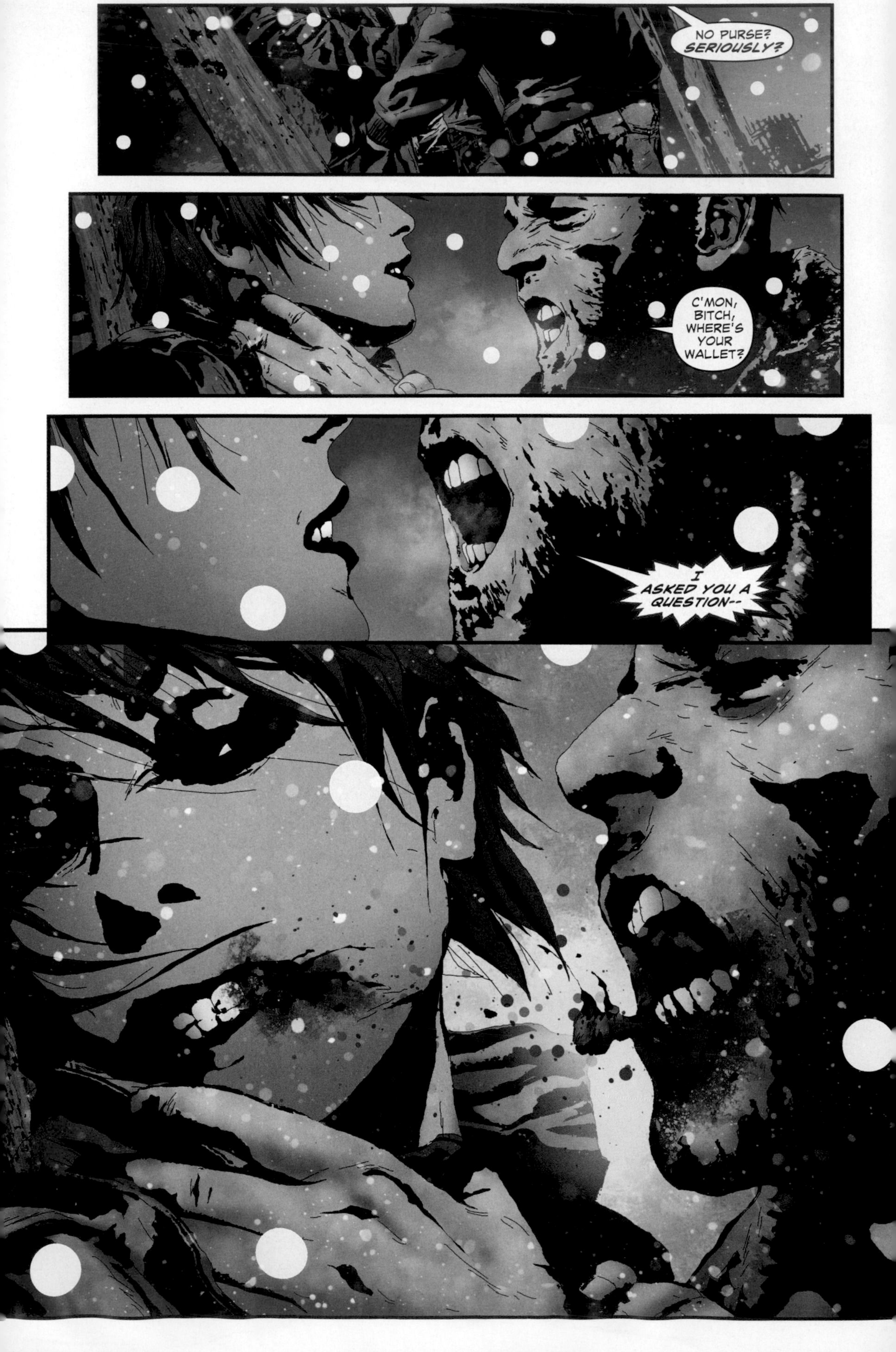
NO PURSE? SERIOUSLY?
C'MON, BITCH, WHERE'S YOUR WALLET?
I ASKED YOU A QUESTION--

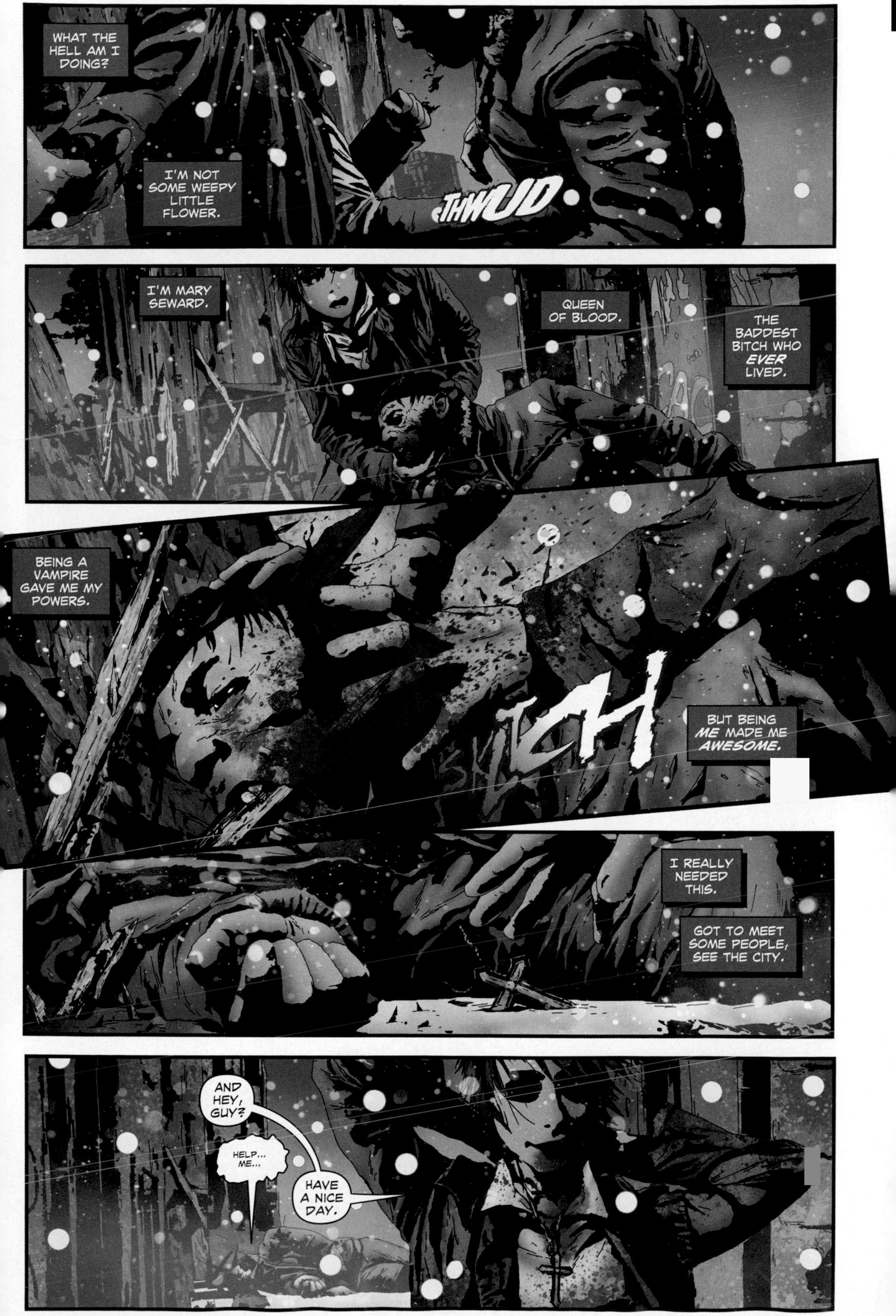
WHAT THE HELL AM I DOING?
I'M NOT SOME WEEPY LITTLE FLOWER.
THWUD
I'M MARY SEWARD.
QUEEN OF BLOOD.
THE BADDEST BITCH WHO EVER LIVED.
BEING A VAMPIRE GAVE ME MY POWERS.
SKLICH
BUT BEING ME MADE ME AWESOME.
I REALLY NEEDED THIS.
GOT TO MEET SOME PEOPLE, SEE THE CITY.
AND HEY, GUY?
HELP... ME...
HAVE A NICE DAY.

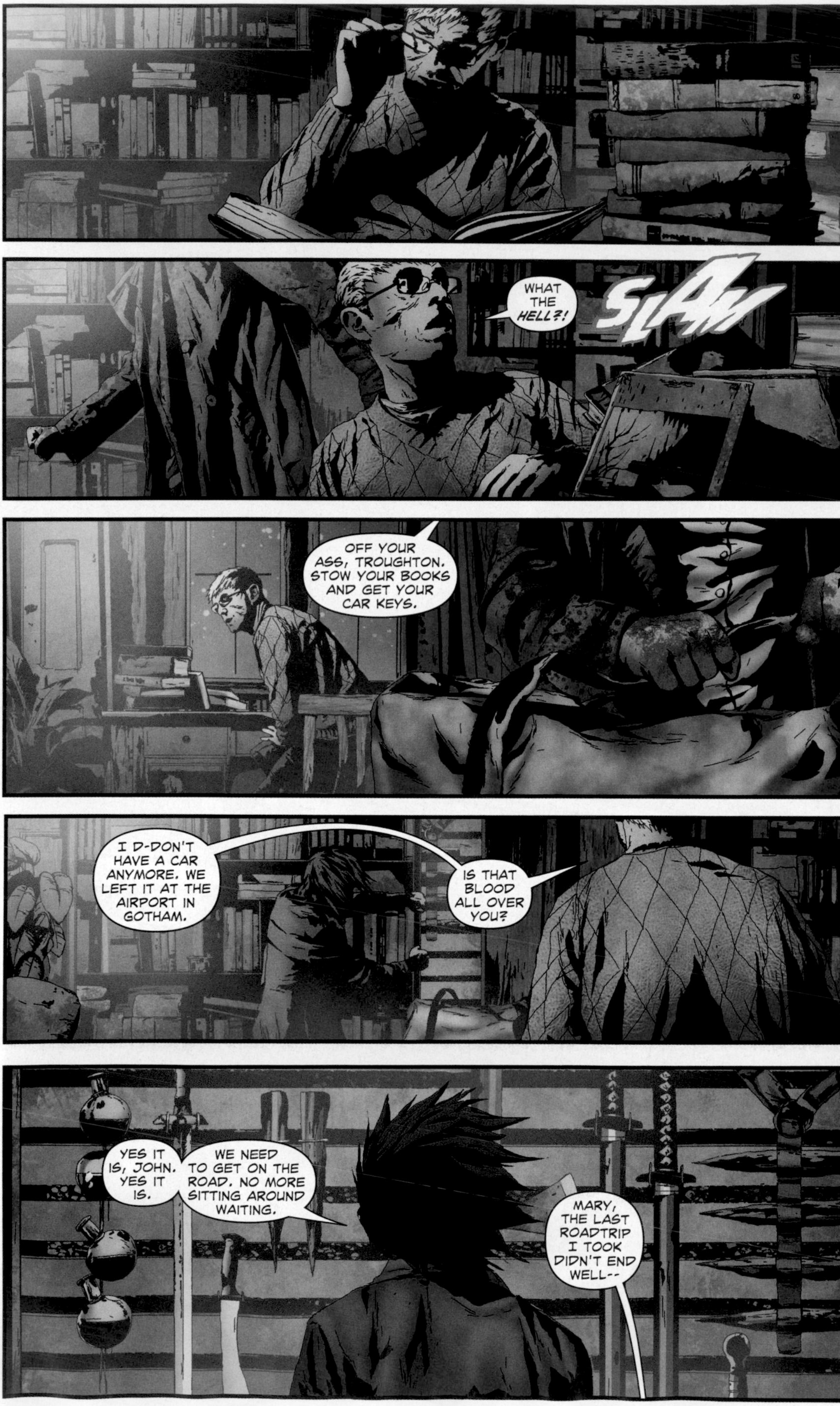
WHAT THE HELL?!
SLAM
OFF YOUR ASS, TROUGHTON. STOW YOUR BOOKS AND GET YOUR CAR KEYS.
I D-DON'T HAVE A CAR ANYMORE. WE LEFT IT AT THE AIRPORT IN GOTHAM.
IS THAT BLOOD ALL OVER YOU?
YES IT IS, JOHN. YES IT IS.
WE NEED TO GET ON THE ROAD. NO MORE SITTING AROUND WAITING.
MARY, THE LAST ROADTRIP I TOOK DIDN'T END WELL--

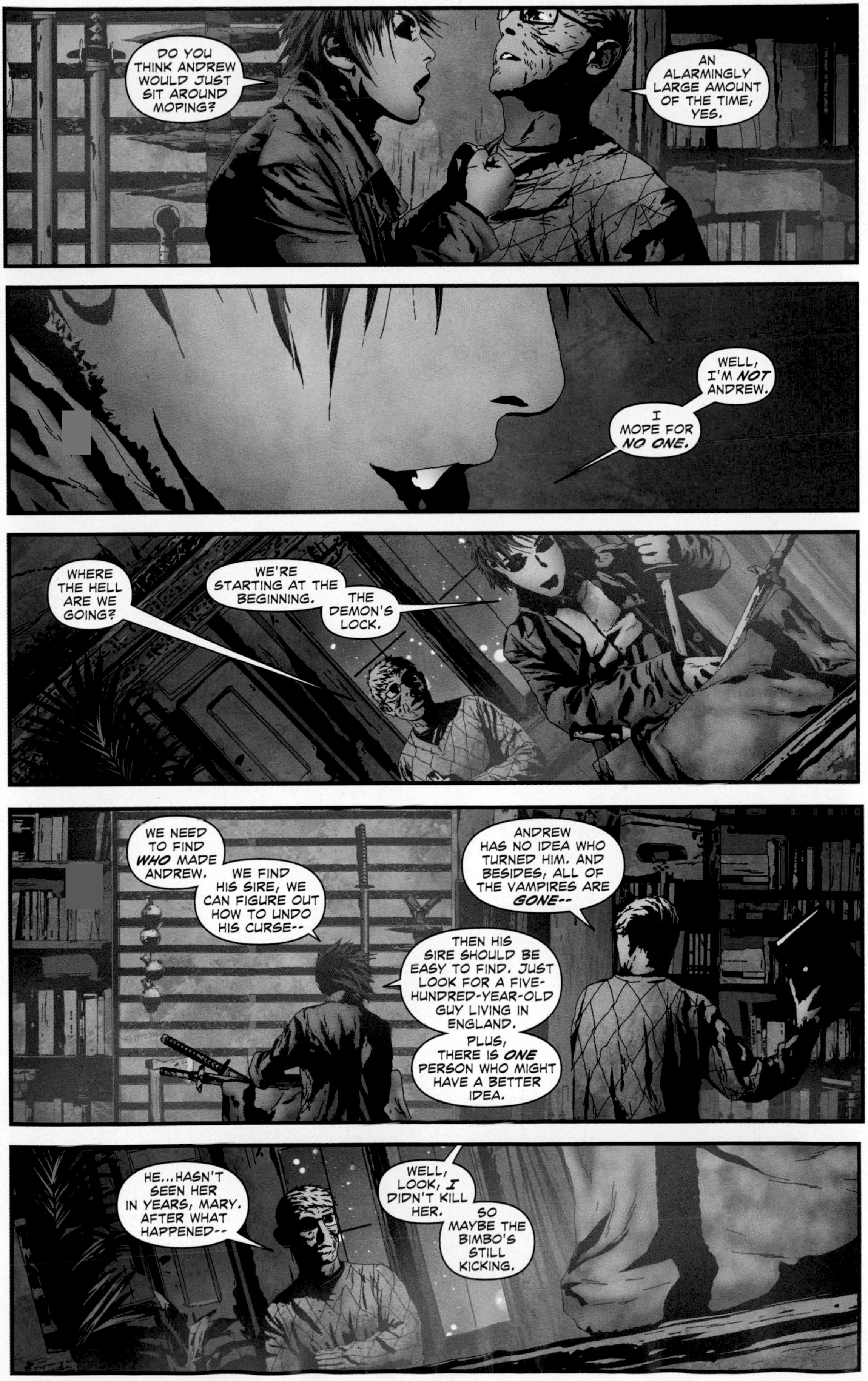
DO YOU THINK ANDREW WOULD JUST SIT AROUND MOPING?
AN ALARMINGLY LARGE AMOUNT OF THE TIME, YES.
WELL, I'M *NOT* ANDREW.
I MOPE FOR *NO ONE.*
WHERE THE HELL ARE WE GOING?
WE'RE STARTING AT THE BEGINNING.
THE DEMON'S LOCK.
WE NEED TO FIND *WHO* MADE ANDREW.
WE FIND HIS SIRE, WE CAN FIGURE OUT HOW TO UNDO HIS CURSE--
ANDREW HAS NO IDEA WHO TURNED HIM. AND BESIDES, ALL OF THE VAMPIRES ARE *GONE--*
THEN HIS SIRE SHOULD BE EASY TO FIND. JUST LOOK FOR A FIVE-HUNDRED-YEAR-OLD GUY LIVING IN ENGLAND.
PLUS, THERE IS *ONE* PERSON WHO MIGHT HAVE A BETTER IDEA.
HE...HASN'T SEEN HER IN YEARS, MARY. AFTER WHAT HAPPENED--
WELL, LOOK, *I* DIDN'T KILL HER.
SO MAYBE THE BIMBO'S STILL KICKING.

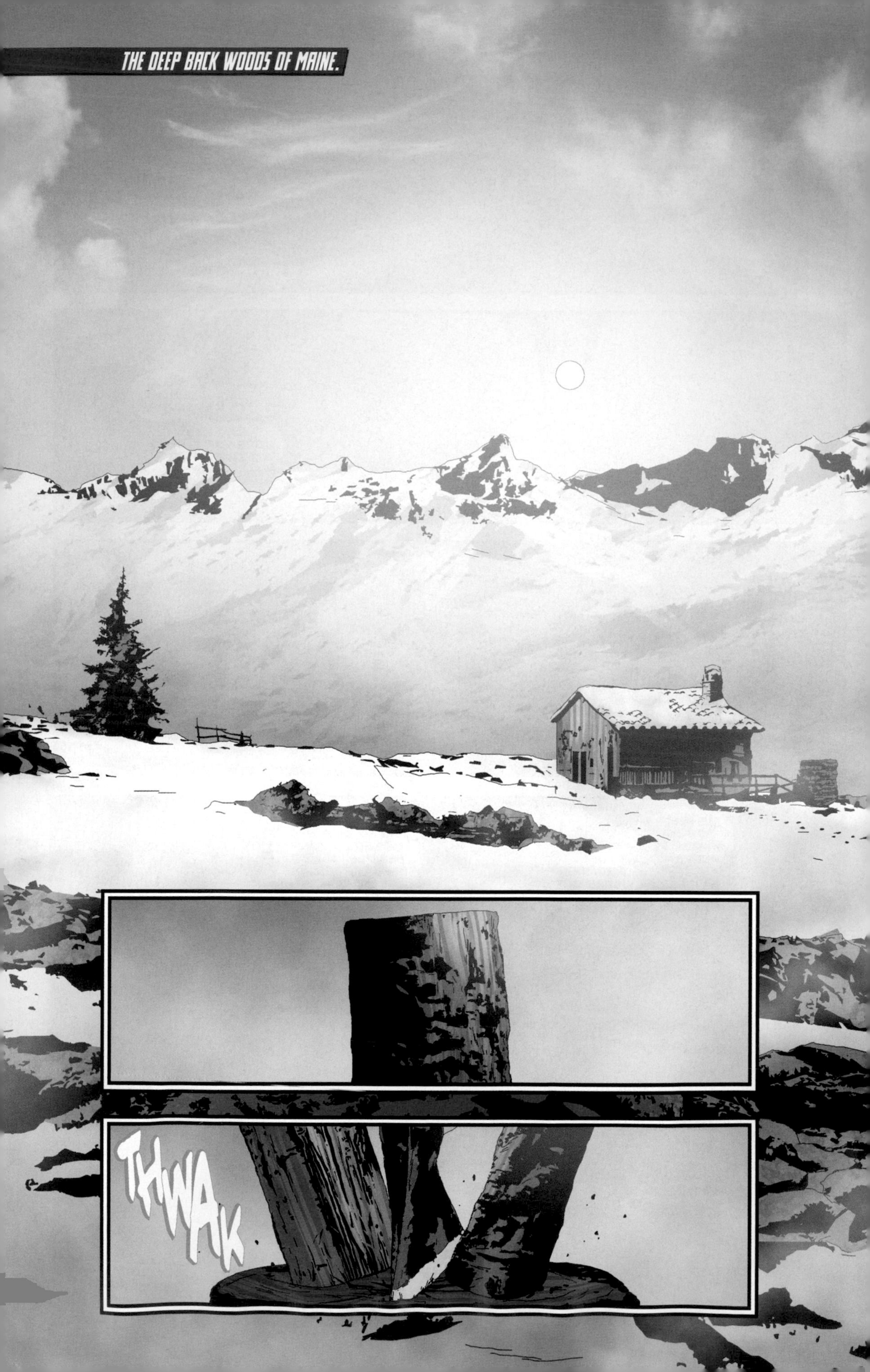
THE DEEP BACK WOODS OF MAINE.
THWAK

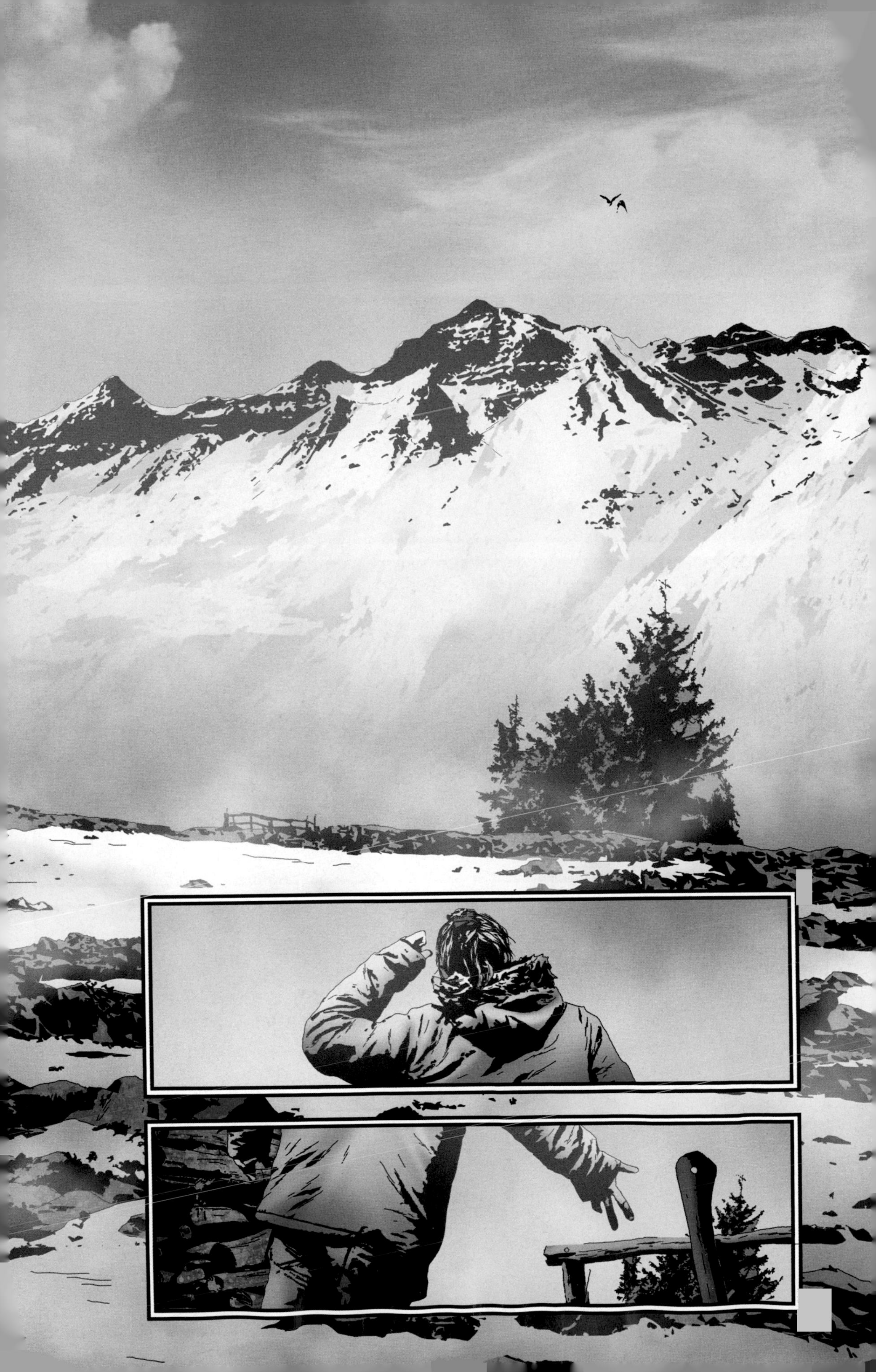

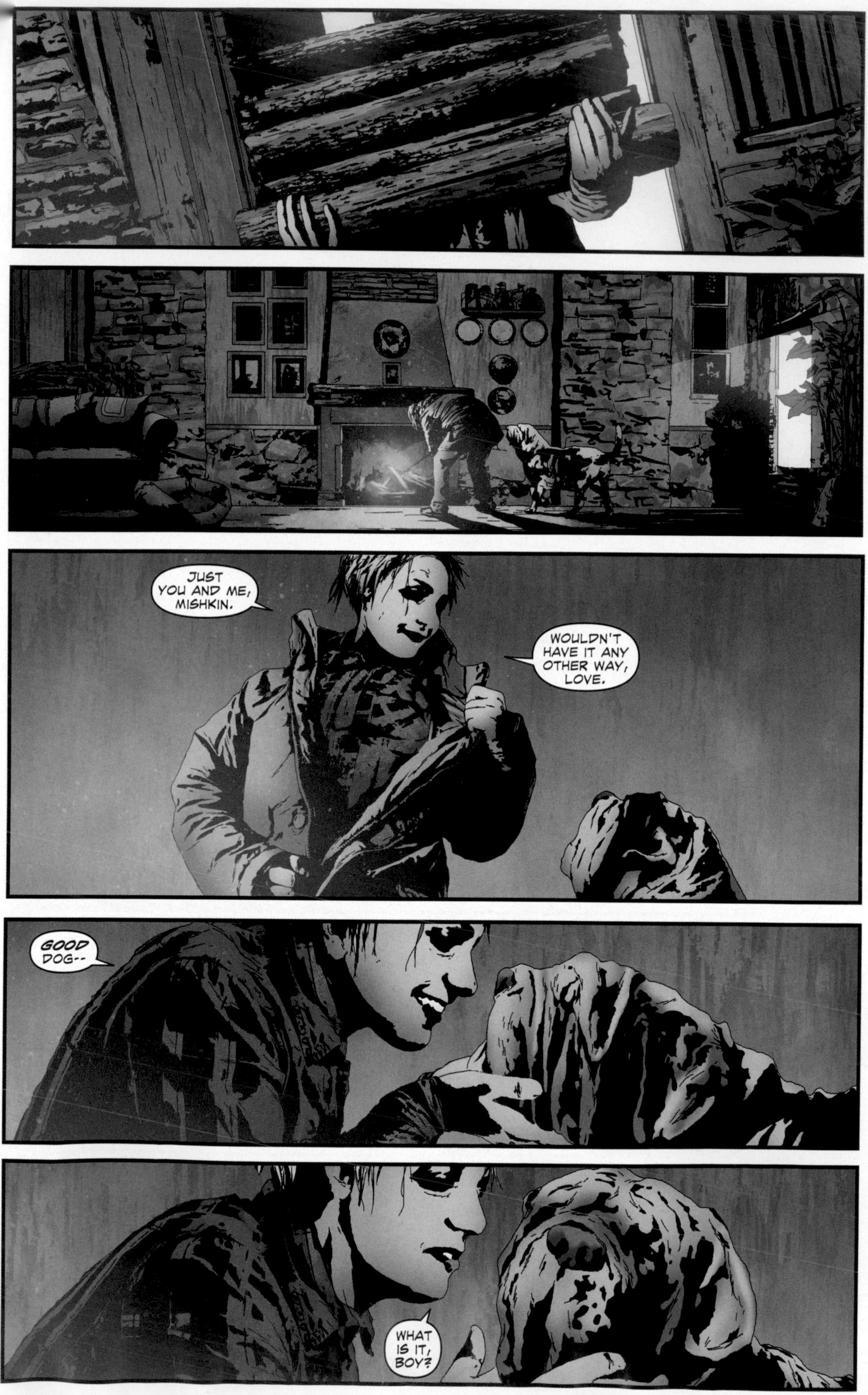
JUST YOU AND ME, MISHKIN.
WOULDN'T HAVE IT ANY OTHER WAY, LOVE.
GOOD DOG--
WHAT IS IT, BOY?

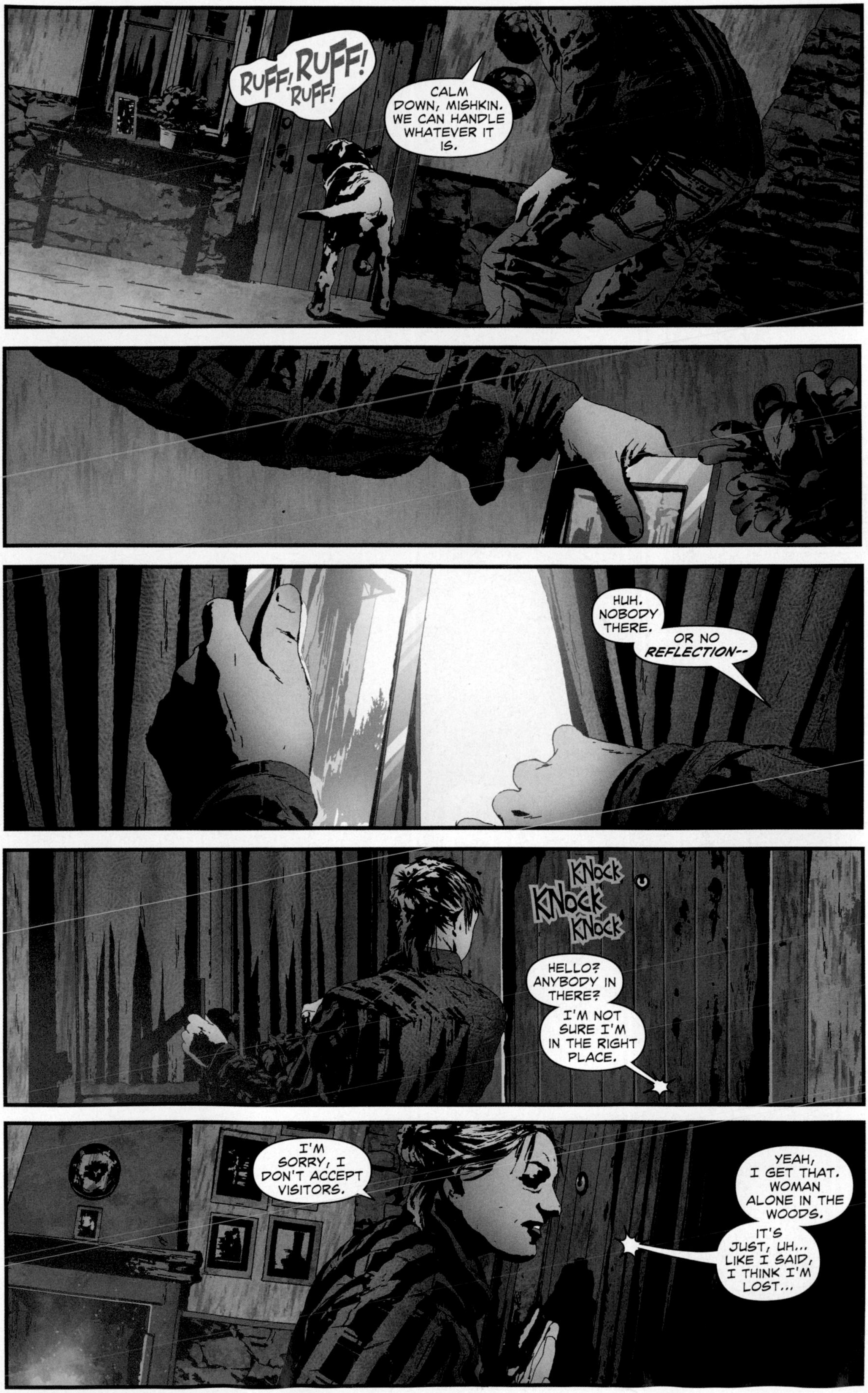
RUFF! RUFF! RUFF!
CALM DOWN, MISHKIN. WE CAN HANDLE WHATEVER IT IS.
HUH. NOBODY THERE.
OR NO REFLECTION--
KNOCK KNOCK KNOCK
HELLO? ANYBODY IN THERE?
I'M NOT SURE I'M IN THE RIGHT PLACE.
I'M SORRY, I DON'T ACCEPT VISITORS.
YEAH, I GET THAT. WOMAN ALONE IN THE WOODS.
IT'S JUST, UH... LIKE I SAID, I THINK I'M LOST...

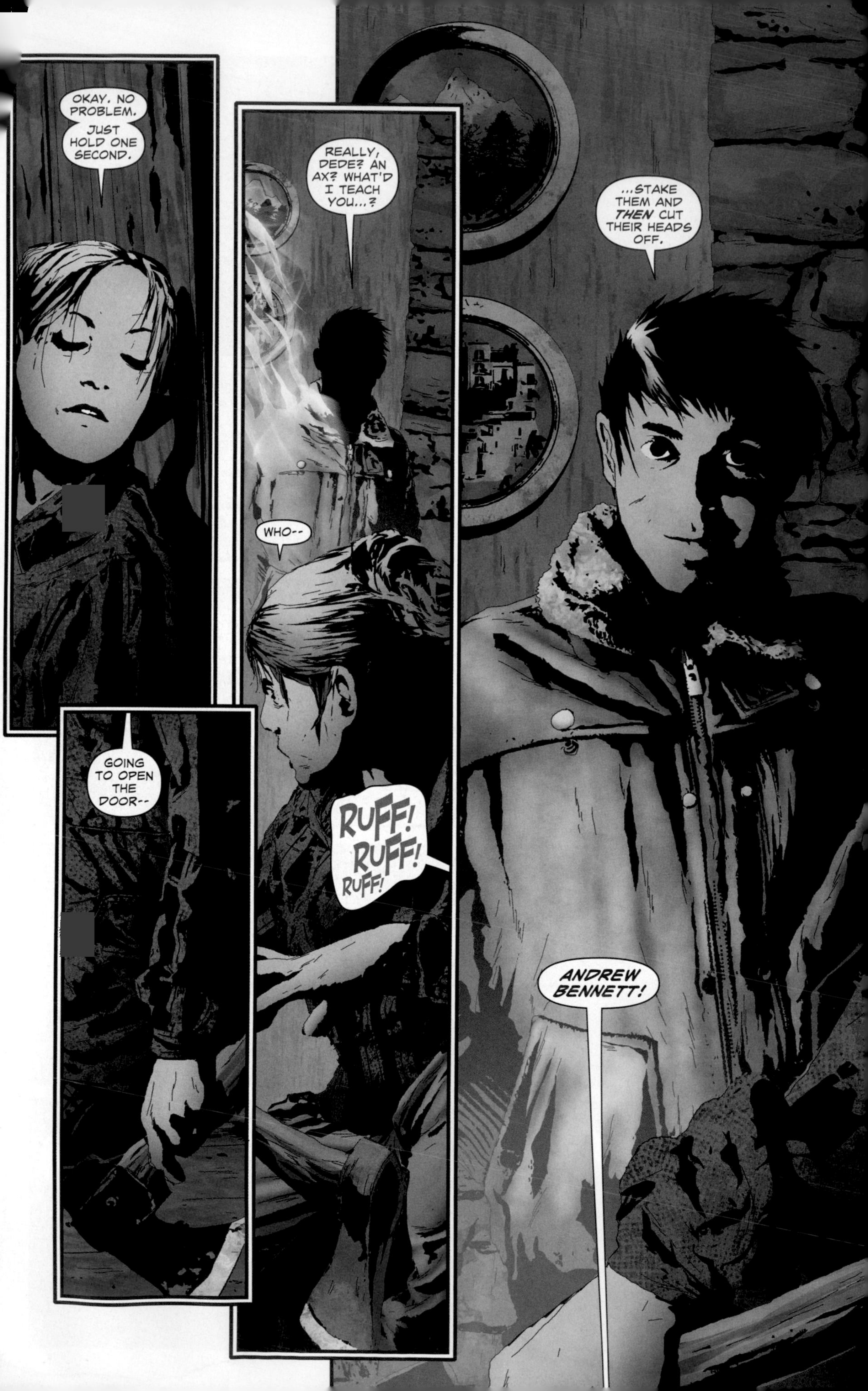
OKAY. NO PROBLEM. JUST HOLD ONE SECOND.
GOING TO OPEN THE DOOR--
REALLY, DEDE? AN AX? WHAT'D I TEACH YOU...?
WHO--
RUFF! RUFF! RUFF!
...STAKE THEM AND *THEN* CUT THEIR HEADS OFF.
ANDREW BENNETT!

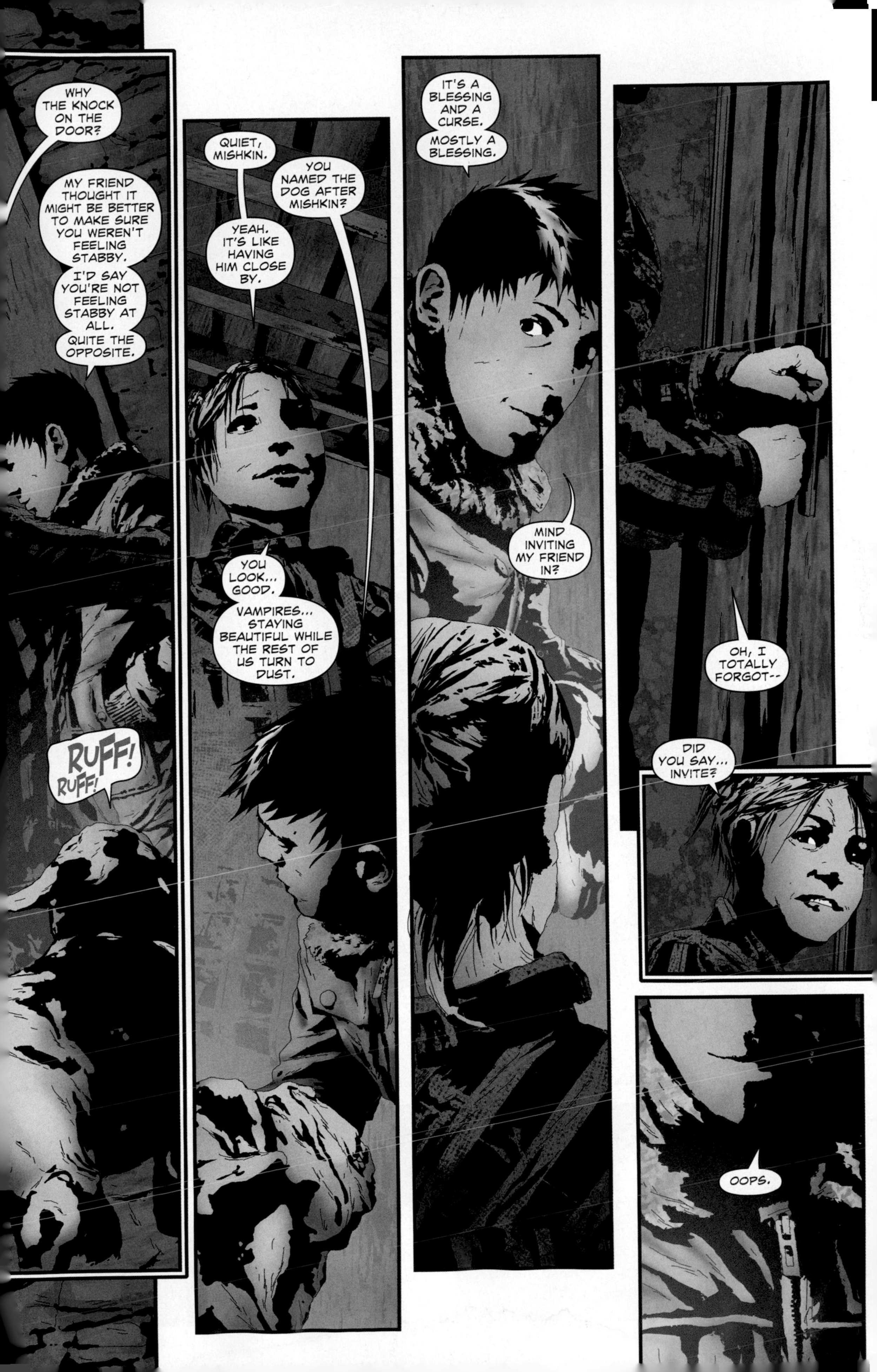
WHY THE KNOCK ON THE DOOR?
MY FRIEND THOUGHT IT MIGHT BE BETTER TO MAKE SURE YOU WEREN'T FEELING STABBY.
I'D SAY YOU'RE NOT FEELING STABBY AT ALL.
QUITE THE OPPOSITE.
RUFF! RUFF!
QUIET, MISHKIN.
YOU NAMED THE DOG AFTER MISHKIN?
YEAH. IT'S LIKE HAVING HIM CLOSE BY.
YOU LOOK... GOOD.
VAMPIRES... STAYING BEAUTIFUL WHILE THE REST OF US TURN TO DUST.
IT'S A BLESSING AND A CURSE.
MOSTLY A BLESSING.
MIND INVITING MY FRIEND IN?
OH, I TOTALLY FORGOT--
DID YOU SAY... INVITE?
OOPS.

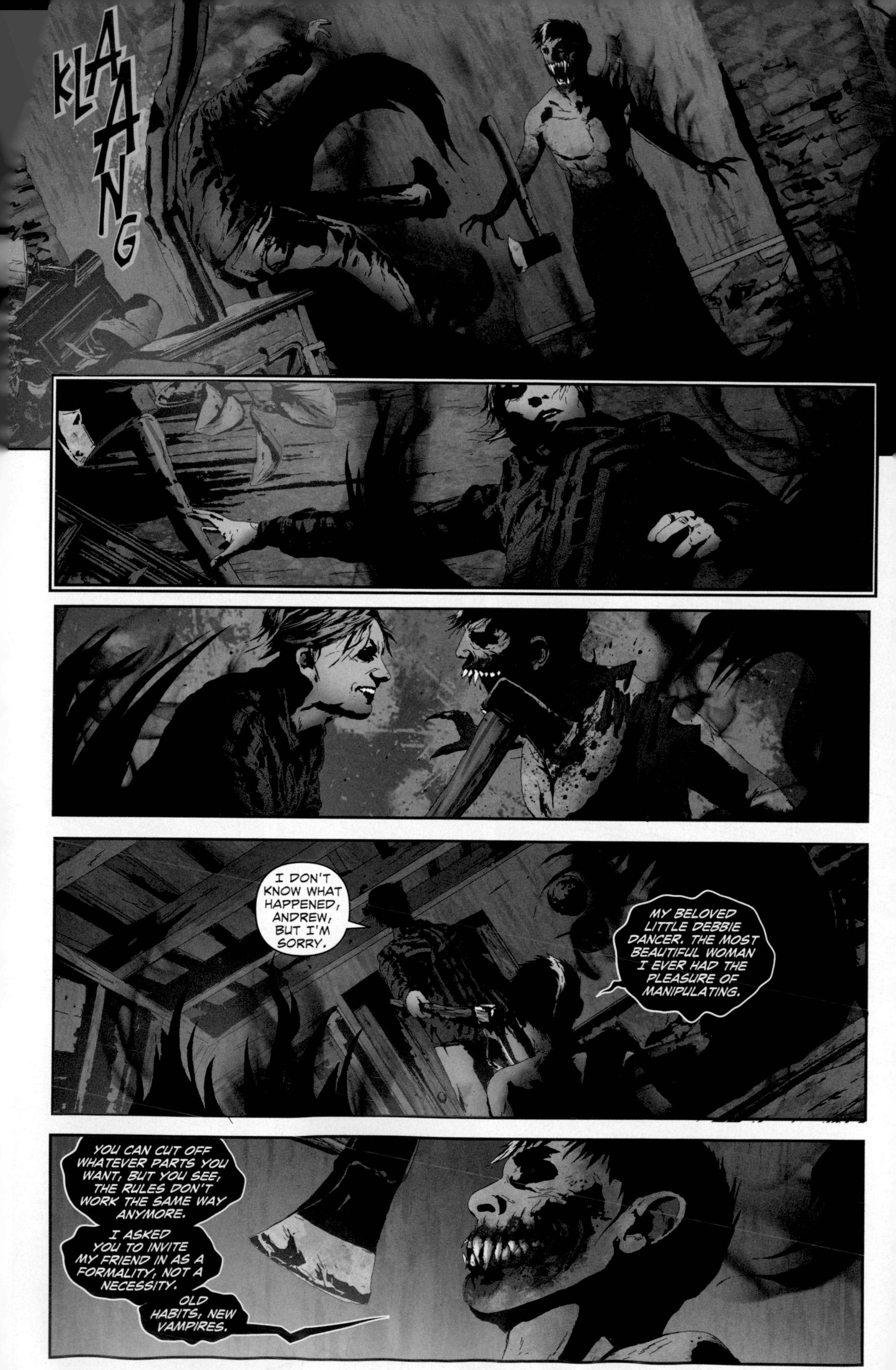
KLAAANG
I DON'T KNOW WHAT HAPPENED, ANDREW, BUT I'M SORRY.
MY BELOVED LITTLE DEBBIE DANCER. THE MOST BEAUTIFUL WOMAN I EVER HAD THE PLEASURE OF MANIPULATING.
YOU CAN CUT OFF WHATEVER PARTS YOU WANT, BUT YOU SEE, THE RULES DON'T WORK THE SAME WAY ANYMORE.
I ASKED YOU TO INVITE MY FRIEND IN AS A FORMALITY, NOT A NECESSITY.
OLD HABITS, NEW VAMPIRES.

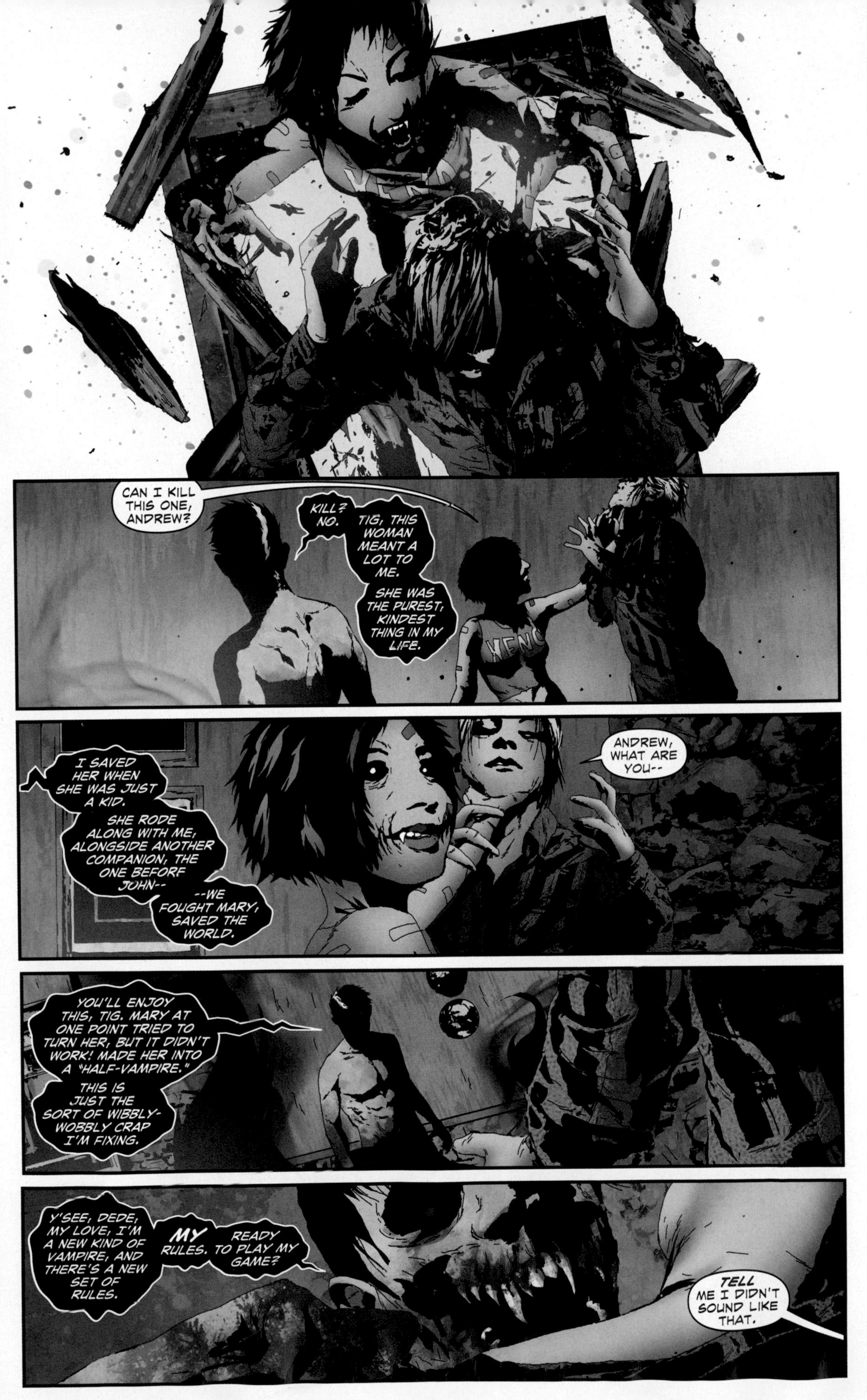
CAN I KILL THIS ONE, ANDREW?
KILL? NO.
TIG, THIS WOMAN MEANT A LOT TO ME.
SHE WAS THE PUREST, KINDEST THING IN MY LIFE.
I SAVED HER WHEN SHE WAS JUST A KID.
SHE RODE ALONG WITH ME, ALONGSIDE ANOTHER COMPANION, THE ONE BEFORE JOHN--
--WE FOUGHT MARY, SAVED THE WORLD.
ANDREW, WHAT ARE YOU--
YOU'LL ENJOY THIS, TIG. MARY AT ONE POINT TRIED TO TURN HER, BUT IT DIDN'T WORK! MADE HER INTO A "HALF-VAMPIRE."
THIS IS JUST THE SORT OF WIBBLY-WOBBLY CRAP I'M FIXING.
Y'SEE, DEDE, MY LOVE, I'M A NEW KIND OF VAMPIRE, AND THERE'S A NEW SET OF RULES.
MY RULES.
READY TO PLAY MY GAME?
TELL ME I DIDN'T SOUND LIKE THAT.

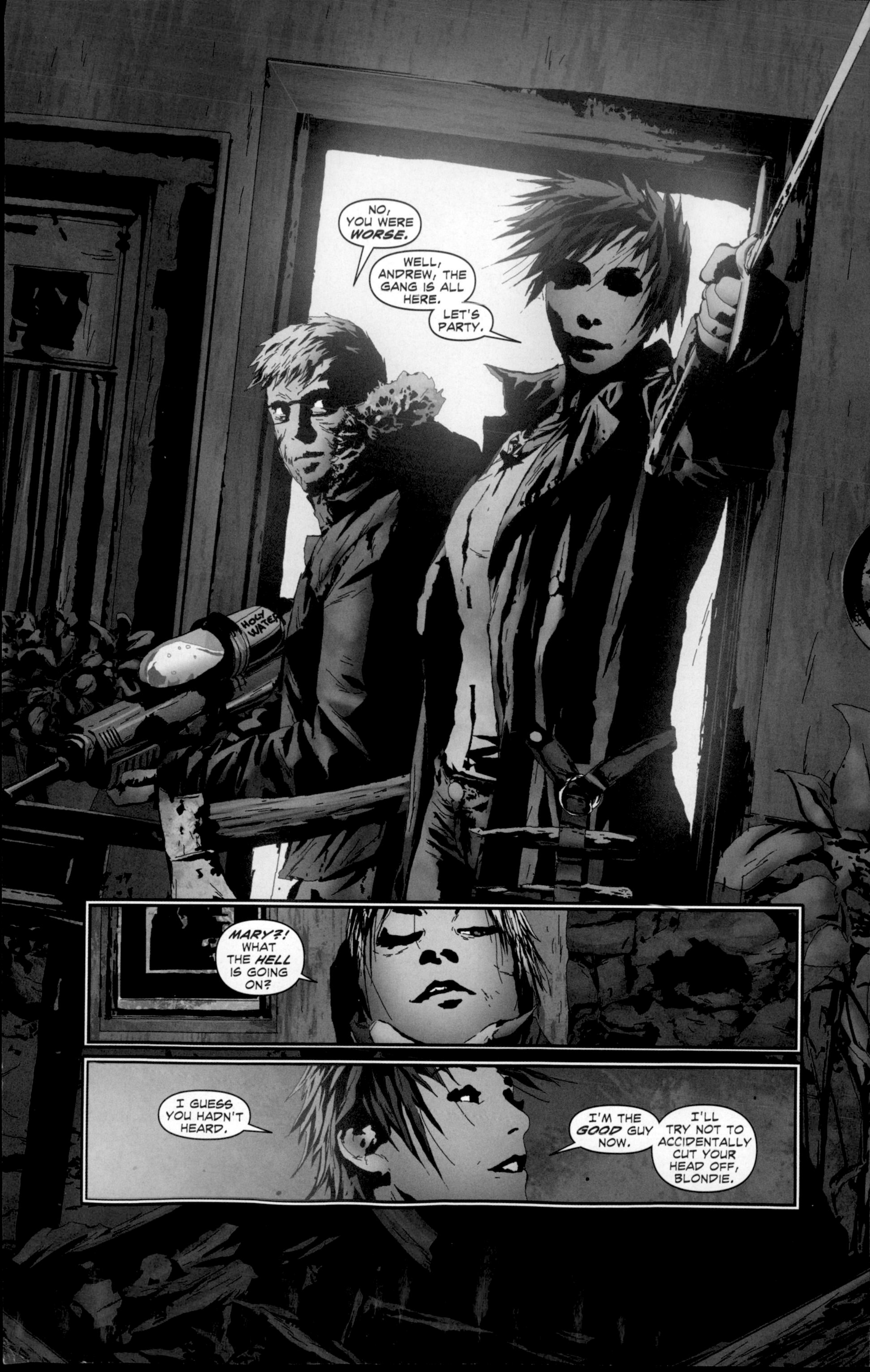
NO, YOU WERE WORSE.
WELL, ANDREW, THE GANG IS ALL HERE.
LET'S PARTY.
HOLY WATER
MARY?! WHAT THE HELL IS GOING ON?
I GUESS YOU HADN'T HEARD.
I'M THE GOOD GUY NOW.
I'LL TRY NOT TO ACCIDENTALLY CUT YOUR HEAD OFF, BLONDIE.

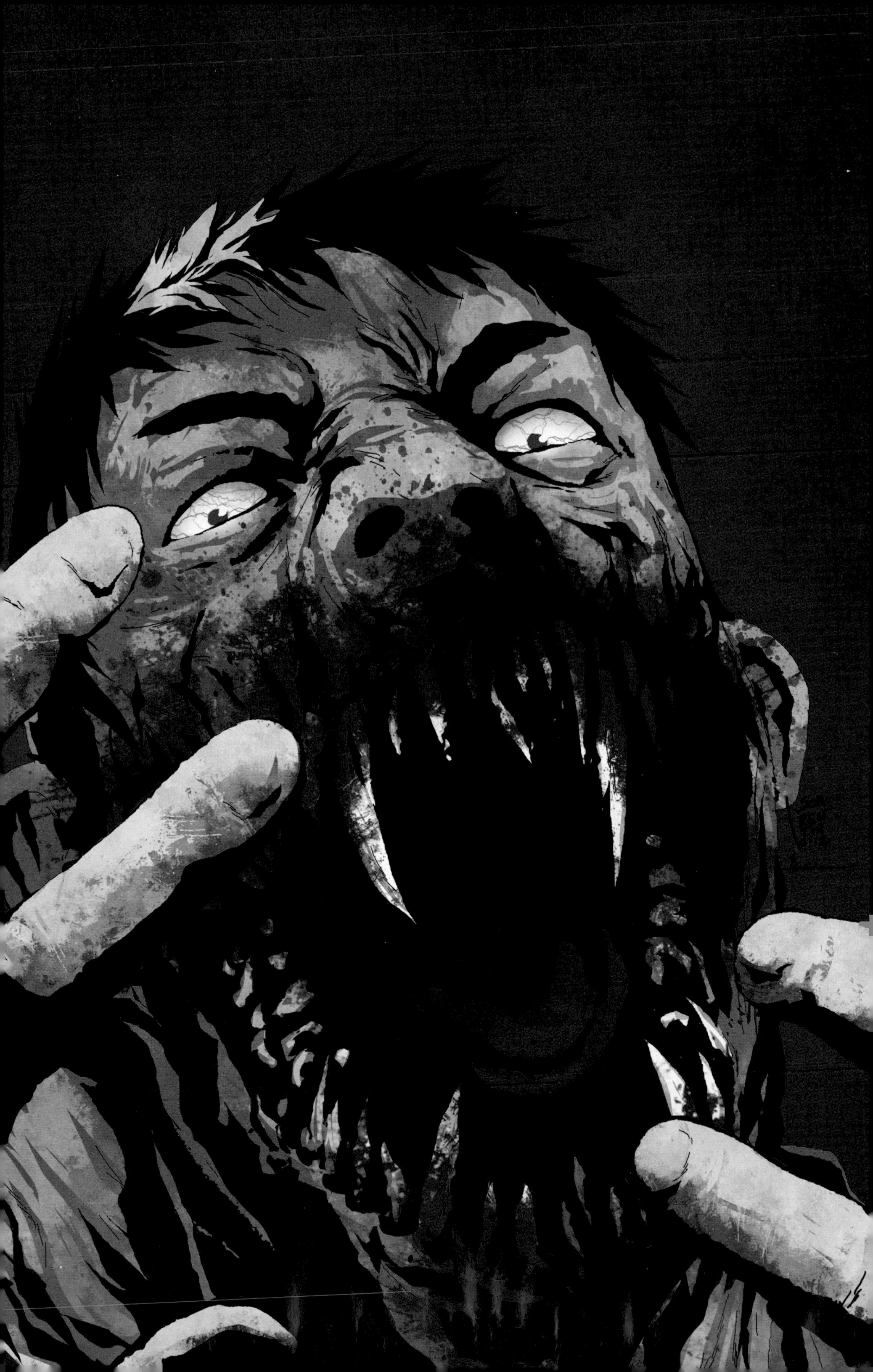

WINTERLONG

JOSHUA HALE FIALKOV writer ANDREA SORRENTINO artist cover art by ANDREA SORRENTINO & MARCELO MAIOLO

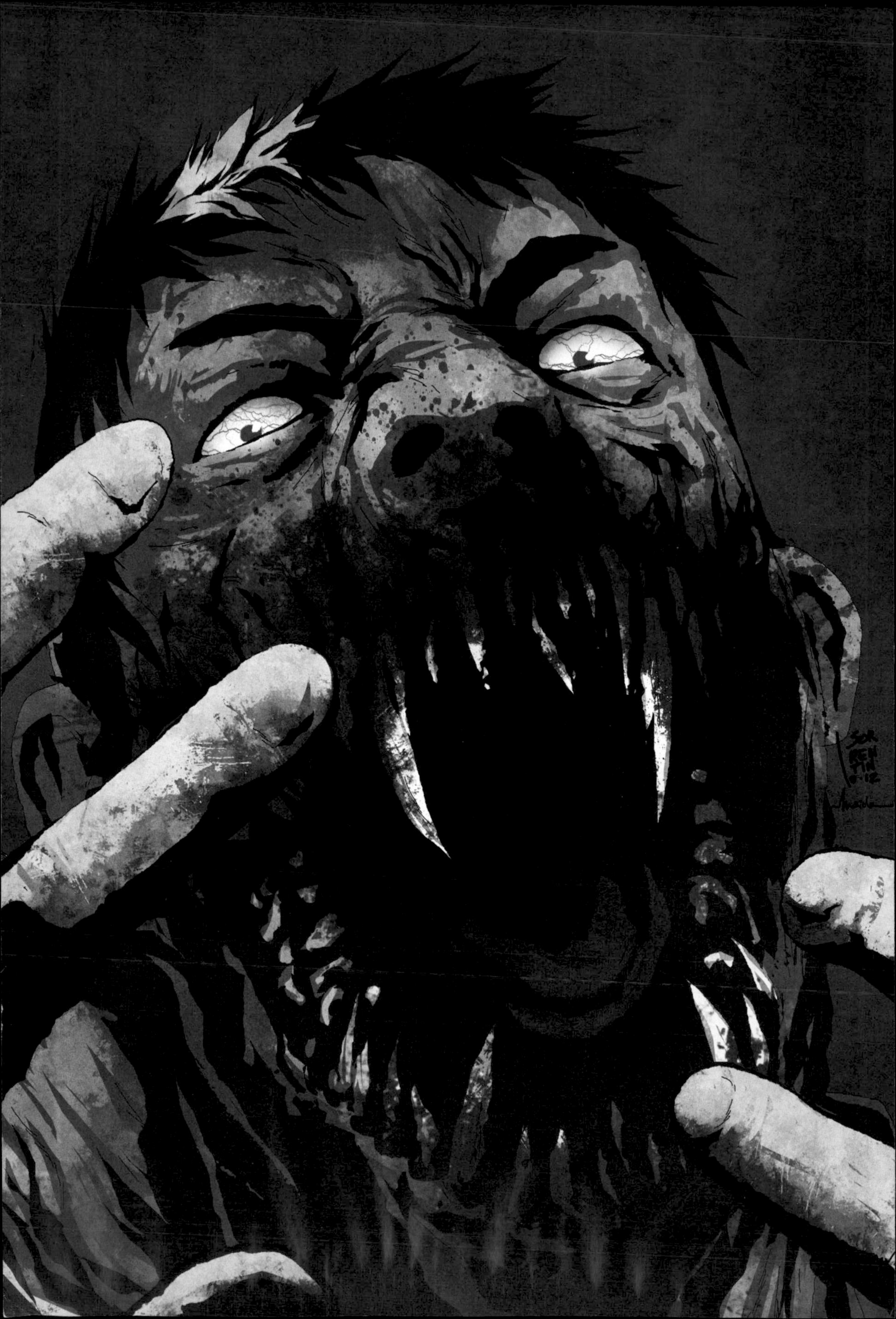

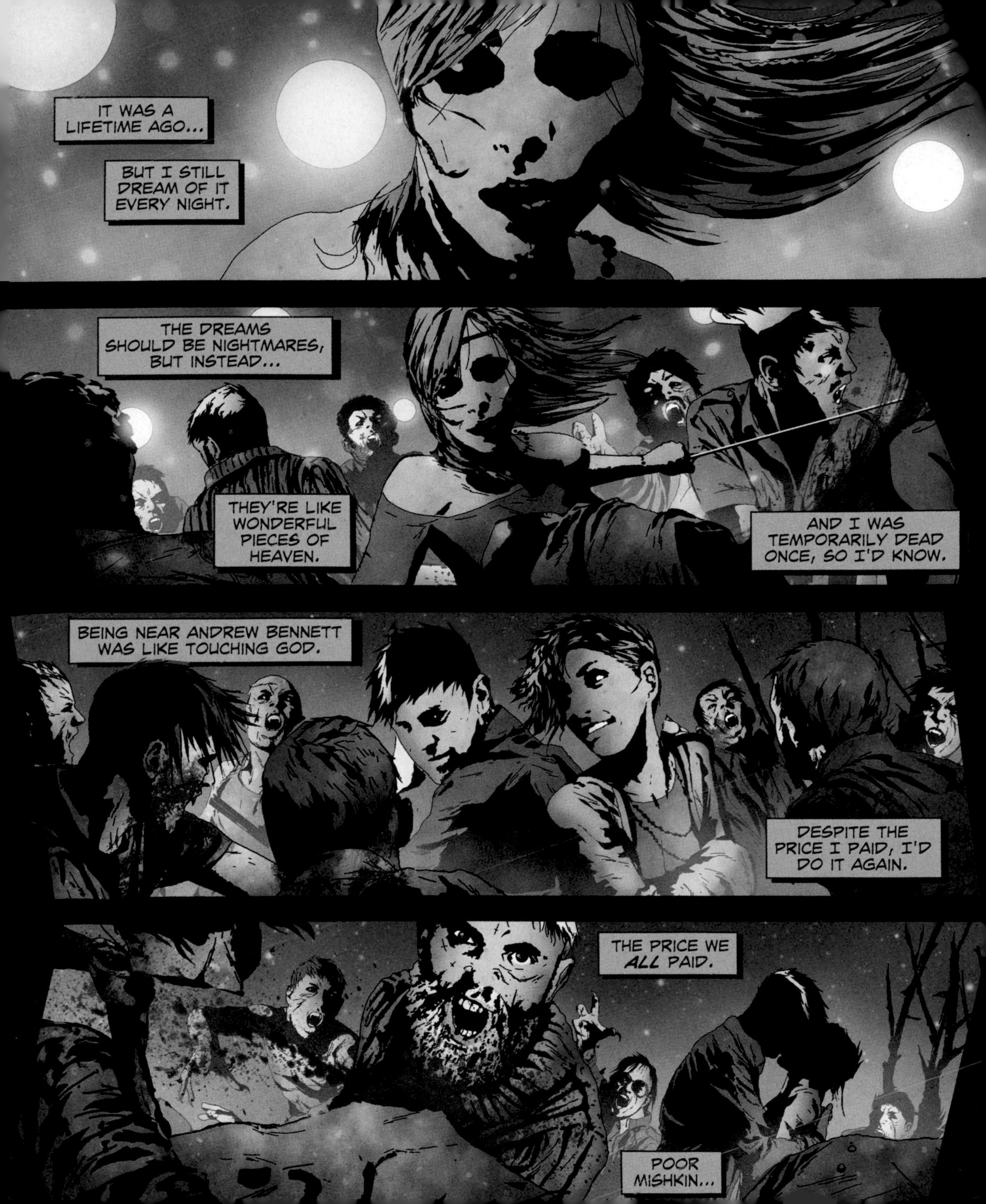
IT WAS A LIFETIME AGO...
BUT I STILL DREAM OF IT EVERY NIGHT.
THE DREAMS SHOULD BE NIGHTMARES, BUT INSTEAD...
THEY'RE LIKE WONDERFUL PIECES OF HEAVEN.
AND I WAS TEMPORARILY DEAD ONCE, SO I'D KNOW.
BEING NEAR ANDREW BENNETT WAS LIKE TOUCHING GOD.
DESPITE THE PRICE I PAID, I'D DO IT AGAIN.
THE PRICE WE *ALL* PAID.
POOR MISHKIN...

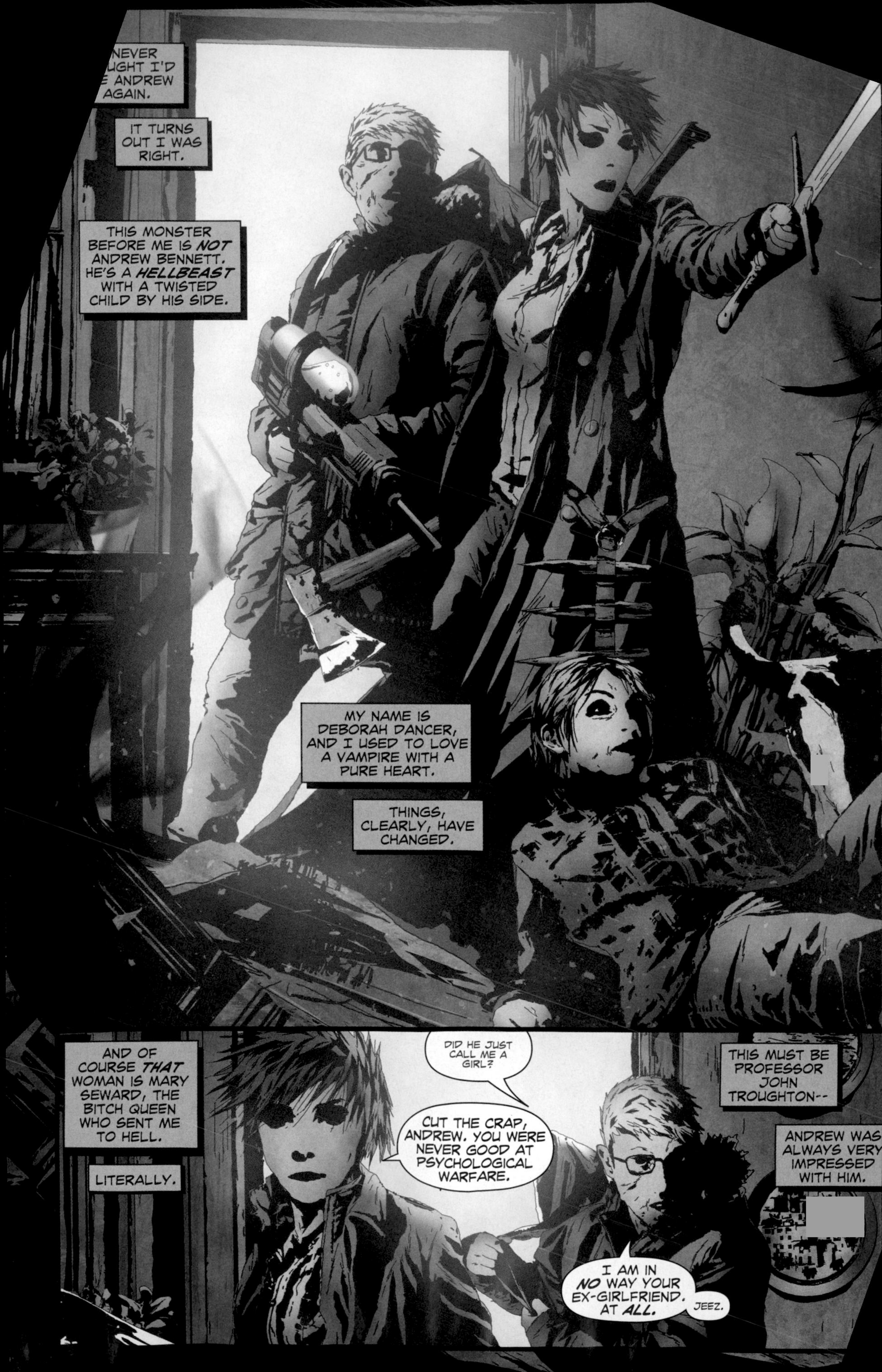
NEVER UGHT I'D E ANDREW AGAIN.
IT TURNS OUT I WAS RIGHT.
THIS MONSTER BEFORE ME IS NOT ANDREW BENNETT. HE'S A HELLBEAST WITH A TWISTED CHILD BY HIS SIDE.
MY NAME IS DEBORAH DANCER, AND I USED TO LOVE A VAMPIRE WITH A PURE HEART.
THINGS, CLEARLY, HAVE CHANGED.
AND OF COURSE THAT WOMAN IS MARY SEWARD, THE BITCH QUEEN WHO SENT ME TO HELL.
LITERALLY.
DID HE JUST CALL ME A GIRL?
CUT THE CRAP, ANDREW. YOU WERE NEVER GOOD AT PSYCHOLOGICAL WARFARE.
THIS MUST BE PROFESSOR JOHN TROUGHTON--
ANDREW WAS ALWAYS VERY IMPRESSED WITH HIM.
I AM IN NO WAY YOUR EX-GIRLFRIEND. AT ALL.
JEEZ.

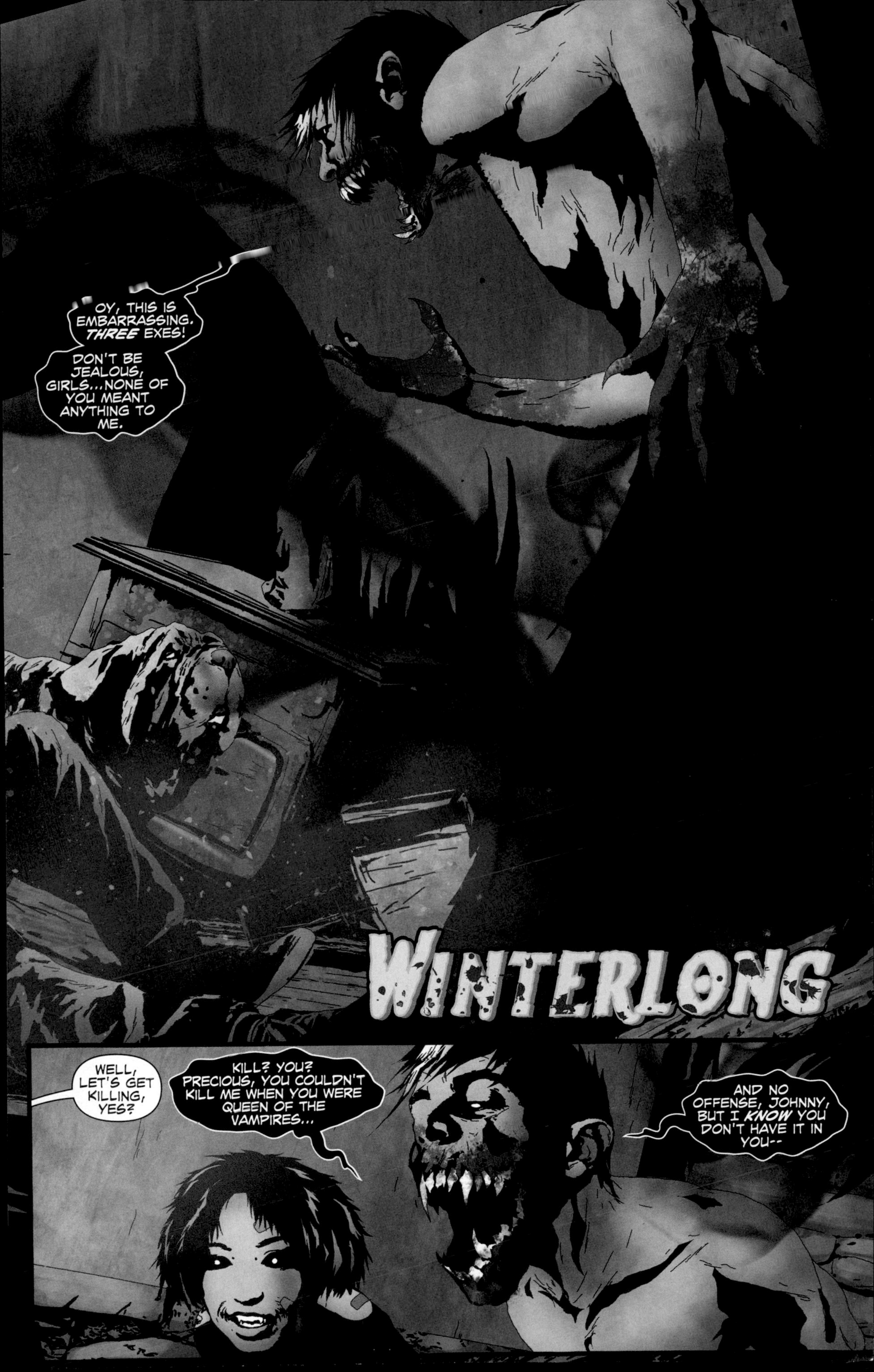
OY, THIS IS EMBARRASSING. *THREE* EXES!
DON'T BE JEALOUS, GIRLS...NONE OF YOU MEANT ANYTHING TO ME.
WINTERLONG
WELL, LET'S GET KILLING, YES?
KILL? YOU? PRECIOUS, YOU COULDN'T KILL ME WHEN YOU WERE QUEEN OF THE VAMPIRES...
AND NO OFFENSE, JOHNNY, BUT I *KNOW* YOU DON'T HAVE IT IN YOU--

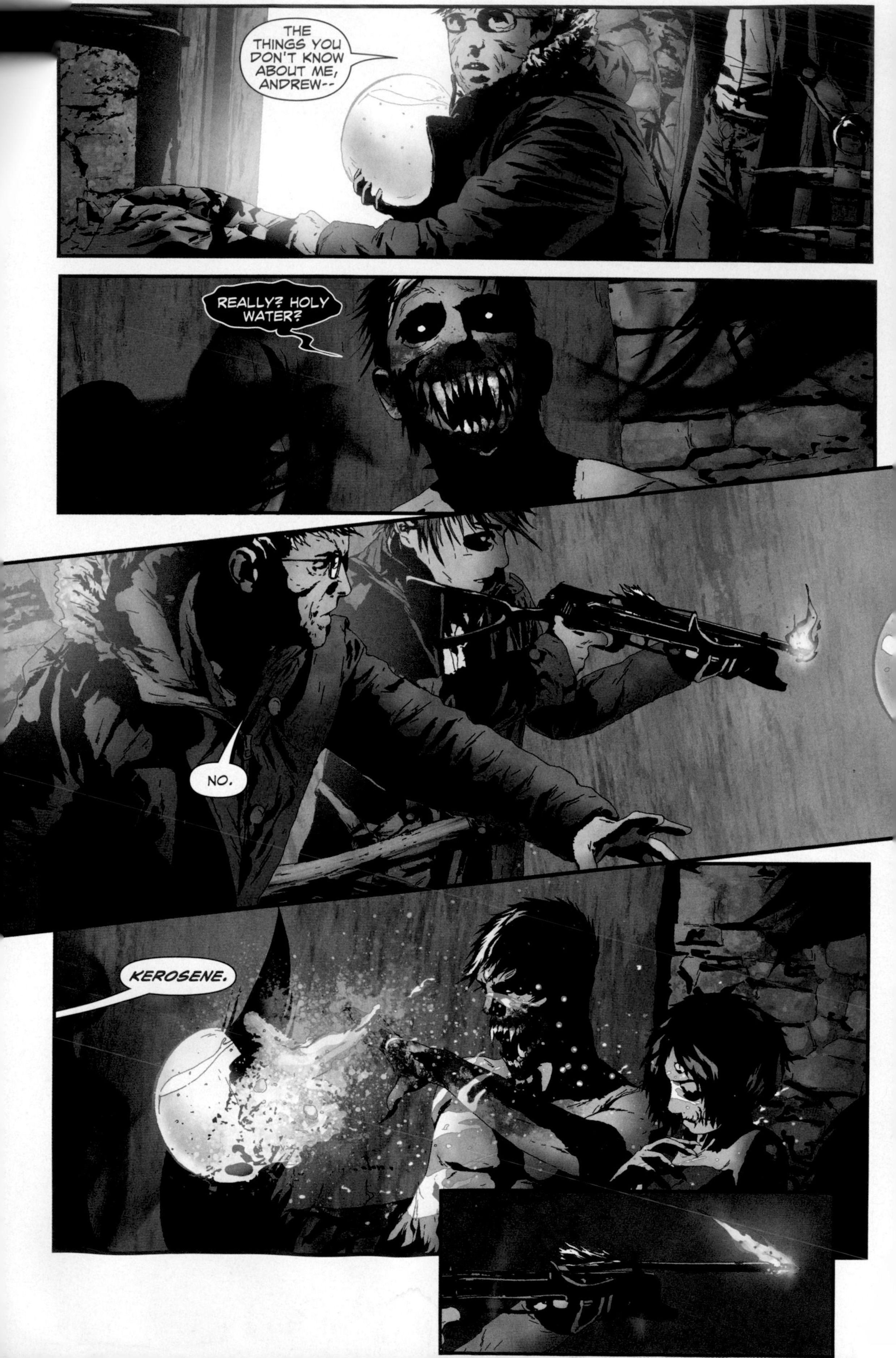
THE THINGS YOU DON'T KNOW ABOUT ME, ANDREW--
REALLY? HOLY WATER?
NO.
KEROSENE.

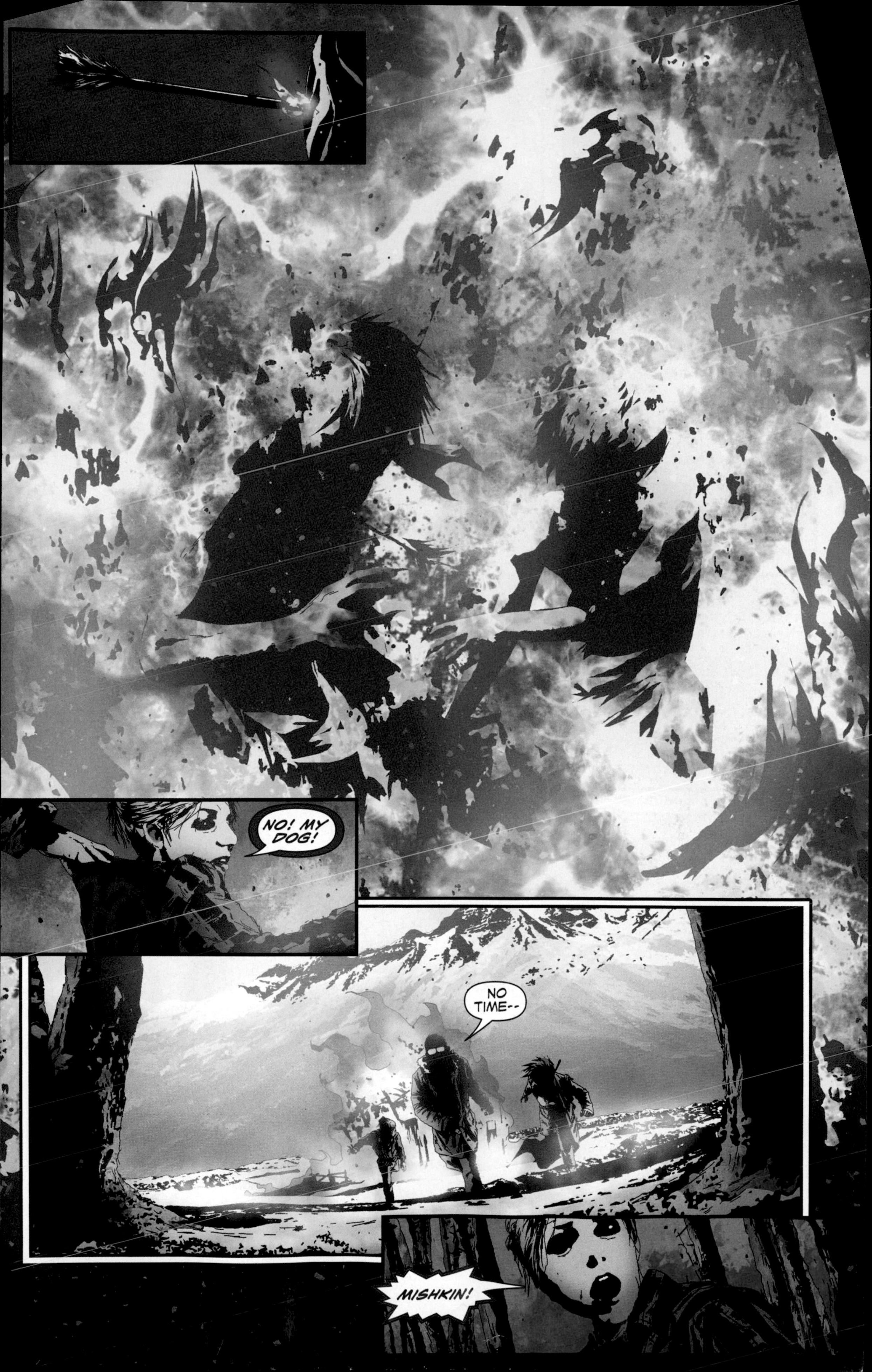
NO! MY DOG!
NO TIME--
MISHKIN!

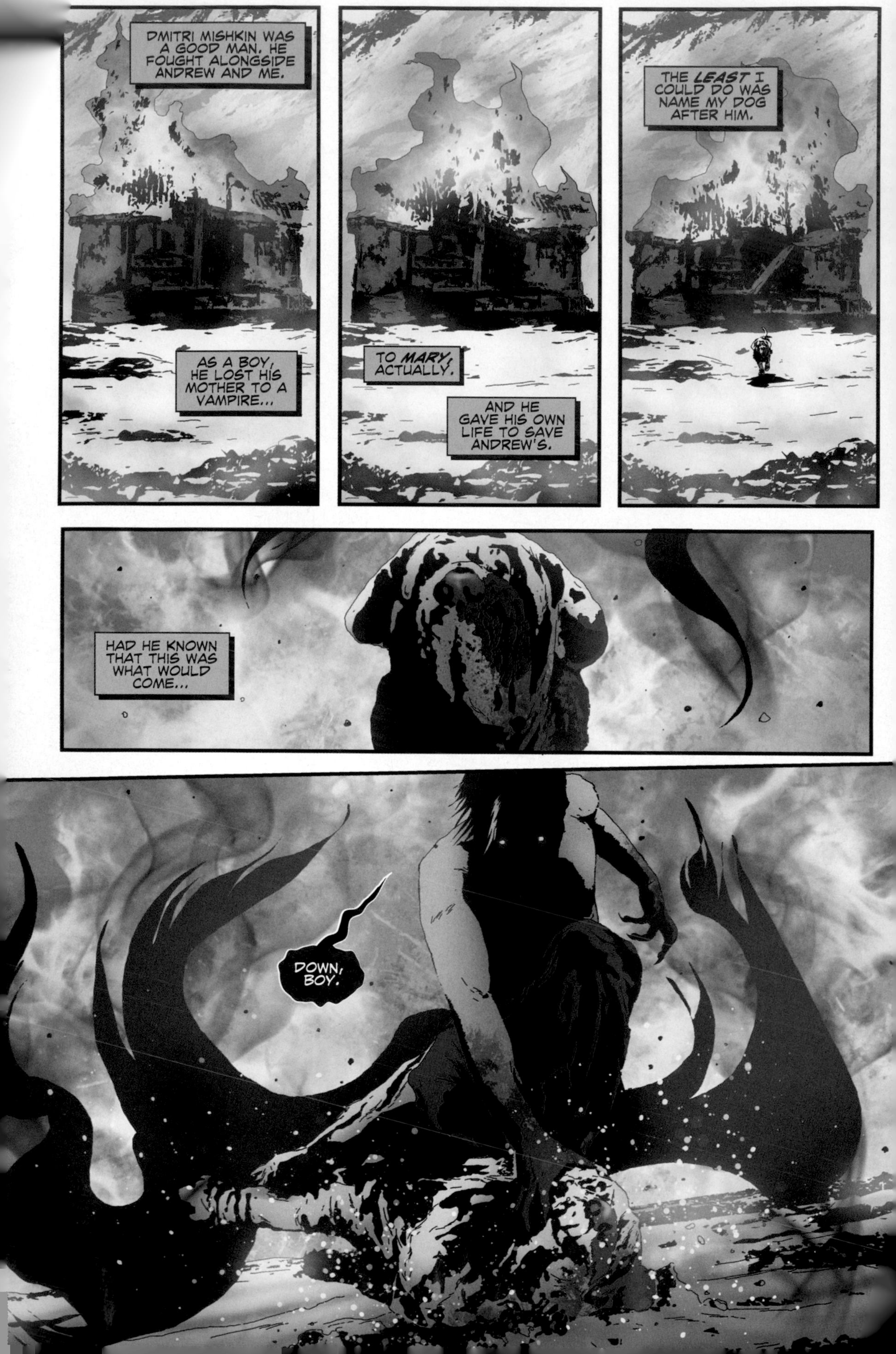
DMITRI MISHKIN WAS A GOOD MAN. HE FOUGHT ALONGSIDE ANDREW AND ME.
AS A BOY, HE LOST HIS MOTHER TO A VAMPIRE...
TO MARY, ACTUALLY.
AND HE GAVE HIS OWN LIFE TO SAVE ANDREW'S.
THE LEAST I COULD DO WAS NAME MY DOG AFTER HIM.
HAD HE KNOWN THAT THIS WAS WHAT WOULD COME...
DOWN, BOY.

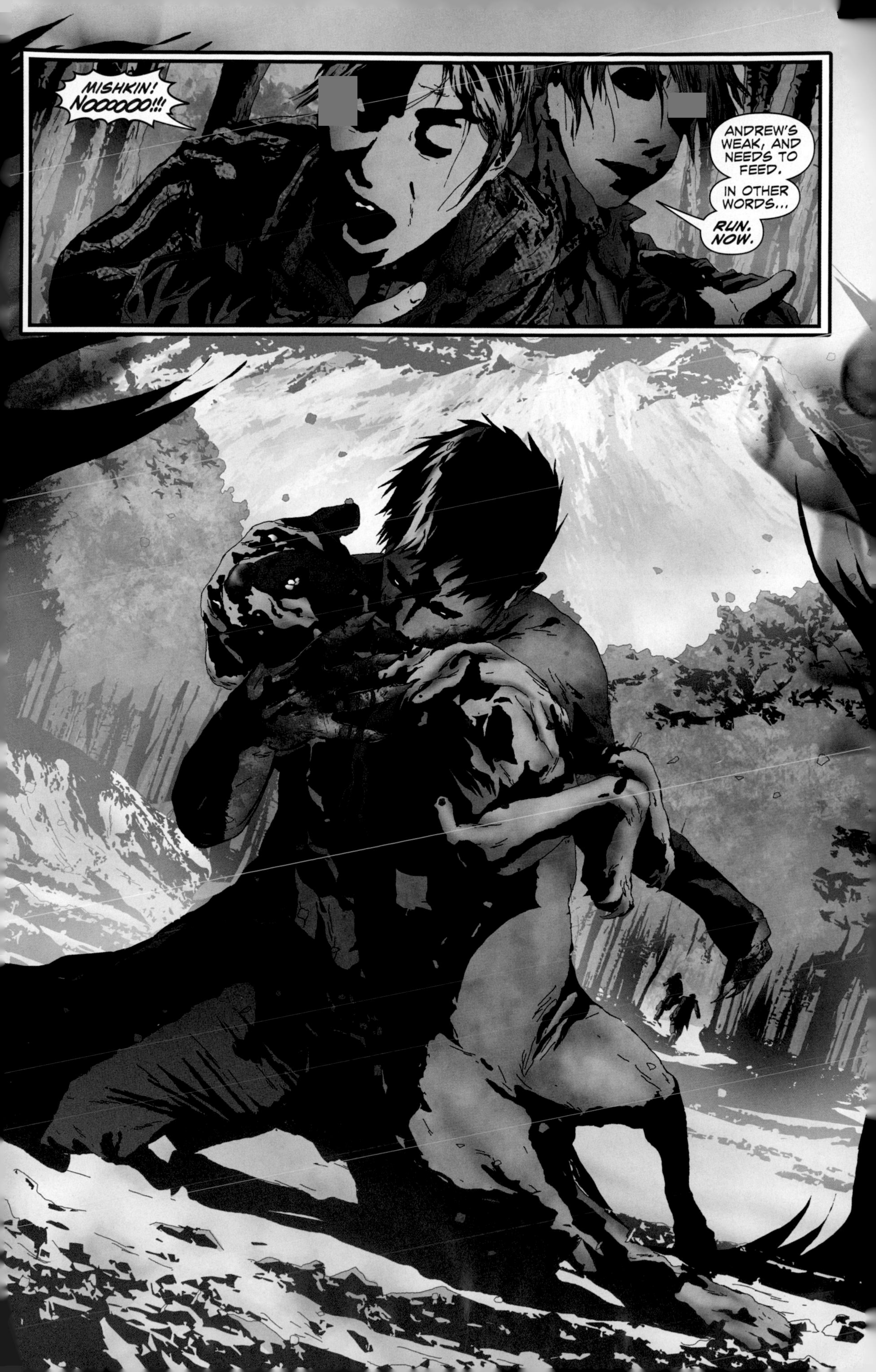
MISHKIN! NOOOOOO!!!
ANDREW'S WEAK, AND NEEDS TO FEED.
IN OTHER WORDS...
RUN. NOW.

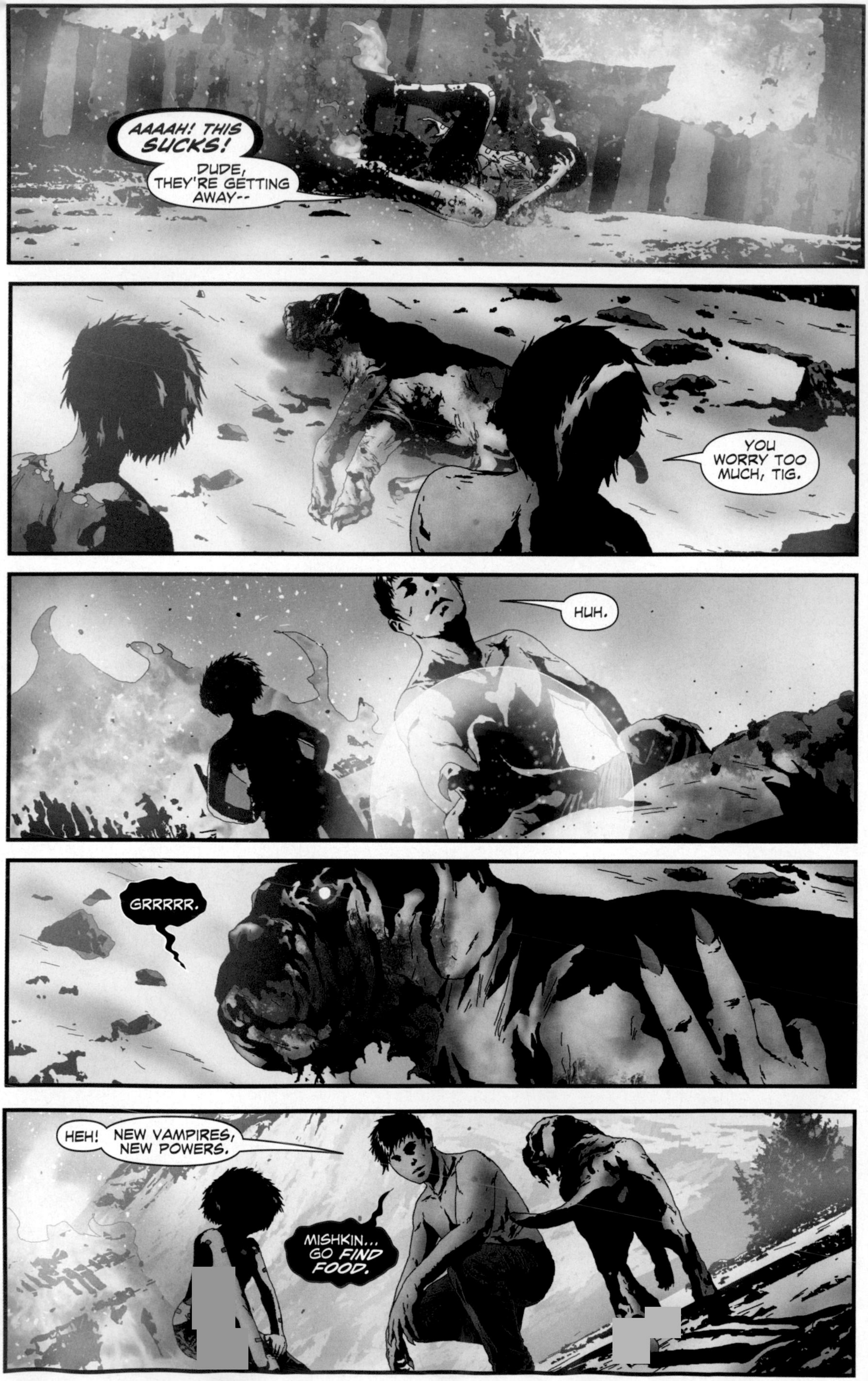
AAAAH! THIS SUCKS!
DUDE, THEY'RE GETTING AWAY--
YOU WORRY TOO MUCH, TIG.
HUH.
GRRRRR.
HEH!
NEW VAMPIRES, NEW POWERS.
MISHKIN... GO FIND FOOD.

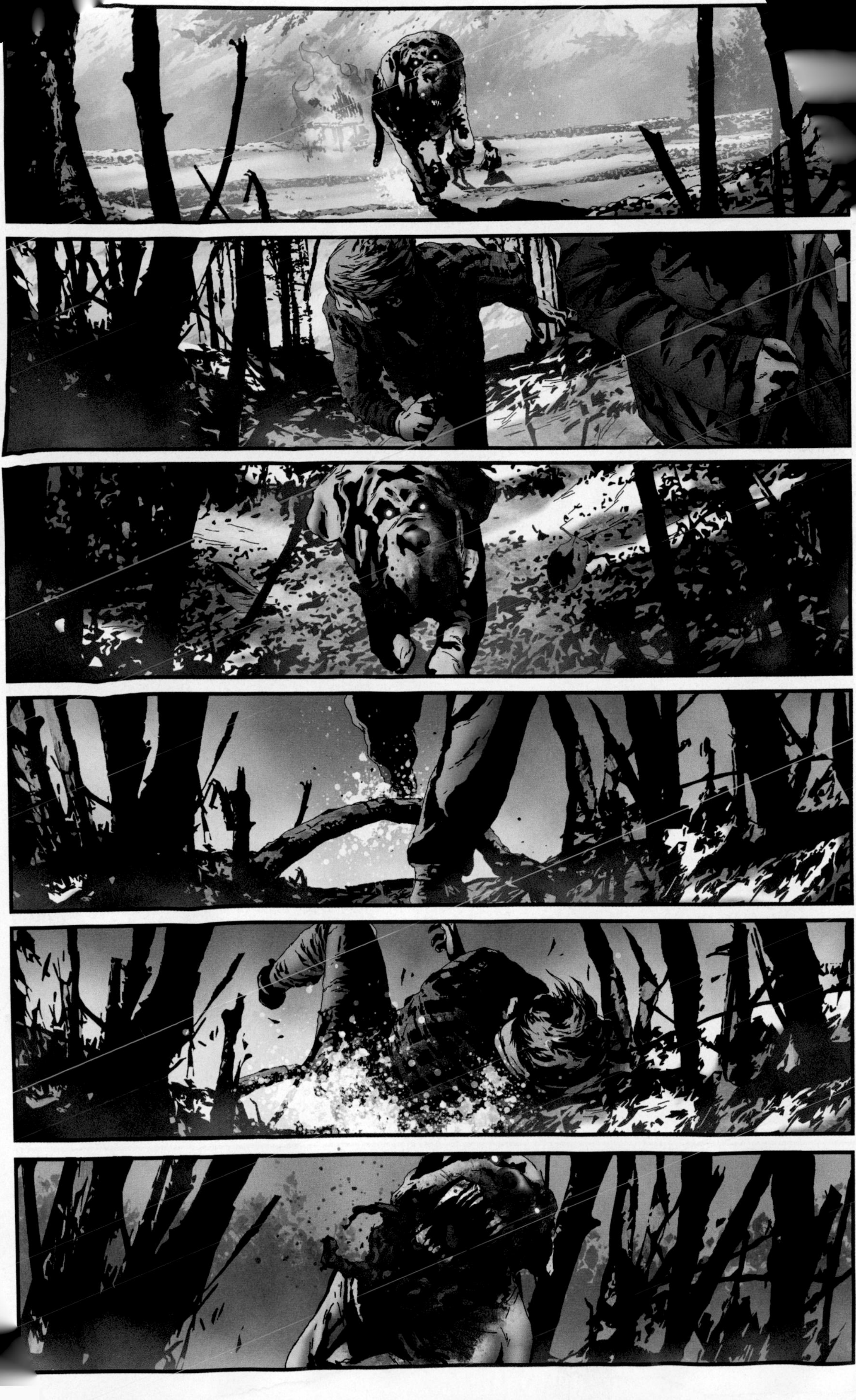

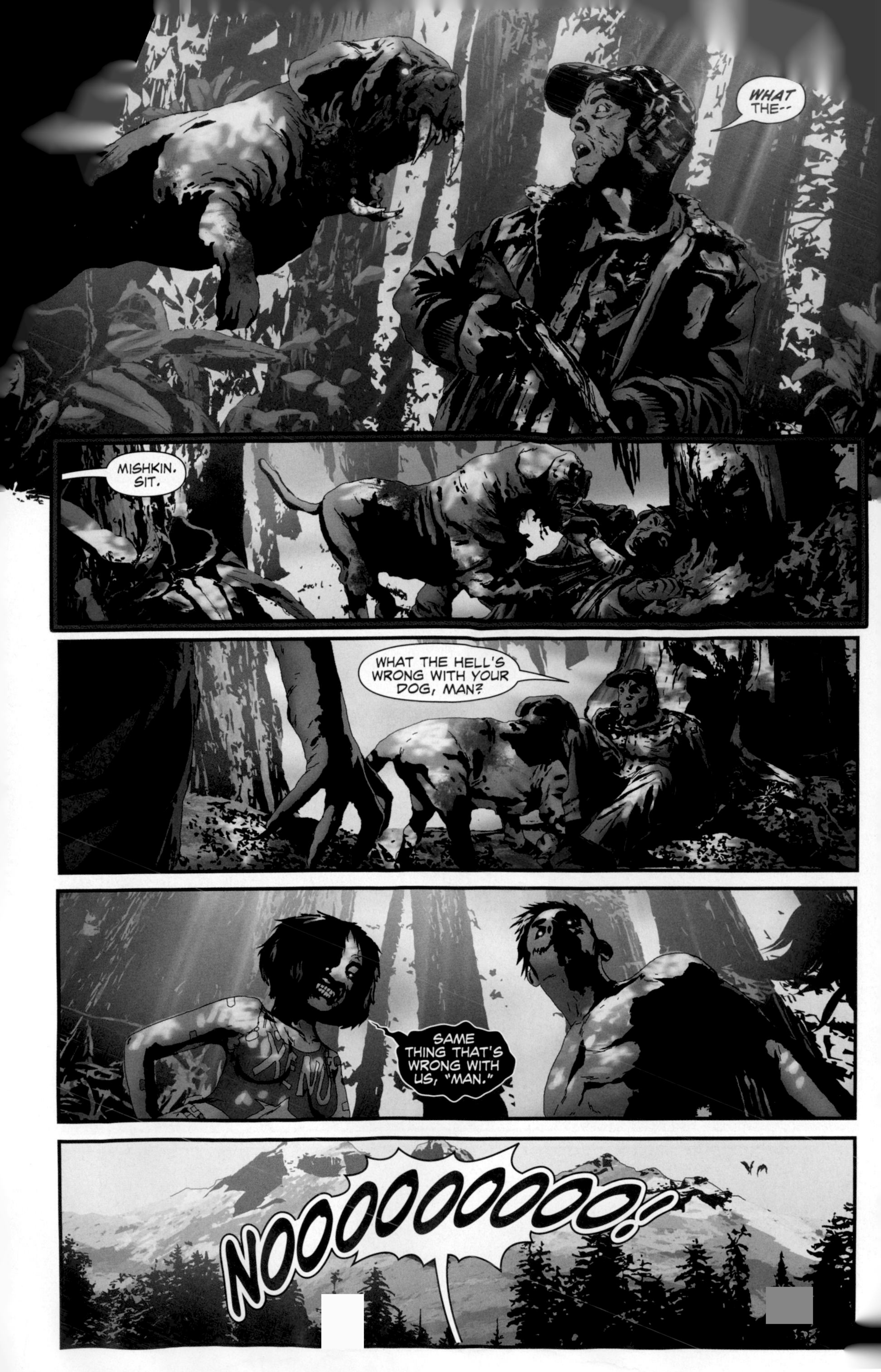
WHAT THE--
MISHKIN. SIT.
WHAT THE HELL'S WRONG WITH YOUR DOG, MAN?
SAME THING THAT'S WRONG WITH US, "MAN."
NOOOOOOOOO!

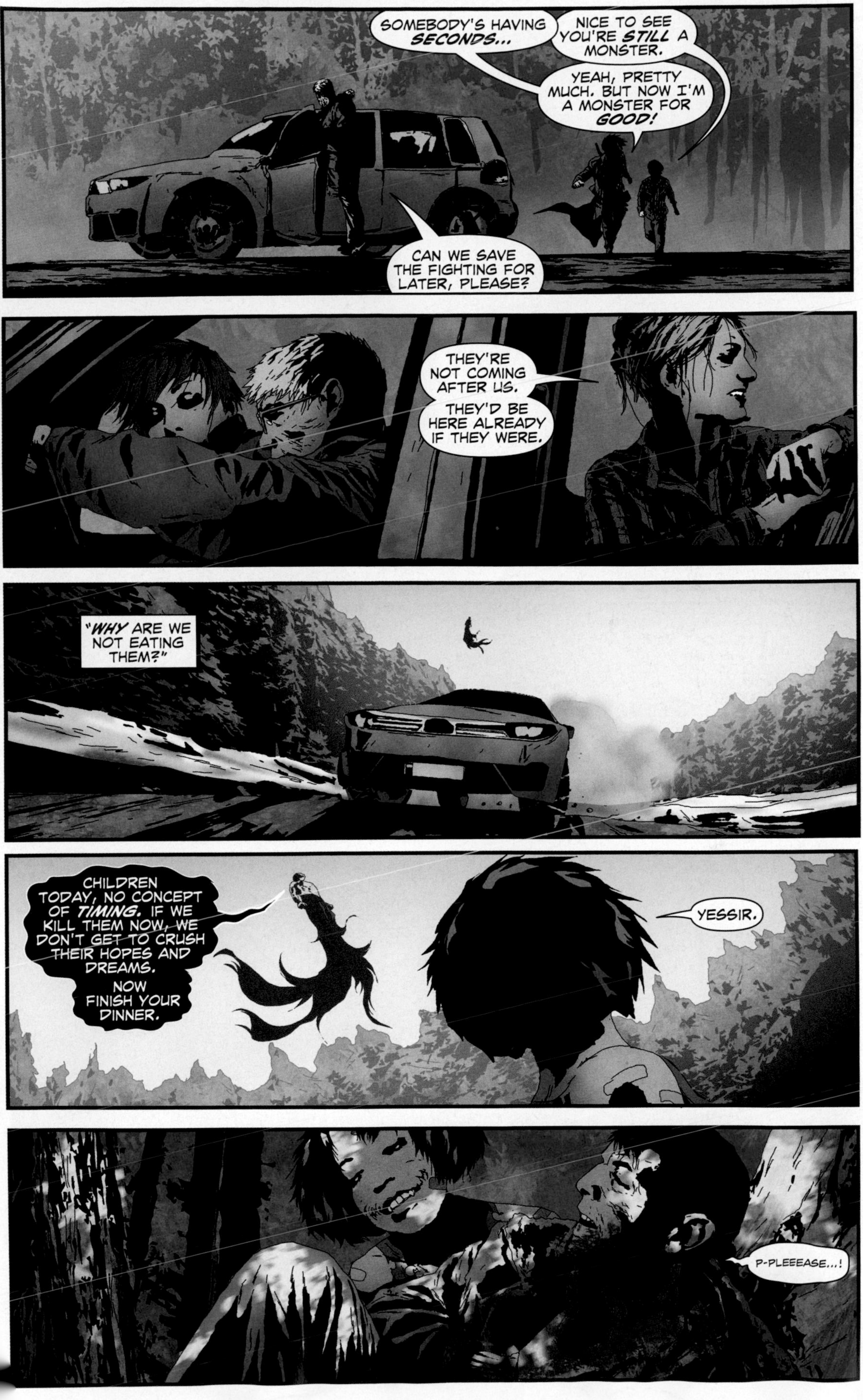
SOMEBODY'S HAVING SECONDS...
NICE TO SEE YOU'RE STILL A MONSTER.
YEAH, PRETTY MUCH. BUT NOW I'M A MONSTER FOR GOOD!
CAN WE SAVE THE FIGHTING FOR LATER, PLEASE?
THEY'RE NOT COMING AFTER US.
THEY'D BE HERE ALREADY IF THEY WERE.
"WHY ARE WE NOT EATING THEM?"
CHILDREN TODAY, NO CONCEPT OF TIMING. IF WE KILL THEM NOW, WE DON'T GET TO CRUSH THEIR HOPES AND DREAMS.
NOW FINISH YOUR DINNER.
YESSIR.
P-PLEEEASE...!

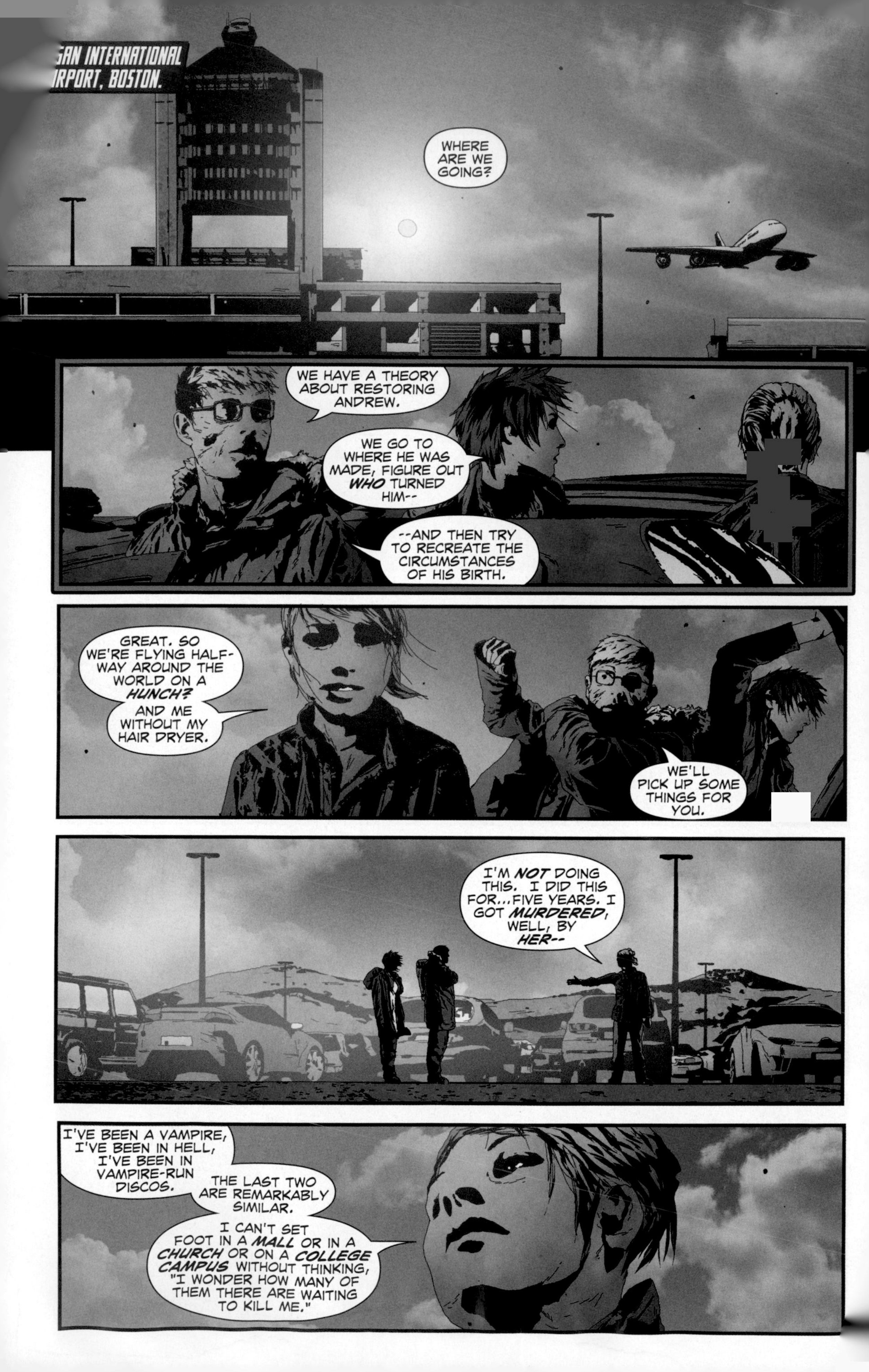

GAN INTERNATIONAL
IRPORT, BOSTON.
WHERE ARE WE GOING?
WE HAVE A THEORY ABOUT RESTORING ANDREW.
WE GO TO WHERE HE WAS MADE, FIGURE OUT WHO TURNED HIM--
--AND THEN TRY TO RECREATE THE CIRCUMSTANCES OF HIS BIRTH.
GREAT. SO WE'RE FLYING HALF-WAY AROUND THE WORLD ON A HUNCH?
AND ME WITHOUT MY HAIR DRYER.
WE'LL PICK UP SOME THINGS FOR YOU.
I'M NOT DOING THIS. I DID THIS FOR...FIVE YEARS. I GOT MURDERED, WELL, BY HER--
I'VE BEEN A VAMPIRE, I'VE BEEN IN HELL, I'VE BEEN IN VAMPIRE-RUN DISCOS.
THE LAST TWO ARE REMARKABLY SIMILAR.
I CAN'T SET FOOT IN A MALL OR IN A CHURCH OR ON A COLLEGE CAMPUS WITHOUT THINKING, "I WONDER HOW MANY OF THEM THERE ARE WAITING TO KILL ME."

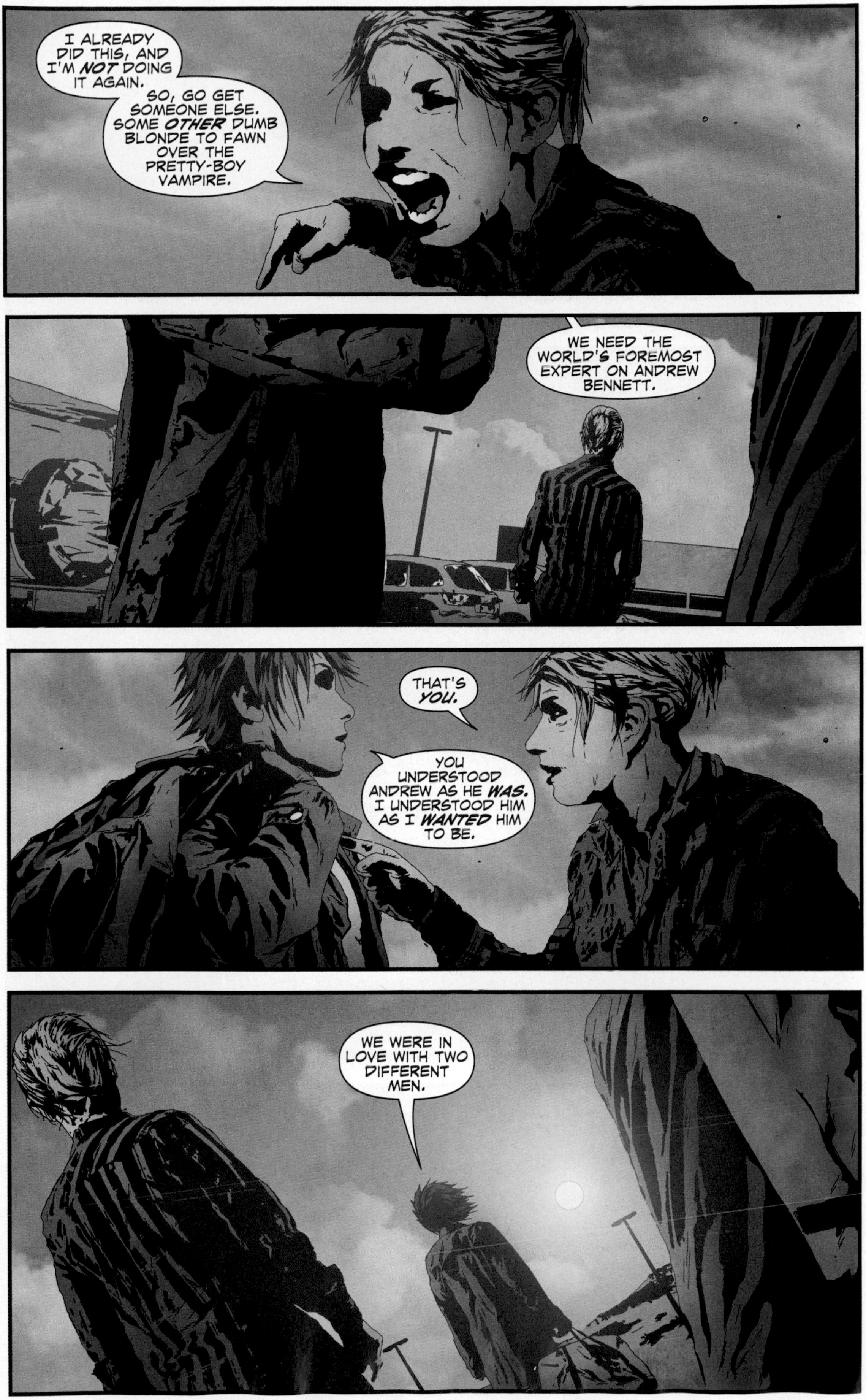
I ALREADY DID THIS, AND I'M NOT DOING IT AGAIN.
SO, GO GET SOMEONE ELSE. SOME OTHER DUMB BLONDE TO FAWN OVER THE PRETTY-BOY VAMPIRE.
WE NEED THE WORLD'S FOREMOST EXPERT ON ANDREW BENNETT.
THAT'S YOU.
YOU UNDERSTOOD ANDREW AS HE WAS. I UNDERSTOOD HIM AS I WANTED HIM TO BE.
WE WERE IN LOVE WITH TWO DIFFERENT MEN.

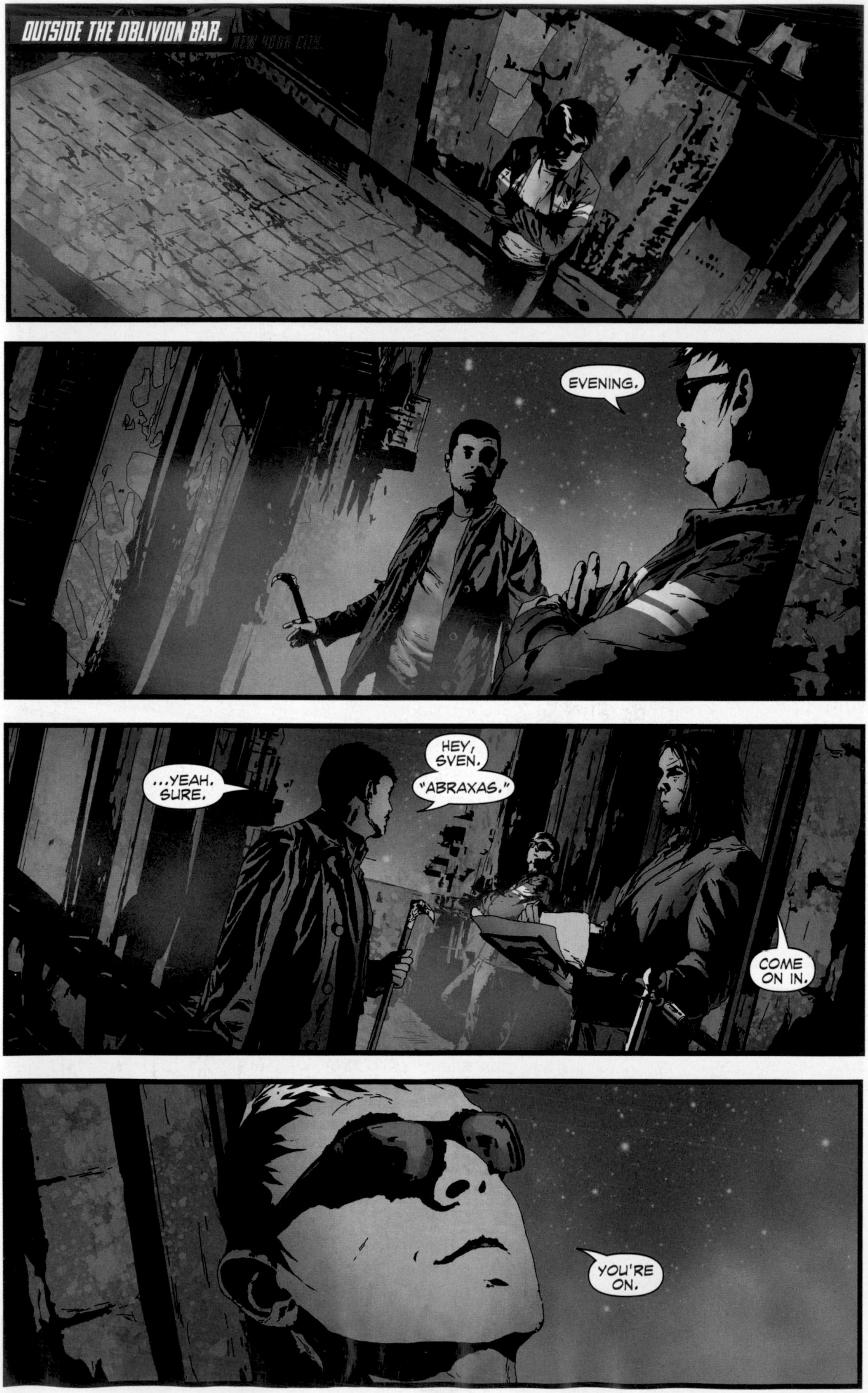
OUTSIDE THE OBLIVION BAR.
NEW YORK CITY.
EVENING.
...YEAH. SURE.
HEY, SVEN. "ABRAXAS."
COME ON IN.
YOU'RE ON.

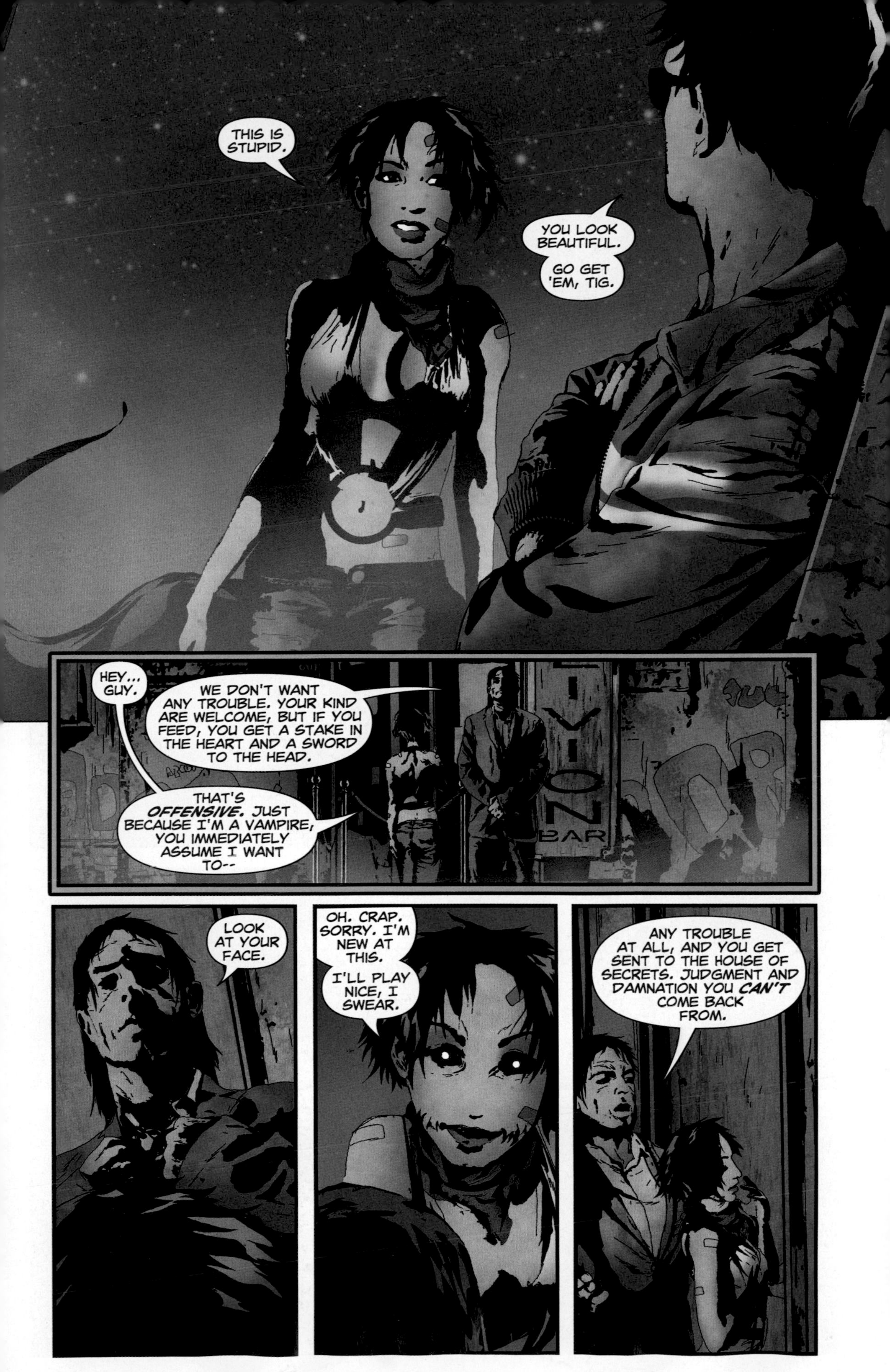
THIS IS STUPID.
YOU LOOK BEAUTIFUL.
GO GET 'EM, TIG.
HEY... GUY.
WE DON'T WANT ANY TROUBLE. YOUR KIND ARE WELCOME, BUT IF YOU FEED, YOU GET A STAKE IN THE HEART AND A SWORD TO THE HEAD.
THAT'S *OFFENSIVE.* JUST BECAUSE I'M A VAMPIRE, YOU IMMEDIATELY ASSUME I WANT TO--
BAR
LOOK AT YOUR FACE.
OH. CRAP. SORRY. I'M NEW AT THIS.
I'LL PLAY NICE, I SWEAR.
ANY TROUBLE AT ALL, AND YOU GET SENT TO THE HOUSE OF SECRETS. JUDGMENT AND DAMNATION YOU *CAN'T* COME BACK FROM.

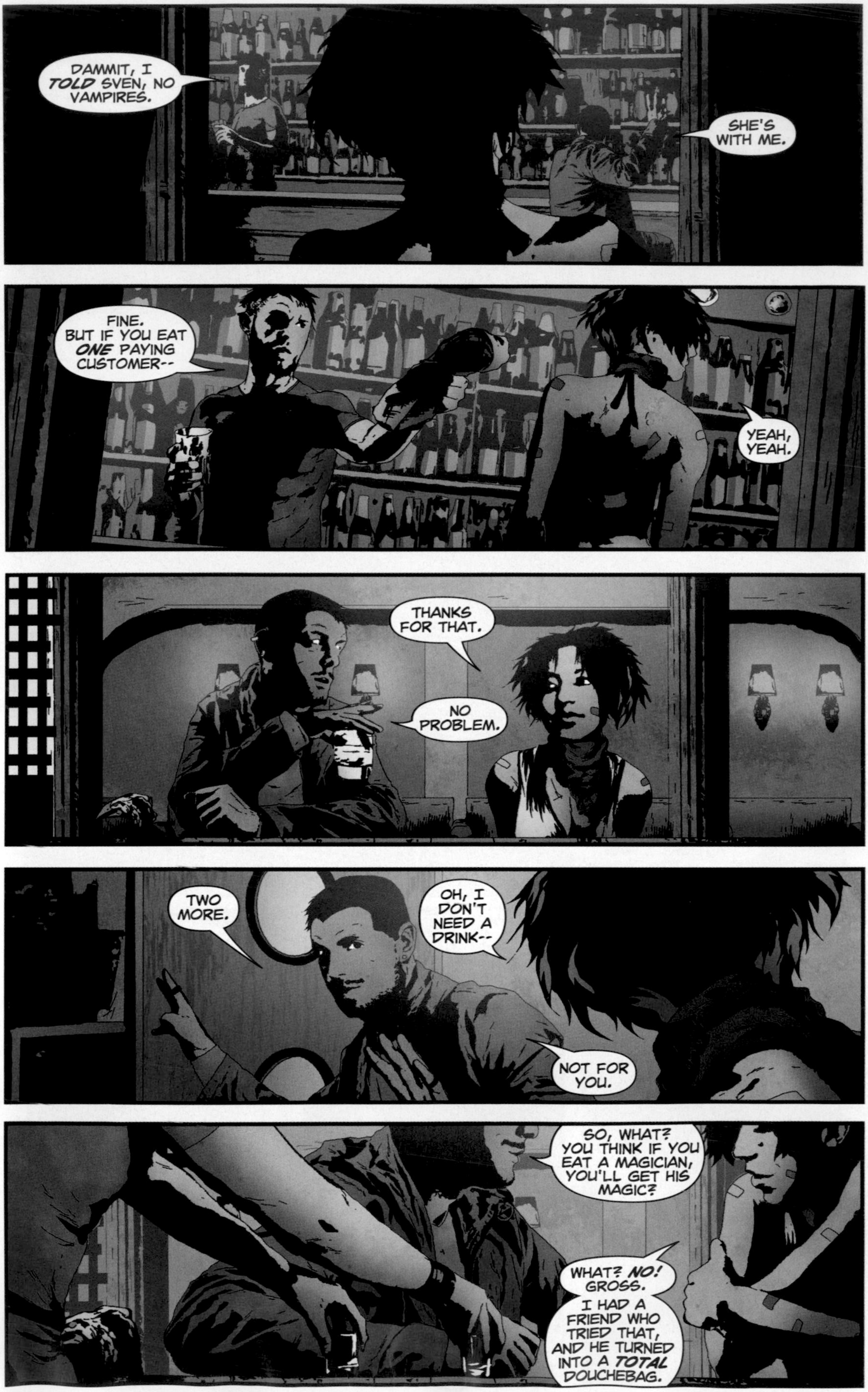
DAMMIT, I TOLD SVEN, NO VAMPIRES.
SHE'S WITH ME.
FINE. BUT IF YOU EAT ONE PAYING CUSTOMER--
YEAH, YEAH.
THANKS FOR THAT.
NO PROBLEM.
TWO MORE.
OH, I DON'T NEED A DRINK--
NOT FOR YOU.
SO, WHAT? YOU THINK IF YOU EAT A MAGICIAN, YOU'LL GET HIS MAGIC?
WHAT? NO! GROSS.
I HAD A FRIEND WHO TRIED THAT, AND HE TURNED INTO A TOTAL DOUCHEBAG.

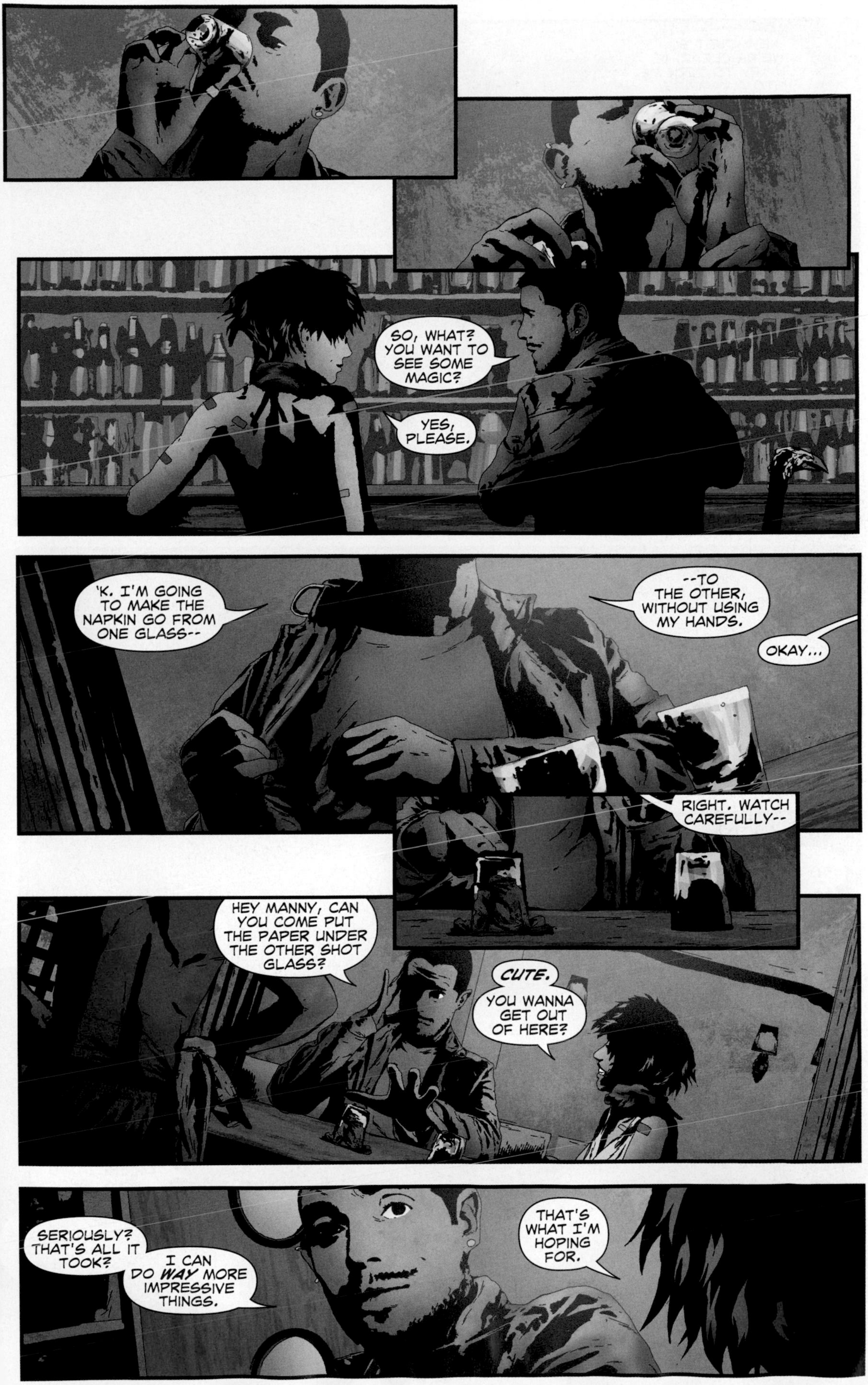
SO, WHAT? YOU WANT TO SEE SOME MAGIC?
YES, PLEASE.
'K. I'M GOING TO MAKE THE NAPKIN GO FROM ONE GLASS--
--TO THE OTHER, WITHOUT USING MY HANDS.
OKAY...
RIGHT. WATCH CAREFULLY--
HEY MANNY, CAN YOU COME PUT THE PAPER UNDER THE OTHER SHOT GLASS?
CUTE.
YOU WANNA GET OUT OF HERE?
SERIOUSLY? THAT'S ALL IT TOOK?
I CAN DO WAY MORE IMPRESSIVE THINGS.
THAT'S WHAT I'M HOPING FOR.

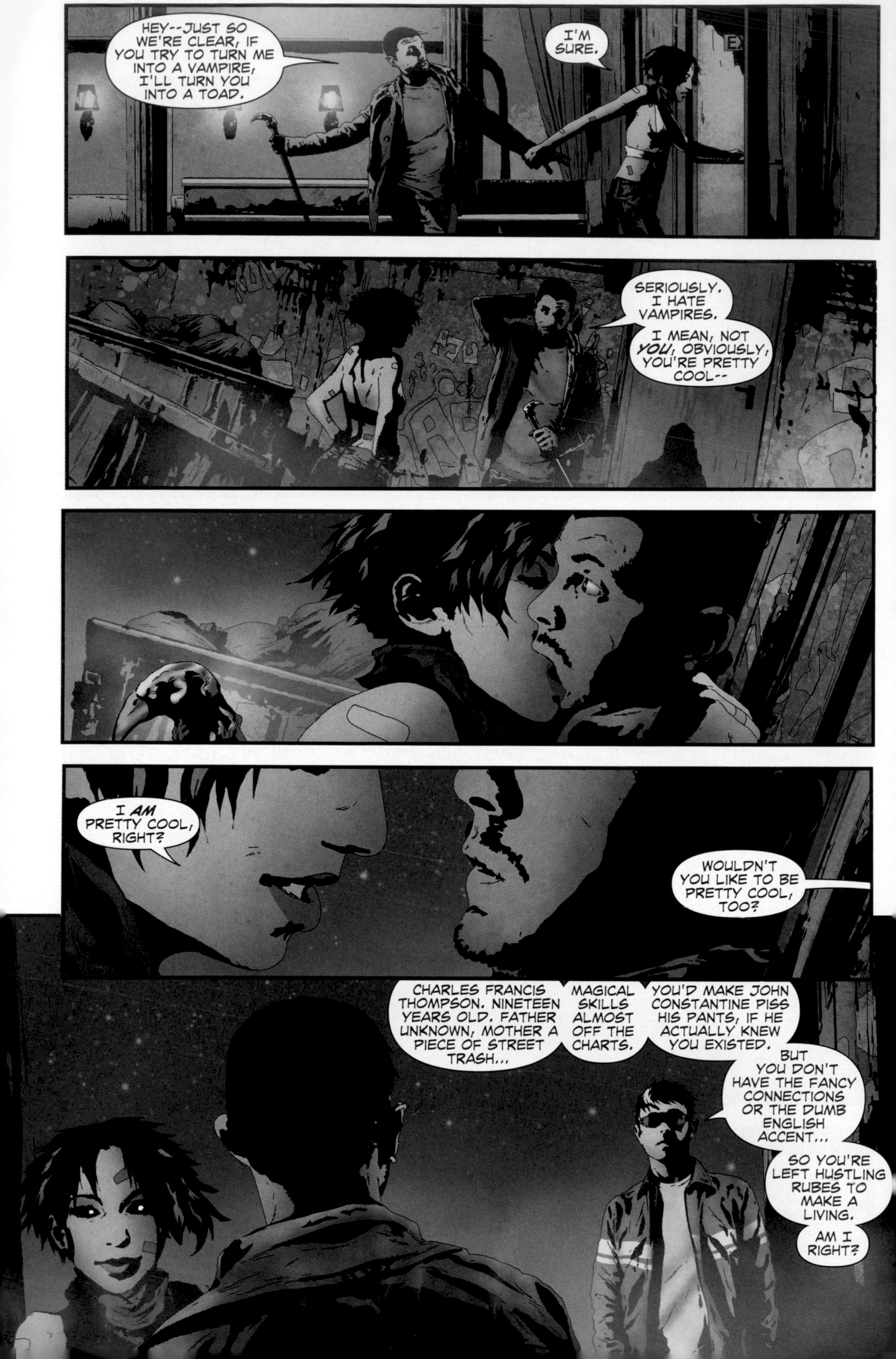
HEY--JUST SO WE'RE CLEAR, IF YOU TRY TO TURN ME INTO A VAMPIRE, I'LL TURN YOU INTO A TOAD.
I'M SURE.
SERIOUSLY. I HATE VAMPIRES.
I MEAN, NOT *YOU*, OBVIOUSLY, YOU'RE PRETTY COOL--
I *AM* PRETTY COOL, RIGHT?
WOULDN'T YOU LIKE TO BE PRETTY COOL, TOO?
CHARLES FRANCIS THOMPSON. NINETEEN YEARS OLD. FATHER UNKNOWN, MOTHER A PIECE OF STREET TRASH...
MAGICAL SKILLS ALMOST OFF THE CHARTS.
YOU'D MAKE JOHN CONSTANTINE PISS HIS PANTS, IF HE ACTUALLY KNEW YOU EXISTED.
BUT YOU DON'T HAVE THE FANCY CONNECTIONS OR THE DUMB ENGLISH ACCENT...
SO YOU'RE LEFT HUSTLING RUBES TO MAKE A LIVING.
AM I RIGHT?

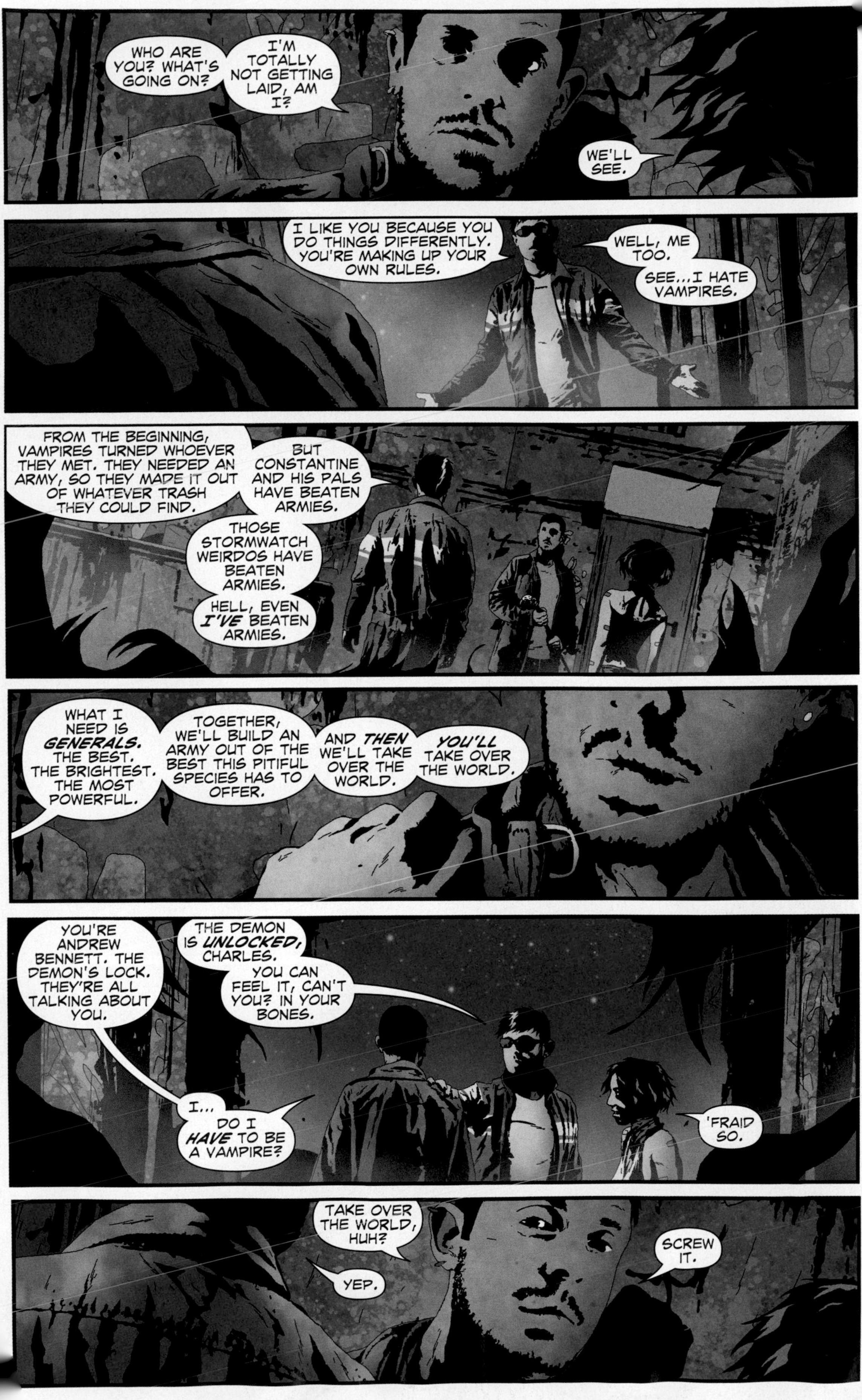
WHO ARE YOU? WHAT'S GOING ON?
I'M TOTALLY NOT GETTING LAID, AM I?
WE'LL SEE.
I LIKE YOU BECAUSE YOU DO THINGS DIFFERENTLY. YOU'RE MAKING UP YOUR OWN RULES.
WELL, ME TOO.
SEE...I HATE VAMPIRES.
FROM THE BEGINNING, VAMPIRES TURNED WHOEVER THEY MET. THEY NEEDED AN ARMY, SO THEY MADE IT OUT OF WHATEVER TRASH THEY COULD FIND.
BUT CONSTANTINE AND HIS PALS HAVE BEATEN ARMIES.
THOSE STORMWATCH WEIRDOS HAVE BEATEN ARMIES.
HELL, EVEN *I'VE* BEATEN ARMIES.
WHAT I NEED IS **GENERALS.** THE BEST. THE BRIGHTEST. THE MOST POWERFUL.
TOGETHER, WE'LL BUILD AN ARMY OUT OF THE BEST THIS PITIFUL SPECIES HAS TO OFFER.
AND **THEN** WE'LL TAKE OVER THE WORLD.
YOU'LL TAKE OVER THE WORLD.
YOU'RE ANDREW BENNETT. THE DEMON'S LOCK. THEY'RE ALL TALKING ABOUT YOU.
THE DEMON IS **UNLOCKED,** CHARLES.
YOU CAN FEEL IT, CAN'T YOU? IN YOUR BONES.
I... DO I **HAVE** TO BE A VAMPIRE?
'FRAID SO.
TAKE OVER THE WORLD, HUH?
YEP.
SCREW IT.

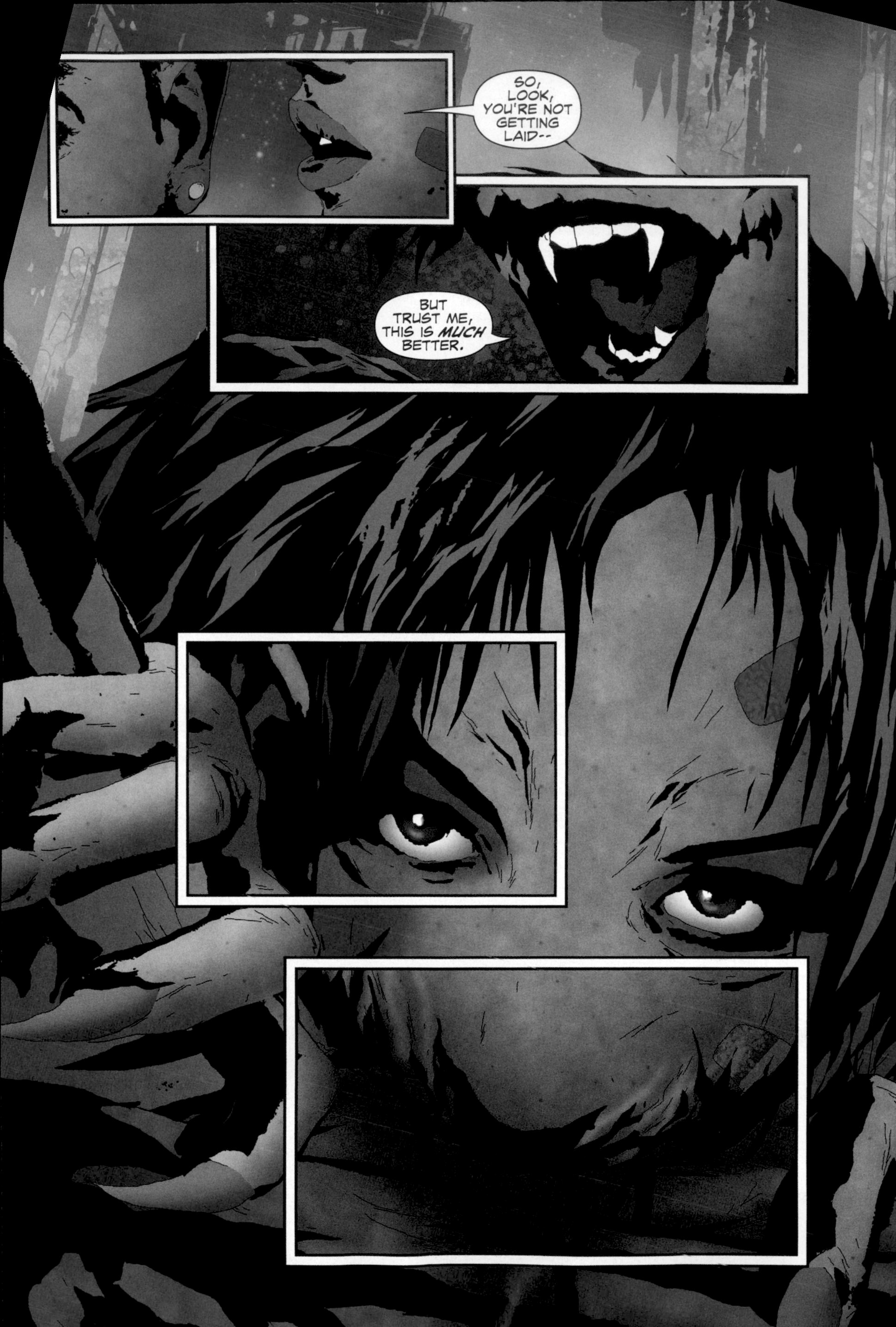
SO, LOOK, YOU'RE NOT GETTING LAID--
BUT TRUST ME, THIS IS *MUCH* BETTER.

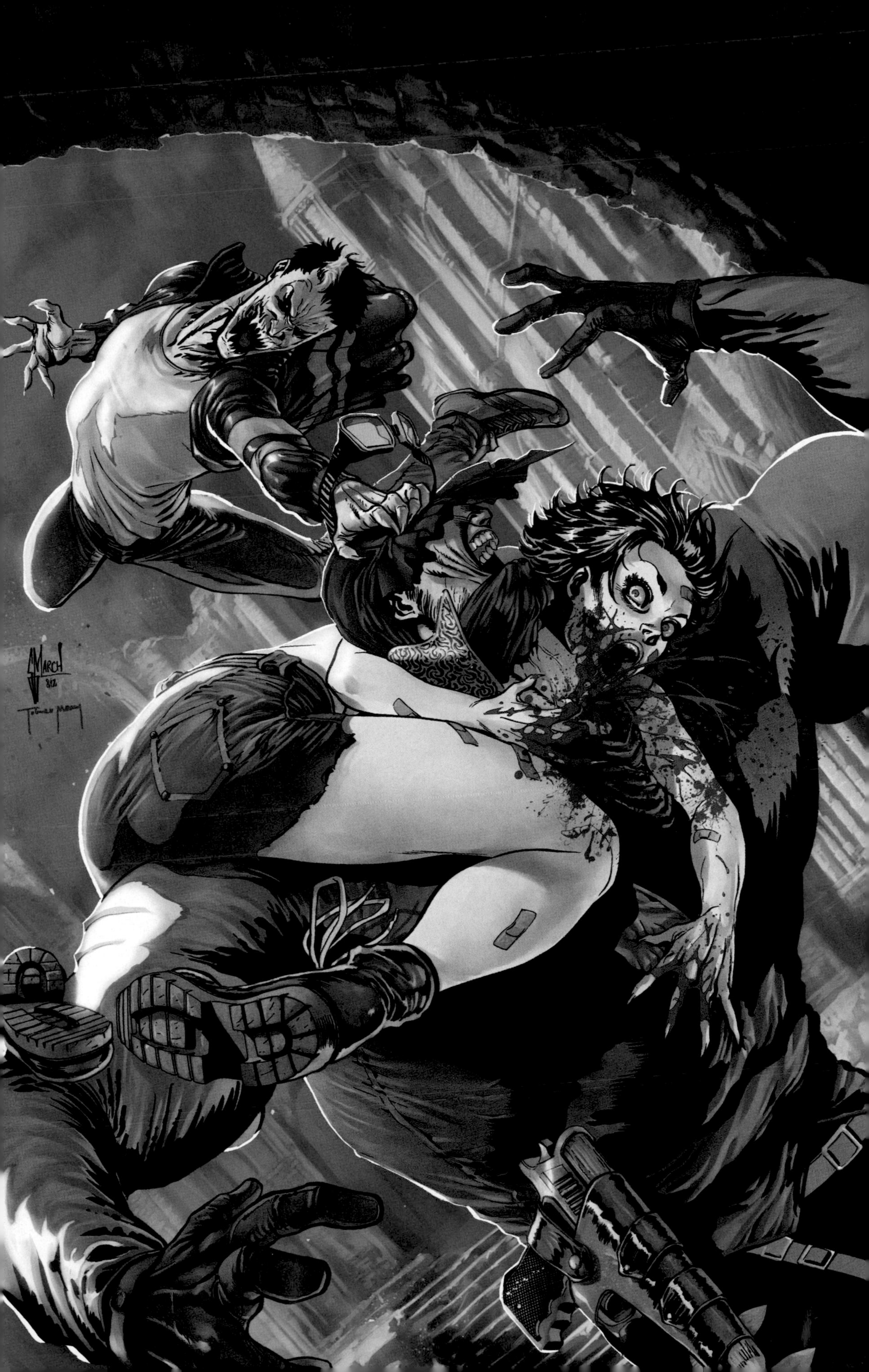
MARCH
8/12

HERE COMES YOUR MAN

JOSHUA HALE FIALKOV writer DENNIS CALERO artist cover art by GUILLEM MARCH & TOMEU MOREY

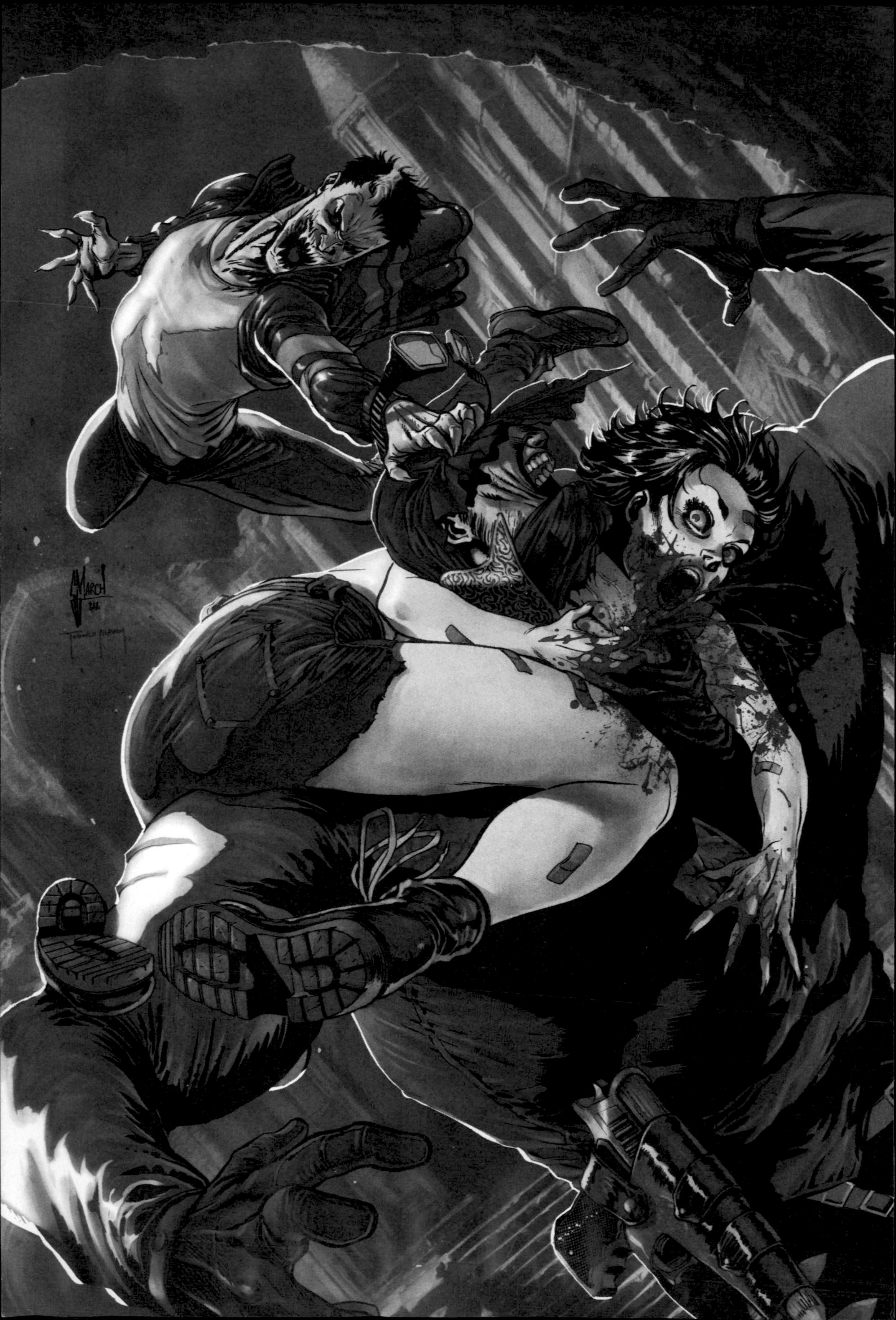

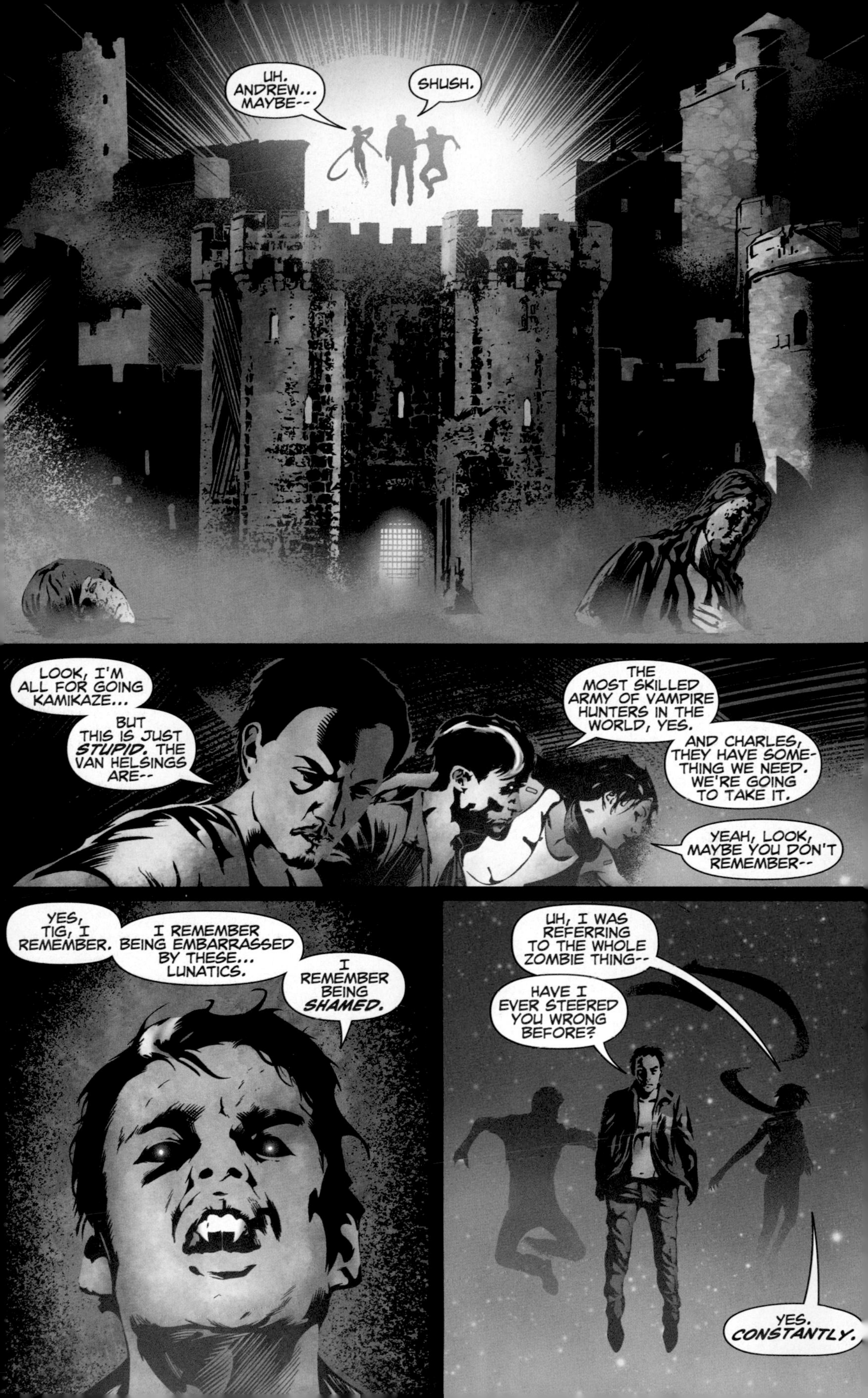
UH. ANDREW... MAYBE--
SHUSH.
LOOK, I'M ALL FOR GOING KAMIKAZE...
BUT THIS IS JUST STUPID. THE VAN HELSINGS ARE--
THE MOST SKILLED ARMY OF VAMPIRE HUNTERS IN THE WORLD, YES.
AND CHARLES, THEY HAVE SOMETHING WE NEED. WE'RE GOING TO TAKE IT.
YEAH, LOOK, MAYBE YOU DON'T REMEMBER--
YES, TIG, I REMEMBER.
I REMEMBER BEING EMBARRASSED BY THESE... LUNATICS.
I REMEMBER BEING SHAMED.
UH, I WAS REFERRING TO THE WHOLE ZOMBIE THING--
HAVE I EVER STEERED YOU WRONG BEFORE?
YES. CONSTANTLY.

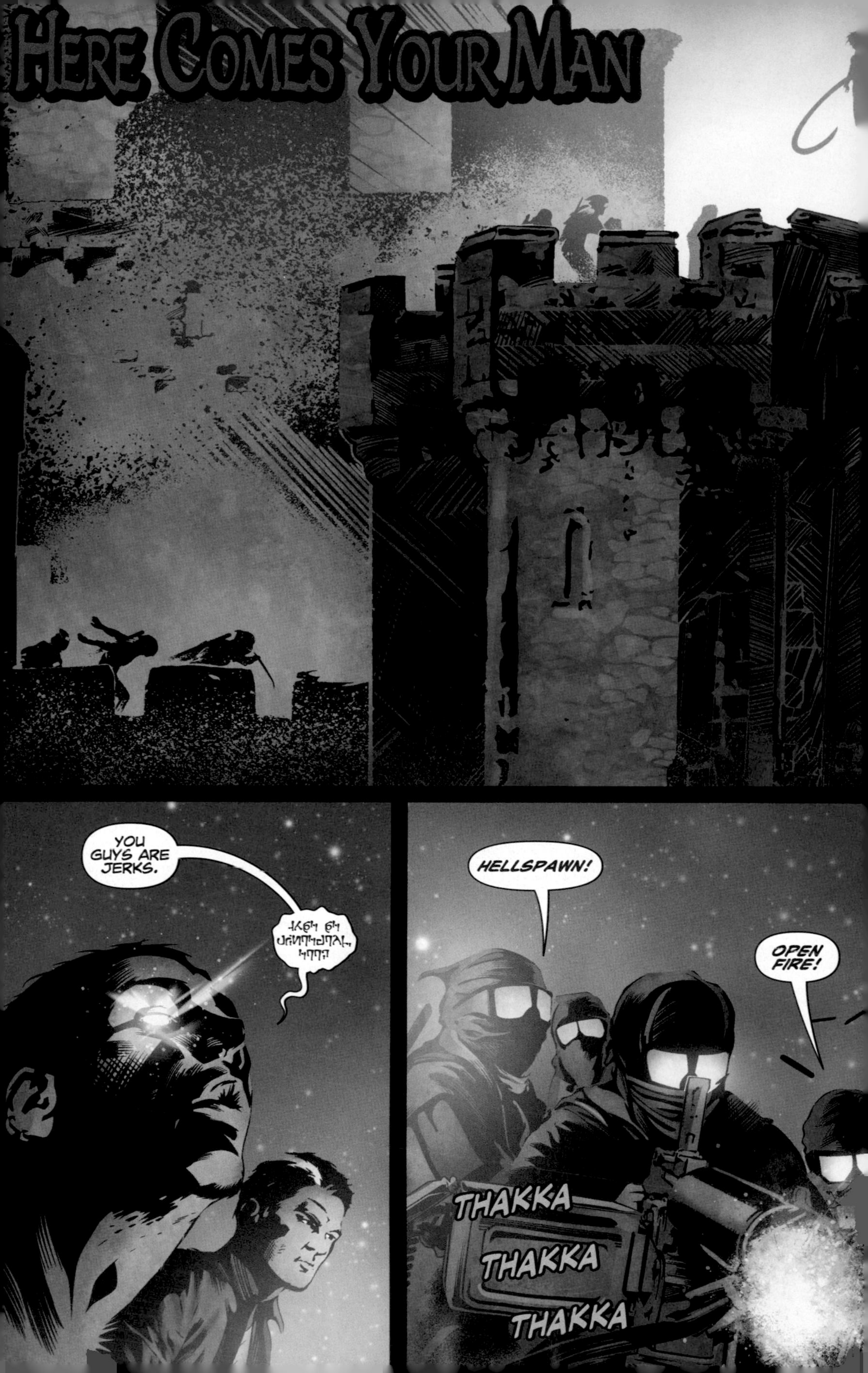
HERE COMES YOUR MAN
YOU GUYS ARE JERKS.
HELLSPAWN!
OPEN FIRE!
THAKKA
THAKKA
THAKKA

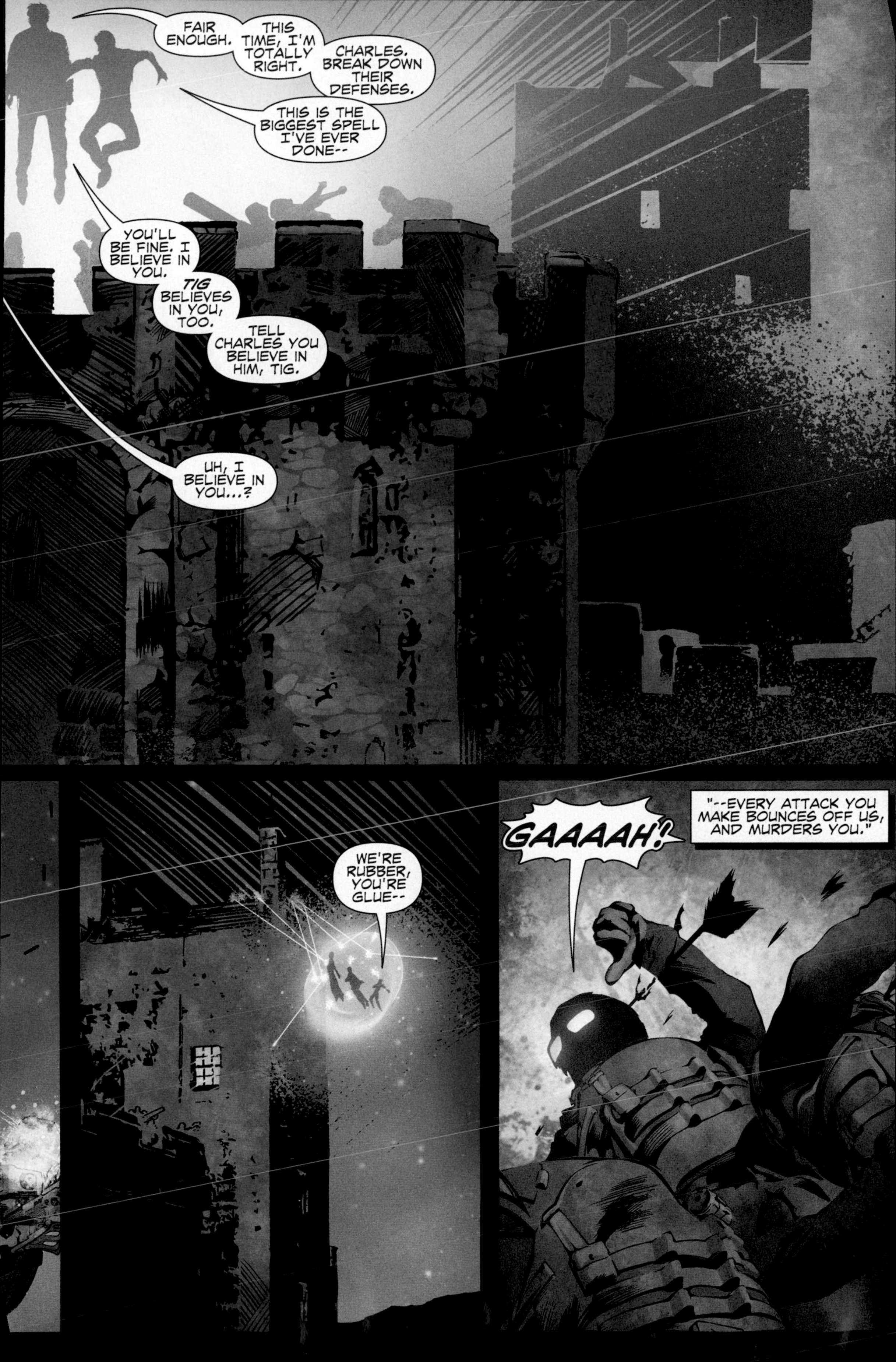
FAIR ENOUGH.
THIS TIME, I'M TOTALLY RIGHT.
CHARLES. BREAK DOWN THEIR DEFENSES.
THIS IS THE BIGGEST SPELL I'VE EVER DONE--
YOU'LL BE FINE. I BELIEVE IN YOU.
TIG BELIEVES IN YOU, TOO.
TELL CHARLES YOU BELIEVE IN HIM, TIG.
UH, I BELIEVE IN YOU...?
WE'RE RUBBER, YOU'RE GLUE--
"--EVERY ATTACK YOU MAKE BOUNCES OFF US, AND MURDERS YOU."
GAAAAH!

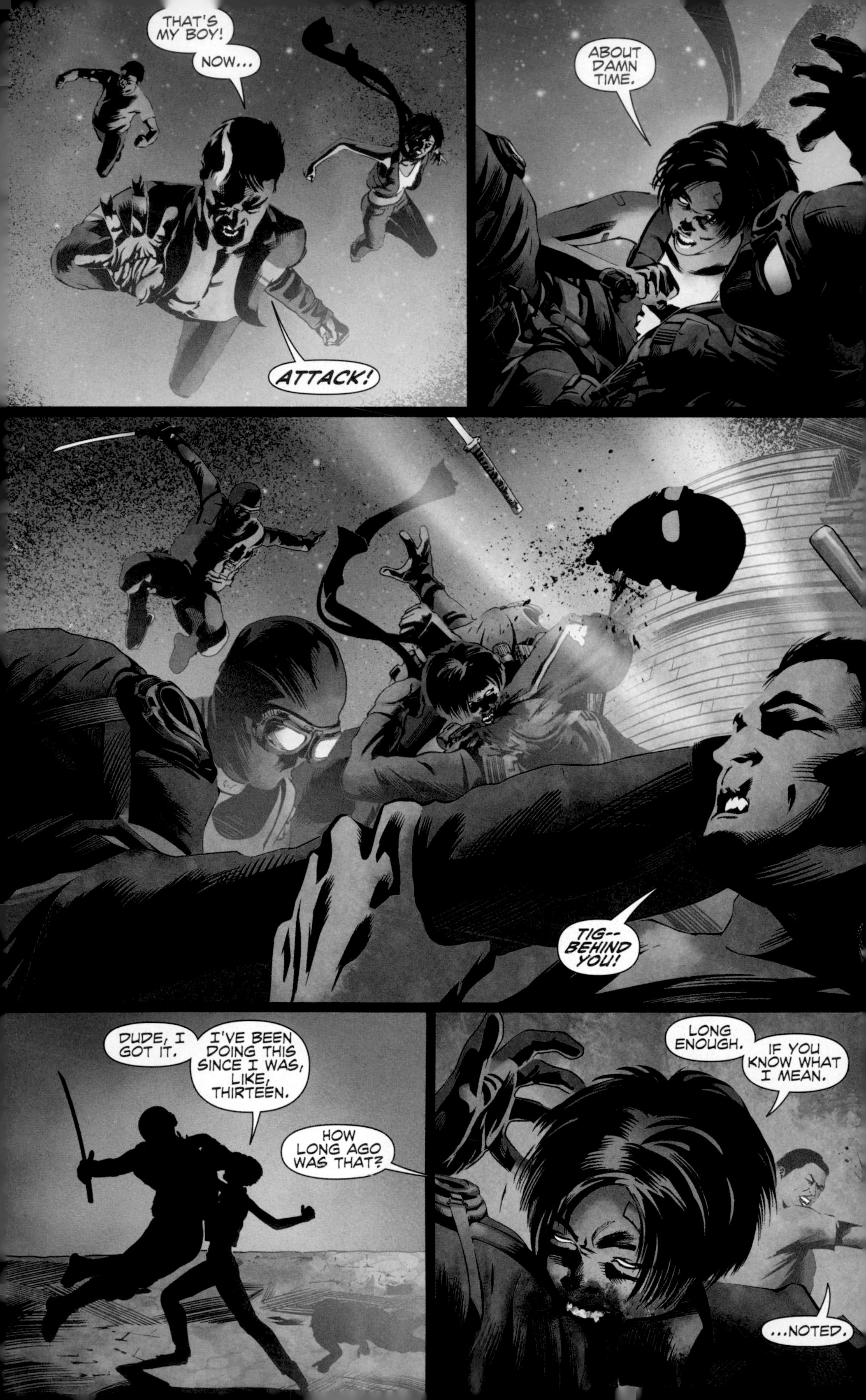
THAT'S MY BOY!
NOW...
ATTACK!
ABOUT DAMN TIME.
TIG-- BEHIND YOU!
DUDE, I GOT IT.
I'VE BEEN DOING THIS SINCE I WAS, LIKE, THIRTEEN.
HOW LONG AGO WAS THAT?
LONG ENOUGH.
IF YOU KNOW WHAT I MEAN.
...NOTED.

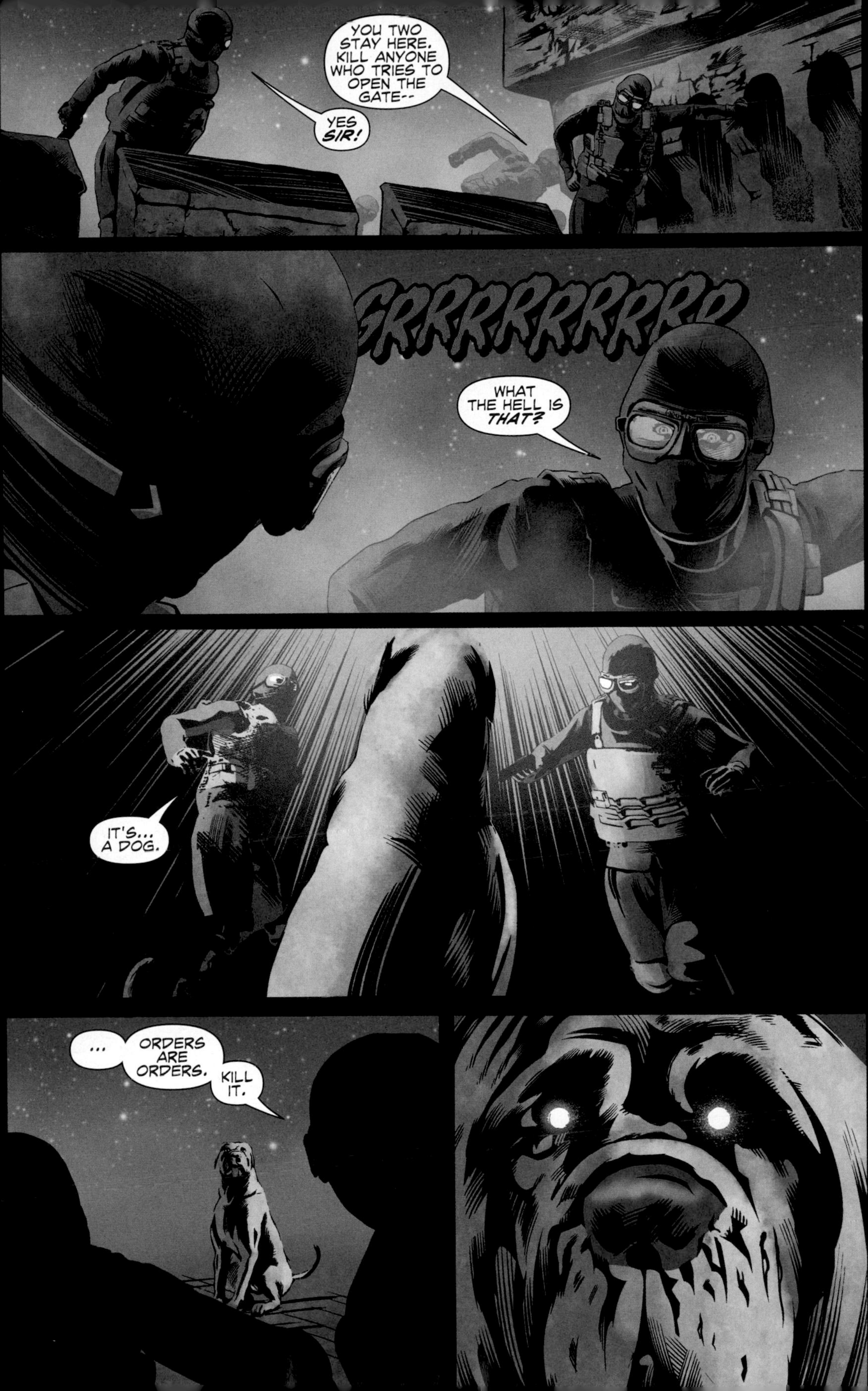
YOU TWO STAY HERE. KILL ANYONE WHO TRIES TO OPEN THE GATE--
YES SIR!
GRRRRRRRRRR
WHAT THE HELL IS THAT?
IT'S... A DOG.
...
ORDERS ARE ORDERS.
KILL IT.

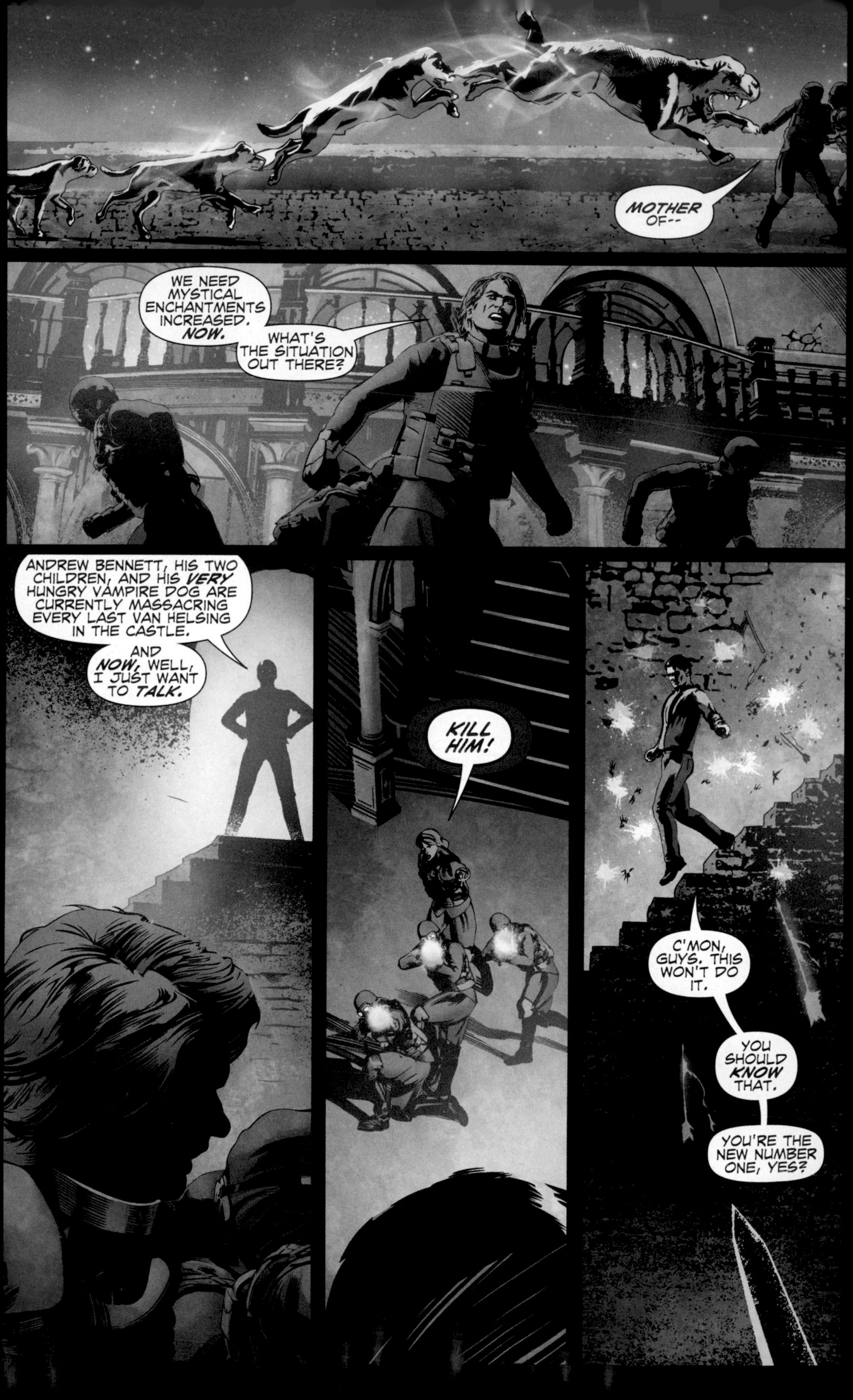
MOTHER OF--
WE NEED MYSTICAL ENCHANTMENTS INCREASED. NOW.
WHAT'S THE SITUATION OUT THERE?
ANDREW BENNETT, HIS TWO CHILDREN, AND HIS VERY HUNGRY VAMPIRE DOG ARE CURRENTLY MASSACRING EVERY LAST VAN HELSING IN THE CASTLE.
AND NOW, WELL, I JUST WANT TO TALK.
KILL HIM!
C'MON, GUYS. THIS WON'T DO IT.
YOU SHOULD KNOW THAT.
YOU'RE THE NEW NUMBER ONE, YES?

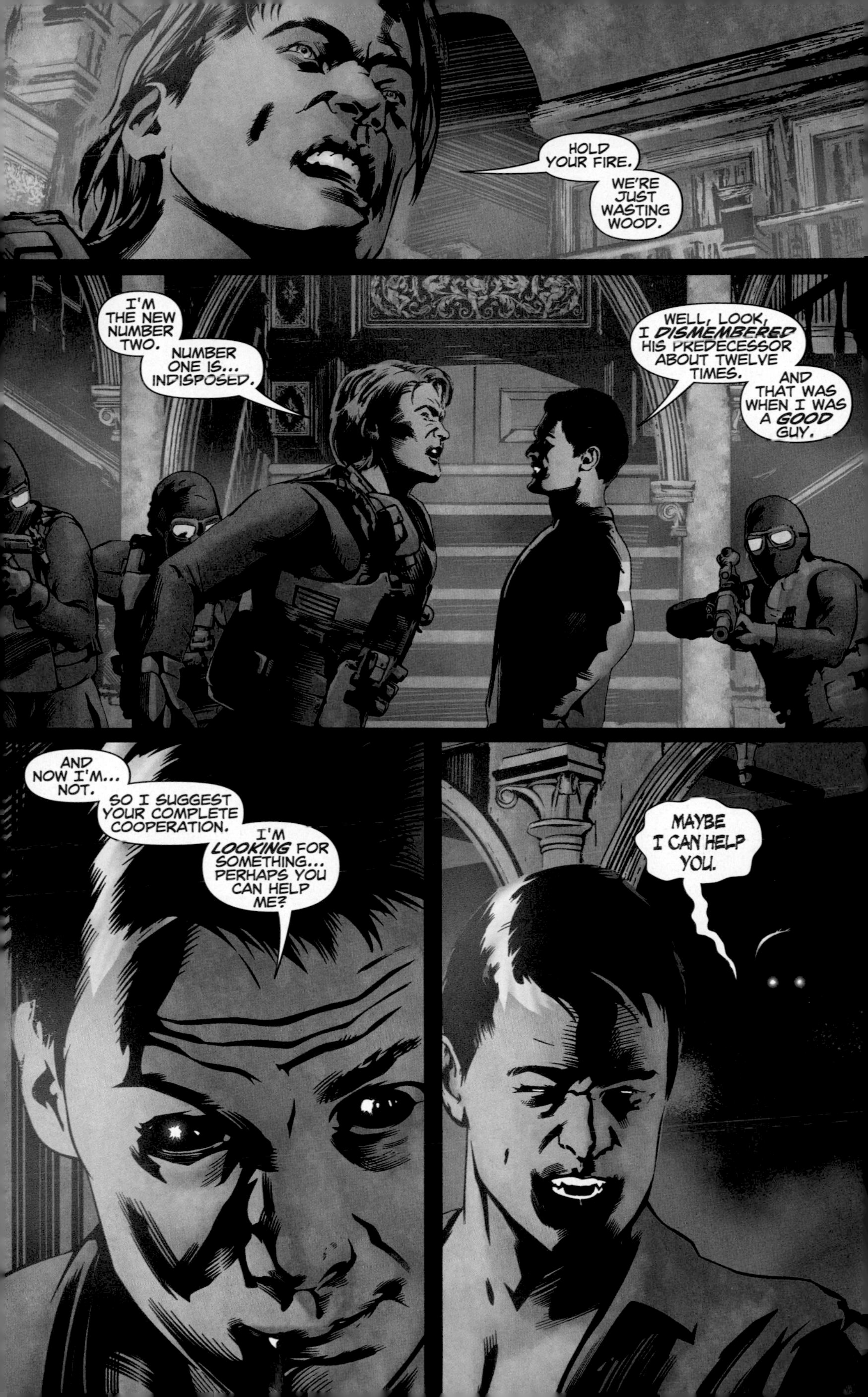
HOLD YOUR FIRE.
WE'RE JUST WASTING WOOD.
I'M THE NEW NUMBER TWO.
NUMBER ONE IS... INDISPOSED.
WELL, LOOK, I DISMEMBERED HIS PREDECESSOR ABOUT TWELVE TIMES.
AND THAT WAS WHEN I WAS A GOOD GUY.
AND NOW I'M... NOT.
SO I SUGGEST YOUR COMPLETE COOPERATION.
I'M LOOKING FOR SOMETHING... PERHAPS YOU CAN HELP ME?
MAYBE I CAN HELP YOU.

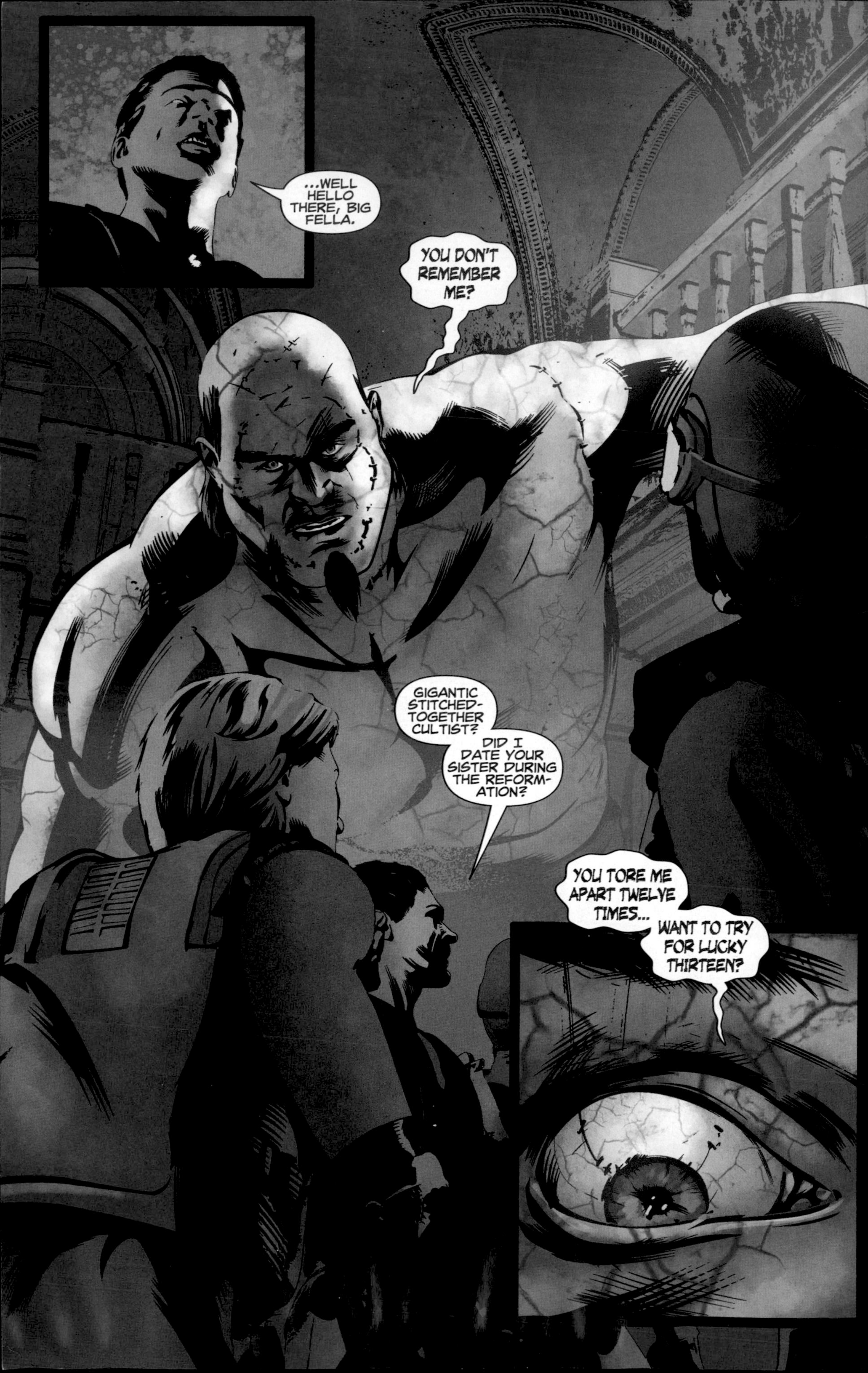
...WELL HELLO THERE, BIG FELLA.
YOU DON'T REMEMBER ME?
GIGANTIC STITCHED-TOGETHER CULTIST?
DID I DATE YOUR SISTER DURING THE REFORMATION?
YOU TORE ME APART TWELVE TIMES...
WANT TO TRY FOR LUCKY THIRTEEN?

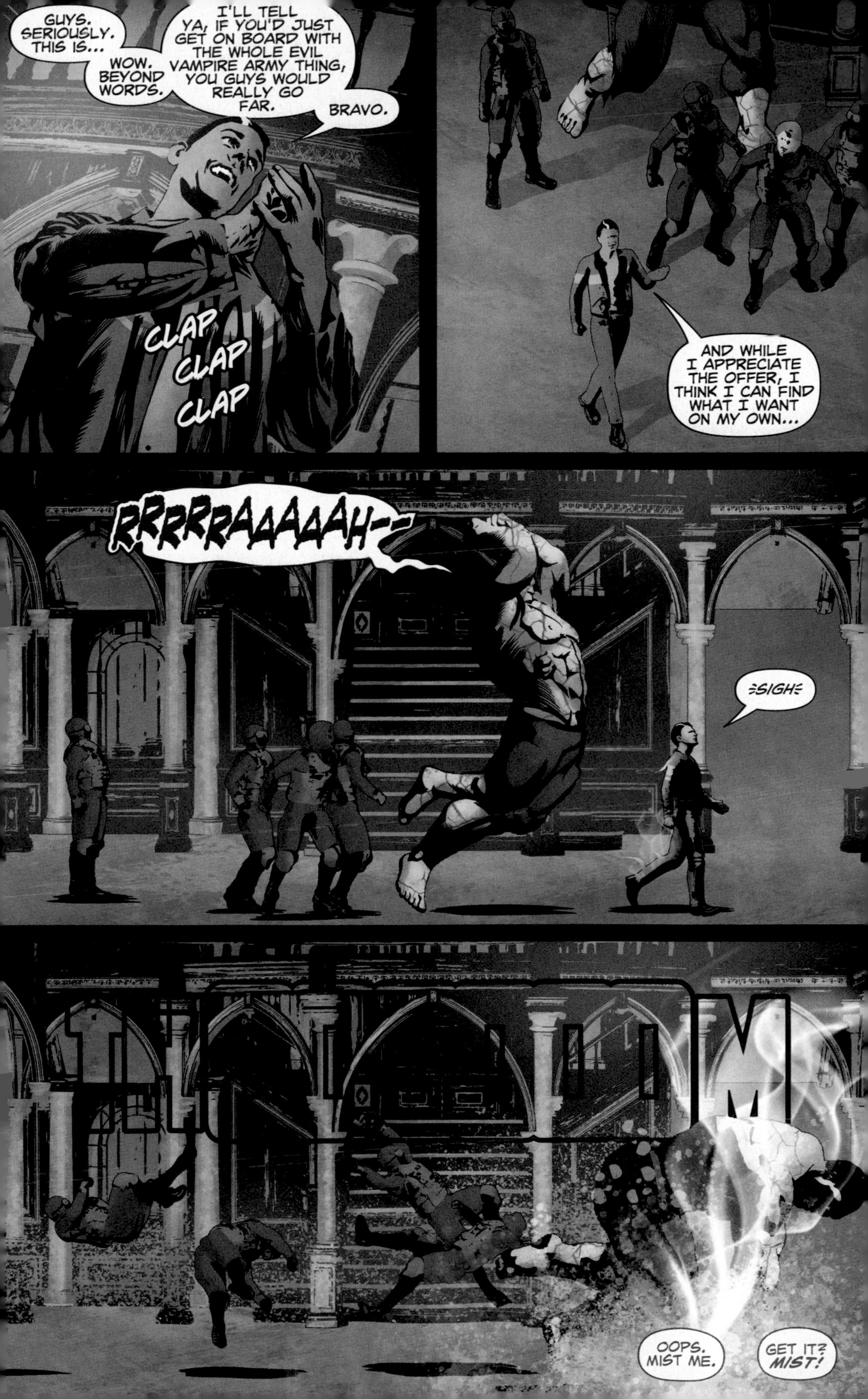
GUYS. SERIOUSLY. THIS IS...
WOW. BEYOND WORDS.
I'LL TELL YA, IF YOU'D JUST GET ON BOARD WITH THE WHOLE EVIL VAMPIRE ARMY THING, YOU GUYS WOULD REALLY GO FAR.
BRAVO.
CLAP
CLAP
CLAP
AND WHILE I APPRECIATE THE OFFER, I THINK I CAN FIND WHAT I WANT ON MY OWN...
RRRRRAAAAAH--
=SIGH=
OOPS. MIST ME.
GET IT? MIST!

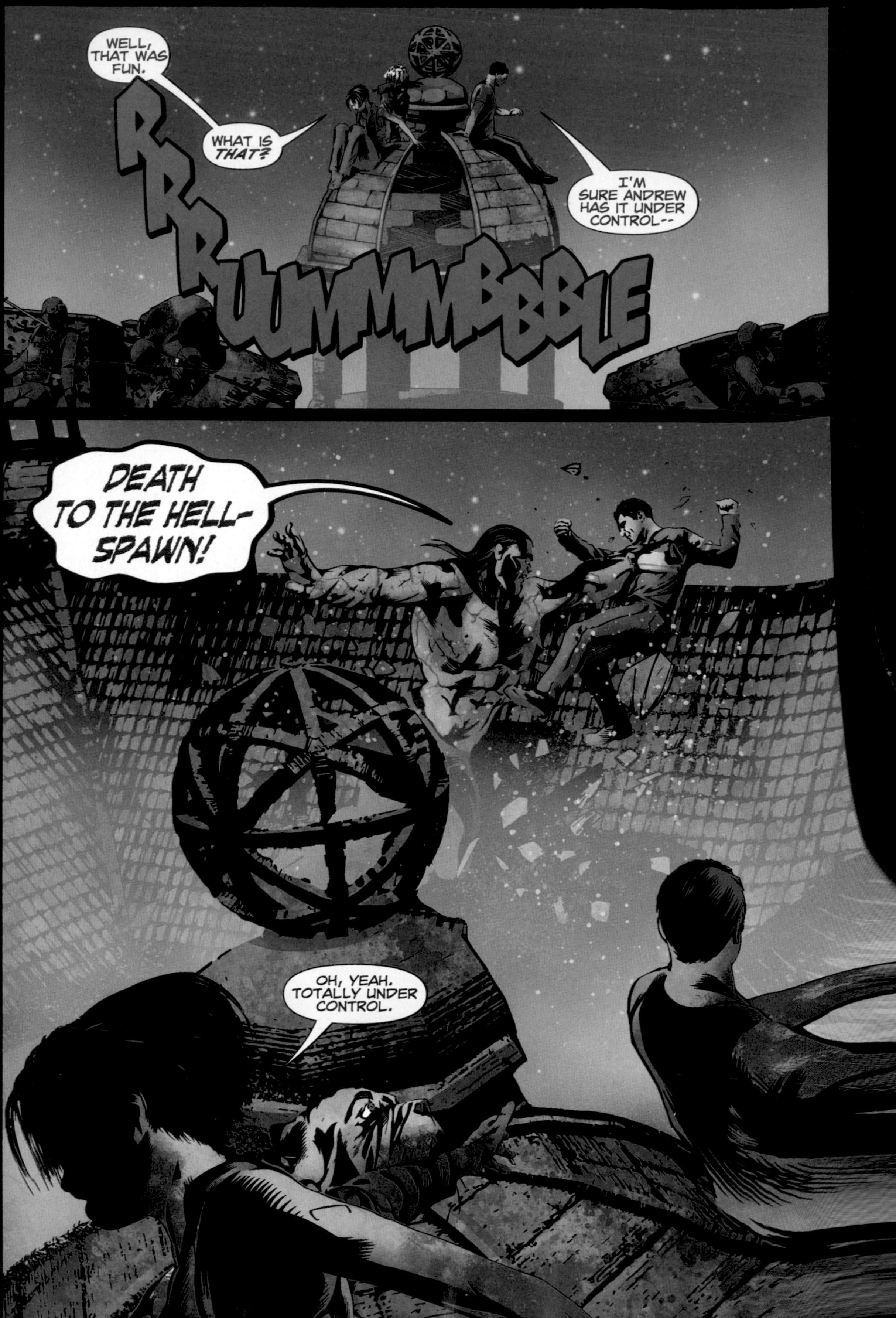
WELL, THAT WAS FUN.
WHAT IS THAT?
I'M SURE ANDREW HAS IT UNDER CONTROL--
RRRUUMMMBBBLE
DEATH TO THE HELL-SPAWN!
OH, YEAH. TOTALLY UNDER CONTROL.

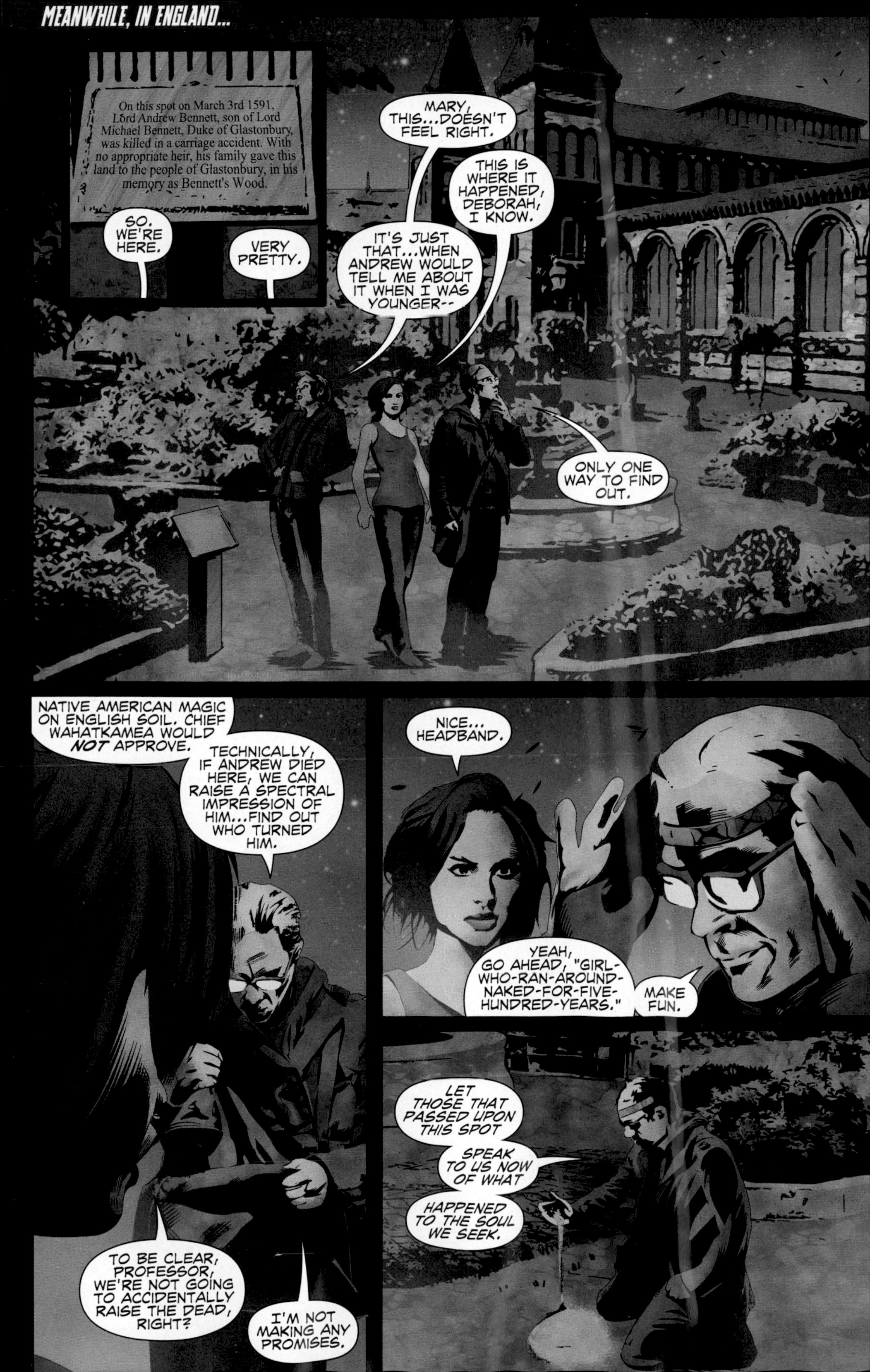
MEANWHILE, IN ENGLAND...
On this spot on March 3rd 1591, Lord Andrew Bennett, son of Lord Michael Bennett, Duke of Glastonbury, was killed in a carriage accident. With no appropriate heir, his family gave this land to the people of Glastonbury, in his memory as Bennett's Wood.
SO. WE'RE HERE.
VERY PRETTY.
MARY, THIS...DOESN'T FEEL RIGHT.
IT'S JUST THAT...WHEN ANDREW WOULD TELL ME ABOUT IT WHEN I WAS YOUNGER--
THIS IS WHERE IT HAPPENED, DEBORAH, I KNOW.
ONLY ONE WAY TO FIND OUT.
NATIVE AMERICAN MAGIC ON ENGLISH SOIL. CHIEF WAHATKAMEA WOULD NOT APPROVE.
TECHNICALLY, IF ANDREW DIED HERE, WE CAN RAISE A SPECTRAL IMPRESSION OF HIM...FIND OUT WHO TURNED HIM.
TO BE CLEAR, PROFESSOR, WE'RE NOT GOING TO ACCIDENTALLY RAISE THE DEAD, RIGHT?
I'M NOT MAKING ANY PROMISES.
NICE... HEADBAND.
YEAH, GO AHEAD, "GIRL-WHO-RAN-AROUND-NAKED-FOR-FIVE-HUNDRED-YEARS."
MAKE FUN.
LET THOSE THAT PASSED UPON THIS SPOT
SPEAK TO US NOW OF WHAT
HAPPENED TO THE SOUL WE SEEK.

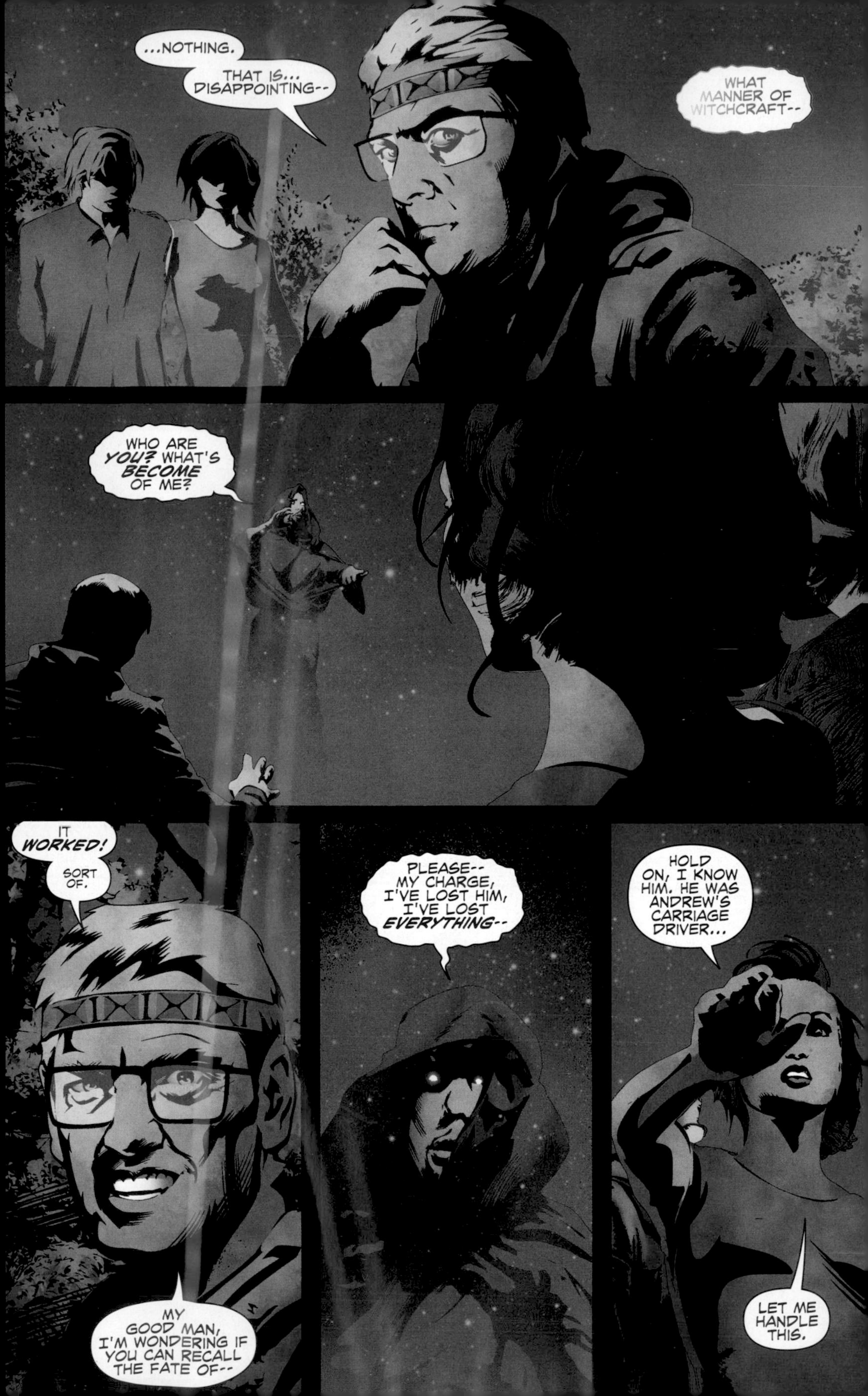
...NOTHING.
THAT IS... DISAPPOINTING--
WHAT MANNER OF WITCHCRAFT--
WHO ARE YOU? WHAT'S BECOME OF ME?
IT WORKED!
SORT OF.
MY GOOD MAN, I'M WONDERING IF YOU CAN RECALL THE FATE OF--
PLEASE-- MY CHARGE, I'VE LOST HIM, I'VE LOST EVERYTHING--
HOLD ON, I KNOW HIM. HE WAS ANDREW'S CARRIAGE DRIVER...
LET ME HANDLE THIS.

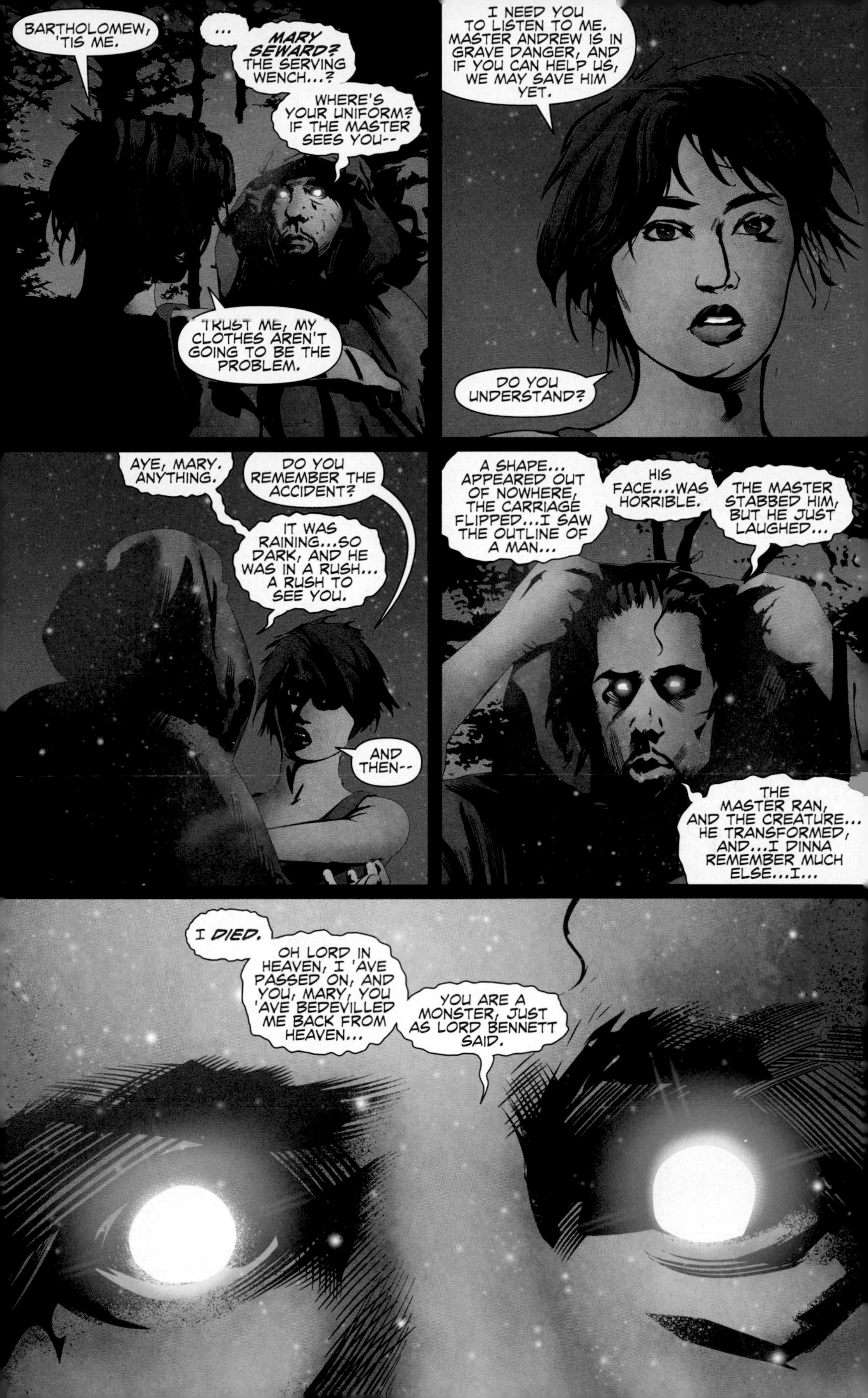
BARTHOLOMEW, 'TIS ME.
... *MARY SEWARD?* THE SERVING WENCH...?
WHERE'S YOUR UNIFORM? IF THE MASTER SEES YOU--
TRUST ME, MY CLOTHES AREN'T GOING TO BE THE PROBLEM.
I NEED YOU TO LISTEN TO ME. MASTER ANDREW IS IN GRAVE DANGER, AND IF YOU CAN HELP US, WE MAY SAVE HIM YET.
DO YOU UNDERSTAND?
AYE, MARY. ANYTHING.
DO YOU REMEMBER THE ACCIDENT?
IT WAS RAINING...SO DARK, AND HE WAS IN A RUSH... A RUSH TO SEE YOU.
AND THEN--
A SHAPE... APPEARED OUT OF NOWHERE, THE CARRIAGE FLIPPED...I SAW THE OUTLINE OF A MAN...
HIS FACE....WAS HORRIBLE.
THE MASTER STABBED HIM, BUT HE JUST LAUGHED...
THE MASTER RAN, AND THE CREATURE... HE TRANSFORMED, AND...I DINNA REMEMBER MUCH ELSE...I...
I *DIED.*
OH LORD IN HEAVEN, I 'AVE PASSED ON, AND YOU, MARY, YOU 'AVE BEDEVILLED ME BACK FROM HEAVEN...
YOU ARE A MONSTER, JUST AS LORD BENNETT SAID.

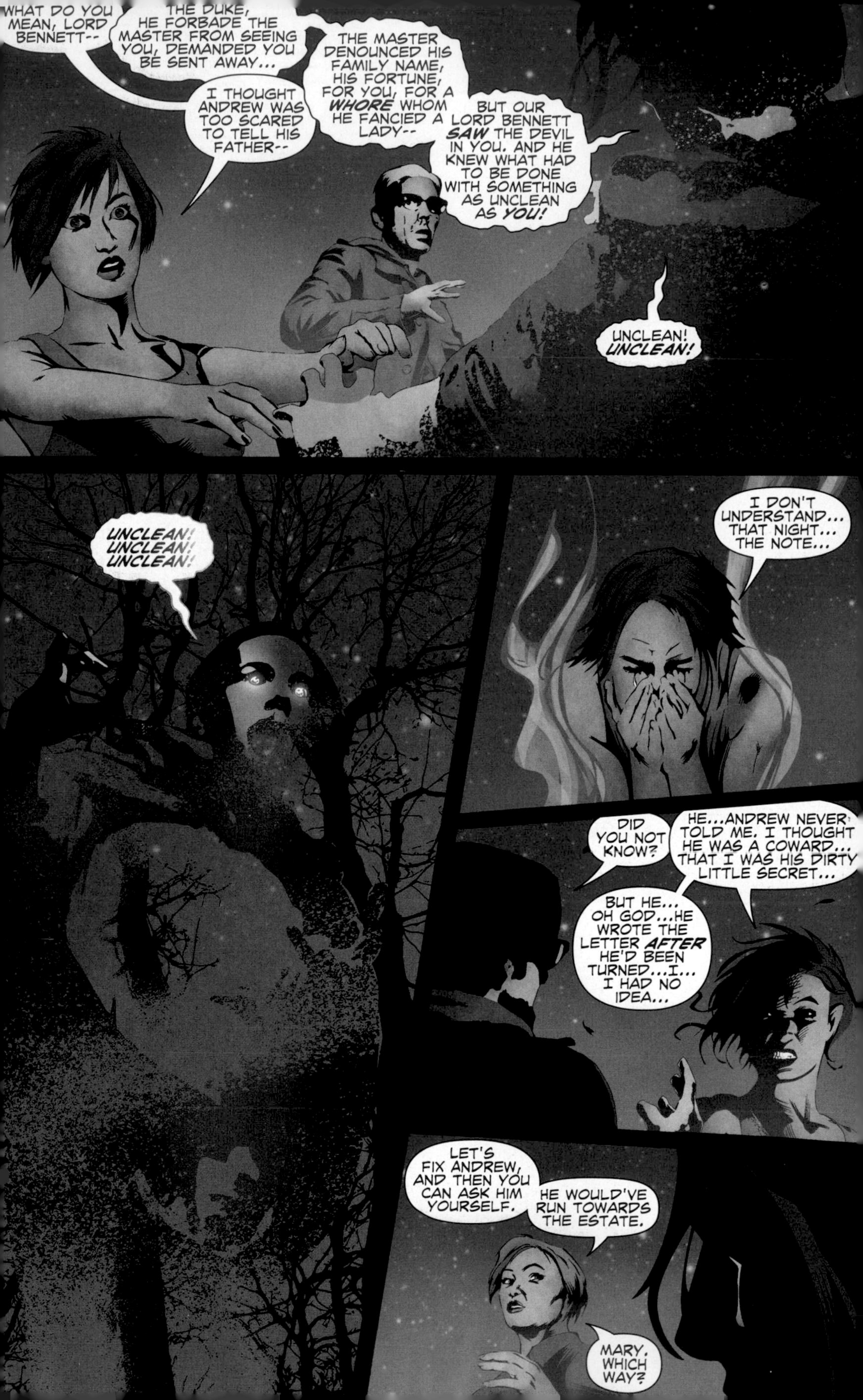
WHAT DO YOU MEAN, LORD BENNETT--
THE DUKE, HE FORBADE THE MASTER FROM SEEING YOU, DEMANDED YOU BE SENT AWAY...
I THOUGHT ANDREW WAS TOO SCARED TO TELL HIS FATHER--
THE MASTER DENOUNCED HIS FAMILY NAME, HIS FORTUNE, FOR YOU, FOR A WHORE WHOM HE FANCIED A LADY--
BUT OUR LORD BENNETT SAW THE DEVIL IN YOU. AND HE KNEW WHAT HAD TO BE DONE WITH SOMETHING AS UNCLEAN AS YOU!
UNCLEAN! UNCLEAN!
UNCLEAN! UNCLEAN! UNCLEAN!
I DON'T UNDERSTAND... THAT NIGHT... THE NOTE...
DID YOU NOT KNOW?
HE...ANDREW NEVER TOLD ME. I THOUGHT HE WAS A COWARD... THAT I WAS HIS DIRTY LITTLE SECRET...
BUT HE... OH GOD...HE WROTE THE LETTER AFTER HE'D BEEN TURNED...I... I HAD NO IDEA...
LET'S FIX ANDREW, AND THEN YOU CAN ASK HIM YOURSELF.
HE WOULD'VE RUN TOWARDS THE ESTATE.
MARY. WHICH WAY?

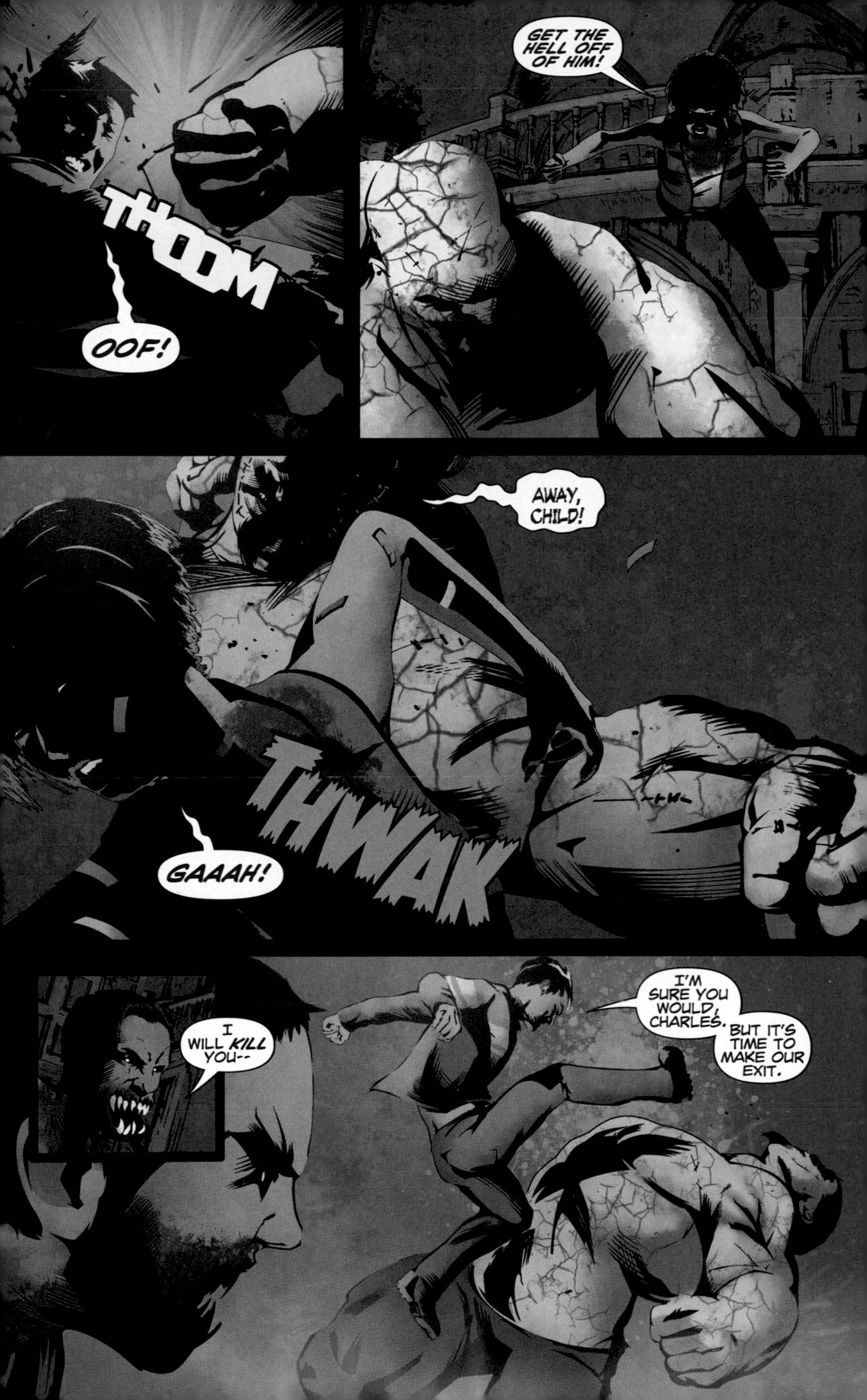
THOOM
OOF!
GET THE HELL OFF OF HIM!
AWAY, CHILD!
THWAK
GAAAH!
I WILL KILL YOU--
I'M SURE YOU WOULD, CHARLES.
BUT IT'S TIME TO MAKE OUR EXIT.

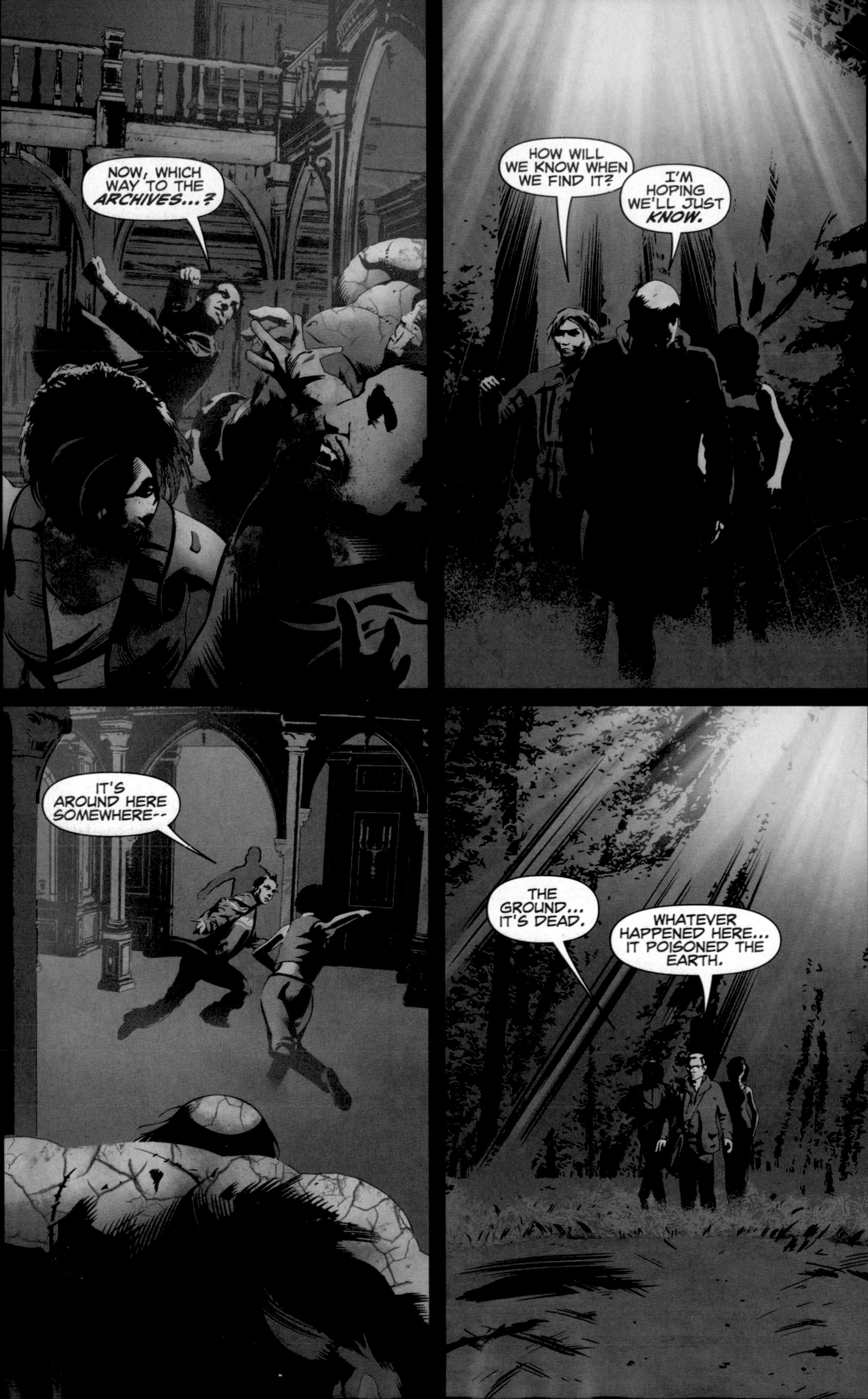
NOW, WHICH WAY TO THE ARCHIVES...?
HOW WILL WE KNOW WHEN WE FIND IT?
I'M HOPING WE'LL JUST KNOW.
IT'S AROUND HERE SOMEWHERE--
THE GROUND... IT'S DEAD.
WHATEVER HAPPENED HERE... IT POISONED THE EARTH.

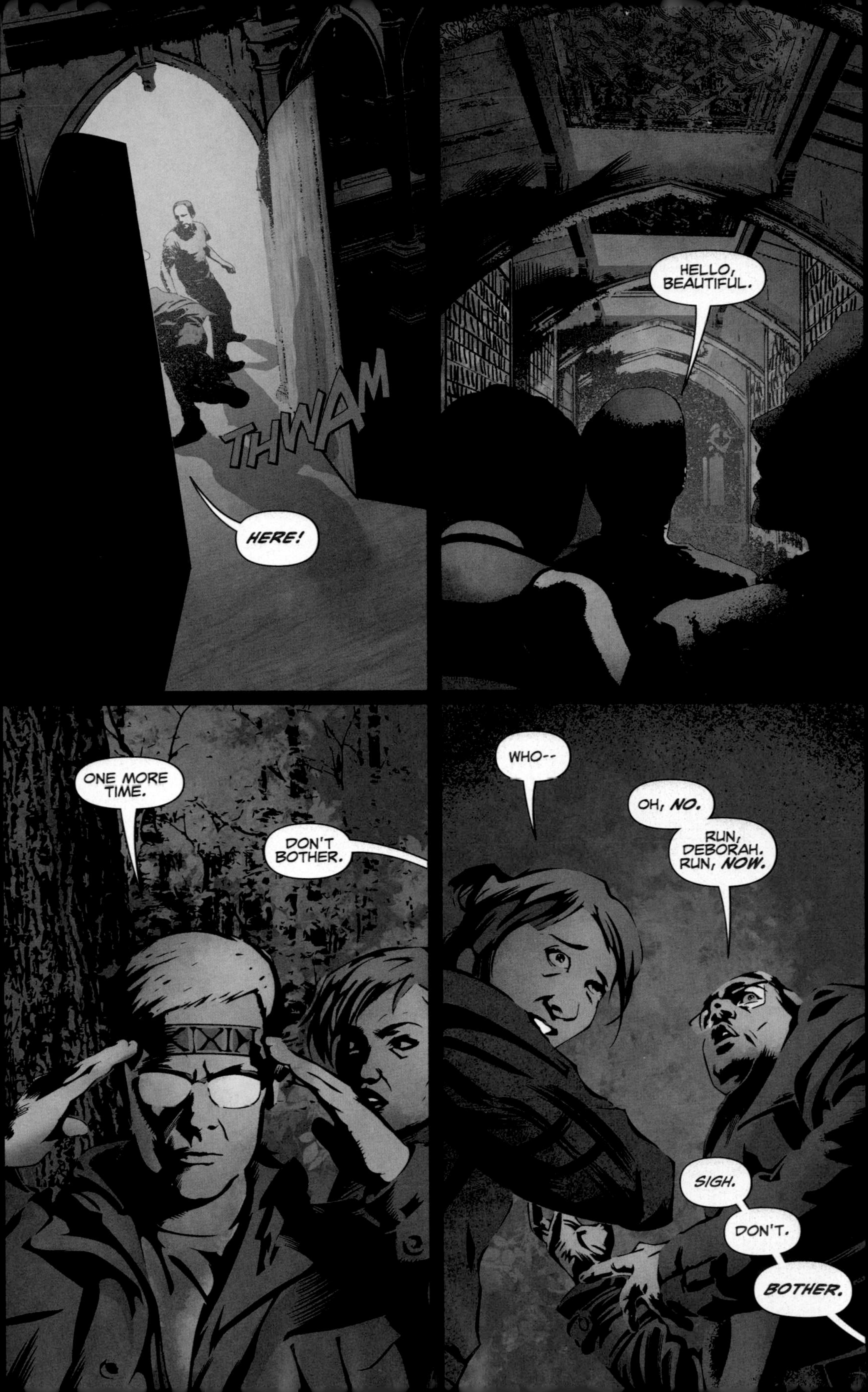
THWAM
HERE!
HELLO, BEAUTIFUL.
ONE MORE TIME.
DON'T BOTHER.
WHO--
OH, NO.
RUN, DEBORAH. RUN, NOW.
SIGH.
DON'T.
BOTHER.

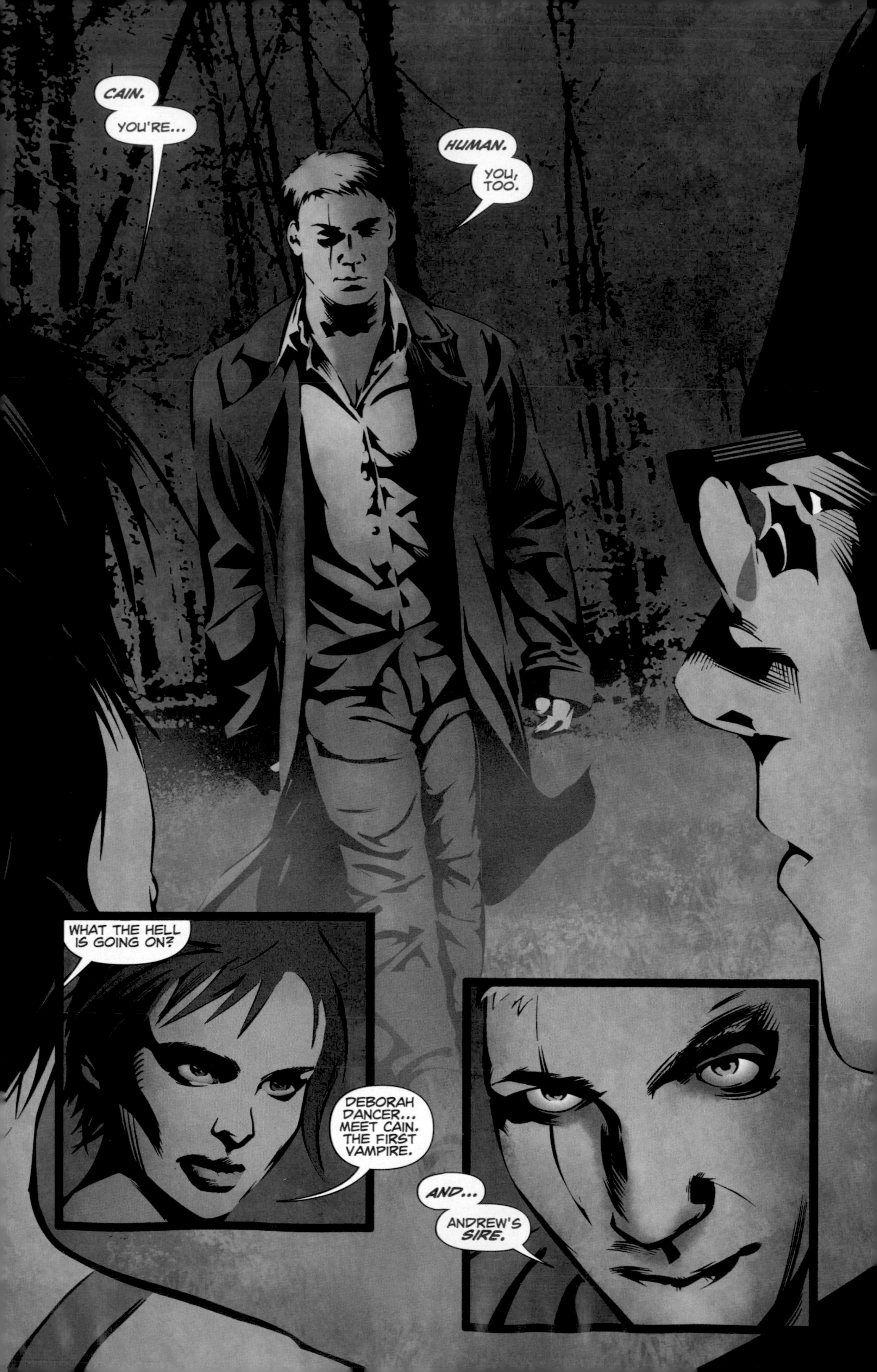

CAIN.
YOU'RE...
HUMAN.
YOU, TOO.
WHAT THE HELL IS GOING ON?
DEBORAH DANCER... MEET CAIN. THE FIRST VAMPIRE.
AND...
ANDREW'S SIRE.

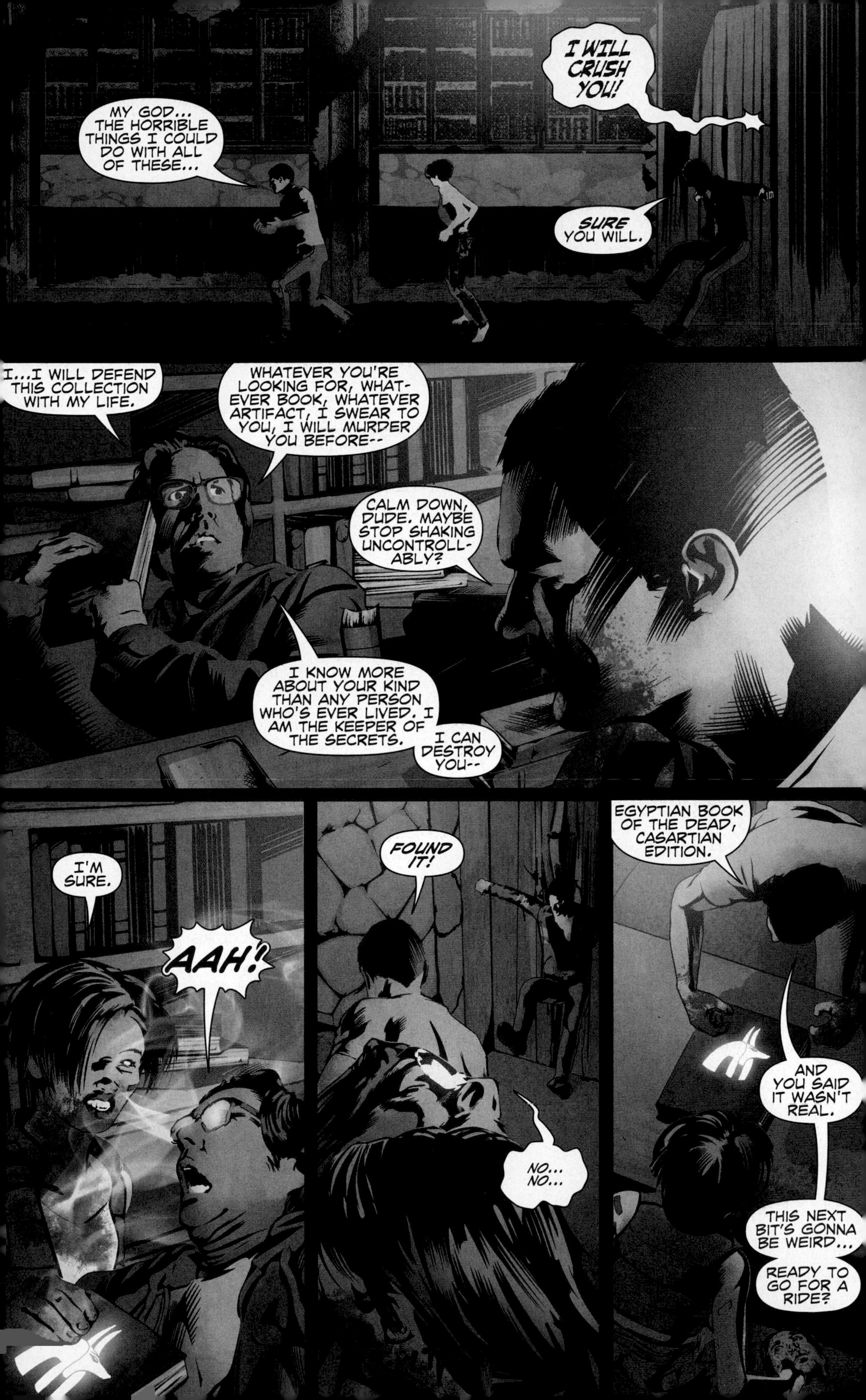
MY GOD... THE HORRIBLE THINGS I COULD DO WITH ALL OF THESE...
I WILL CRUSH YOU!
SURE YOU WILL.
I...I WILL DEFEND THIS COLLECTION WITH MY LIFE.
WHATEVER YOU'RE LOOKING FOR, WHATEVER BOOK, WHATEVER ARTIFACT, I SWEAR TO YOU, I WILL MURDER YOU BEFORE--
CALM DOWN, DUDE. MAYBE STOP SHAKING UNCONTROLLABLY?
I KNOW MORE ABOUT YOUR KIND THAN ANY PERSON WHO'S EVER LIVED. I AM THE KEEPER OF THE SECRETS.
I CAN DESTROY YOU--
I'M SURE.
AAH!
FOUND IT!
NO... NO...
EGYPTIAN BOOK OF THE DEAD, CASARTIAN EDITION.
AND YOU SAID IT WASN'T REAL.
THIS NEXT BIT'S GONNA BE WEIRD...
READY TO GO FOR A RIDE?

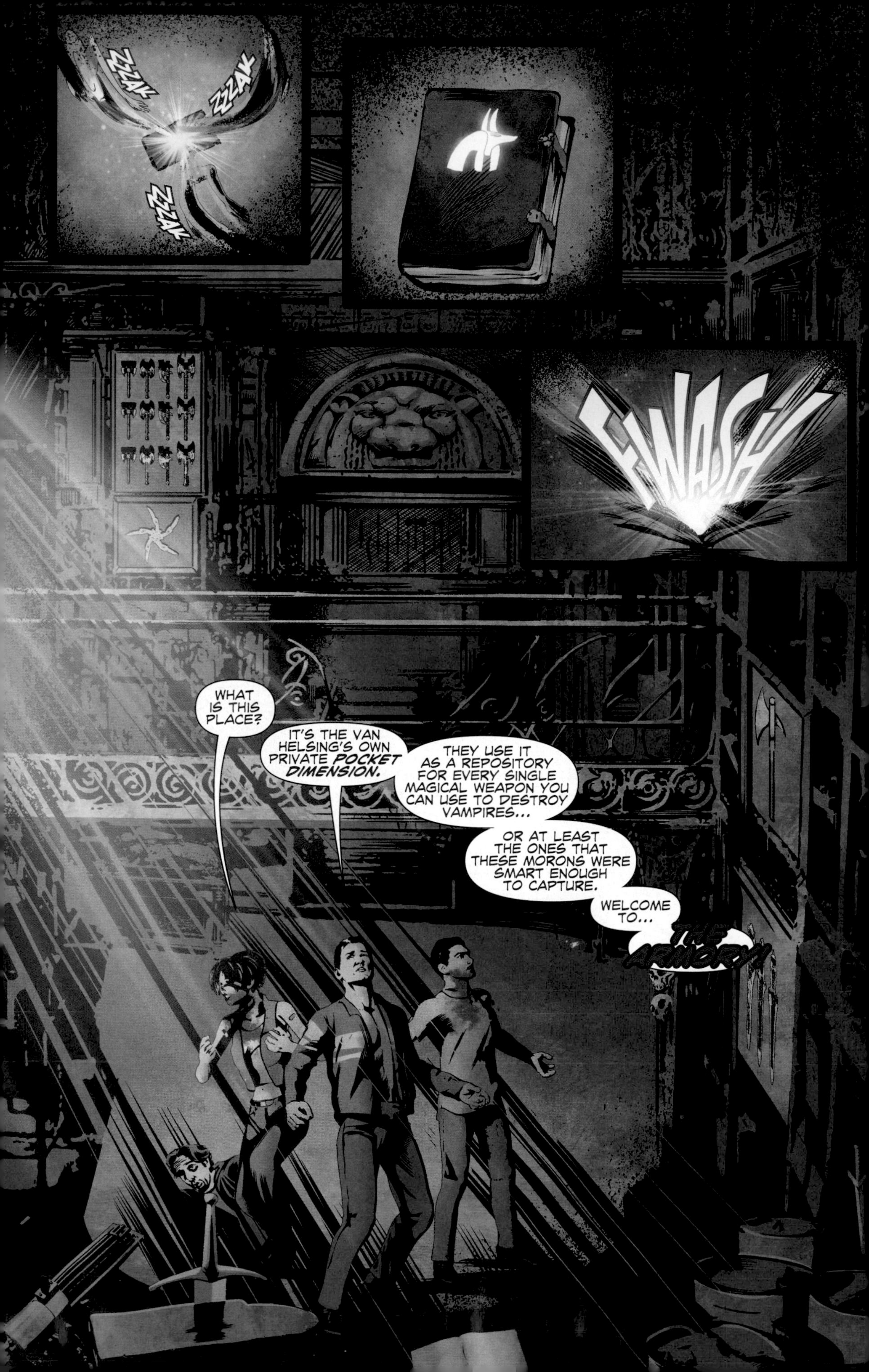
ZZZAK
ZZZAK
ZZZAK
FWASH!
WHAT IS THIS PLACE?
IT'S THE VAN HELSING'S OWN PRIVATE *POCKET DIMENSION.*
THEY USE IT AS A REPOSITORY FOR EVERY SINGLE MAGICAL WEAPON YOU CAN USE TO DESTROY VAMPIRES...
OR AT LEAST THE ONES THAT THESE MORONS WERE SMART ENOUGH TO CAPTURE.
WELCOME TO...
THE ARMORY!

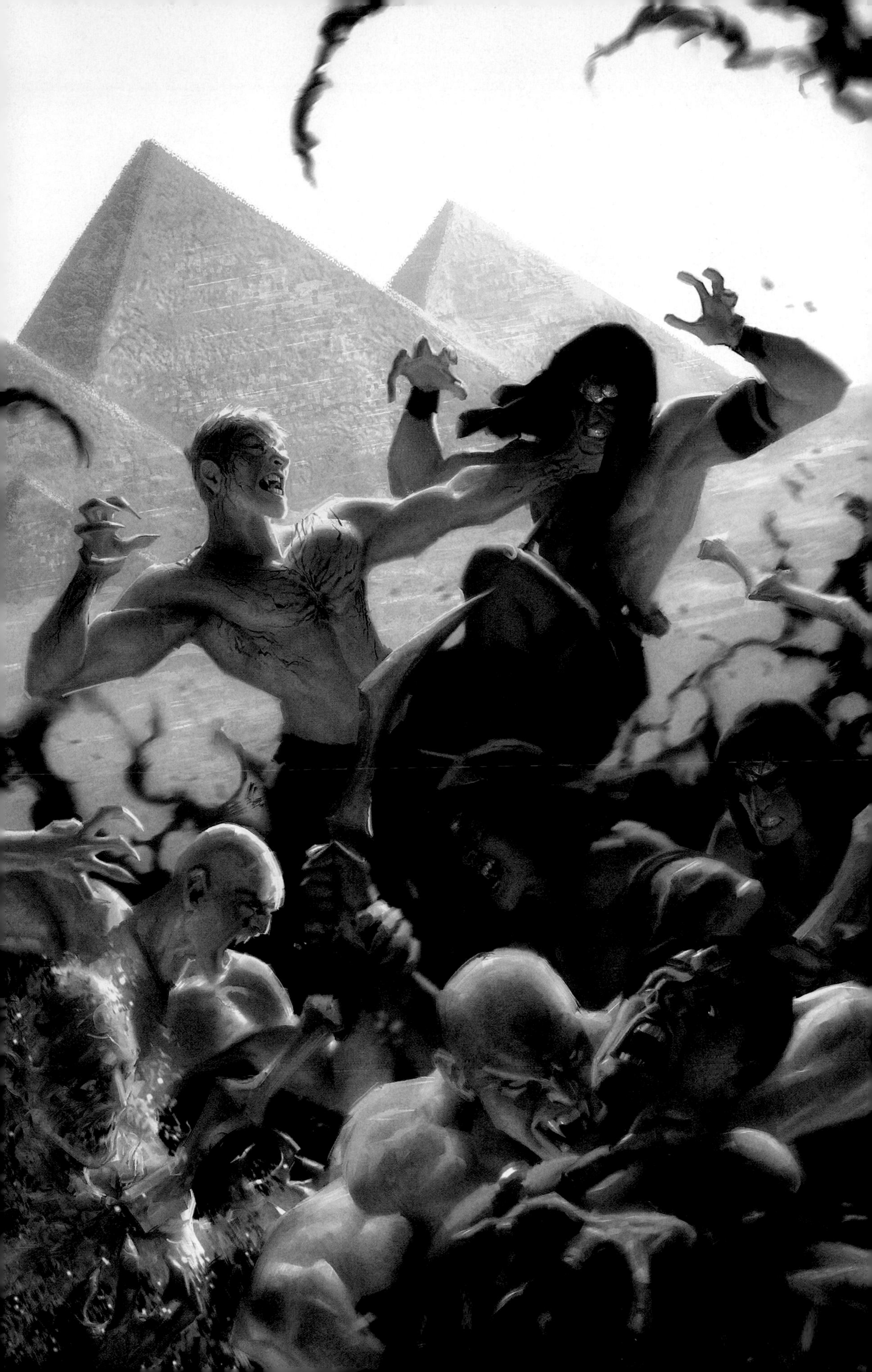

NIMROD'S SON

JOSHUA HALE FIALKOV writer SCOTT CLARK, FERNANDO BLANCO, SZYMON KUDRANSKI & DAVE BEATY artists cover art by ALEX GARNER

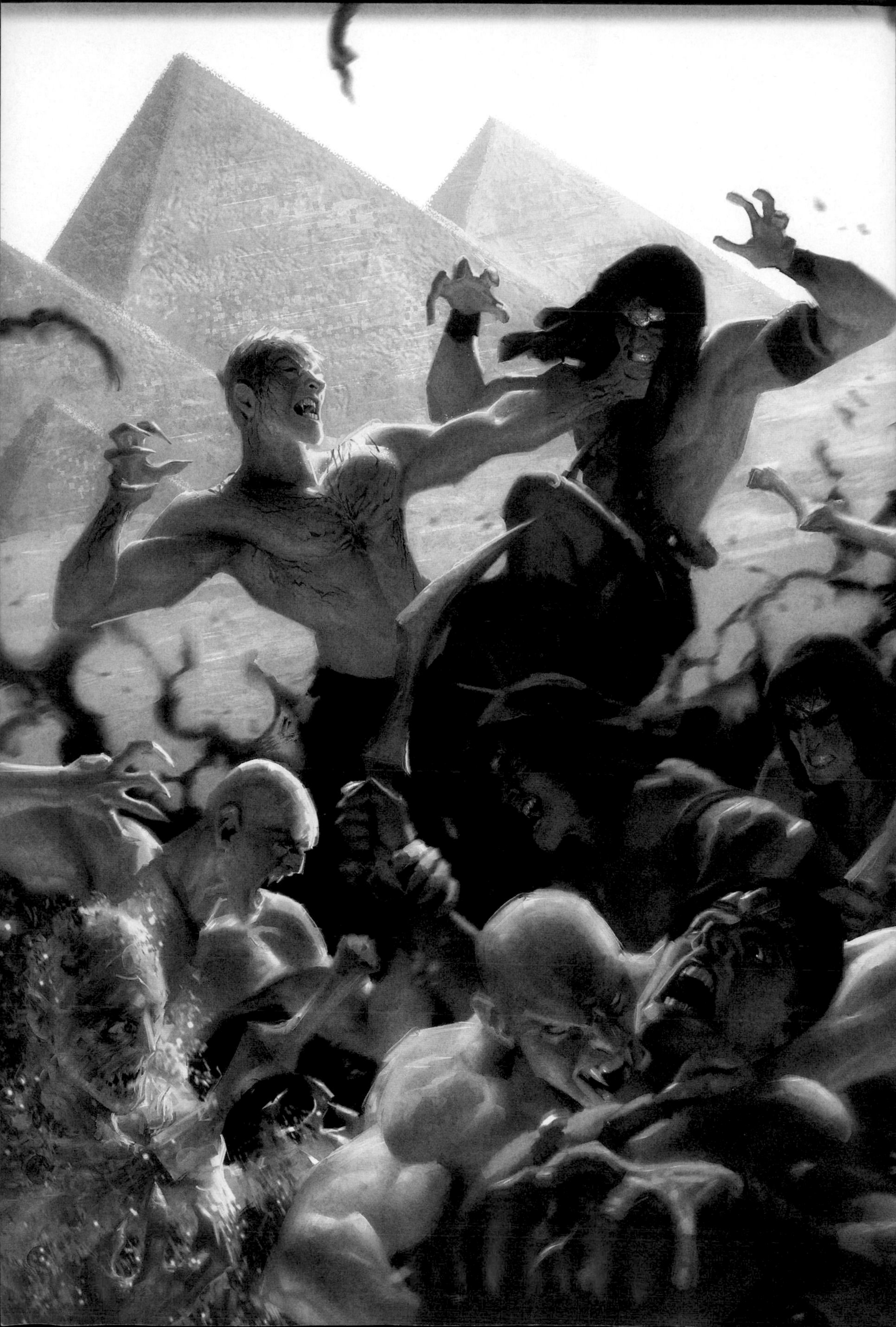

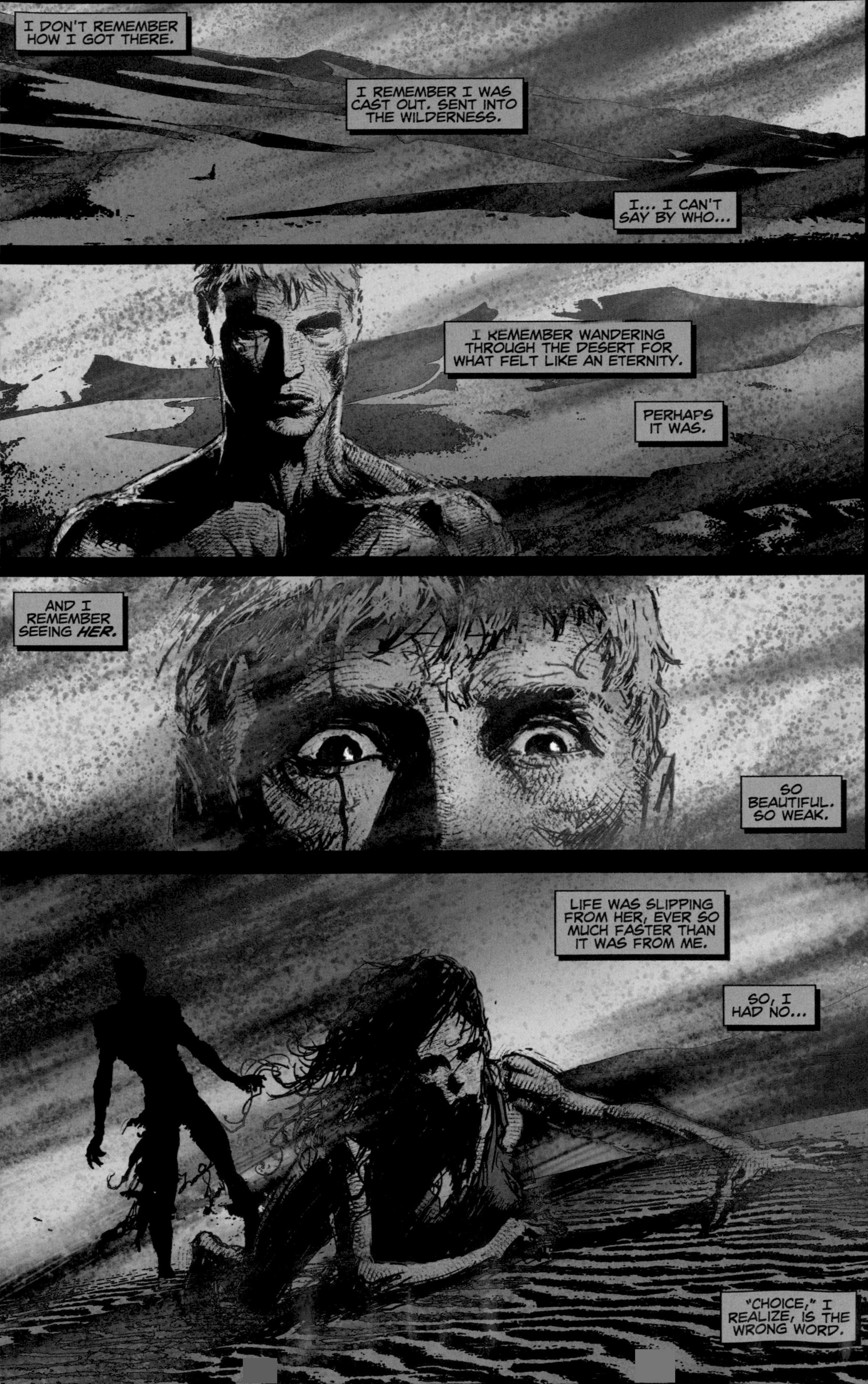
I DON'T REMEMBER HOW I GOT THERE.
I REMEMBER I WAS CAST OUT. SENT INTO THE WILDERNESS.
I... I CAN'T SAY BY WHO...
I KEMEMBER WANDERING THROUGH THE DESERT FOR WHAT FELT LIKE AN ETERNITY.
PERHAPS IT WAS.
AND I REMEMBER SEEING *HER*.
SO BEAUTIFUL. SO WEAK.
LIFE WAS SLIPPING FROM HER, EVER SO MUCH FASTER THAN IT WAS FROM ME.
SO, I HAD NO...
"CHOICE," I REALIZE, IS THE WRONG WORD.

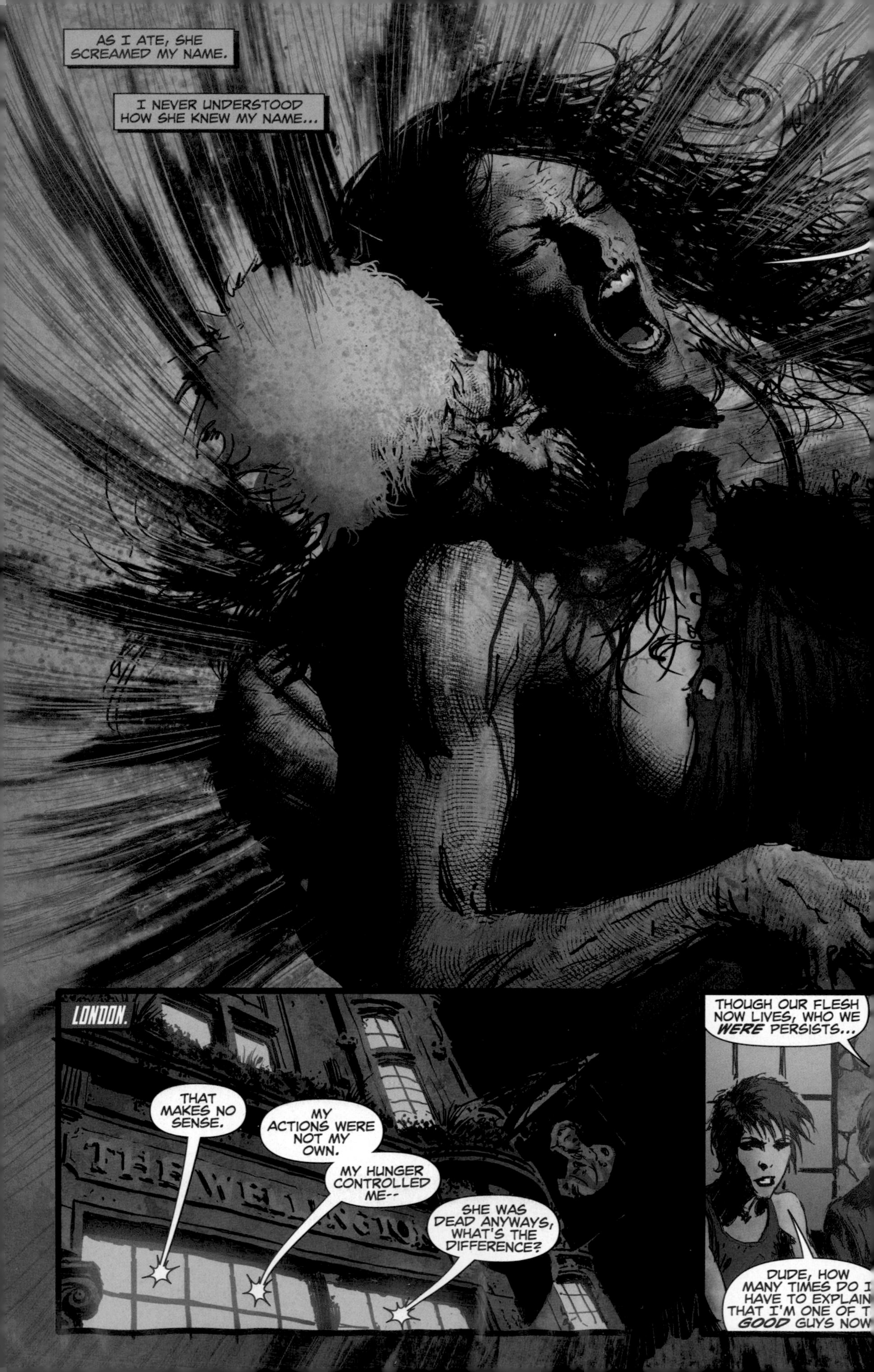
AS I ATE, SHE SCREAMED MY NAME.
I NEVER UNDERSTOOD HOW SHE KNEW MY NAME...
LONDON.
THAT MAKES NO SENSE.
MY ACTIONS WERE NOT MY OWN.
MY HUNGER CONTROLLED ME--
SHE WAS DEAD ANYWAYS, WHAT'S THE DIFFERENCE?
THOUGH OUR FLESH NOW LIVES, WHO WE WERE PERSISTS...
DUDE, HOW MANY TIMES DO I HAVE TO EXPLAIN THAT I'M ONE OF T GOOD GUYS NOW

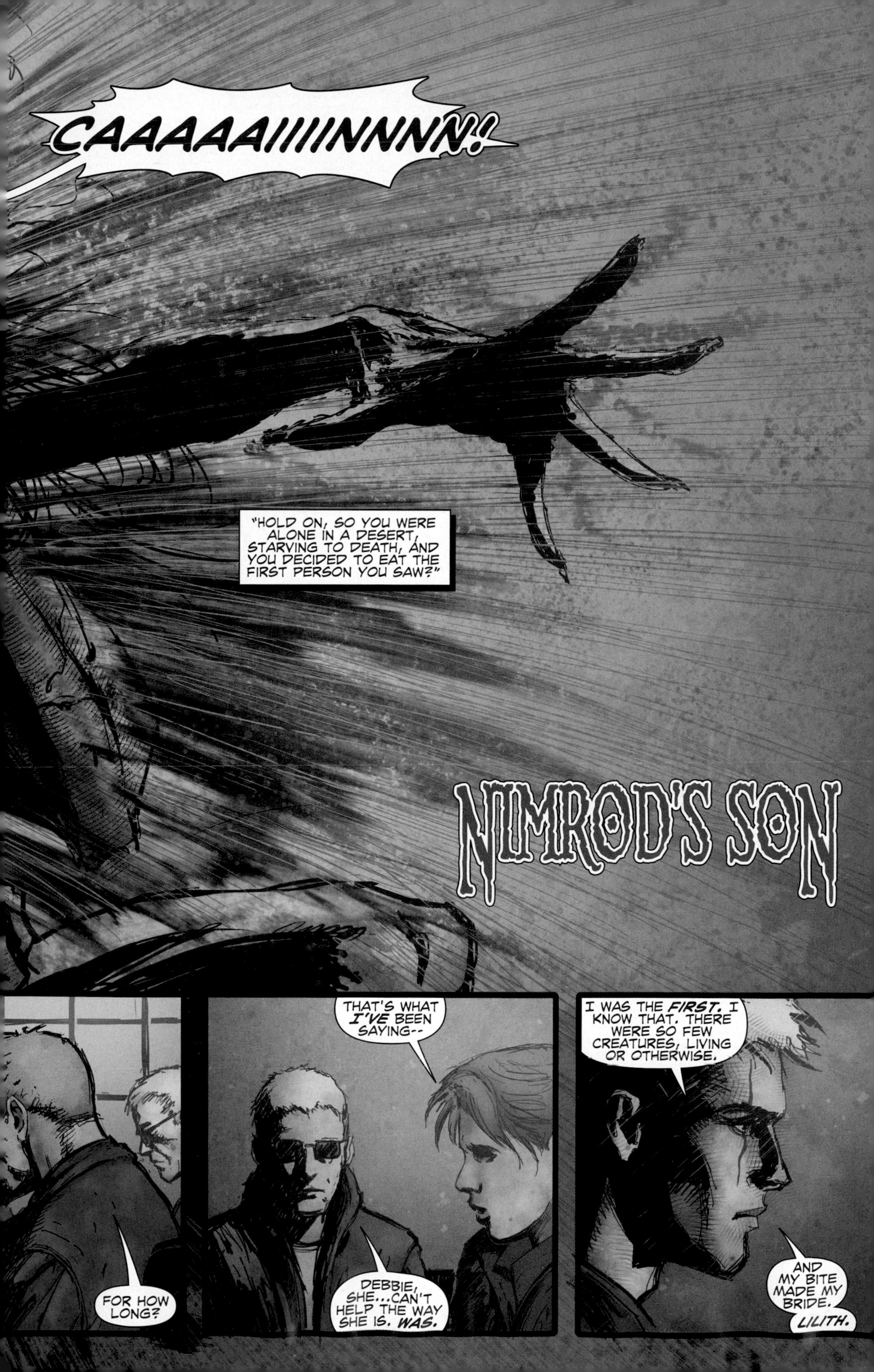
CAAAAAIIIINNNN!
"HOLD ON, SO YOU WERE ALONE IN A DESERT, STARVING TO DEATH, AND YOU DECIDED TO EAT THE FIRST PERSON YOU SAW?"
NIMROD'S SON
FOR HOW LONG?
THAT'S WHAT I'VE BEEN SAYING--
DEBBIE, SHE...CAN'T HELP THE WAY SHE IS. WAS.
I WAS THE FIRST. I KNOW THAT. THERE WERE SO FEW CREATURES, LIVING OR OTHERWISE.
AND MY BITE MADE MY BRIDE. LILITH.

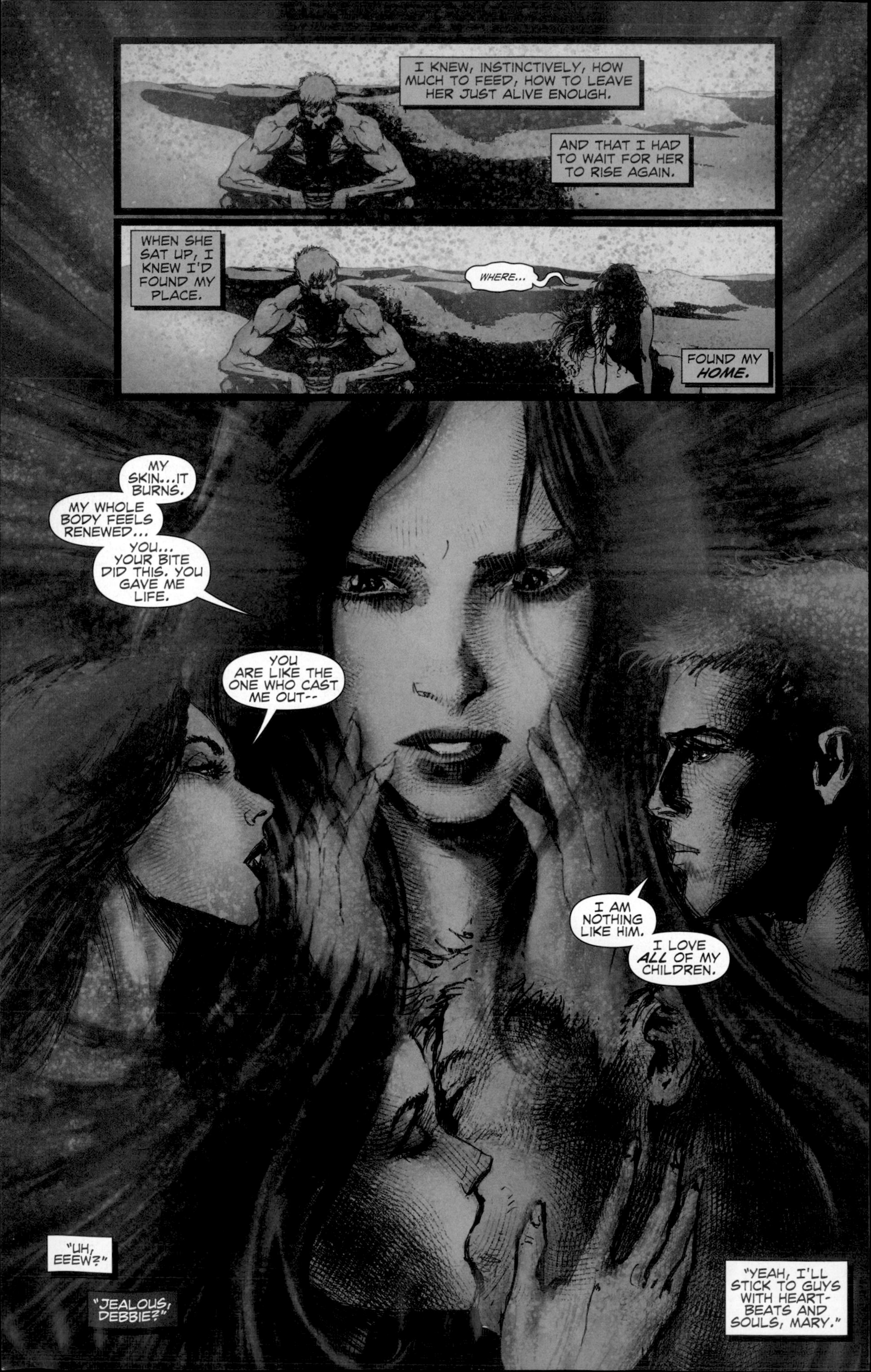
I KNEW, INSTINCTIVELY, HOW MUCH TO FEED, HOW TO LEAVE HER JUST ALIVE ENOUGH.
AND THAT I HAD TO WAIT FOR HER TO RISE AGAIN.
WHEN SHE SAT UP, I KNEW I'D FOUND MY PLACE.
WHERE...
FOUND MY *HOME.*
MY SKIN...IT BURNS.
MY WHOLE BODY FEELS RENEWED...
YOU... YOUR BITE DID THIS. YOU GAVE ME LIFE.
YOU ARE LIKE THE ONE WHO CAST ME OUT--
I AM NOTHING LIKE HIM.
I LOVE *ALL* OF MY CHILDREN.
"UH, EEEW?"
"JEALOUS, DEBBIE?"
"YEAH, I'LL STICK TO GUYS WITH HEART-BEATS AND SOULS, MARY."

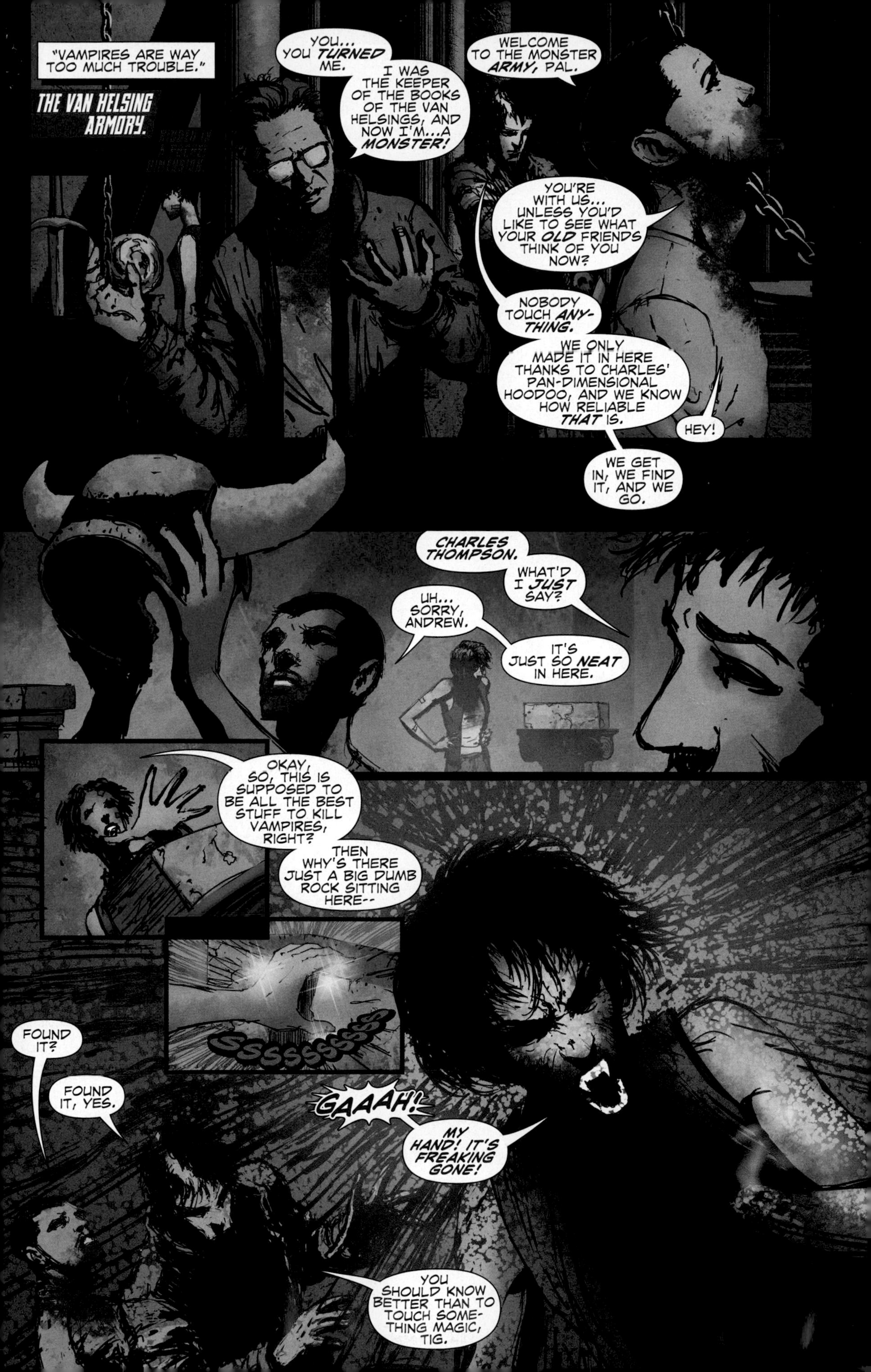
"VAMPIRES ARE WAY TOO MUCH TROUBLE."
THE VAN HELSING ARMORY.
YOU... YOU TURNED ME.
I WAS THE KEEPER OF THE BOOKS OF THE VAN HELSINGS, AND NOW I'M...A MONSTER!
WELCOME TO THE MONSTER ARMY, PAL.
YOU'RE WITH US... UNLESS YOU'D LIKE TO SEE WHAT YOUR OLD FRIENDS THINK OF YOU NOW?
NOBODY TOUCH ANY-THING.
WE ONLY MADE IT IN HERE THANKS TO CHARLES' PAN-DIMENSIONAL HOODOO, AND WE KNOW HOW RELIABLE THAT IS.
HEY!
WE GET IN, WE FIND IT, AND WE GO.
CHARLES THOMPSON.
WHAT'D I JUST SAY?
UH... SORRY, ANDREW.
IT'S JUST SO NEAT IN HERE.
OKAY, SO, THIS IS SUPPOSED TO BE ALL THE BEST STUFF TO KILL VAMPIRES, RIGHT?
THEN WHY'S THERE JUST A BIG DUMB ROCK SITTING HERE--
SSSSSSSSSS
FOUND IT?
FOUND IT, YES.
GAAAH!
MY HAND! IT'S FREAKING GONE!
YOU SHOULD KNOW BETTER THAN TO TOUCH SOME-THING MAGIC, TIG.

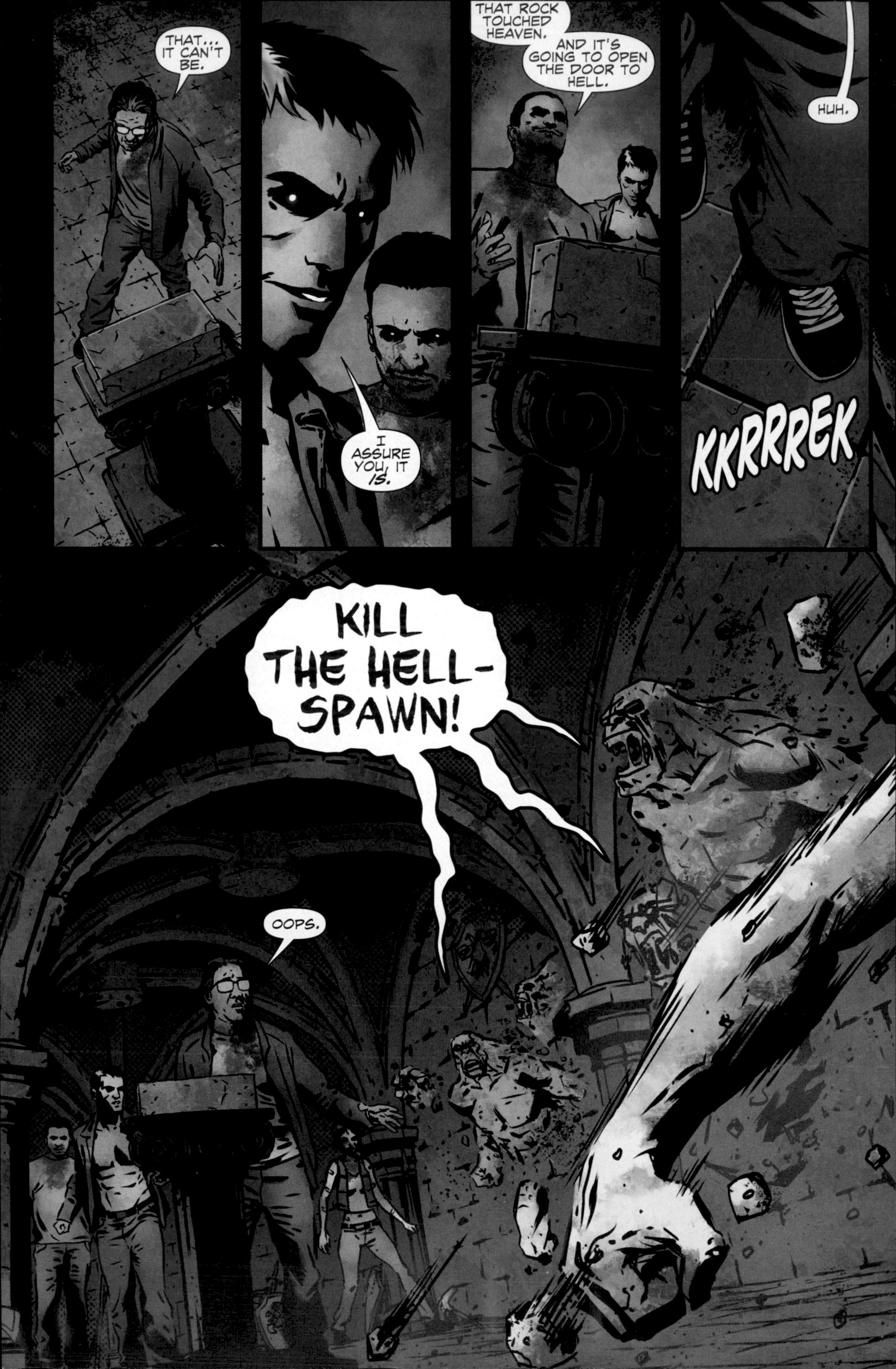
THAT... IT CAN'T BE.
I ASSURE YOU, IT IS.
THAT ROCK TOUCHED HEAVEN.
AND IT'S GOING TO OPEN THE DOOR TO HELL.
HUH.
KKRRREK
KILL THE HELL-SPAWN!
OOPS.

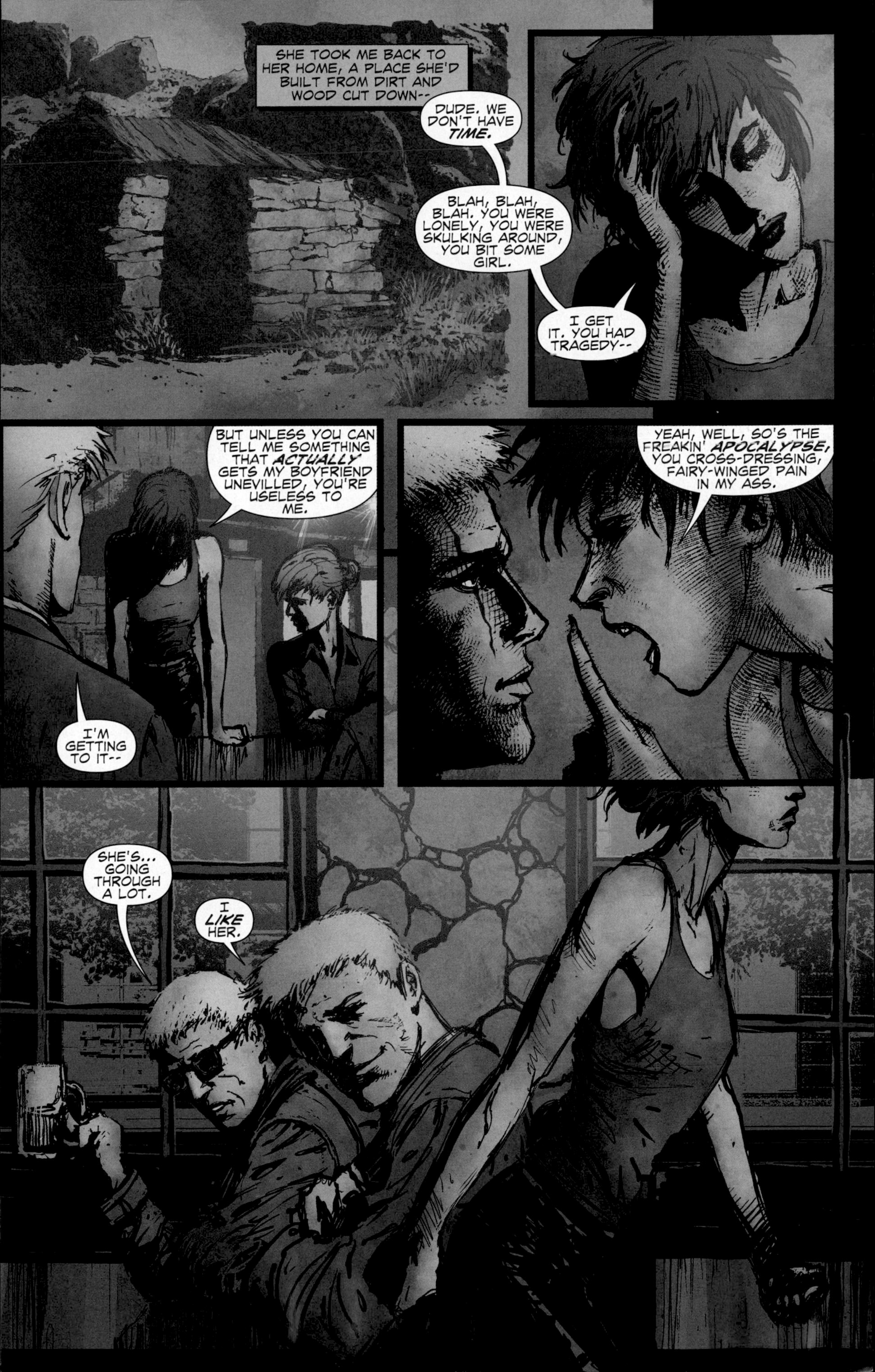
SHE TOOK ME BACK TO HER HOME, A PLACE SHE'D BUILT FROM DIRT AND WOOD CUT DOWN--
DUDE. WE DON'T HAVE TIME.
BLAH, BLAH, BLAH. YOU WERE LONELY, YOU WERE SKULKING AROUND, YOU BIT SOME GIRL.
I GET IT. YOU HAD TRAGEDY--
BUT UNLESS YOU CAN TELL ME SOMETHING THAT ACTUALLY GETS MY BOYFRIEND UNEVILLED, YOU'RE USELESS TO ME.
I'M GETTING TO IT--
YEAH, WELL, SO'S THE FREAKIN' APOCALYPSE, YOU CROSS-DRESSING, FAIRY-WINGED PAIN IN MY ASS.
SHE'S... GOING THROUGH A LOT.
I LIKE HER.

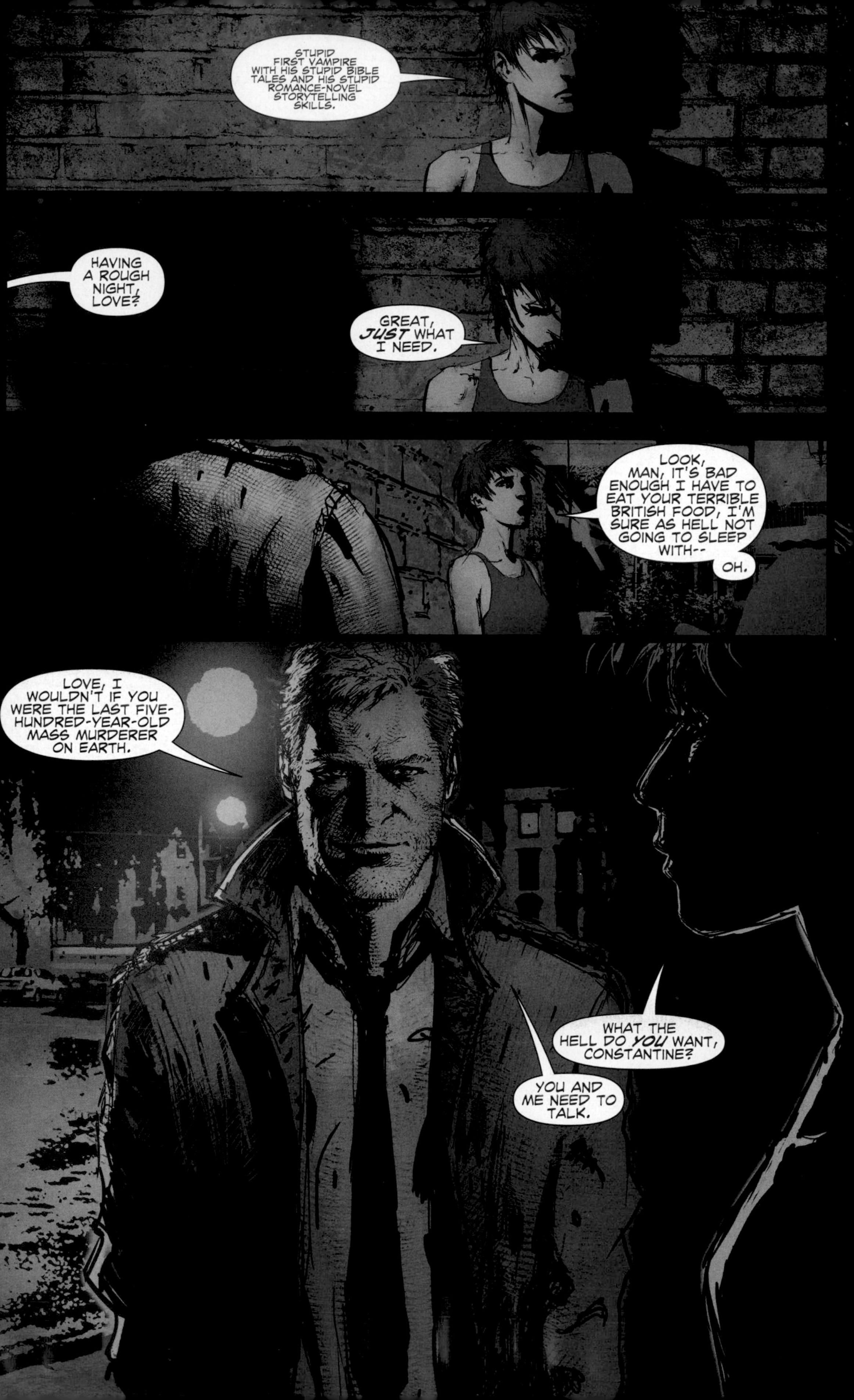
STUPID FIRST VAMPIRE WITH HIS STUPID BIBLE TALES AND HIS STUPID ROMANCE-NOVEL STORYTELLING SKILLS.
HAVING A ROUGH NIGHT, LOVE?
GREAT, JUST WHAT I NEED.
LOOK, MAN, IT'S BAD ENOUGH I HAVE TO EAT YOUR TERRIBLE BRITISH FOOD, I'M SURE AS HELL NOT GOING TO SLEEP WITH--
OH.
LOVE, I WOULDN'T IF YOU WERE THE LAST FIVE-HUNDRED-YEAR-OLD MASS MURDERER ON EARTH.
WHAT THE HELL DO YOU WANT, CONSTANTINE?
YOU AND ME NEED TO TALK.

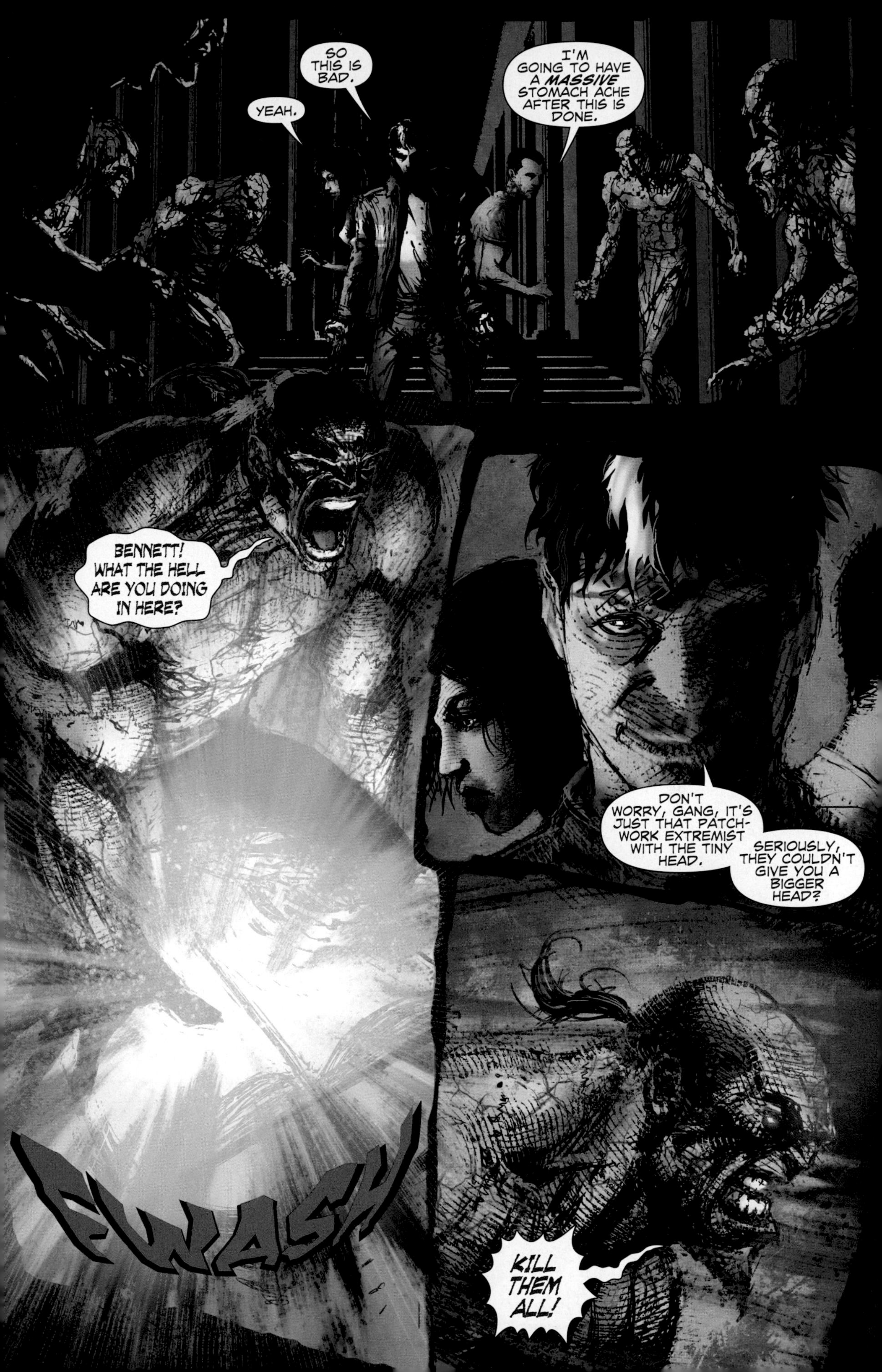
SO THIS IS BAD.
YEAH.
I'M GOING TO HAVE A *MASSIVE* STOMACH ACHE AFTER THIS IS DONE.
BENNETT! WHAT THE HELL ARE YOU DOING IN HERE?
DON'T WORRY, GANG, IT'S JUST THAT PATCH-WORK EXTREMIST WITH THE TINY HEAD.
SERIOUSLY, THEY COULDN'T GIVE YOU A BIGGER HEAD?
FWASH
KILL THEM ALL!

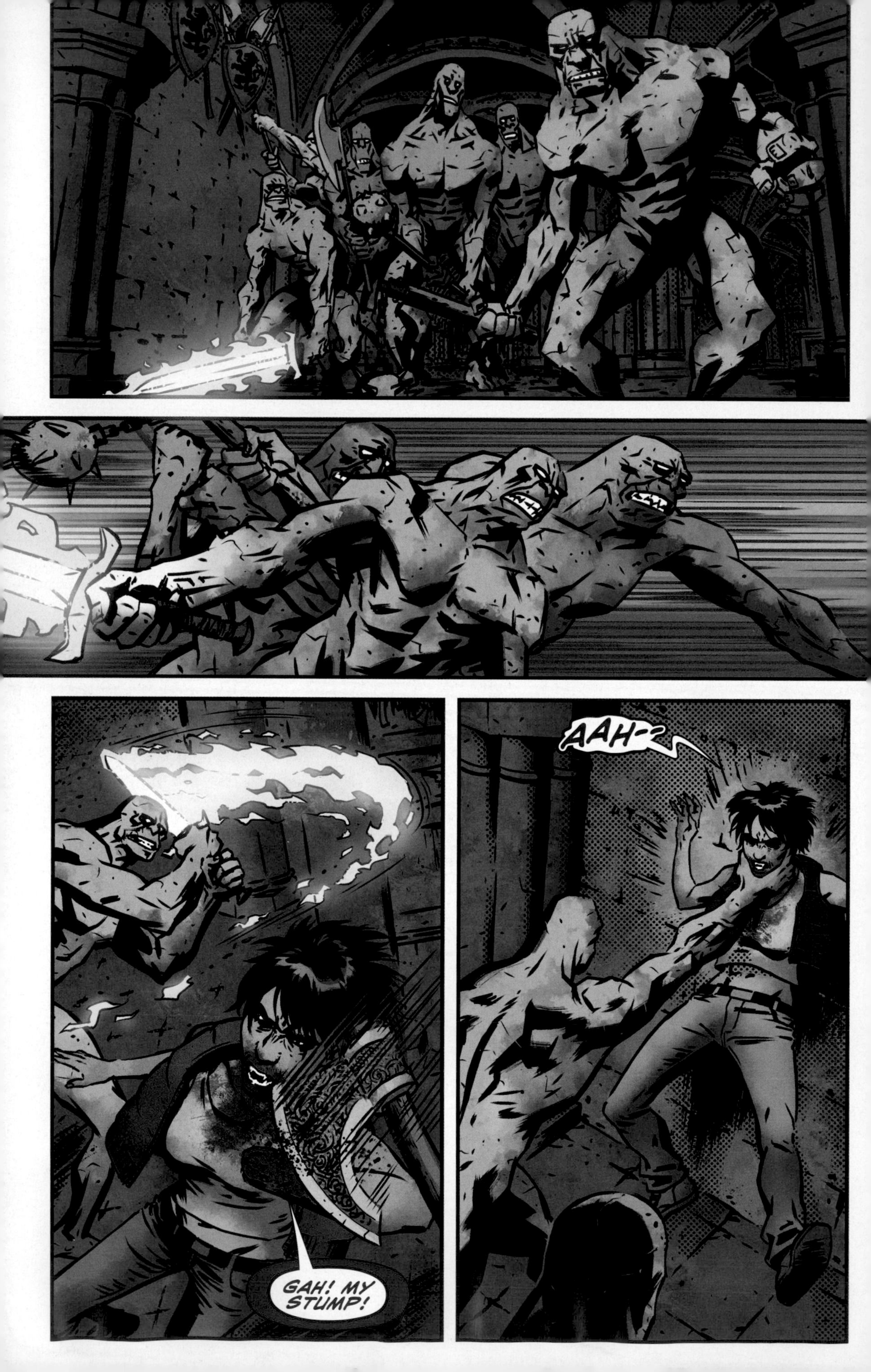
GAH! MY STUMP!
AAH--

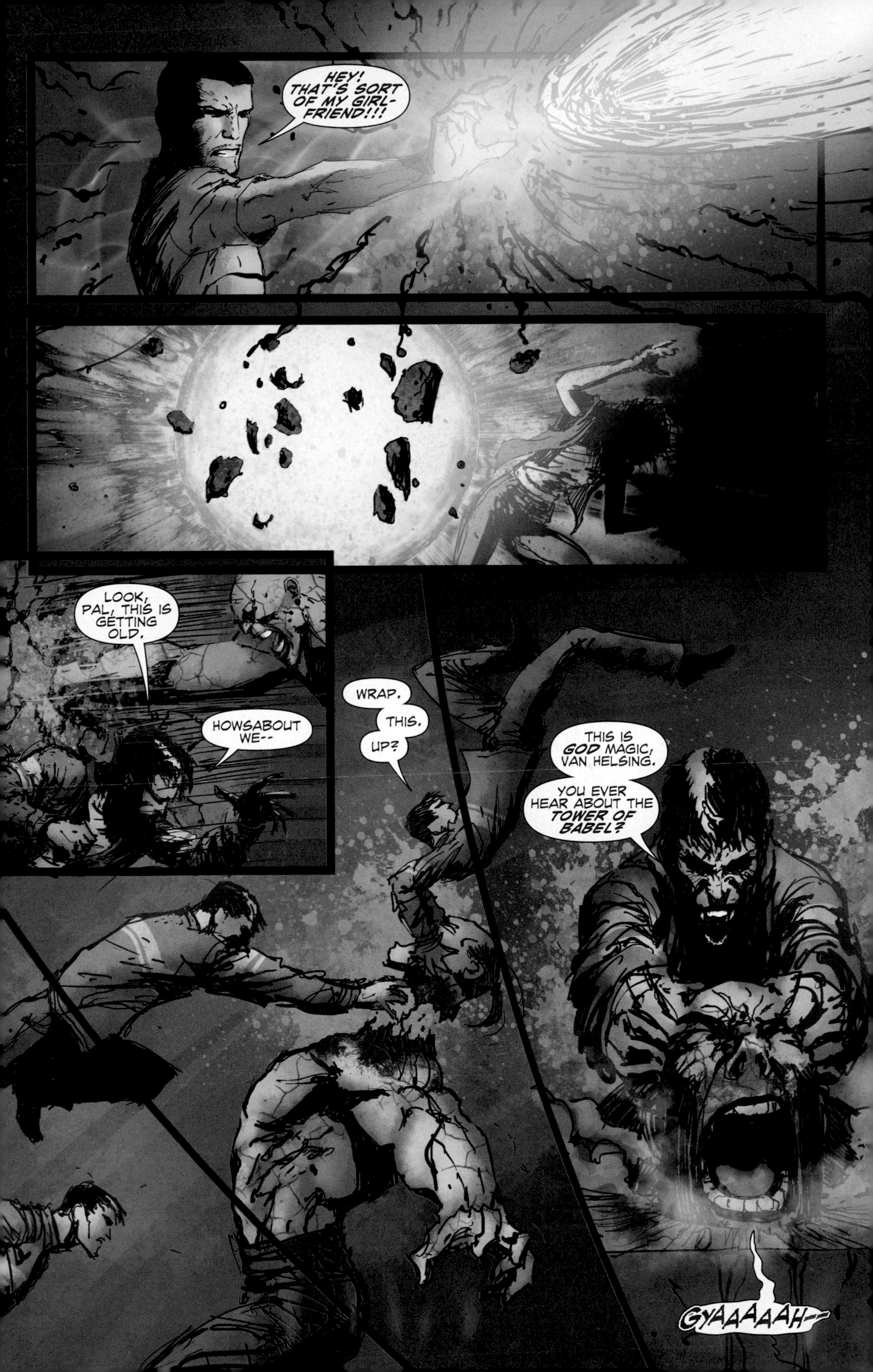
HEY! THAT'S SORT OF MY GIRL-FRIEND!!!
LOOK, PAL, THIS IS GETTING OLD.
HOWSABOUT WE--
WRAP.
THIS.
UP?
THIS IS GOD MAGIC, VAN HELSING.
YOU EVER HEAR ABOUT THE TOWER OF BABEL?
GYAAAAAH--

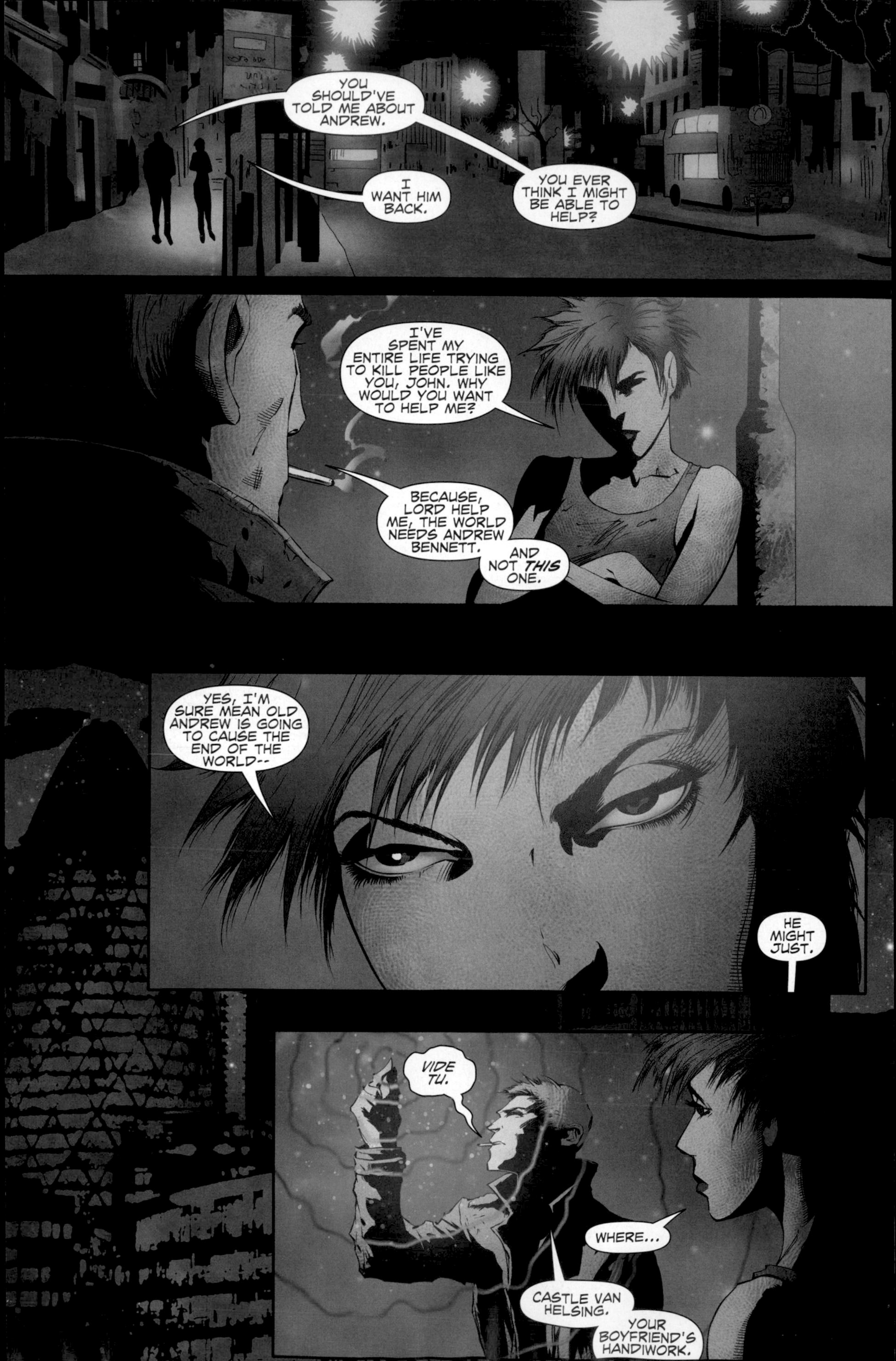
YOU SHOULD'VE TOLD ME ABOUT ANDREW.
I WANT HIM BACK.
YOU EVER THINK I MIGHT BE ABLE TO HELP?
I'VE SPENT MY ENTIRE LIFE TRYING TO KILL PEOPLE LIKE YOU, JOHN. WHY WOULD YOU WANT TO HELP ME?
BECAUSE, LORD HELP ME, THE WORLD NEEDS ANDREW BENNETT.
AND NOT *THIS* ONE.
YES, I'M SURE MEAN OLD ANDREW IS GOING TO CAUSE THE END OF THE WORLD--
HE MIGHT JUST.
VIDE TU.
WHERE...
CASTLE VAN HELSING.
YOUR BOYFRIEND'S HANDIWORK.

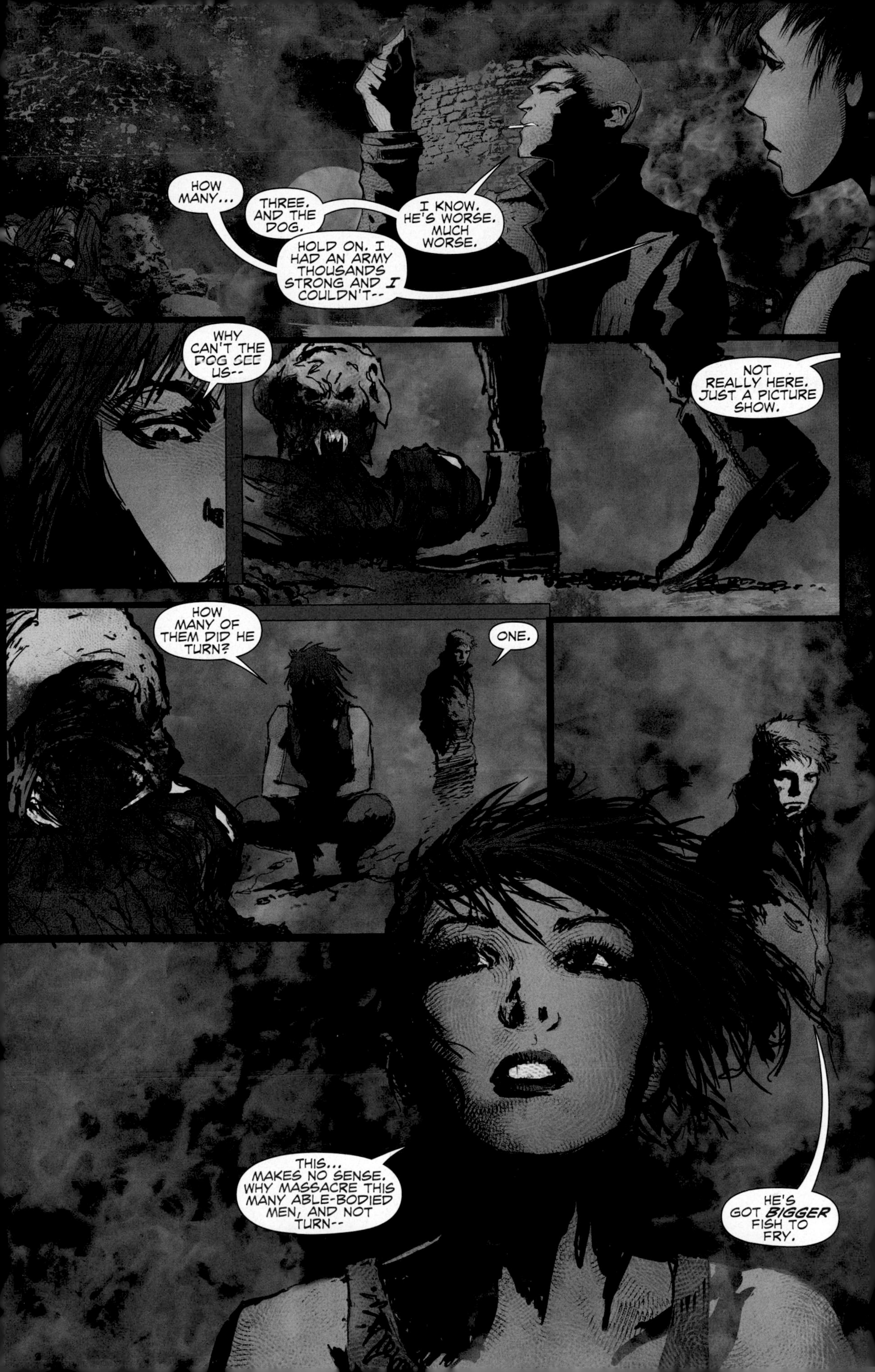
HOW MANY...
THREE. AND THE DOG.
I KNOW. HE'S WORSE. MUCH WORSE.
HOLD ON. I HAD AN ARMY THOUSANDS STRONG AND I COULDN'T--
WHY CAN'T THE DOG SEE US--
NOT REALLY HERE. JUST A PICTURE SHOW.
HOW MANY OF THEM DID HE TURN?
ONE.
THIS... MAKES NO SENSE. WHY MASSACRE THIS MANY ABLE-BODIED MEN, AND NOT TURN--
HE'S GOT BIGGER FISH TO FRY.

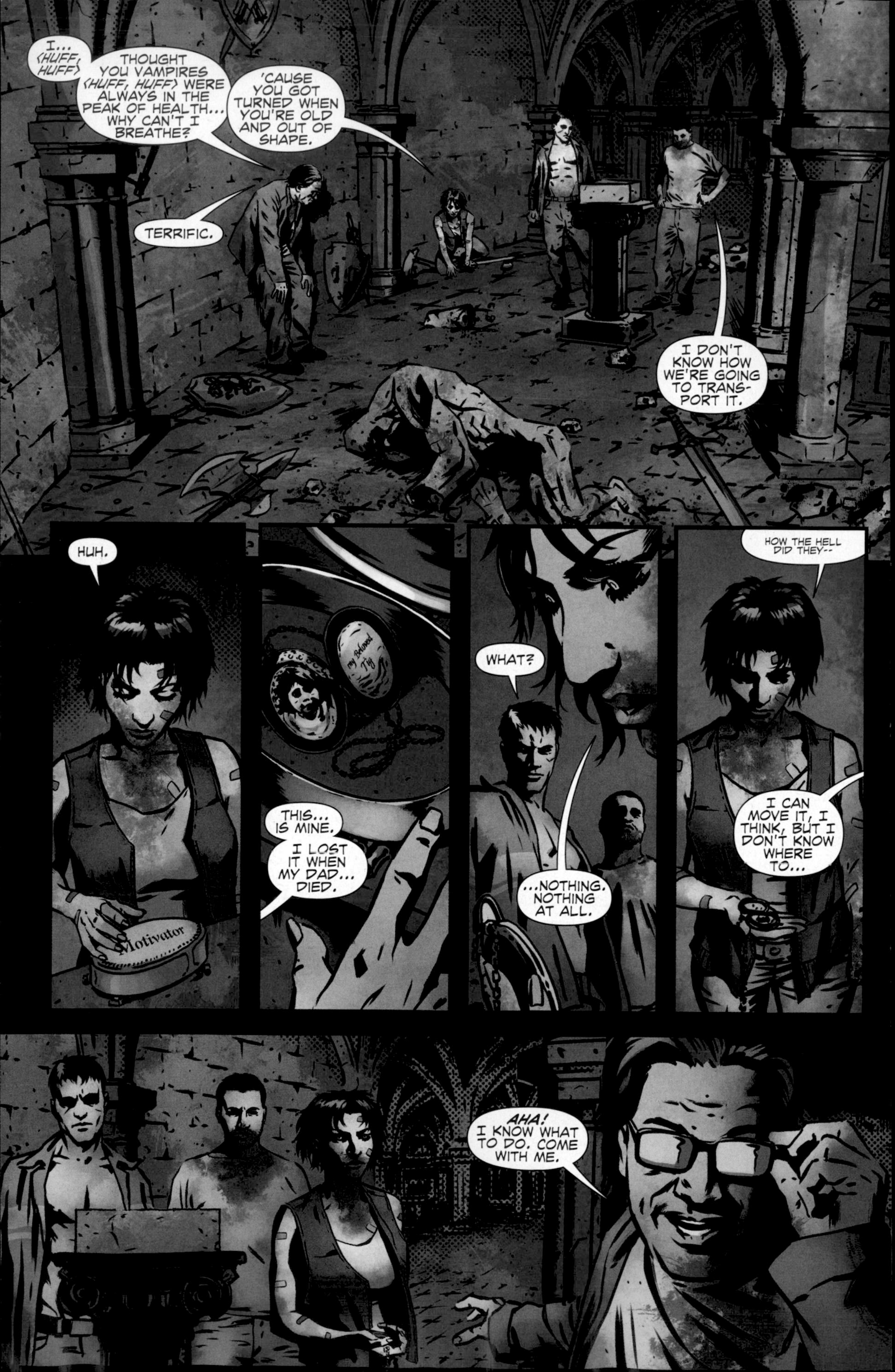
I... ‹HUFF, HUFF› THOUGHT YOU VAMPIRES ‹HUFF, HUFF› WERE ALWAYS IN THE PEAK OF HEALTH... WHY CAN'T I BREATHE?
'CAUSE YOU GOT TURNED WHEN YOU'RE OLD AND OUT OF SHAPE.
TERRIFIC.
I DON'T KNOW HOW WE'RE GOING TO TRANS-PORT IT.
HUH.
Motivator
my Beloved Tig
THIS... IS MINE.
I LOST IT WHEN MY DAD... DIED.
WHAT?
...NOTHING. NOTHING AT ALL.
HOW THE HELL DID THEY--
I CAN MOVE IT, I THINK, BUT I DON'T KNOW WHERE TO...
AHA! I KNOW WHAT TO DO. COME WITH ME.

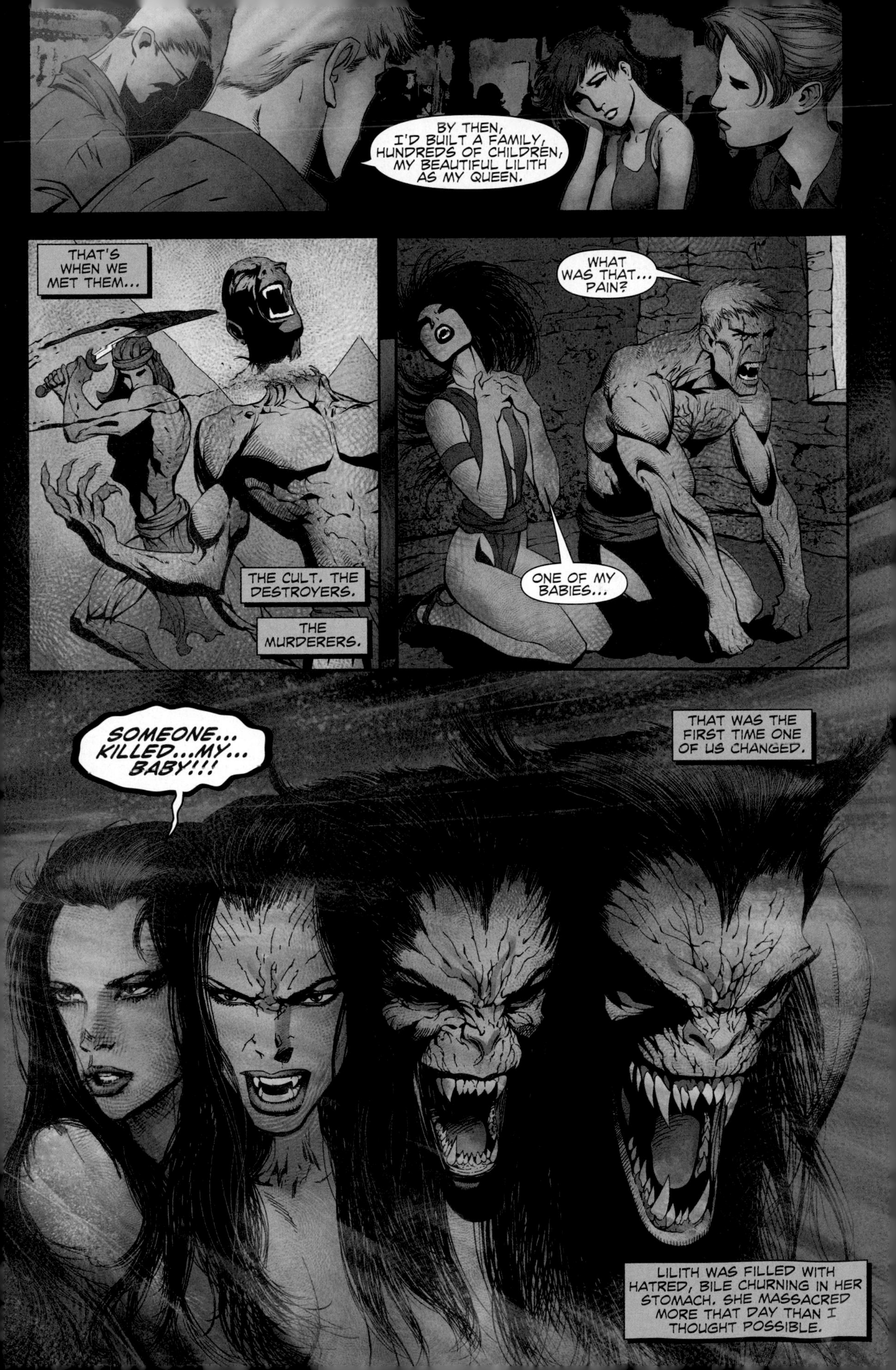
BY THEN, I'D BUILT A FAMILY, HUNDREDS OF CHILDREN, MY BEAUTIFUL LILITH AS MY QUEEN.
THAT'S WHEN WE MET THEM...
THE CULT. THE DESTROYERS.
THE MURDERERS.
WHAT WAS THAT... PAIN?
ONE OF MY BABIES...
SOMEONE... KILLED...MY... BABY!!!
THAT WAS THE FIRST TIME ONE OF US CHANGED.
LILITH WAS FILLED WITH HATRED, BILE CHURNING IN HER STOMACH. SHE MASSACRED MORE THAT DAY THAN I THOUGHT POSSIBLE.

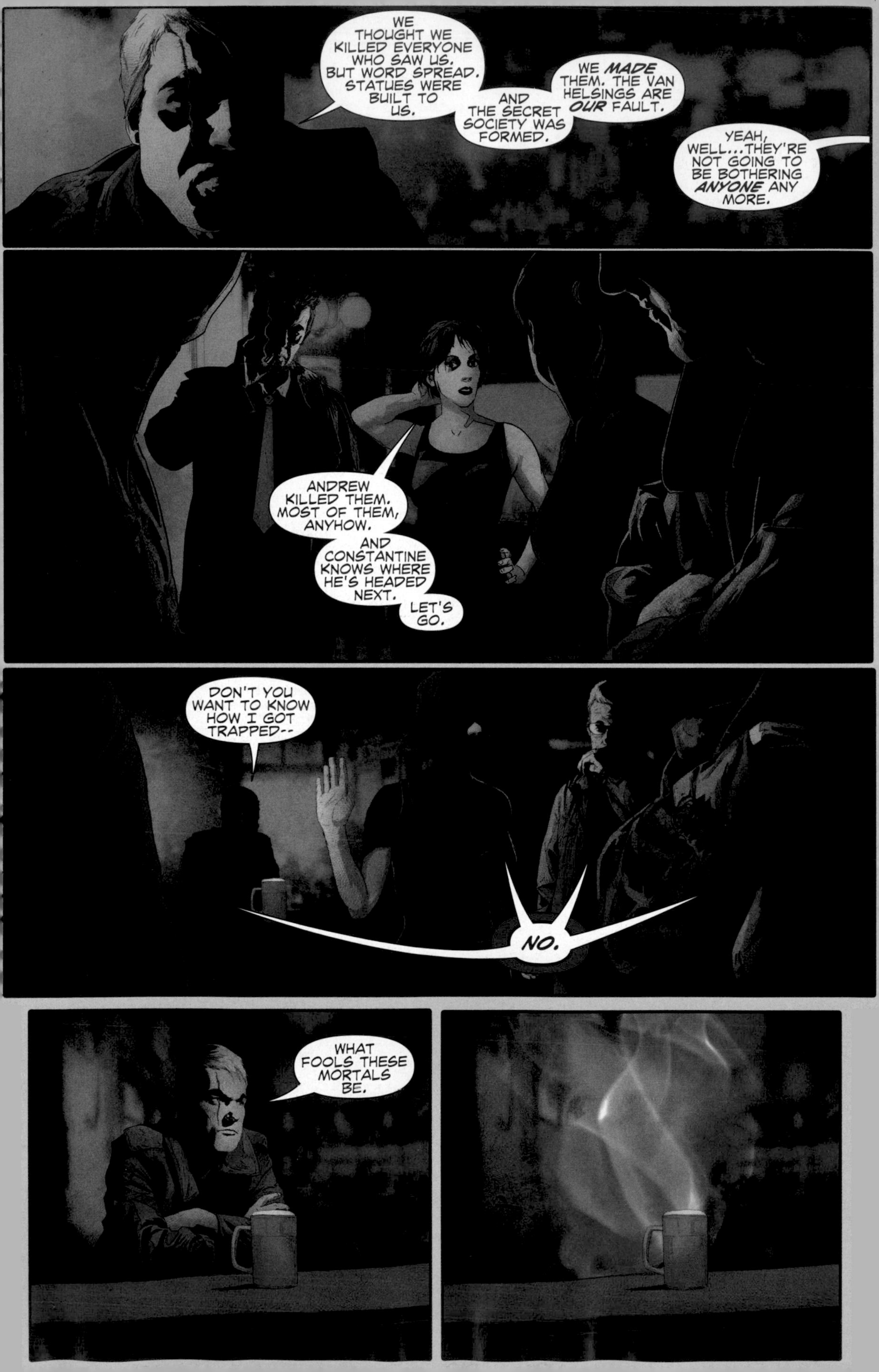
WE THOUGHT WE KILLED EVERYONE WHO SAW US. BUT WORD SPREAD. STATUES WERE BUILT TO US.
AND THE SECRET SOCIETY WAS FORMED.
WE MADE THEM. THE VAN HELSINGS ARE OUR FAULT.
YEAH, WELL...THEY'RE NOT GOING TO BE BOTHERING ANYONE ANY MORE.
ANDREW KILLED THEM. MOST OF THEM, ANYHOW.
AND CONSTANTINE KNOWS WHERE HE'S HEADED NEXT.
LET'S GO.
DON'T YOU WANT TO KNOW HOW I GOT TRAPPED--
NO.
WHAT FOOLS THESE MORTALS BE.

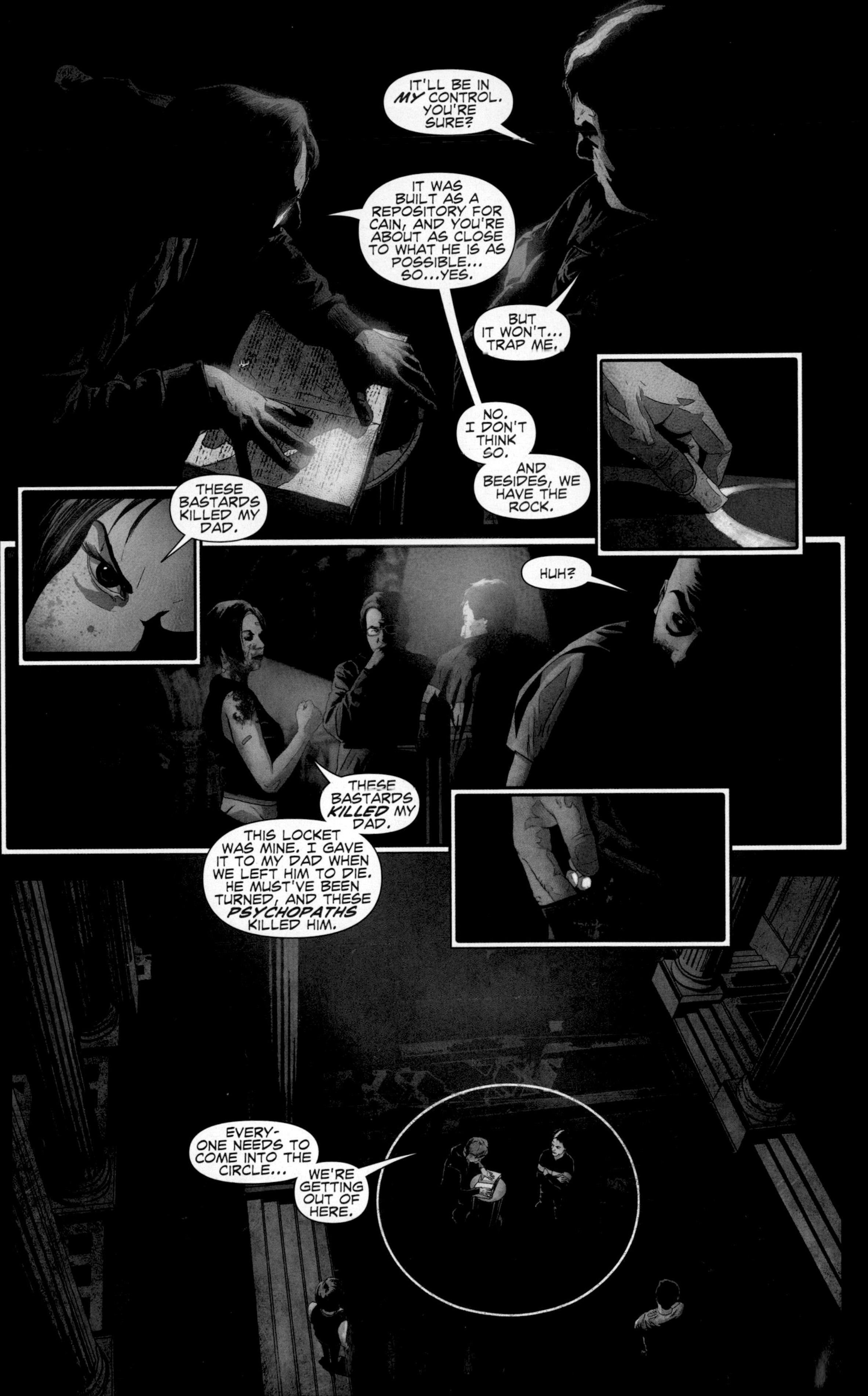
IT'LL BE IN MY CONTROL. YOU'RE SURE?
IT WAS BUILT AS A REPOSITORY FOR CAIN, AND YOU'RE ABOUT AS CLOSE TO WHAT HE IS AS POSSIBLE... SO...YES.
BUT IT WON'T... TRAP ME.
NO. I DON'T THINK SO.
AND BESIDES, WE HAVE THE ROCK.
THESE BASTARDS KILLED MY DAD.
HUH?
THESE BASTARDS KILLED MY DAD.
THIS LOCKET WAS MINE. I GAVE IT TO MY DAD WHEN WE LEFT HIM TO DIE. HE MUST'VE BEEN TURNED, AND THESE PSYCHOPATHS KILLED HIM.
EVERY-ONE NEEDS TO COME INTO THE CIRCLE...
WE'RE GETTING OUT OF HERE.

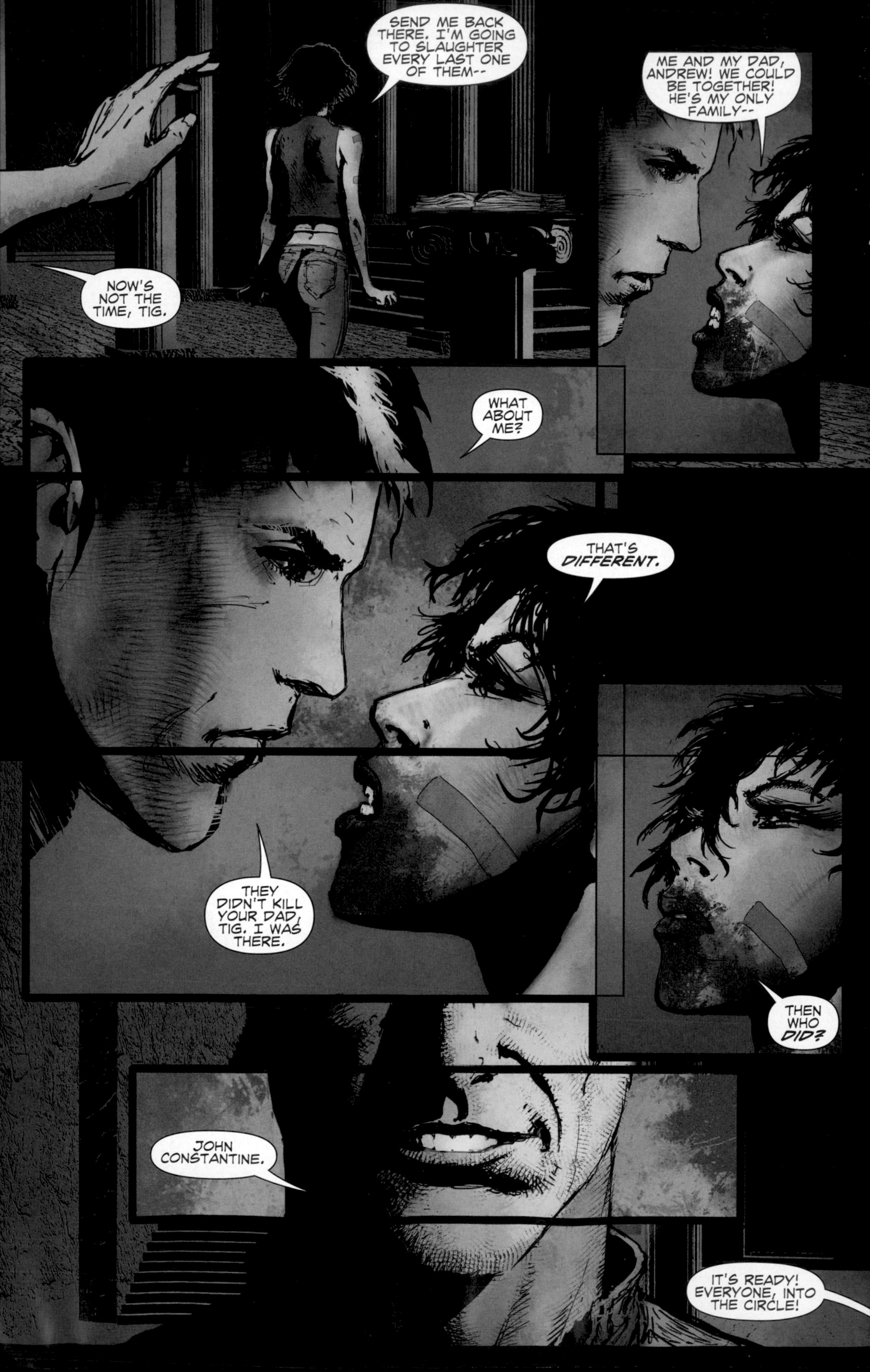
SEND ME BACK THERE. I'M GOING TO SLAUGHTER EVERY LAST ONE OF THEM--
NOW'S NOT THE TIME, TIG.
ME AND MY DAD, ANDREW! WE COULD BE TOGETHER! HE'S MY ONLY FAMILY--
WHAT ABOUT ME?
THAT'S DIFFERENT.
THEY DIDN'T KILL YOUR DAD, TIG. I WAS THERE.
THEN WHO DID?
JOHN CONSTANTINE.
IT'S READY! EVERYONE, INTO THE CIRCLE!

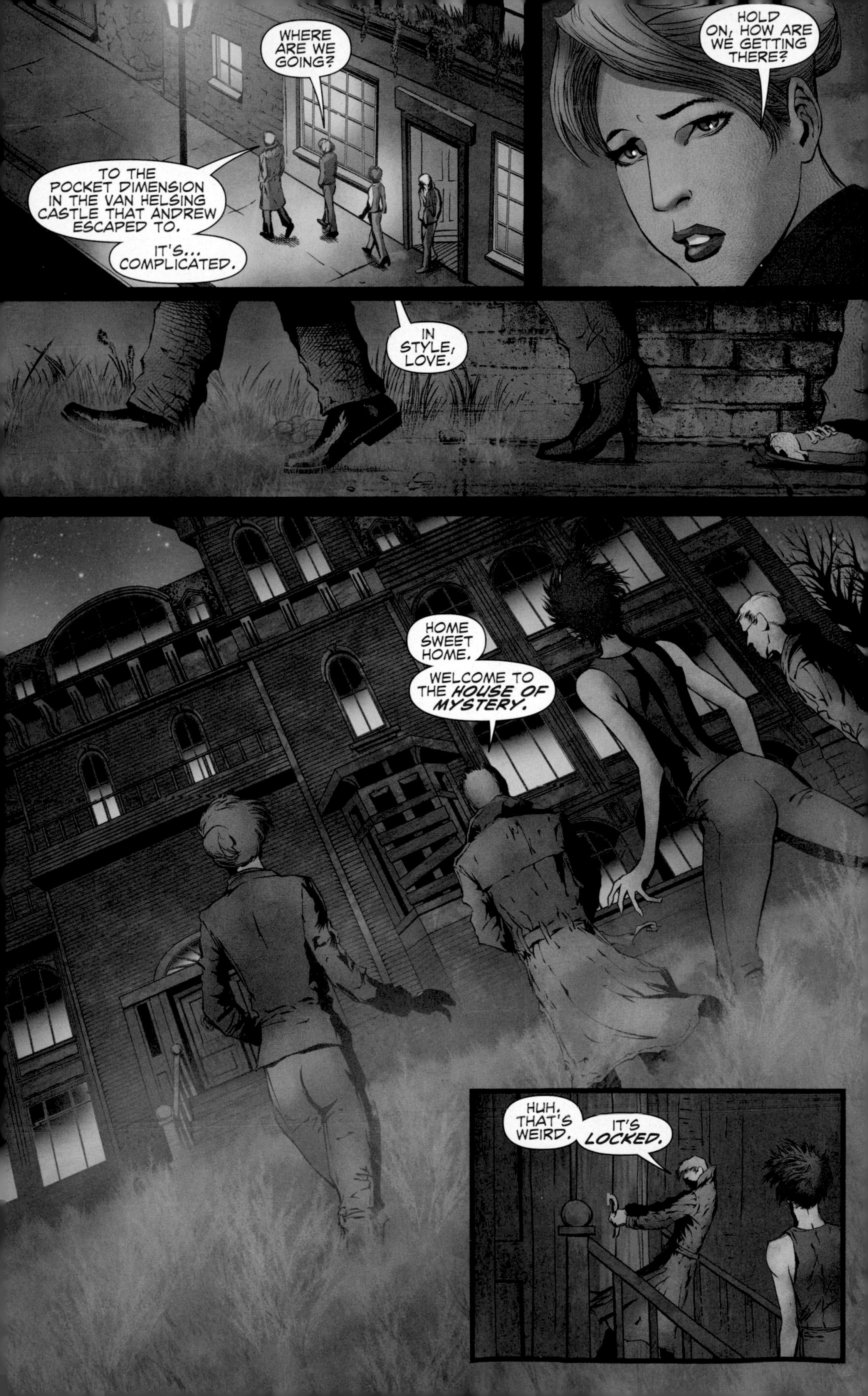
WHERE ARE WE GOING?
TO THE POCKET DIMENSION IN THE VAN HELSING CASTLE THAT ANDREW ESCAPED TO.
IT'S... COMPLICATED.
HOLD ON, HOW ARE WE GETTING THERE?
IN STYLE, LOVE.
HOME SWEET HOME.
WELCOME TO THE *HOUSE OF MYSTERY*.
HUH, THAT'S WEIRD.
IT'S *LOCKED*.

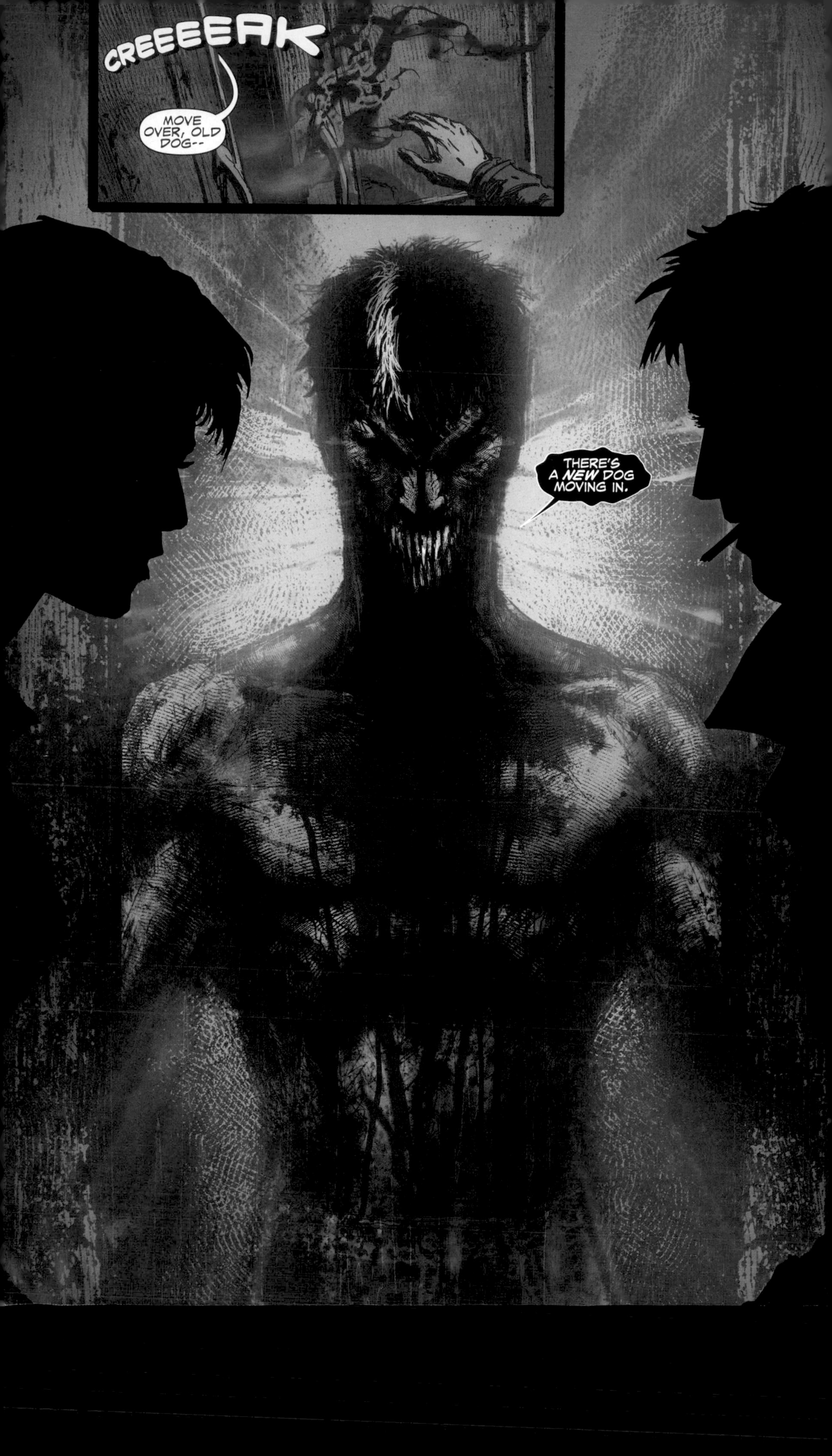
CREEEEAK
MOVE OVER, OLD DOG--
THERE'S A NEW DOG MOVING IN.

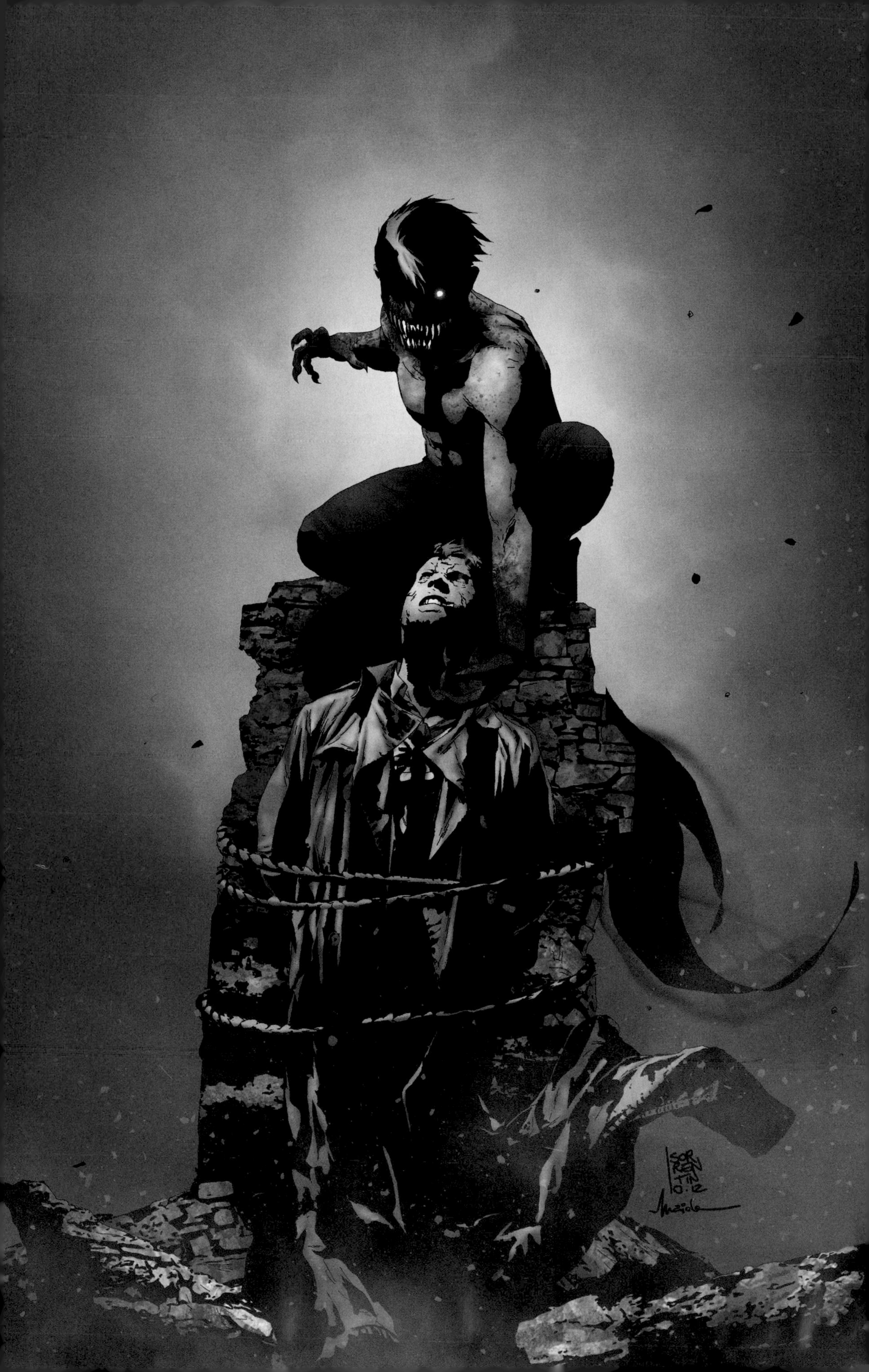

WAVE OF MUTILATION

JOSHUA HALE FIALKOV writer FERNANDO BLANCO artist cover art by ANDREA SORRENTINO & MARCELO MAIOLO

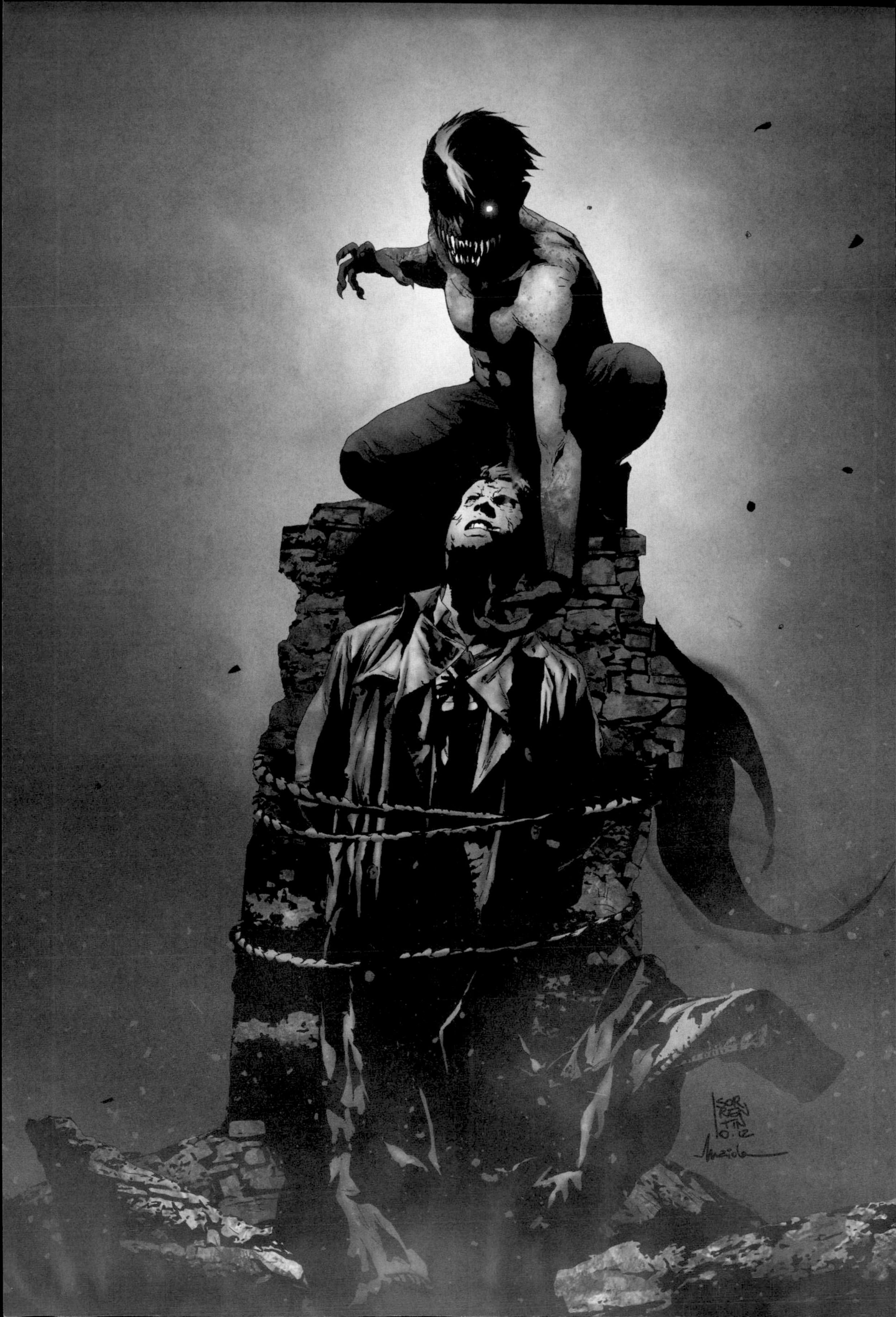
SOR
REN
TIN
10.12

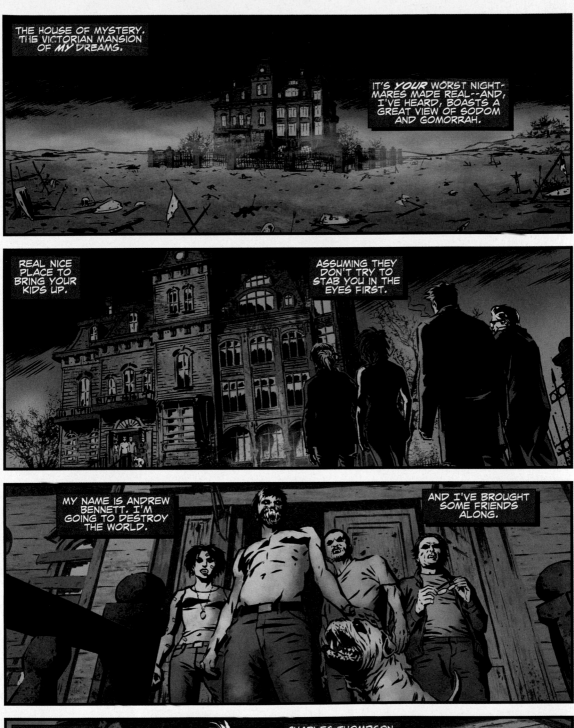

THE HOUSE OF MYSTERY. THE VICTORIAN MANSION OF *MY* DREAMS.

IT'S *YOUR* WORST NIGHTMARES MADE REAL--AND, I'VE HEARD, BOASTS A GREAT VIEW OF SODOM AND GOMORRAH.

REAL NICE PLACE TO BRING YOUR KIDS UP.

ASSUMING THEY DON'T TRY TO STAB YOU IN THE EYES FIRST.

MY NAME IS ANDREW BENNETT. I'M GOING TO DESTROY THE WORLD.

AND I'VE BROUGHT SOME FRIENDS ALONG.

TIG RAFELSON, TEEN VAMPIRE GIRL.

CHARLES THOMPSON, MAGICAL VAMPIRE BOY.

THE KEEPER, ARCHIVIST OF THE ARCANE.

AND MY FAITHFUL DOG, MISHKIN.

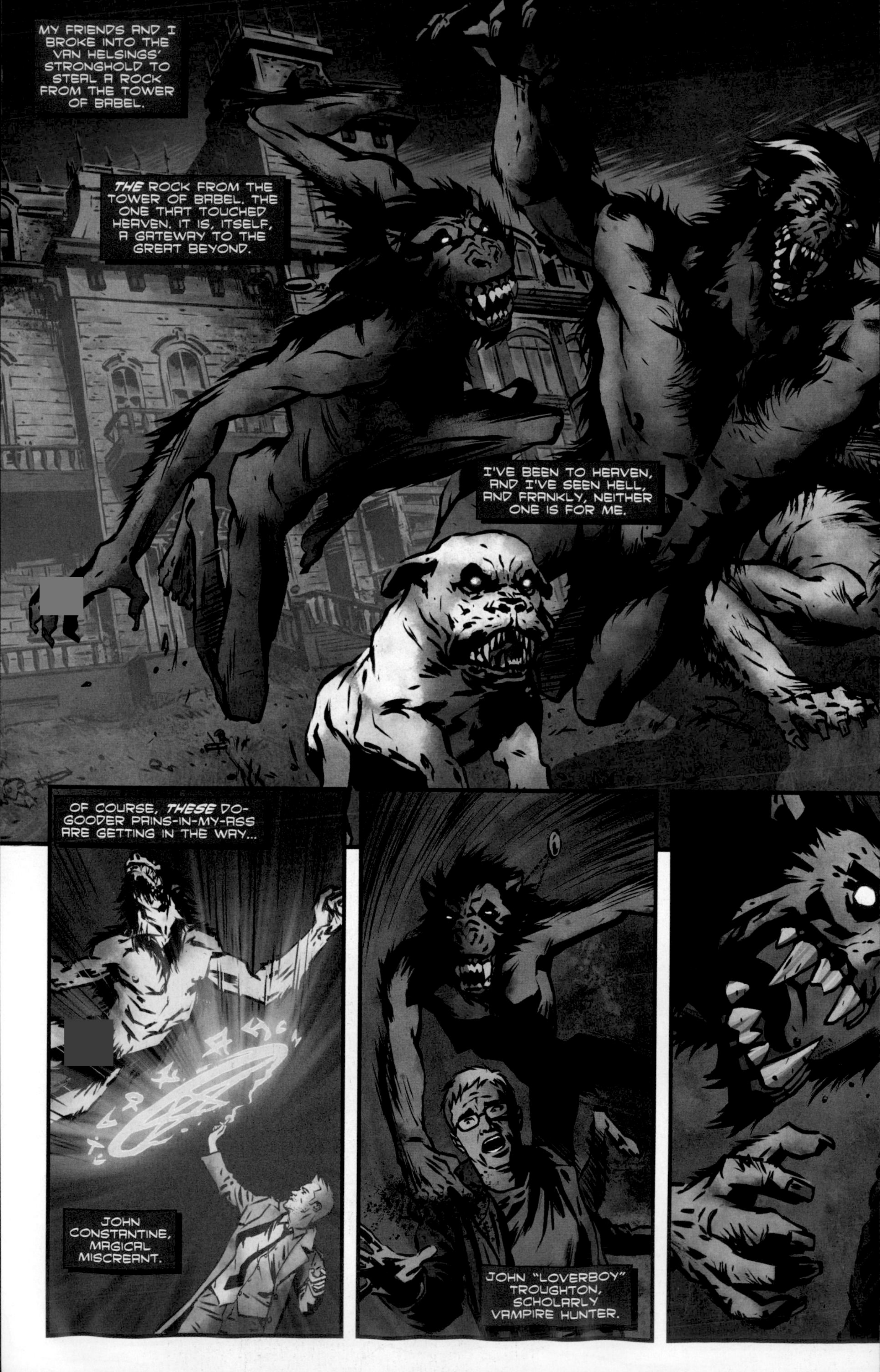
MY FRIENDS AND I BROKE INTO THE VAN HELSINGS' STRONGHOLD TO STEAL A ROCK FROM THE TOWER OF BABEL.
THE ROCK FROM THE TOWER OF BABEL. THE ONE THAT TOUCHED HEAVEN. IT IS, ITSELF, A GATEWAY TO THE GREAT BEYOND.
I'VE BEEN TO HEAVEN, AND I'VE SEEN HELL, AND FRANKLY, NEITHER ONE IS FOR ME.
OF COURSE, *THESE* DO-GOODER PAINS-IN-MY-ASS ARE GETTING IN THE WAY...
JOHN CONSTANTINE, MAGICAL MISCREANT.
JOHN "LOVERBOY" TROUGHTON, SCHOLARLY VAMPIRE HUNTER.

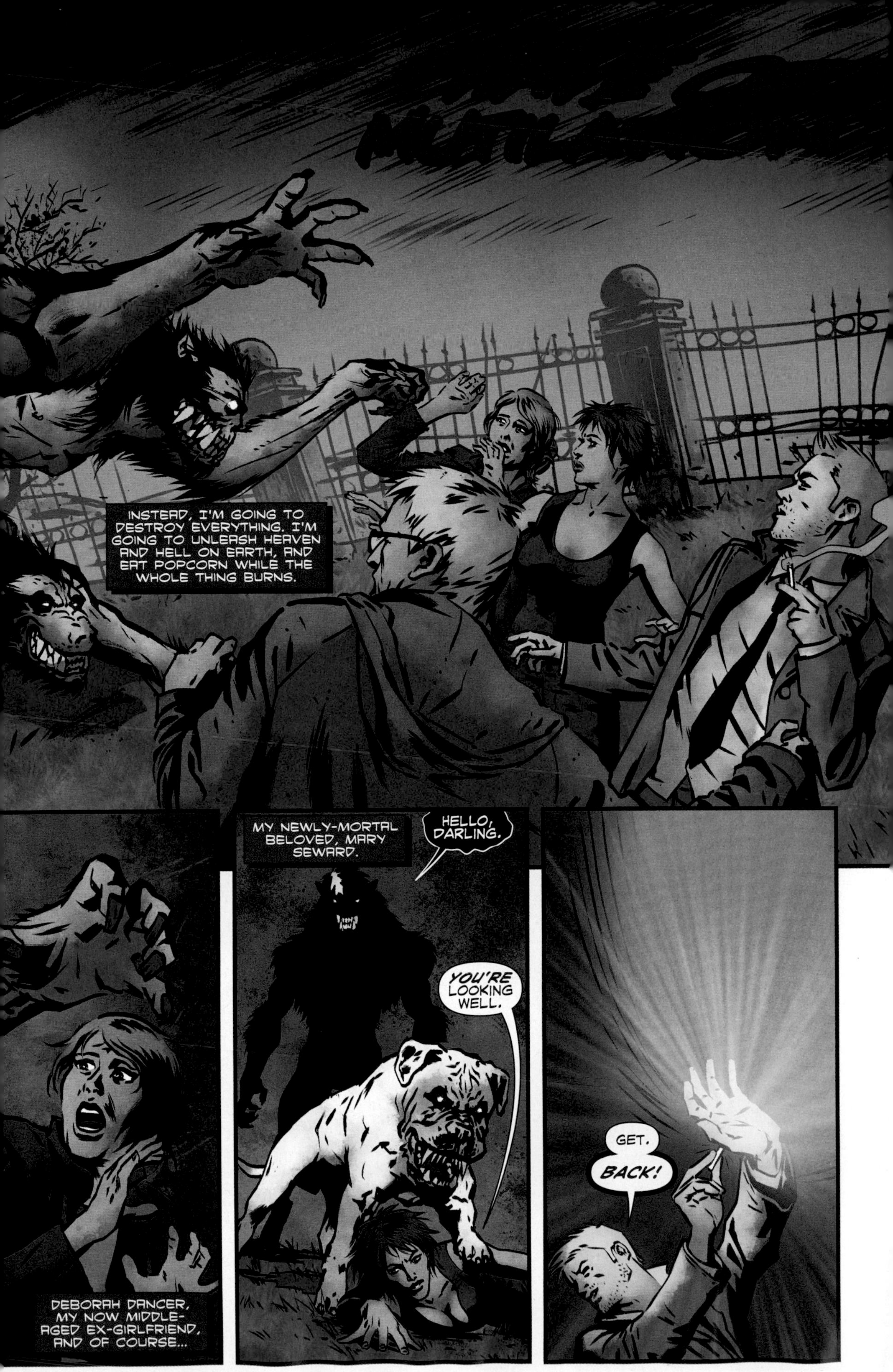
INSTEAD, I'M GOING TO DESTROY EVERYTHING. I'M GOING TO UNLEASH HEAVEN AND HELL ON EARTH, AND EAT POPCORN WHILE THE WHOLE THING BURNS.
DEBORAH DANCER, MY NOW MIDDLE-AGED EX-GIRLFRIEND, AND OF COURSE...
MY NEWLY-MORTAL BELOVED, MARY SEWARD.
HELLO, DARLING.
YOU'RE LOOKING WELL.
GET.
BACK!

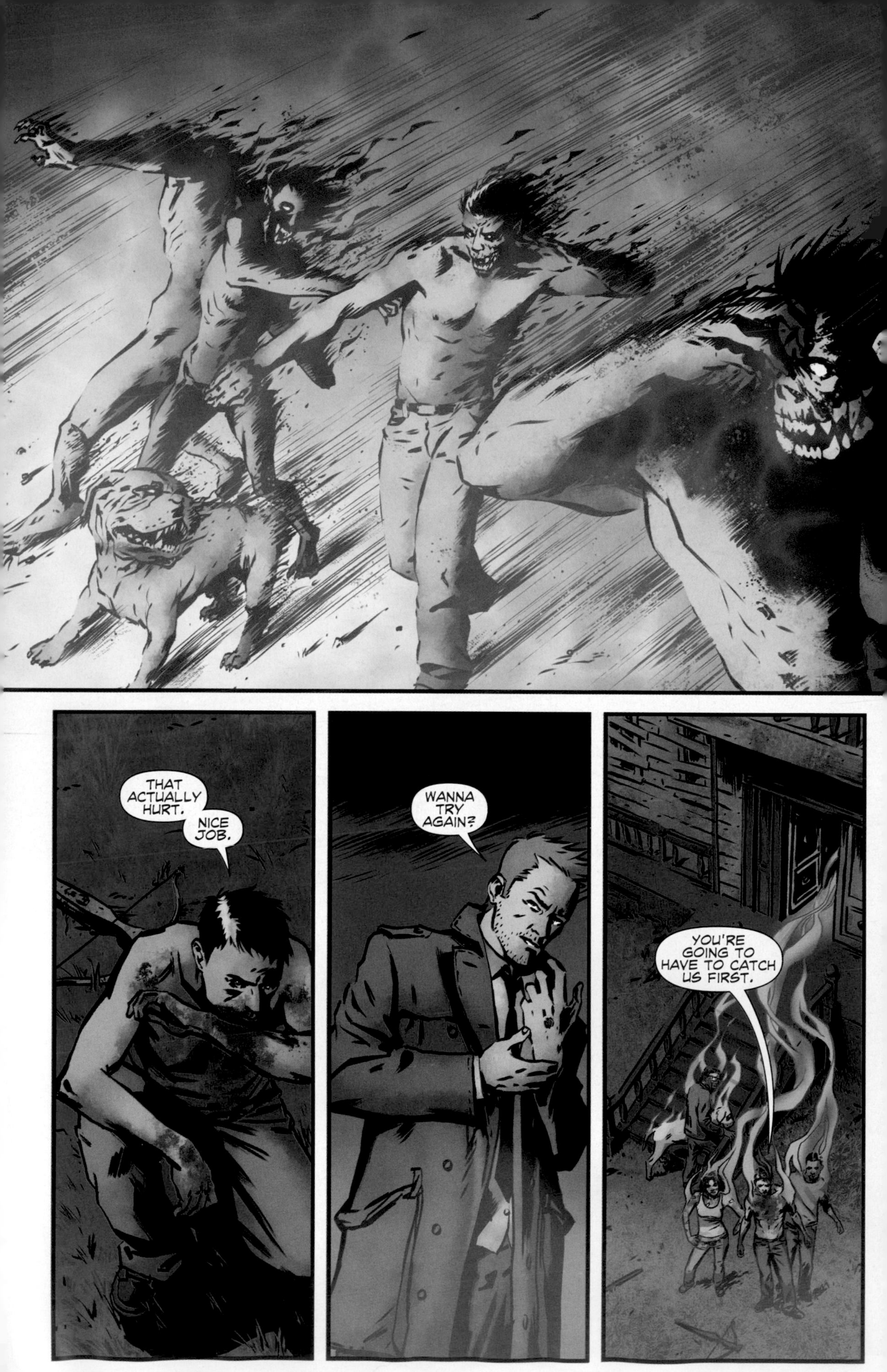
THAT ACTUALLY HURT.
NICE JOB.
WANNA TRY AGAIN?
YOU'RE GOING TO HAVE TO CATCH US FIRST.

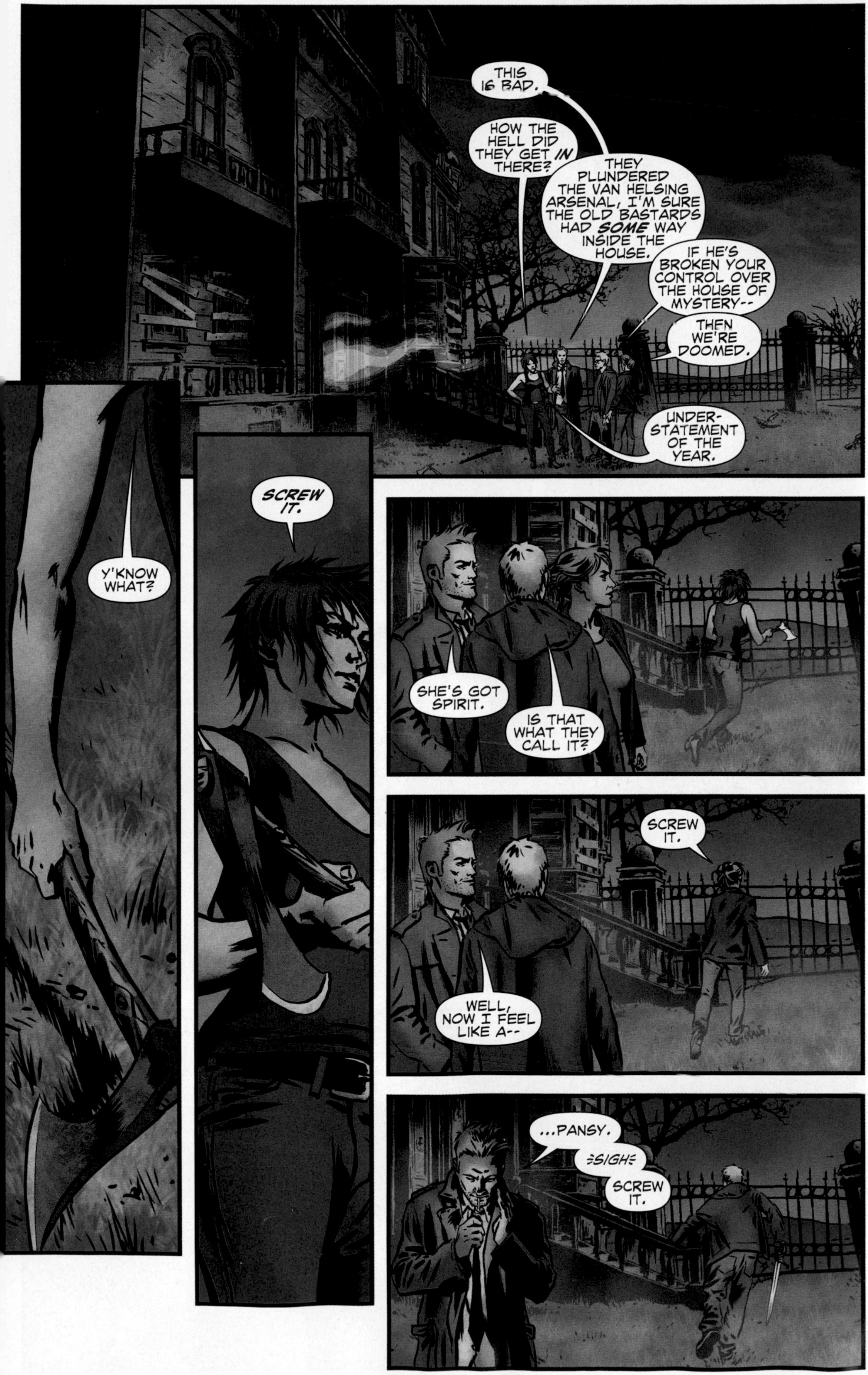
THIS IS BAD.
HOW THE HELL DID THEY GET *IN* THERE?
THEY PLUNDERED THE VAN HELSING ARSENAL, I'M SURE THE OLD BASTARDS HAD *SOME* WAY INSIDE THE HOUSE.
IF HE'S BROKEN YOUR CONTROL OVER THE HOUSE OF MYSTERY--
THEN WE'RE DOOMED.
UNDER-STATEMENT OF THE YEAR.
Y'KNOW WHAT?
SCREW IT.
SHE'S GOT SPIRIT.
IS THAT WHAT THEY CALL IT?
SCREW IT.
WELL, NOW I FEEL LIKE A--
...PANSY.
SIGH
SCREW IT.

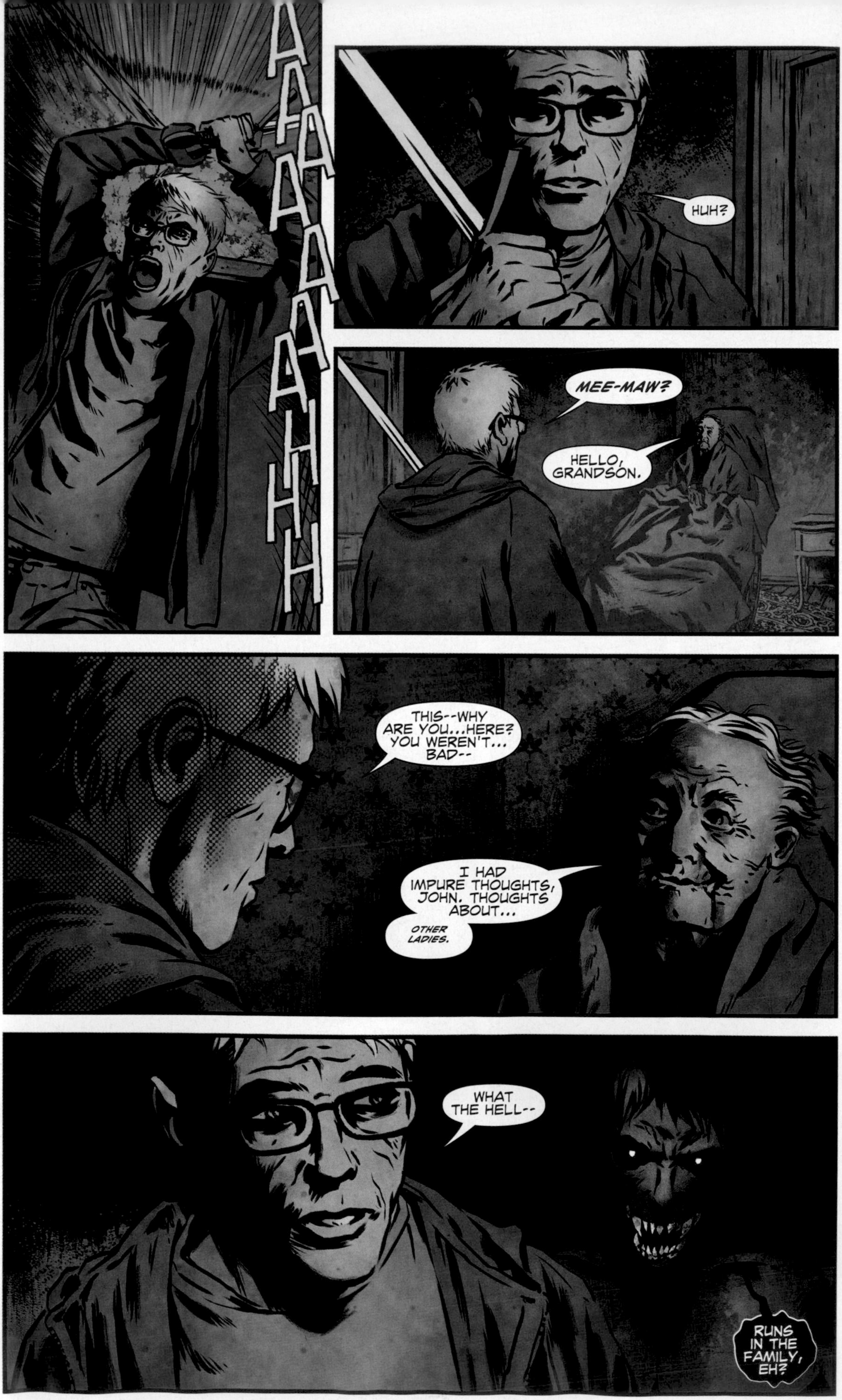
AAAAAAAAAAHHHH
HUH?
MEE-MAW?
HELLO, GRANDSON.
THIS--WHY ARE YOU...HERE? YOU WEREN'T... BAD--
I HAD IMPURE THOUGHTS, JOHN. THOUGHTS ABOUT...
OTHER LADIES.
WHAT THE HELL--
RUNS IN THE FAMILY, EH?

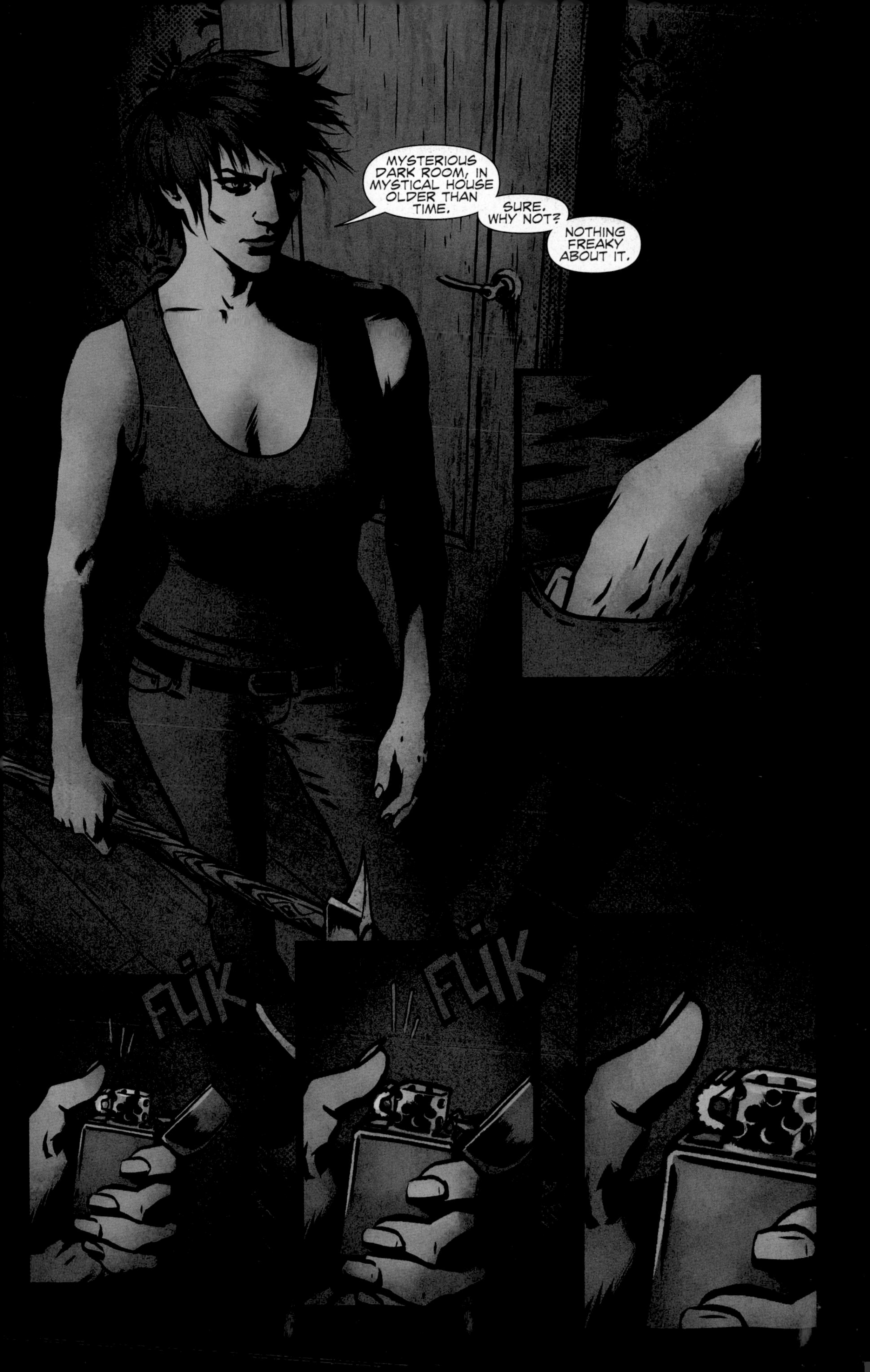
MYSTERIOUS DARK ROOM, IN MYSTICAL HOUSE OLDER THAN TIME.
SURE. WHY NOT?
NOTHING FREAKY ABOUT IT.
FLIK
FLIK

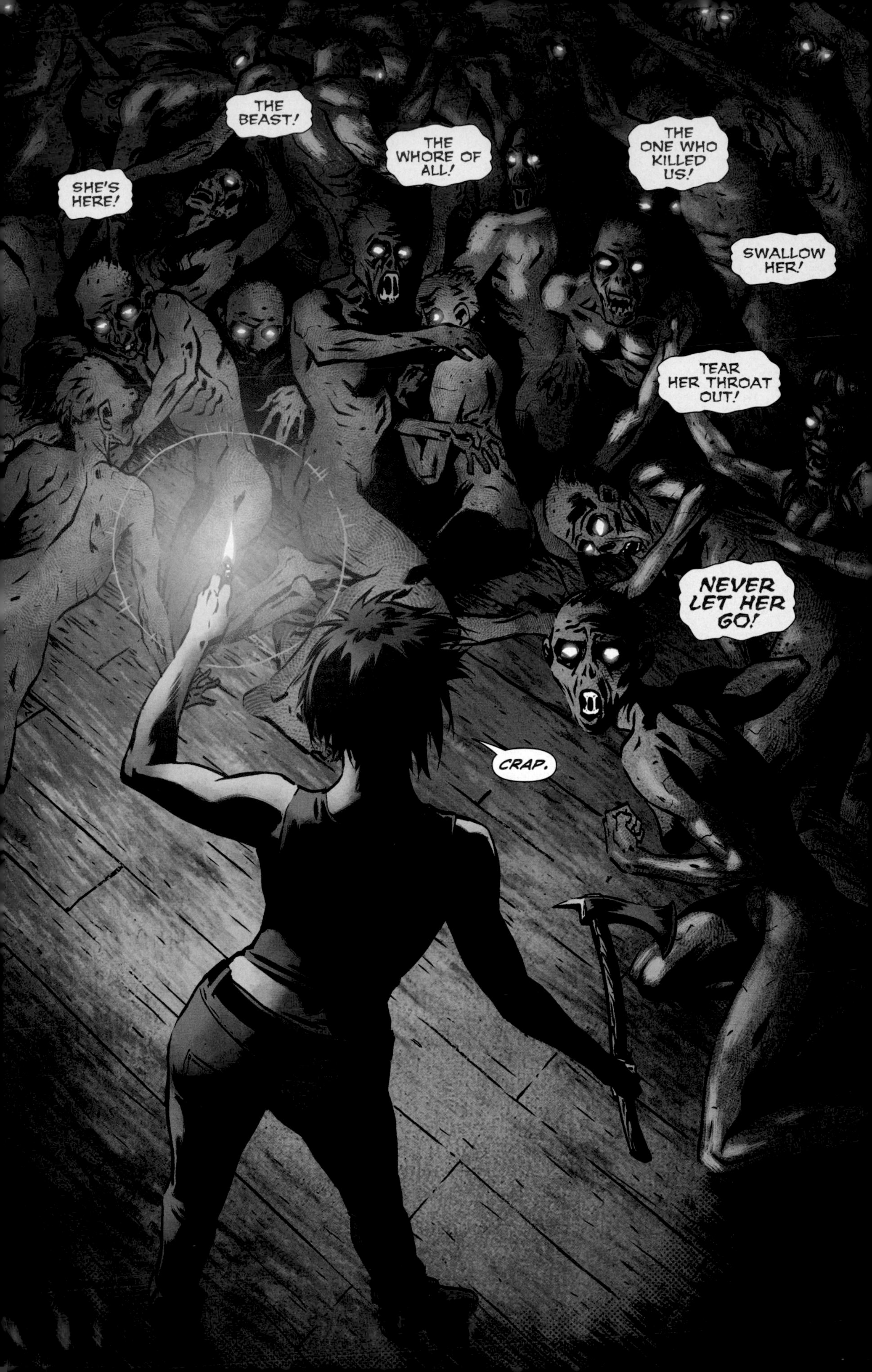
SHE'S HERE!
THE BEAST!
THE WHORE OF ALL!
THE ONE WHO KILLED US!
SWALLOW HER!
TEAR HER THROAT OUT!
NEVER LET HER GO!
CRAP.

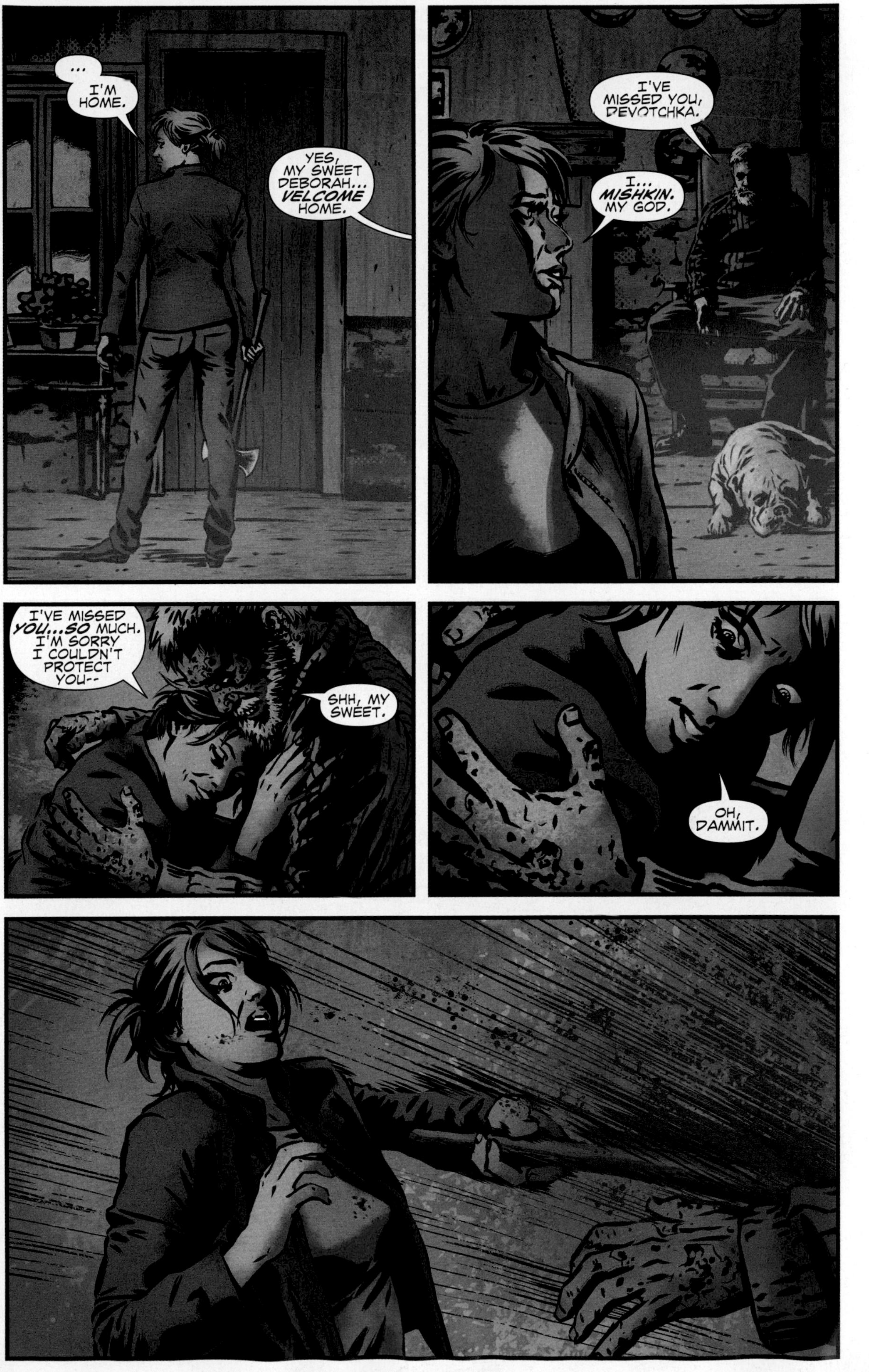
...
I'M HOME.
YES, MY SWEET DEBORAH... VELCOME HOME.
I'VE MISSED YOU, DEVOTCHKA.
I... MISHKIN. MY GOD.
I'VE MISSED YOU...SO MUCH. I'M SORRY I COULDN'T PROTECT YOU--
SHH, MY SWEET.
OH, DAMMIT.

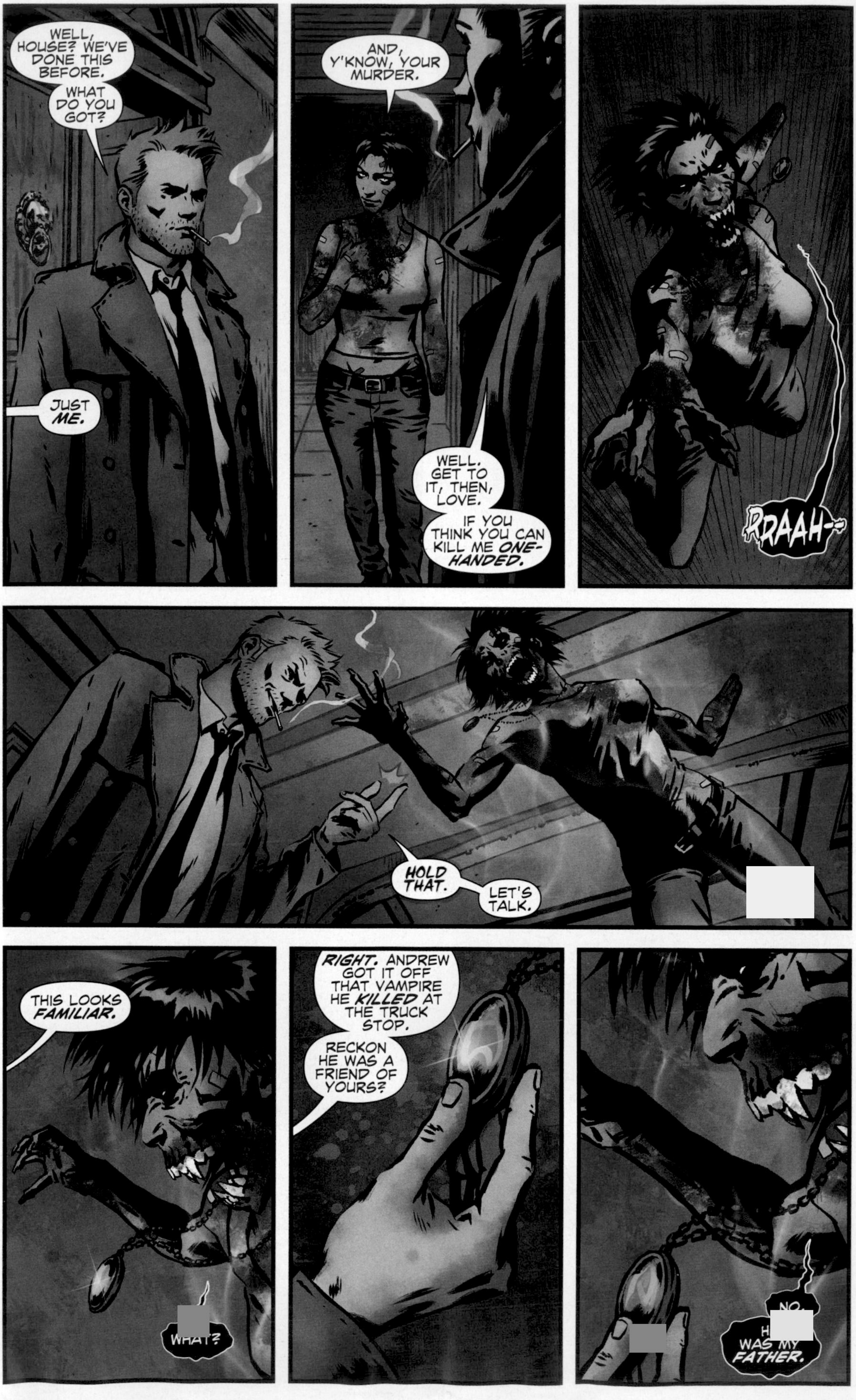
WELL, HOUSE? WE'VE DONE THIS BEFORE.
WHAT DO YOU GOT?
JUST ME.
AND, Y'KNOW, YOUR MURDER.
WELL. GET TO IT, THEN, LOVE.
IF YOU THINK YOU CAN KILL ME ONE-HANDED.
RRAAH--
HOLD THAT.
LET'S TALK.
THIS LOOKS FAMILIAR.
WHAT?
RIGHT. ANDREW GOT IT OFF THAT VAMPIRE HE KILLED AT THE TRUCK STOP.
RECKON HE WAS A FRIEND OF YOURS?
NO.
WAS MY FATHER.

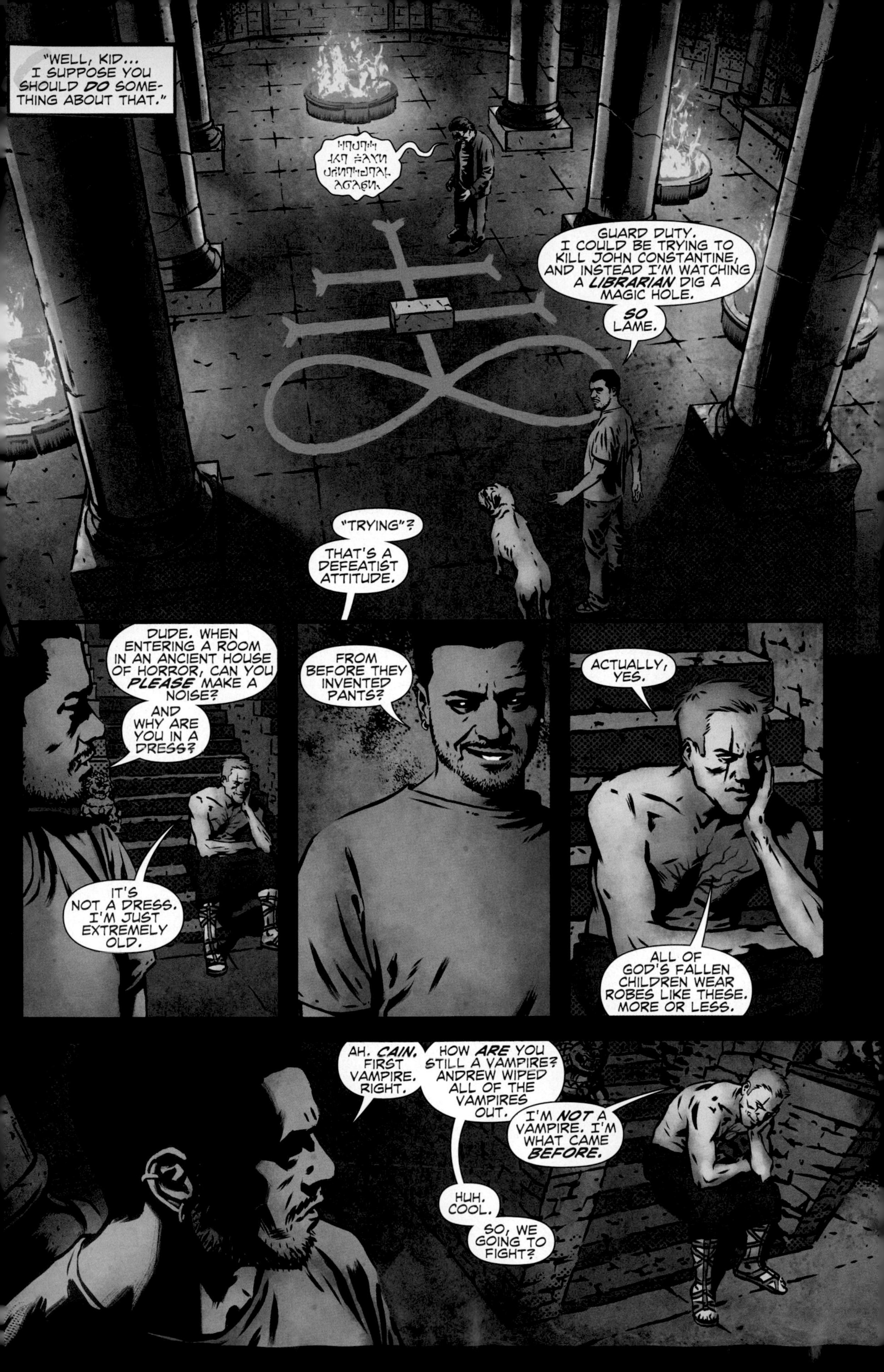

"WELL, KID... I SUPPOSE YOU SHOULD DO SOMETHING ABOUT THAT."
GUARD DUTY. I COULD BE TRYING TO KILL JOHN CONSTANTINE, AND INSTEAD I'M WATCHING A LIBRARIAN DIG A MAGIC HOLE.
SO LAME.
"TRYING"?
THAT'S A DEFEATIST ATTITUDE.
DUDE. WHEN ENTERING A ROOM IN AN ANCIENT HOUSE OF HORROR, CAN YOU PLEASE MAKE A NOISE?
AND WHY ARE YOU IN A DRESS?
IT'S NOT A DRESS. I'M JUST EXTREMELY OLD.
FROM BEFORE THEY INVENTED PANTS?
ACTUALLY, YES.
ALL OF GOD'S FALLEN CHILDREN WEAR ROBES LIKE THESE. MORE OR LESS.
AH. CAIN. FIRST VAMPIRE. RIGHT.
HOW ARE YOU STILL A VAMPIRE? ANDREW WIPED ALL OF THE VAMPIRES OUT.
I'M NOT A VAMPIRE. I'M WHAT CAME BEFORE.
HUH. COOL.
SO, WE GOING TO FIGHT?

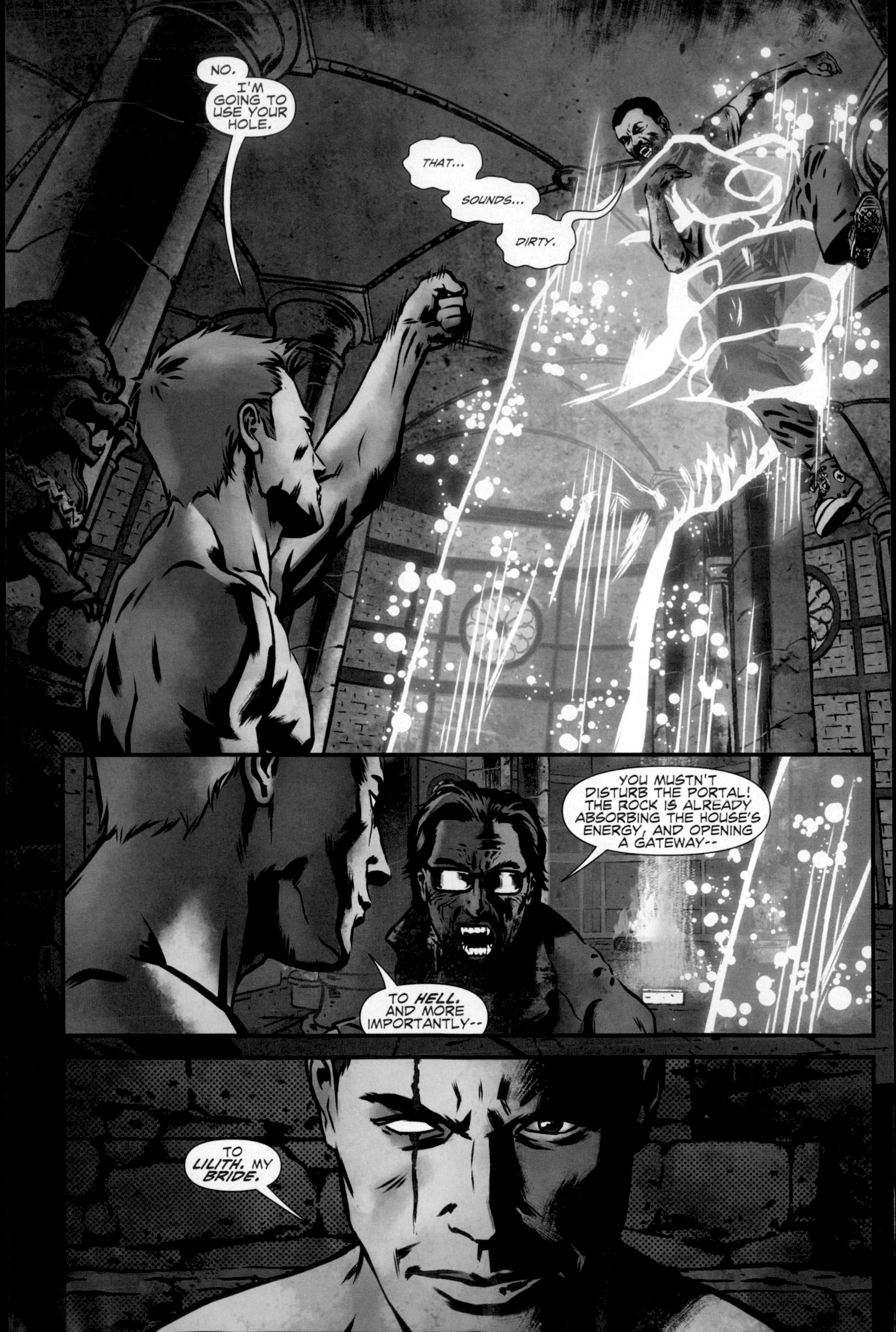
NO. I'M GOING TO USE YOUR HOLE.
THAT...
SOUNDS...
DIRTY.
YOU MUSTN'T DISTURB THE PORTAL! THE ROCK IS ALREADY ABSORBING THE HOUSE'S ENERGY, AND OPENING A GATEWAY--
TO HELL. AND MORE IMPORTANTLY--
TO LILITH. MY BRIDE.

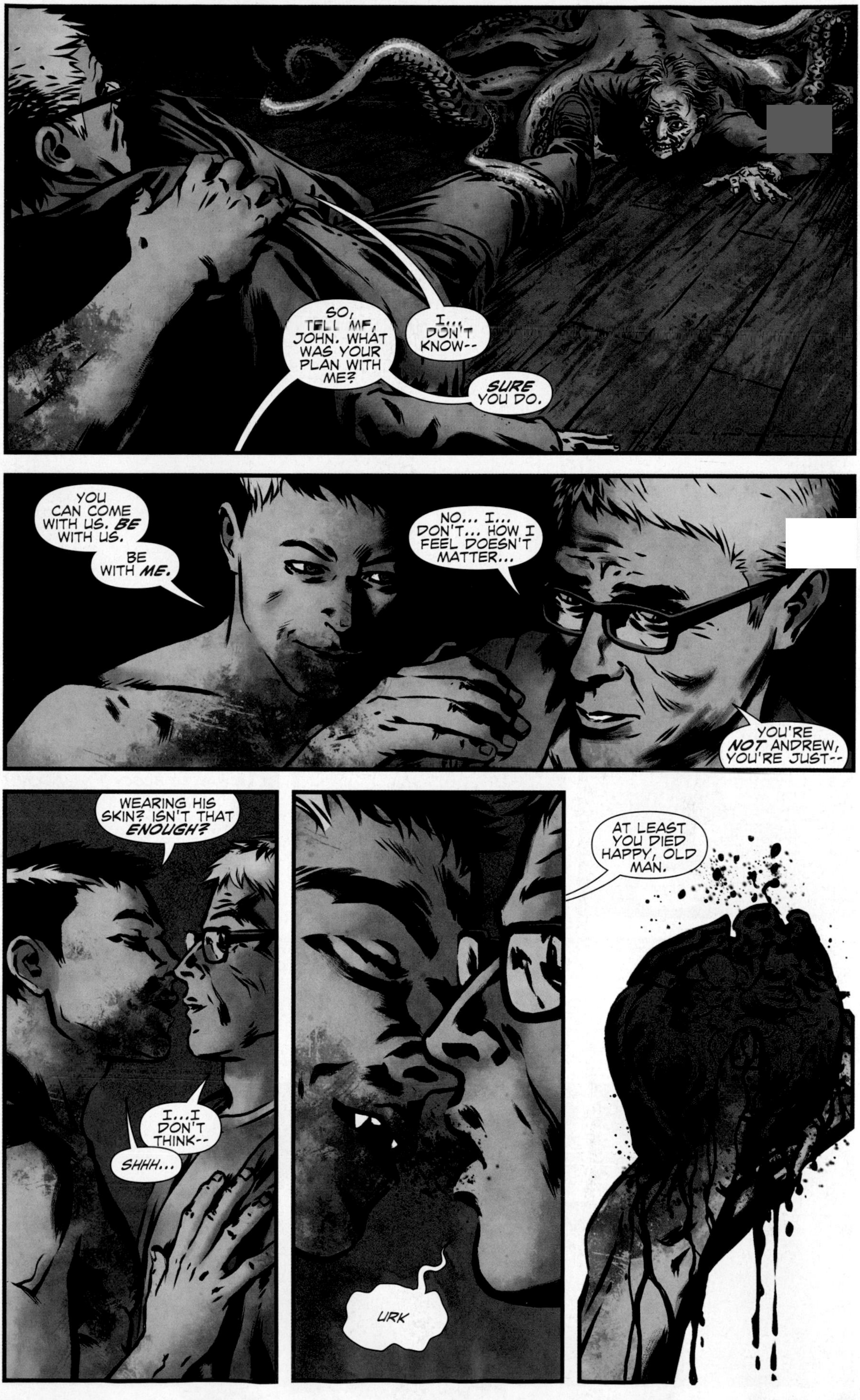
SO, TELL ME, JOHN. WHAT WAS YOUR PLAN WITH ME?
I... DON'T KNOW--
SURE YOU DO.
YOU CAN COME WITH US. *BE* WITH US.
BE WITH *ME.*
NO... I... DON'T... HOW I FEEL DOESN'T MATTER...
YOU'RE *NOT* ANDREW, YOU'RE JUST--
WEARING HIS SKIN? ISN'T THAT *ENOUGH?*
I...I DON'T THINK--
SHHH...
URK
AT LEAST YOU DIED HAPPY, OLD MAN.

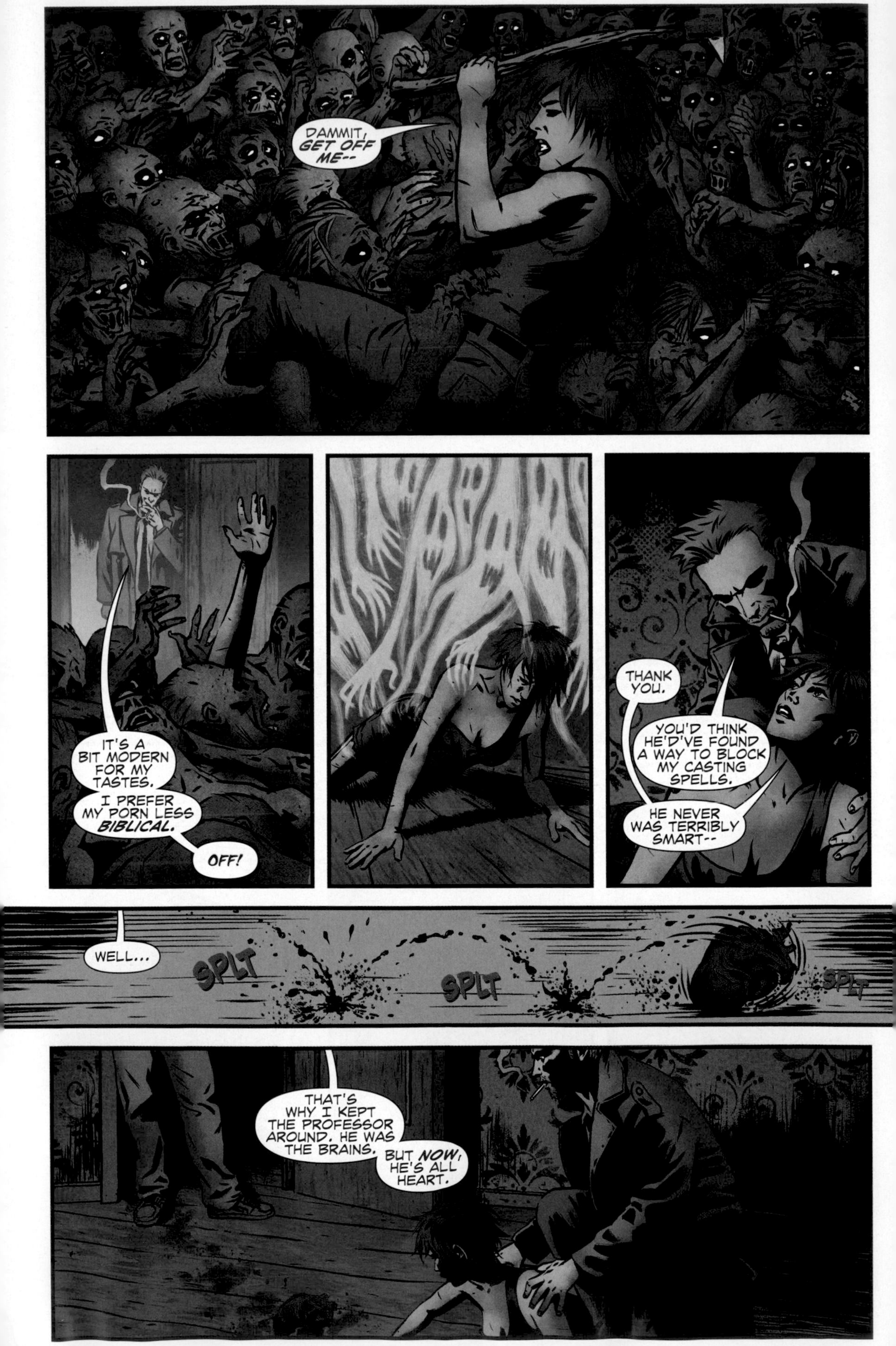
DAMMIT, GET OFF ME--
IT'S A BIT MODERN FOR MY TASTES.
I PREFER MY PORN LESS BIBLICAL.
OFF!
THANK YOU.
YOU'D THINK HE'D'VE FOUND A WAY TO BLOCK MY CASTING SPELLS.
HE NEVER WAS TERRIBLY SMART--
WELL...
SPLT
SPLT
SPLT
THAT'S WHY I KEPT THE PROFESSOR AROUND. HE WAS THE BRAINS.
BUT NOW, HE'S ALL HEART.

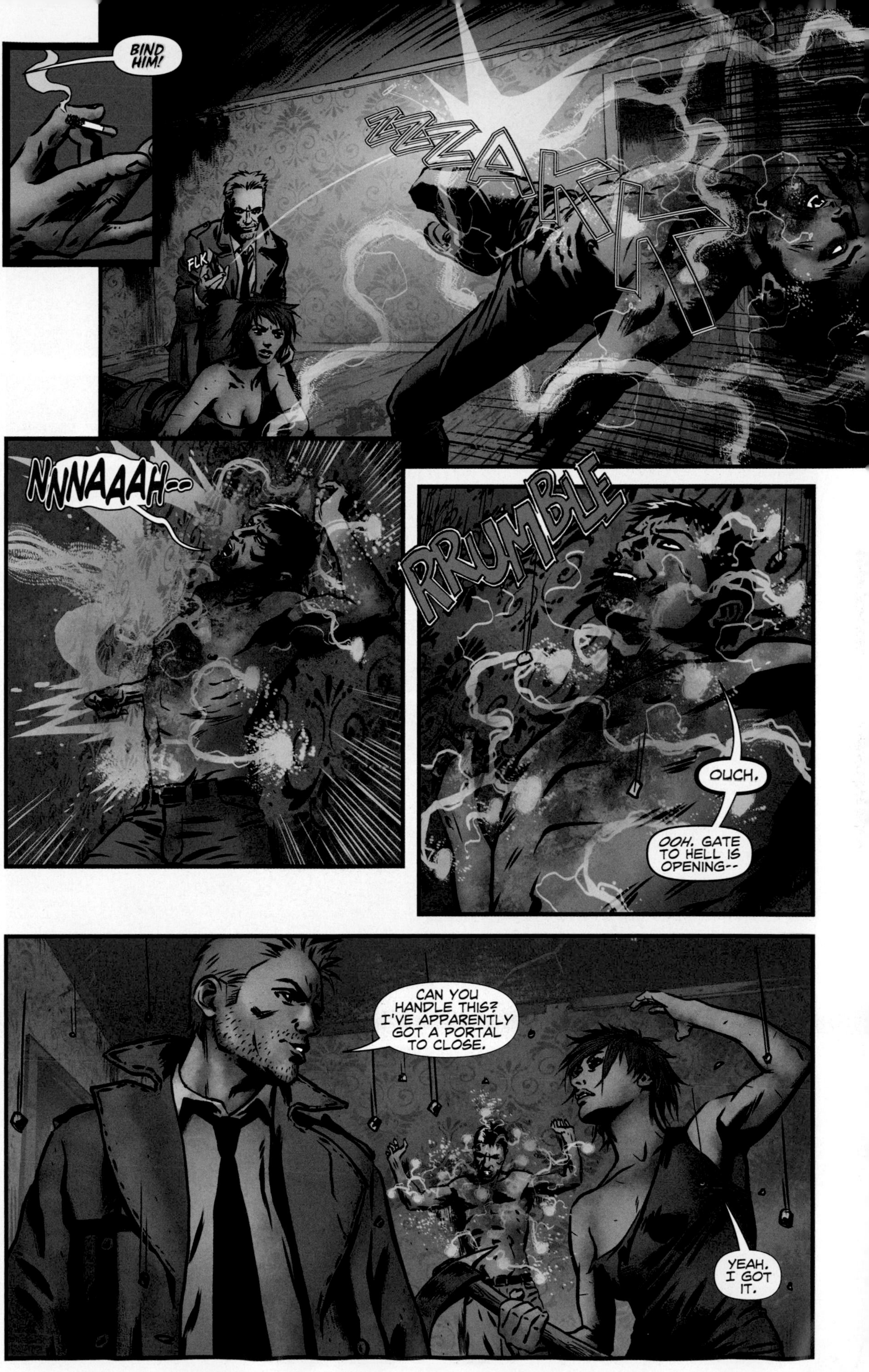
BIND HIM!
FLK
ZZZAKKT
NNNAAAH--
RRUMBLE
OUCH.
OOH. GATE TO HELL IS OPENING--
CAN YOU HANDLE THIS? I'VE APPARENTLY GOT A PORTAL TO CLOSE.
YEAH. I GOT IT.

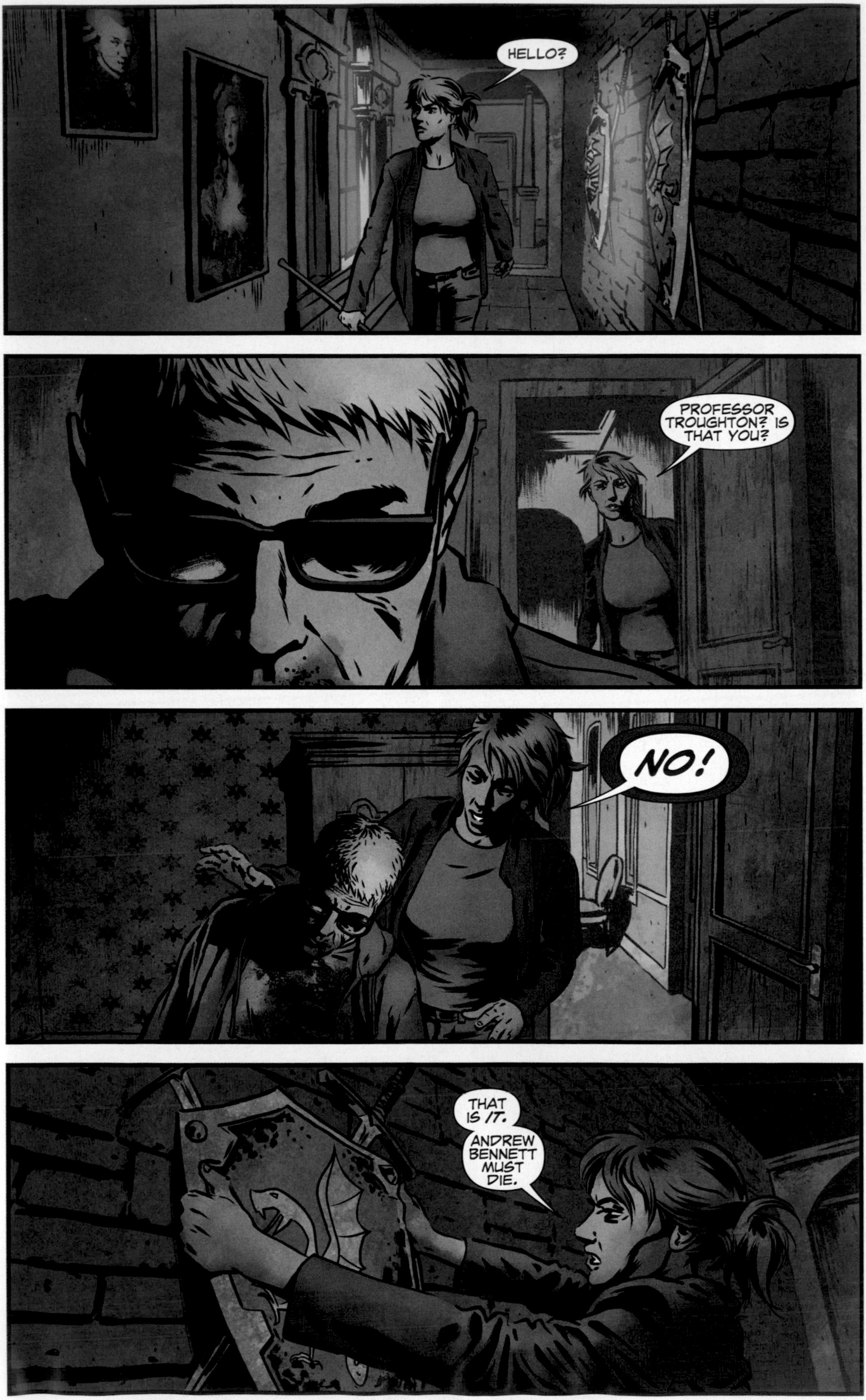
HELLO?
PROFESSOR TROUGHTON? IS THAT YOU?
NO!
THAT IS IT.
ANDREW BENNETT MUST DIE.

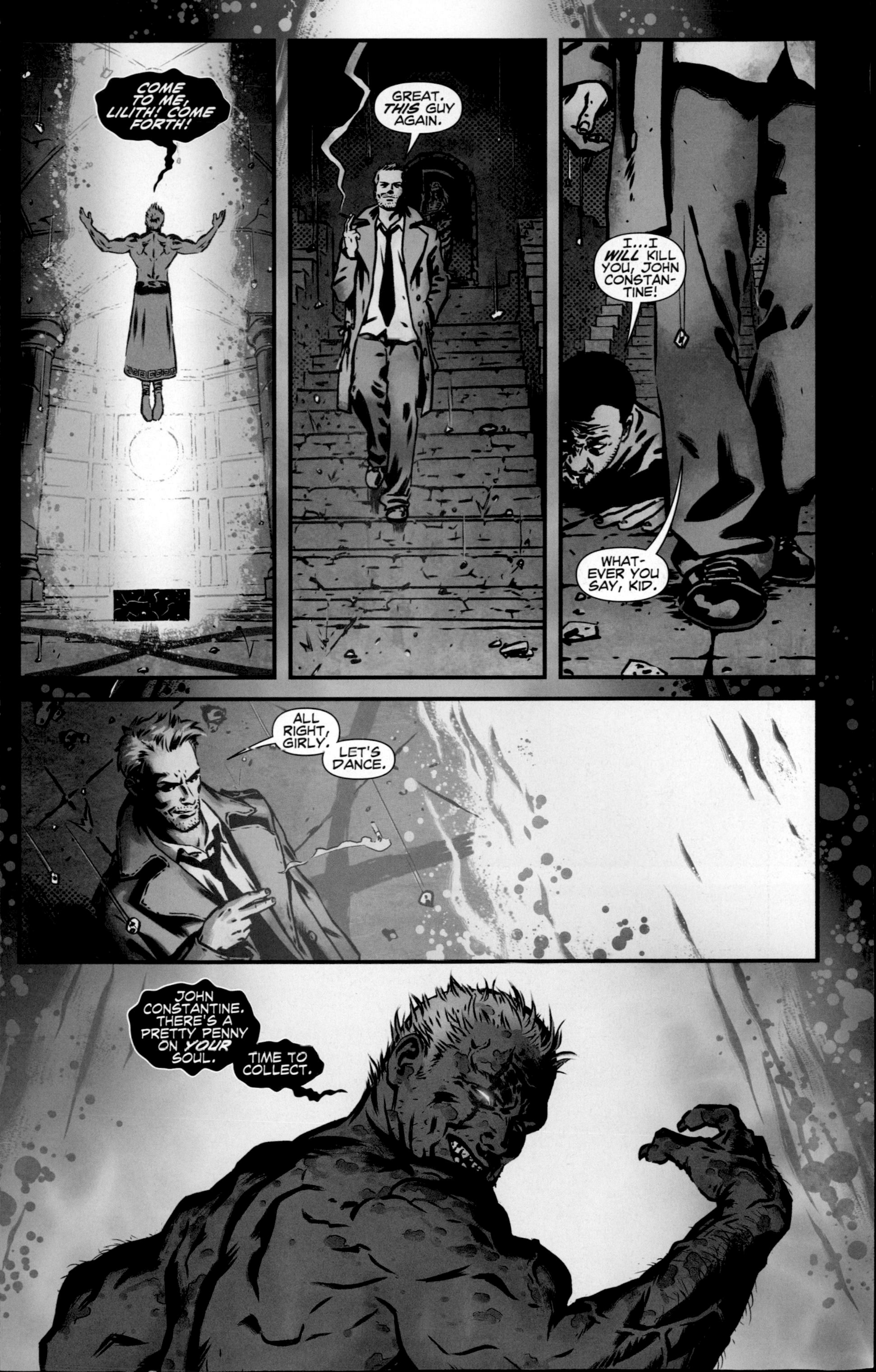
COME TO ME, LILITH! COME FORTH!
GREAT. THIS GUY AGAIN.
I...I WILL KILL YOU, JOHN CONSTAN-TINE!
WHAT-EVER YOU SAY, KID.
ALL RIGHT, GIRLY.
LET'S DANCE.
JOHN CONSTANTINE. THERE'S A PRETTY PENNY ON YOUR SOUL.
TIME TO COLLECT.

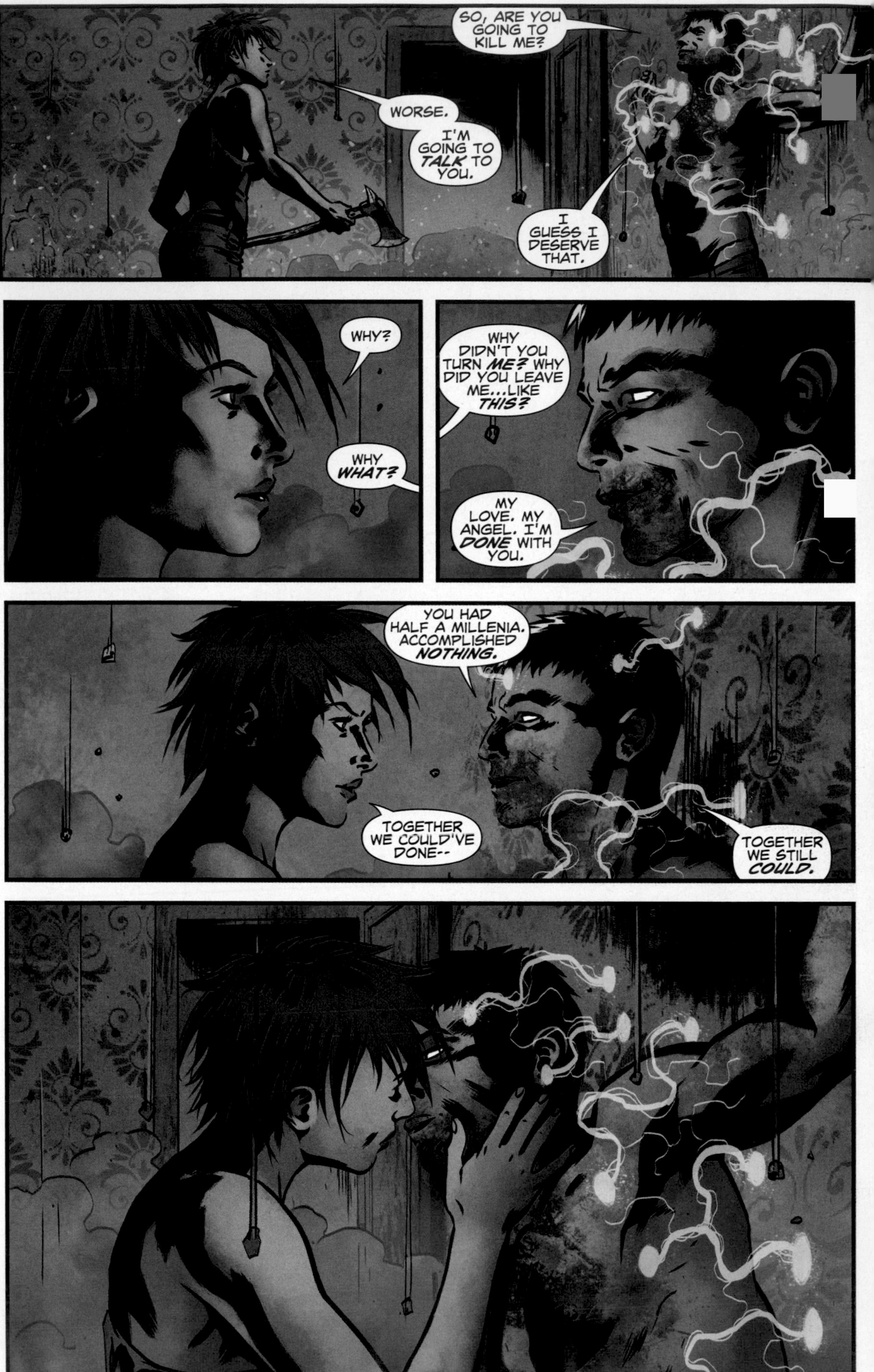
SO, ARE YOU GOING TO KILL ME?
WORSE.
I'M GOING TO TALK TO YOU.
I GUESS I DESERVE THAT.
WHY?
WHY WHAT?
WHY DIDN'T YOU TURN ME? WHY DID YOU LEAVE ME...LIKE THIS?
MY LOVE. MY ANGEL. I'M DONE WITH YOU.
YOU HAD HALF A MILLENIA. ACCOMPLISHED NOTHING.
TOGETHER WE COULD'VE DONE--
TOGETHER WE STILL COULD.

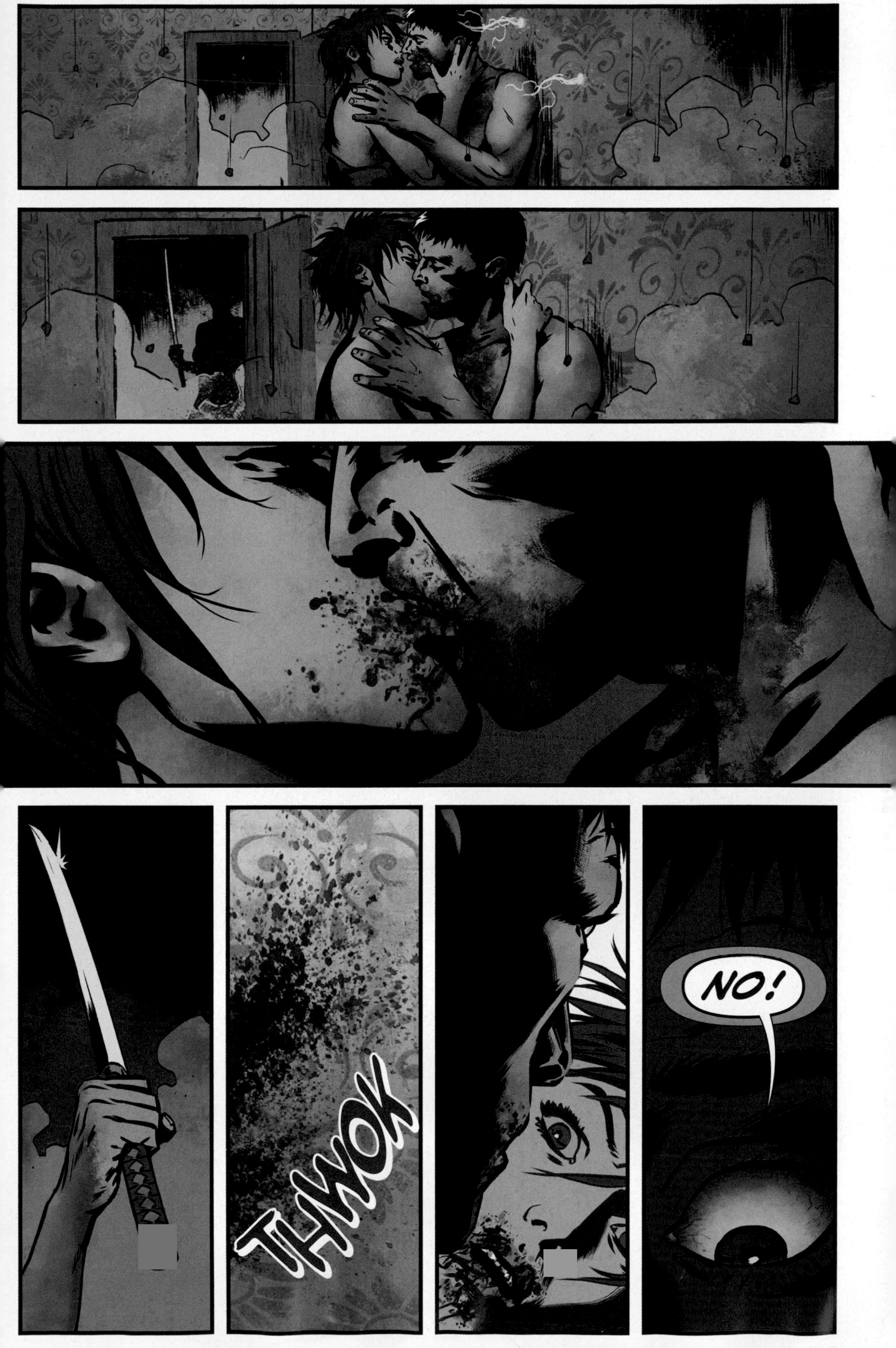
THWOK
NO!

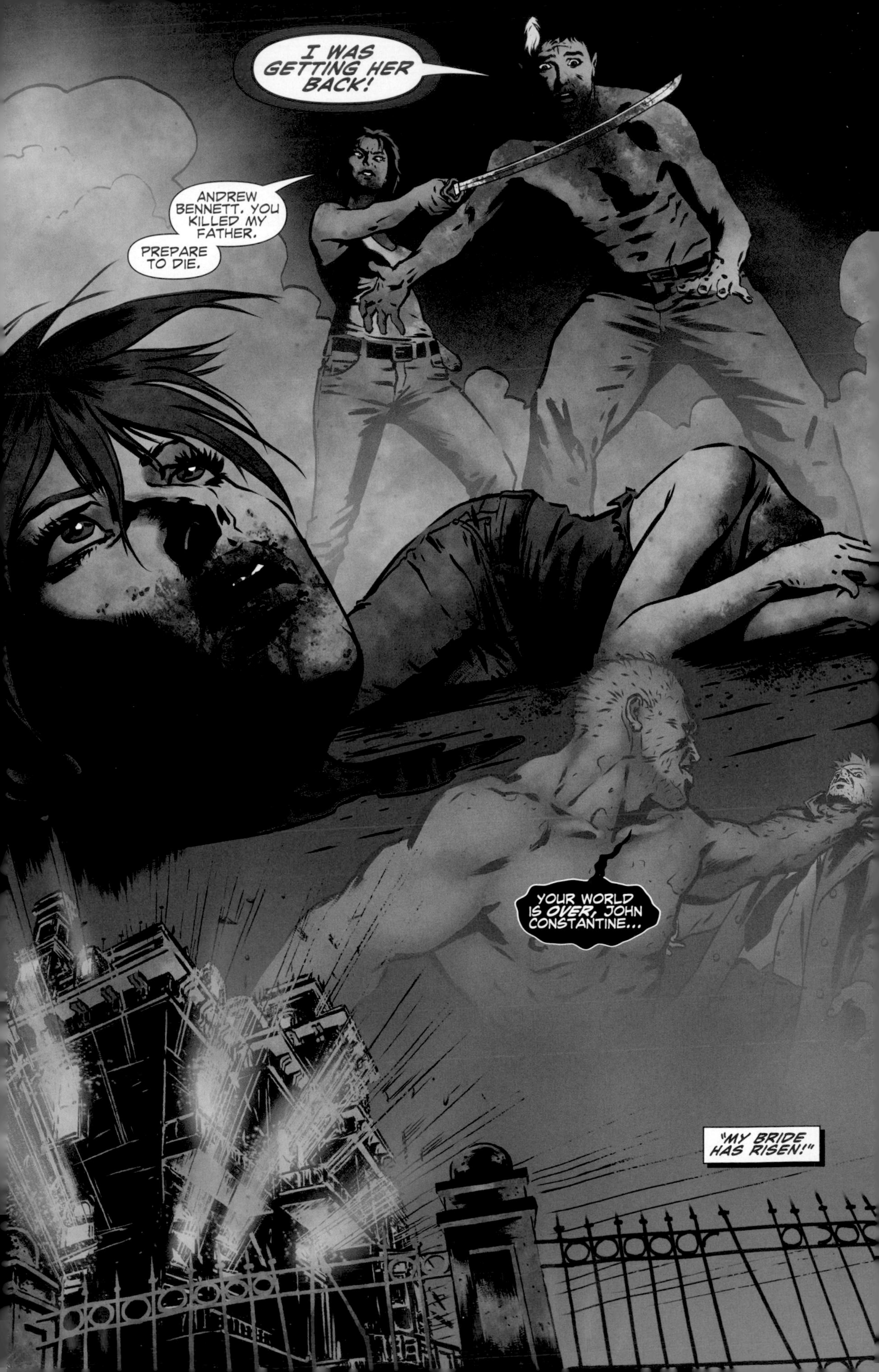
I WAS GETTING HER BACK!
ANDREW BENNETT. YOU KILLED MY FATHER.
PREPARE TO DIE.
YOUR WORLD IS OVER, JOHN CONSTANTINE...
"MY BRIDE HAS RISEN!"

DIG FOR FIRE

JOSHUA HALE FIALKOV writer   FERNANDO BLANCO artist   cover art by ANDREA SORRENTINO & MARCELO MAIOLO

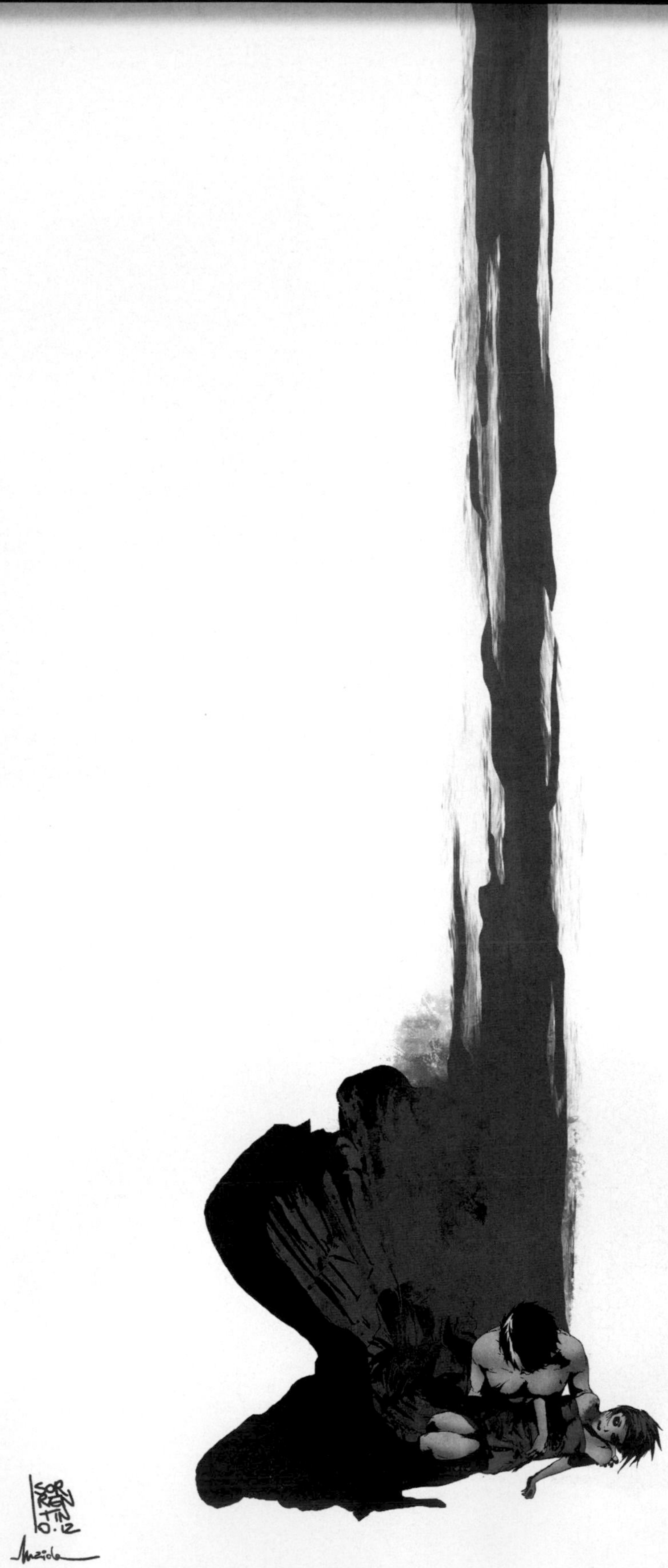

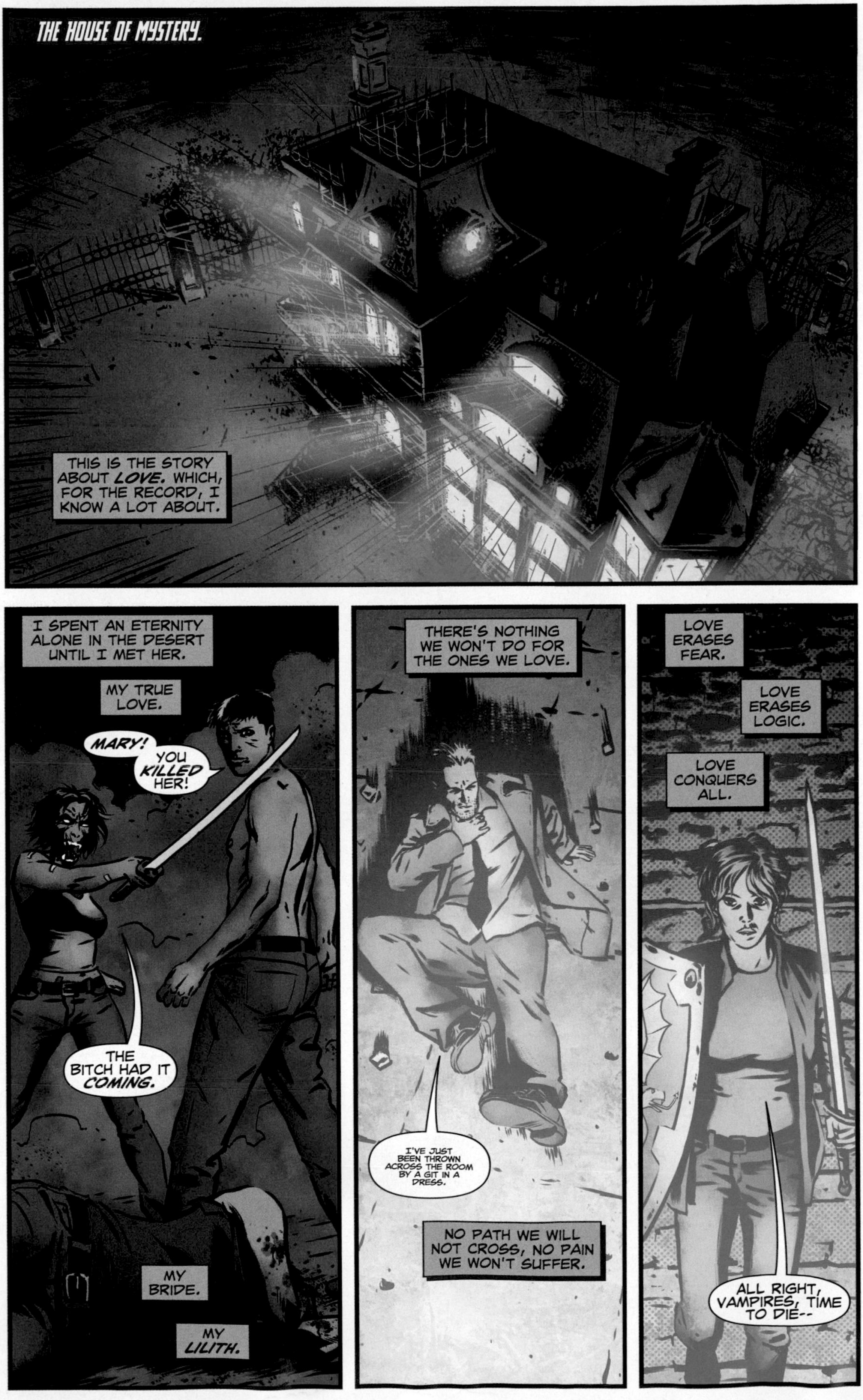
THE HOUSE OF MYSTERY.
THIS IS THE STORY ABOUT LOVE. WHICH, FOR THE RECORD, I KNOW A LOT ABOUT.
I SPENT AN ETERNITY ALONE IN THE DESERT UNTIL I MET HER.
MY TRUE LOVE.
MARY!
YOU KILLED HER!
THE BITCH HAD IT COMING.
MY BRIDE.
MY LILITH.
THERE'S NOTHING WE WON'T DO FOR THE ONES WE LOVE.
I'VE JUST BEEN THROWN ACROSS THE ROOM BY A GIT IN A DRESS.
NO PATH WE WILL NOT CROSS, NO PAIN WE WON'T SUFFER.
LOVE ERASES FEAR.
LOVE ERASES LOGIC.
LOVE CONQUERS ALL.
ALL RIGHT, VAMPIRES, TIME TO DIE--

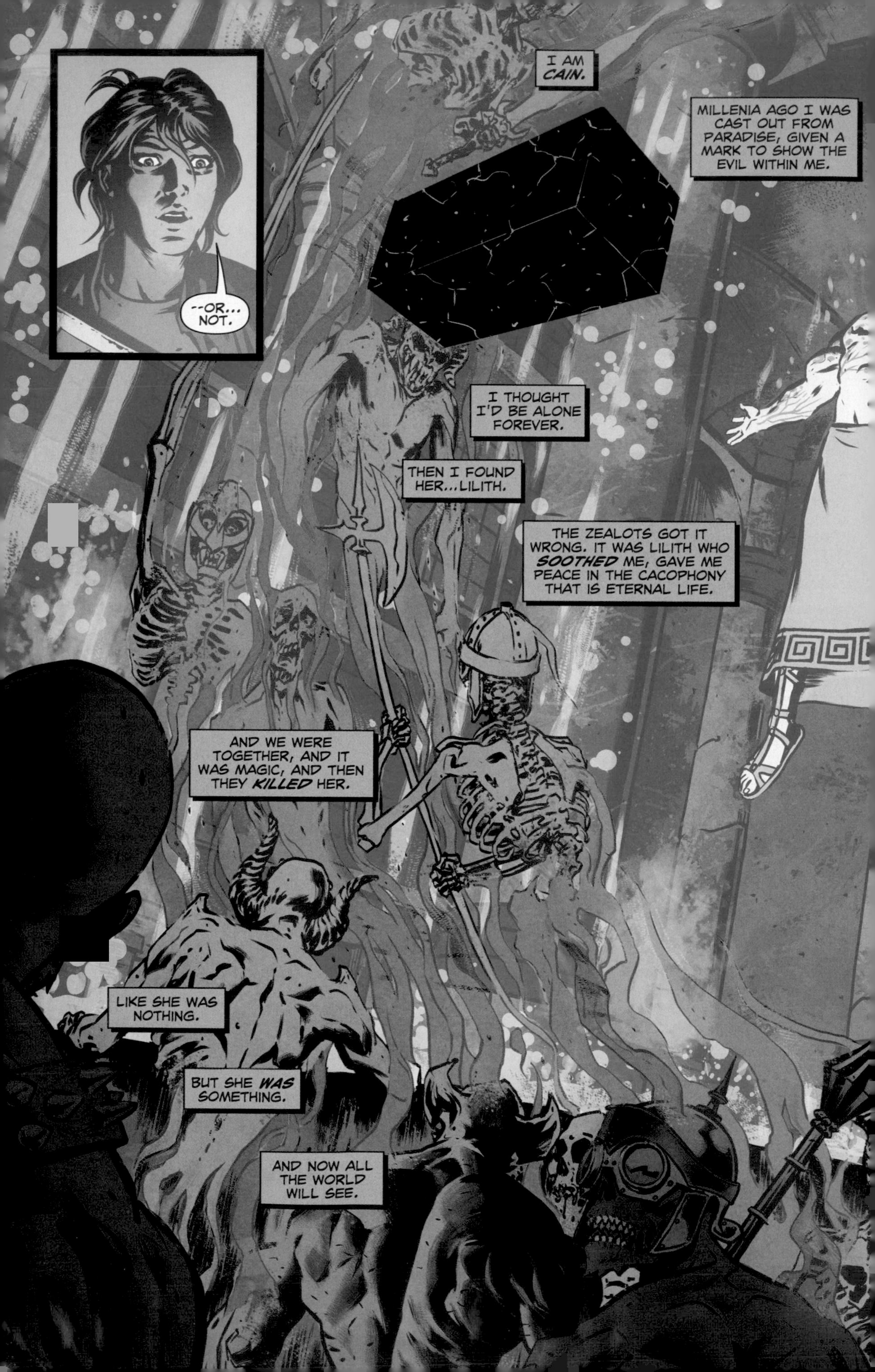
--OR... NOT.
I AM CAIN.
MILLENIA AGO I WAS CAST OUT FROM PARADISE, GIVEN A MARK TO SHOW THE EVIL WITHIN ME.
I THOUGHT I'D BE ALONE FOREVER.
THEN I FOUND HER...LILITH.
THE ZEALOTS GOT IT WRONG. IT WAS LILITH WHO SOOTHED ME, GAVE ME PEACE IN THE CACOPHONY THAT IS ETERNAL LIFE.
AND WE WERE TOGETHER, AND IT WAS MAGIC, AND THEN THEY KILLED HER.
LIKE SHE WAS NOTHING.
BUT SHE WAS SOMETHING.
AND NOW ALL THE WORLD WILL SEE.

DIG FOR FIRE

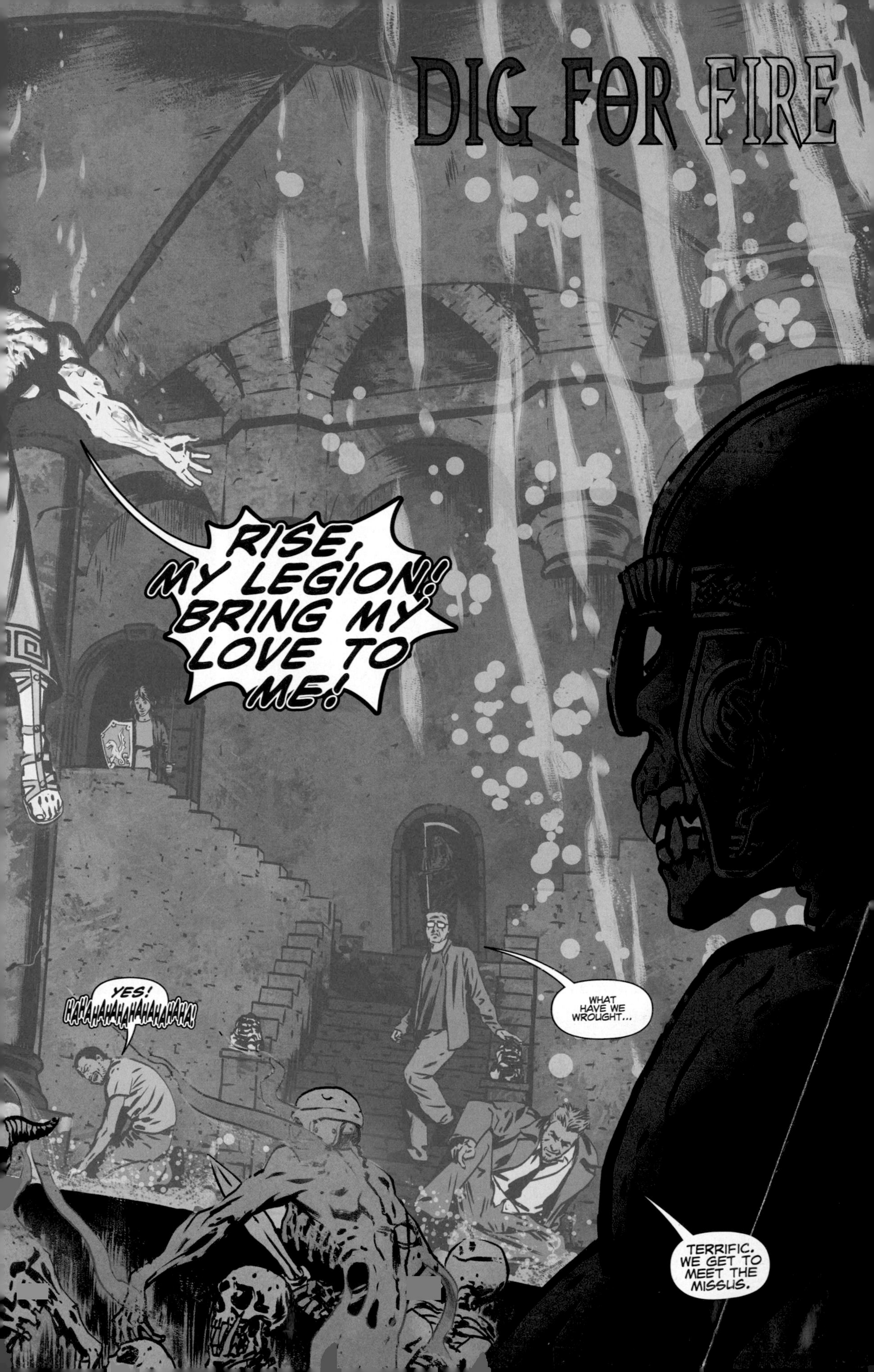
RISE, MY LEGION! BRING MY LOVE TO ME!
YES! HAHAHAHAHAHAHAHAHAHA!
WHAT HAVE WE WROUGHT...
TERRIFIC. WE GET TO MEET THE MISSUS.

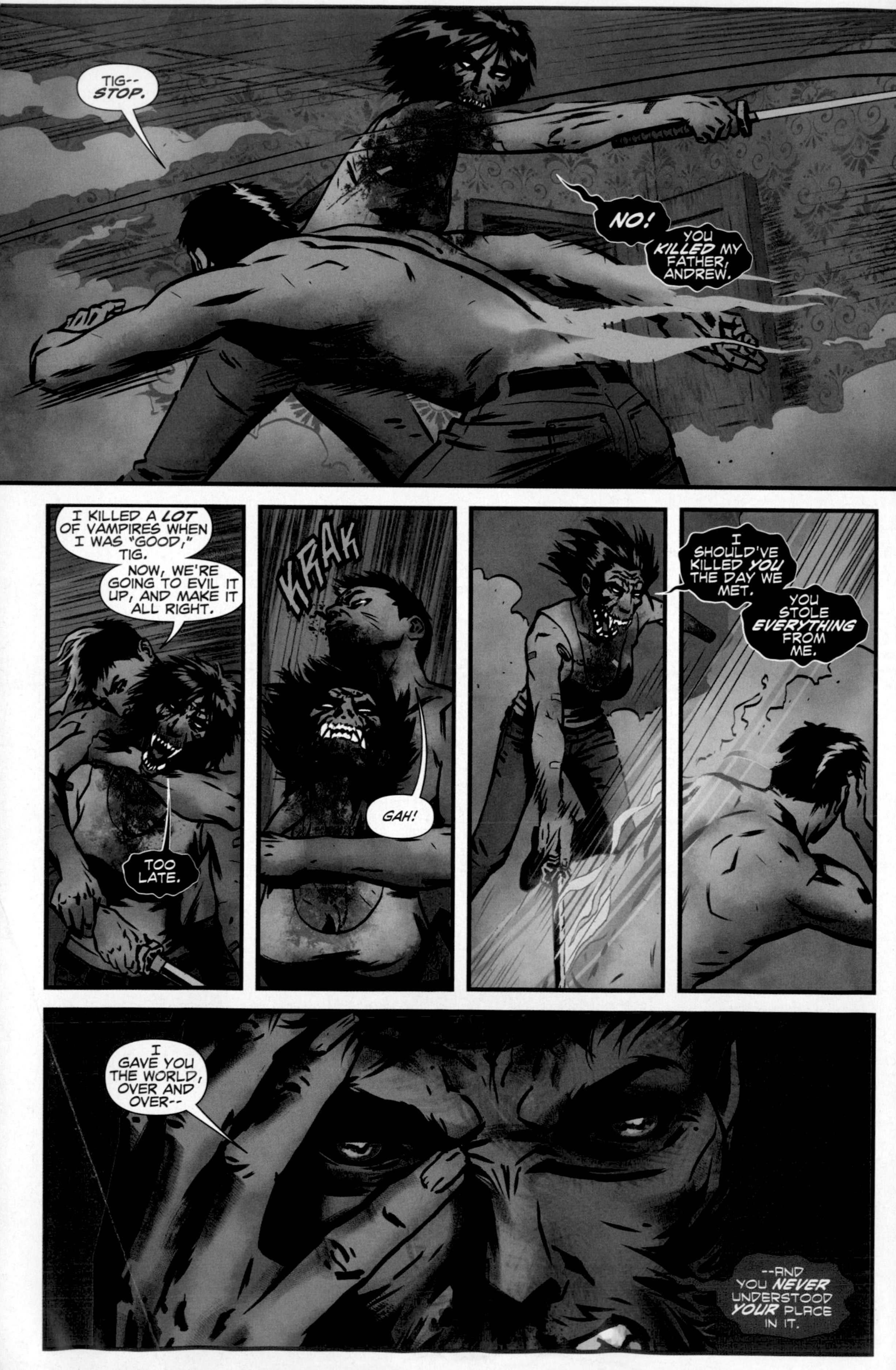
TIG-- STOP.
NO!
YOU KILLED MY FATHER, ANDREW.
I KILLED A LOT OF VAMPIRES WHEN I WAS "GOOD," TIG.
NOW, WE'RE GOING TO EVIL IT UP, AND MAKE IT ALL RIGHT.
TOO LATE.
KRAK
GAH!
I SHOULD'VE KILLED YOU THE DAY WE MET.
YOU STOLE EVERYTHING FROM ME.
I GAVE YOU THE WORLD, OVER AND OVER--
--AND YOU NEVER UNDERSTOOD YOUR PLACE IN IT.

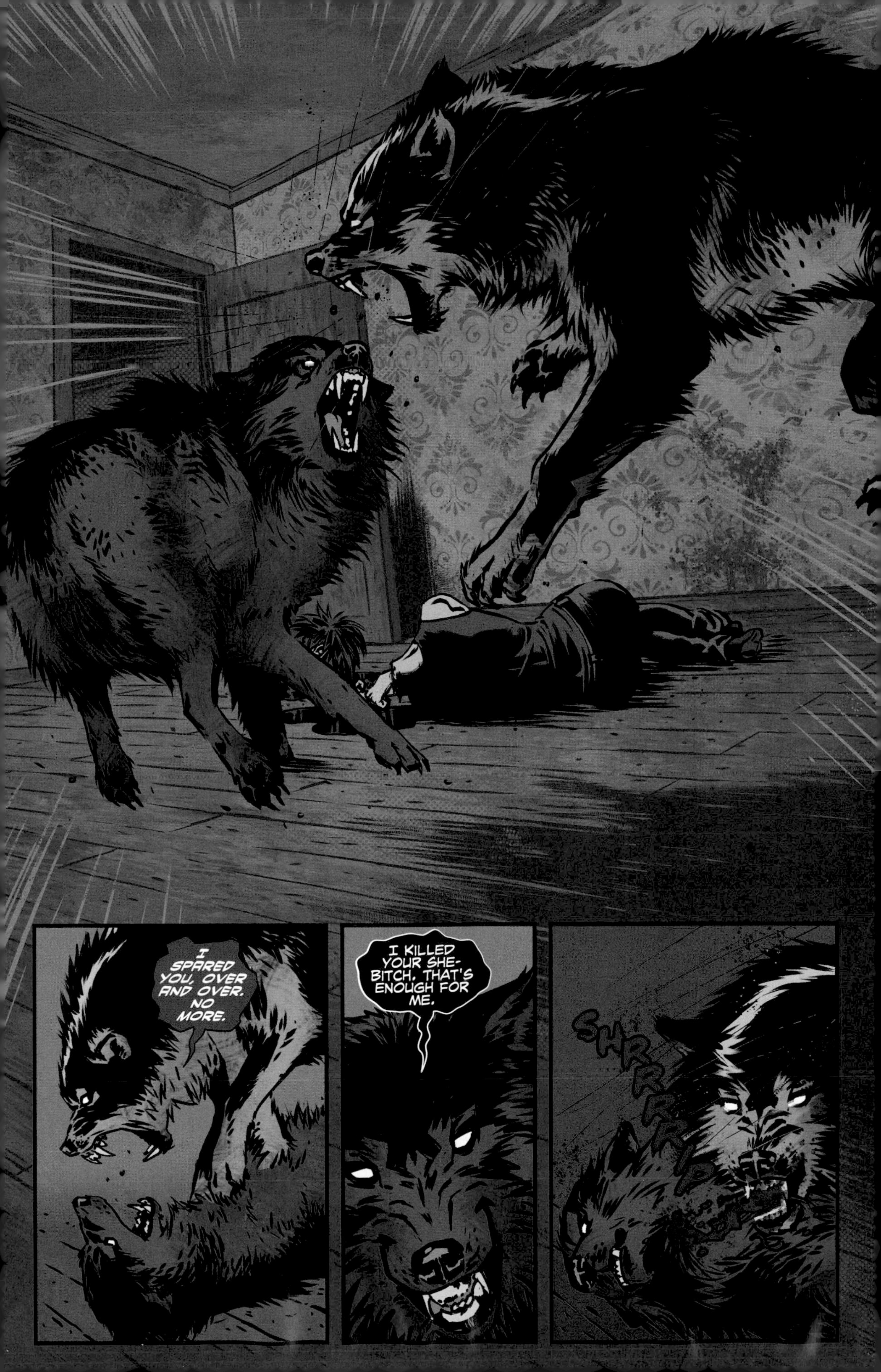
I SPARED YOU, OVER AND OVER. NO MORE.
I KILLED YOUR SHE-BITCH. THAT'S ENOUGH FOR ME.
SHRRRRIP

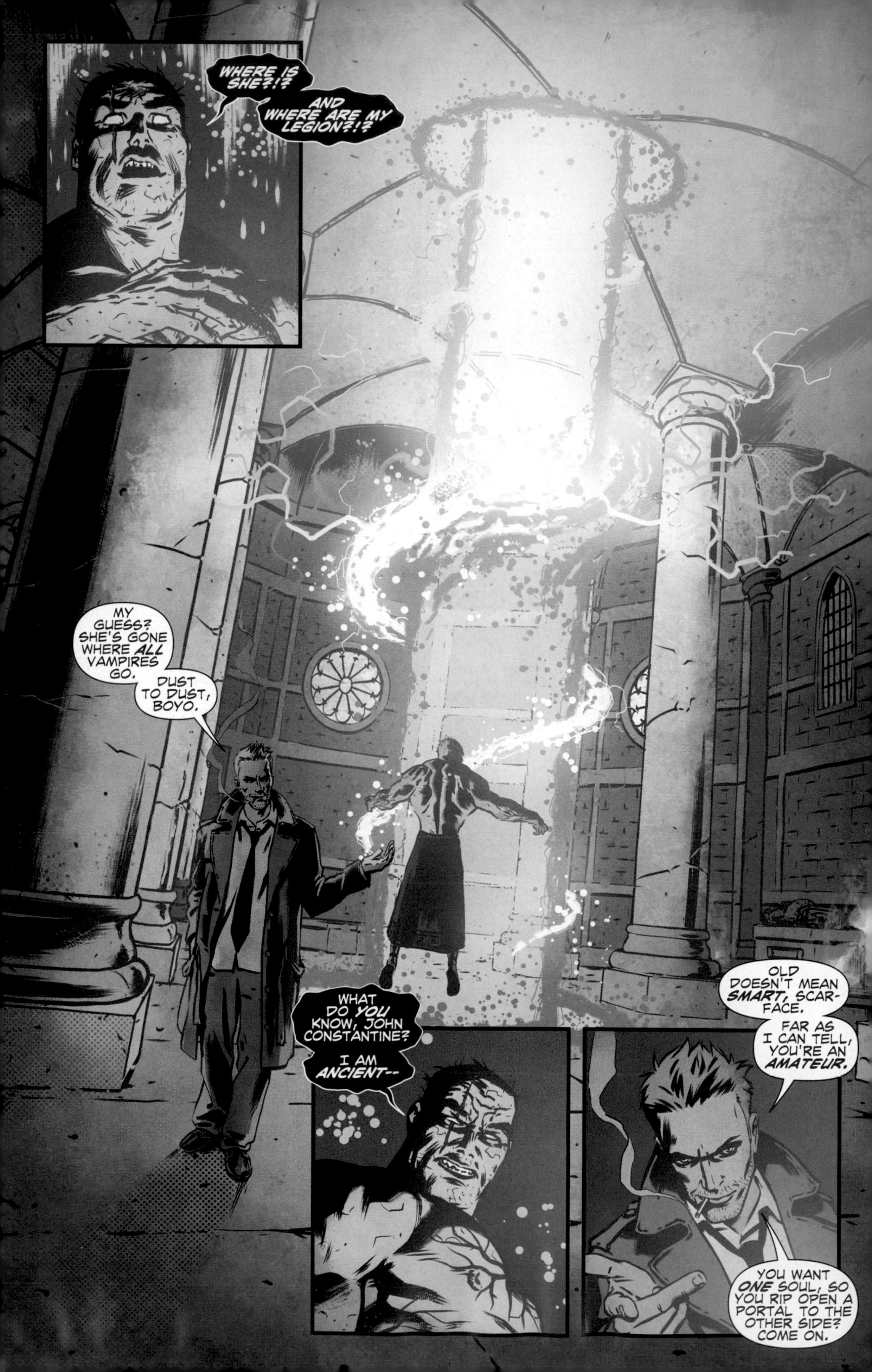
WHERE IS SHE?!?
AND WHERE ARE MY LEGION?!?
MY GUESS? SHE'S GONE WHERE ALL VAMPIRES GO.
DUST TO DUST, BOYO.
WHAT DO YOU KNOW, JOHN CONSTANTINE?
I AM ANCIENT--
OLD DOESN'T MEAN SMART, SCAR-FACE.
FAR AS I CAN TELL, YOU'RE AN AMATEUR.
YOU WANT ONE SOUL, SO YOU RIP OPEN A PORTAL TO THE OTHER SIDE? COME ON.

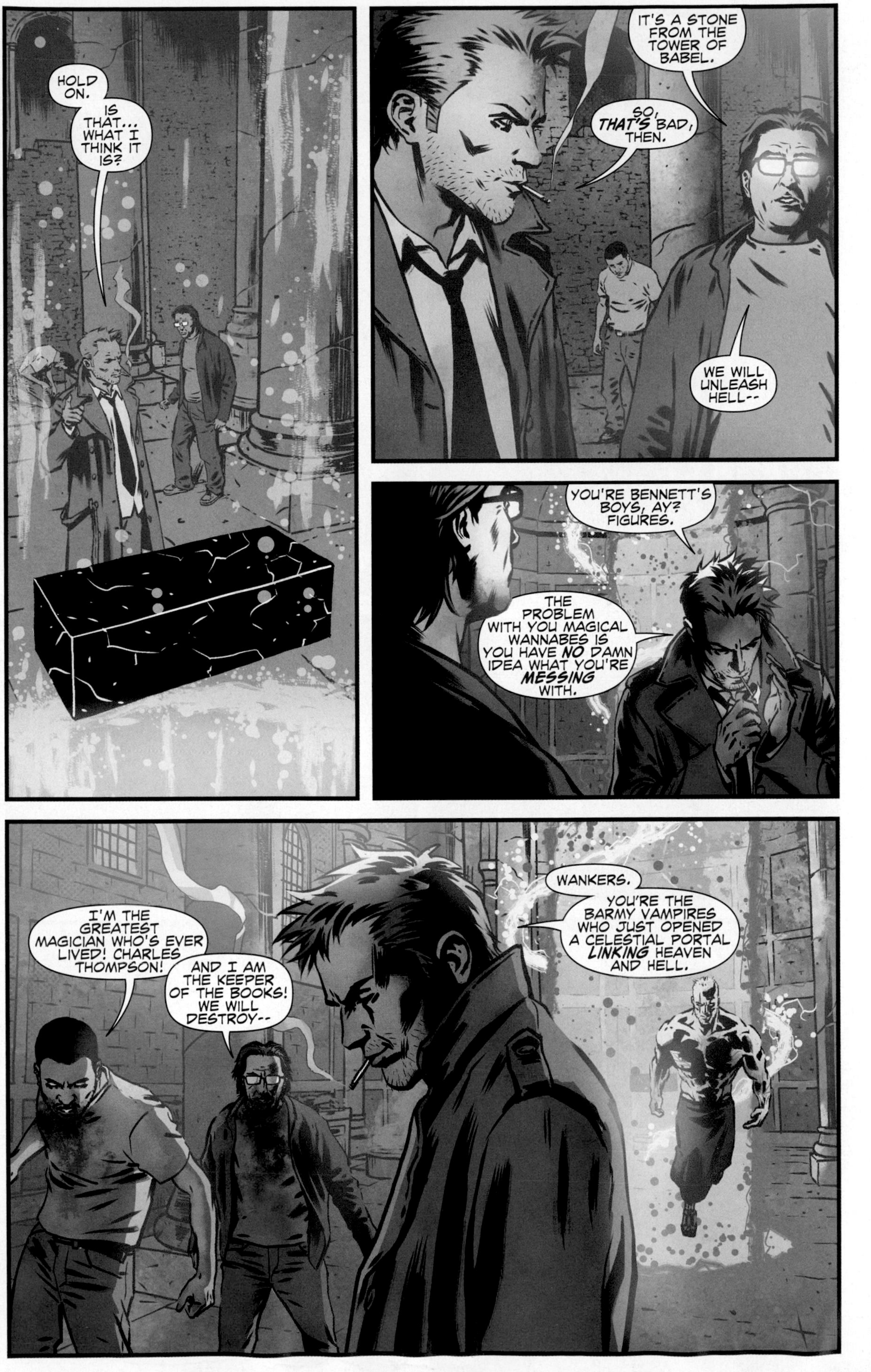
HOLD ON.
IS THAT... WHAT I THINK IT IS?
IT'S A STONE FROM THE TOWER OF BABEL.
SO, *THAT'S* BAD, THEN.
WE WILL UNLEASH HELL--
YOU'RE BENNETT'S BOYS, AY? FIGURES.
THE PROBLEM WITH YOU MAGICAL WANNABES IS YOU HAVE *NO* DAMN IDEA WHAT YOU'RE *MESSING* WITH.
I'M THE GREATEST MAGICIAN WHO'S EVER LIVED! CHARLES THOMPSON!
AND I AM THE KEEPER OF THE BOOKS! WE WILL DESTROY--
WANKERS.
YOU'RE THE BARMY VAMPIRES WHO JUST OPENED A CELESTIAL PORTAL *LINKING* HEAVEN AND HELL.

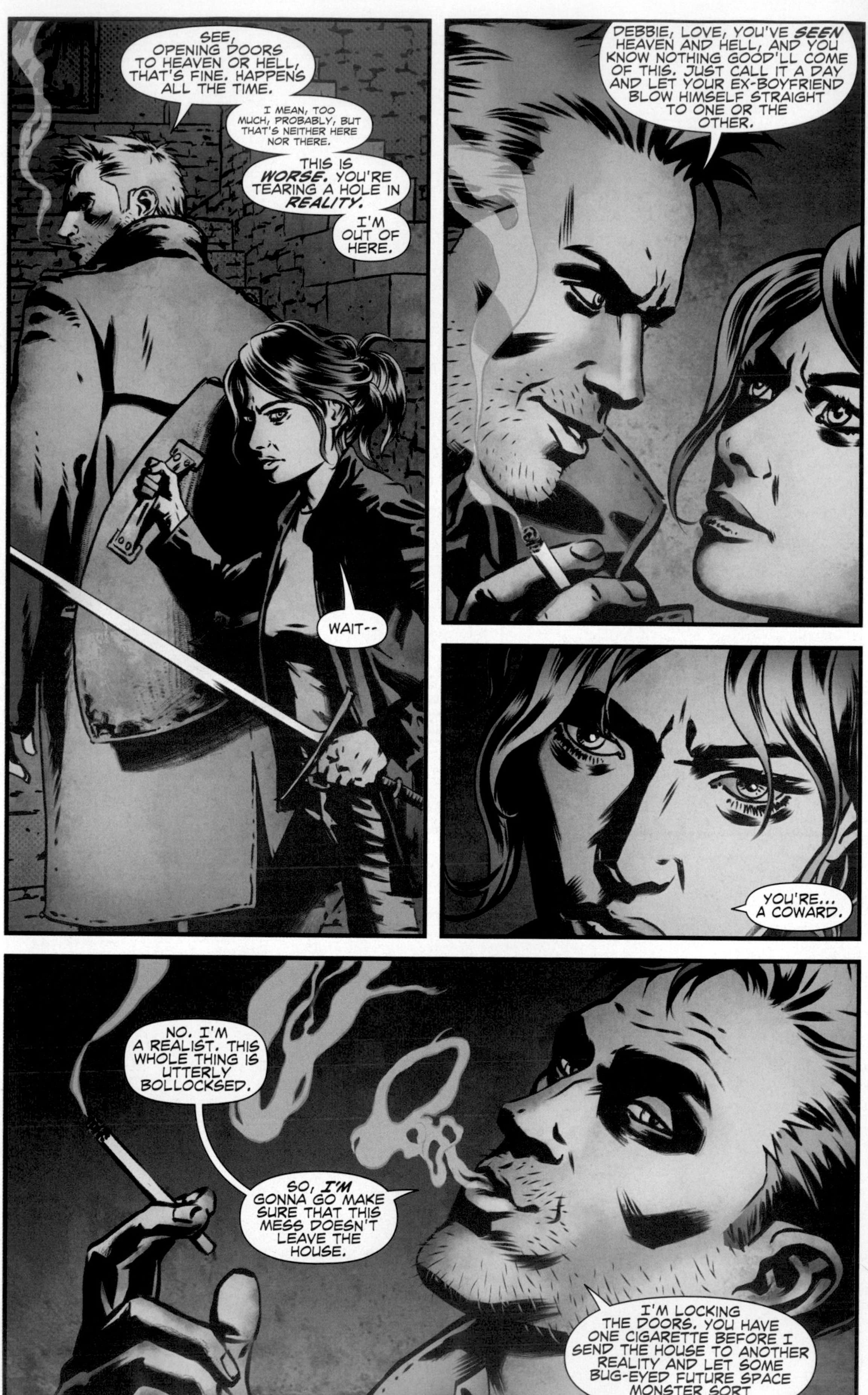
SEE, OPENING DOORS TO HEAVEN OR HELL, THAT'S FINE. HAPPENS ALL THE TIME.
I MEAN, TOO MUCH, PROBABLY, BUT THAT'S NEITHER HERE NOR THERE.
THIS IS WORSE. YOU'RE TEARING A HOLE IN REALITY.
I'M OUT OF HERE.
WAIT--
DEBBIE, LOVE, YOU'VE SEEN HEAVEN AND HELL, AND YOU KNOW NOTHING GOOD'LL COME OF THIS. JUST CALL IT A DAY AND LET YOUR EX-BOYFRIEND BLOW HIMSELF STRAIGHT TO ONE OR THE OTHER.
YOU'RE... A COWARD.
NO. I'M A REALIST. THIS WHOLE THING IS UTTERLY BOLLOCKSED.
SO, I'M GONNA GO MAKE SURE THAT THIS MESS DOESN'T LEAVE THE HOUSE.
I'M LOCKING THE DOORS. YOU HAVE ONE CIGARETTE BEFORE I SEND THE HOUSE TO ANOTHER REALITY AND LET SOME BUG-EYED FUTURE SPACE MONSTER SORT IT OUT.

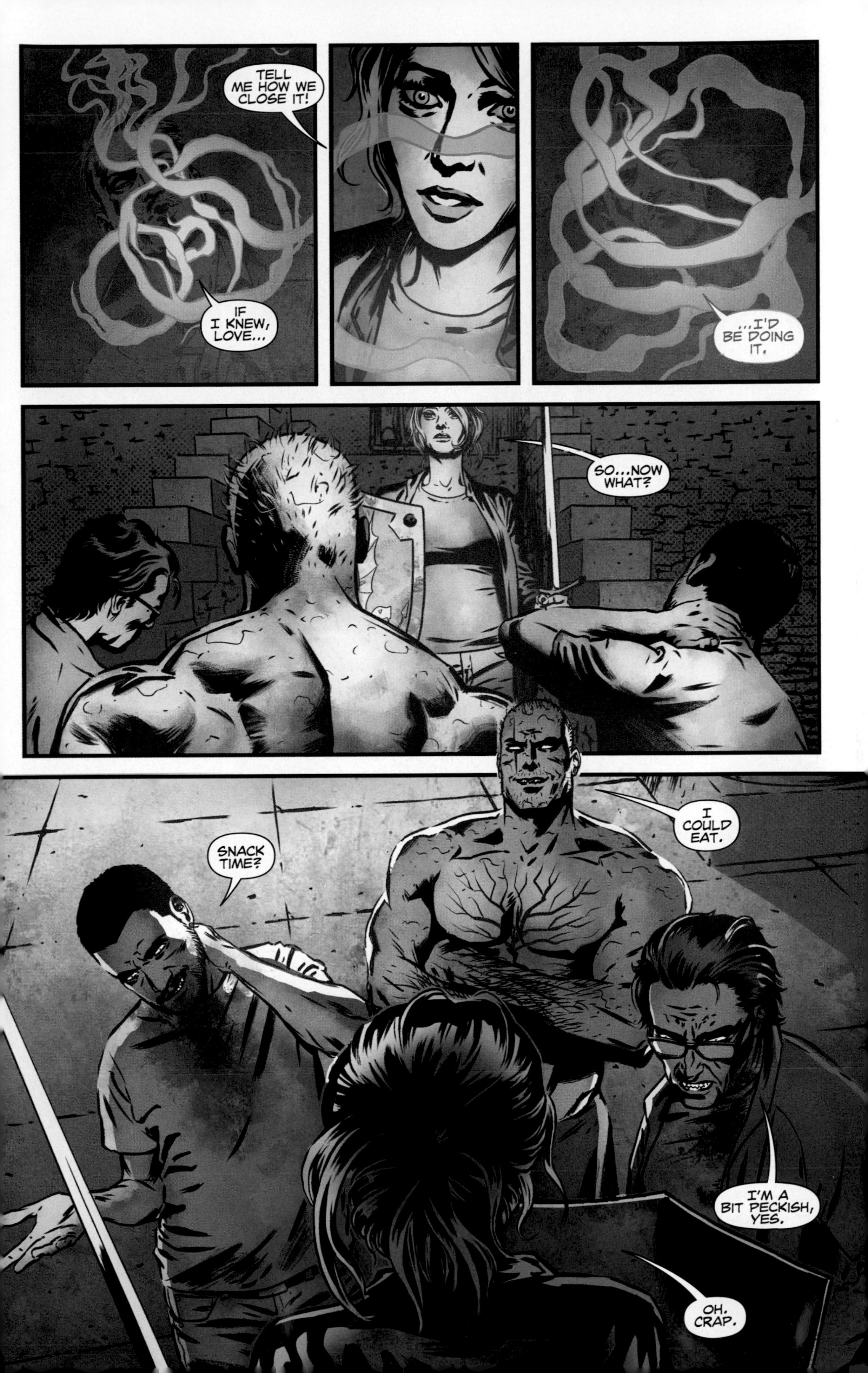
TELL ME HOW WE CLOSE IT!
IF I KNEW, LOVE...
...I'D BE DOING IT.
SO...NOW WHAT?
I COULD EAT.
SNACK TIME?
I'M A BIT PECKISH, YES.
OH. CRAP.

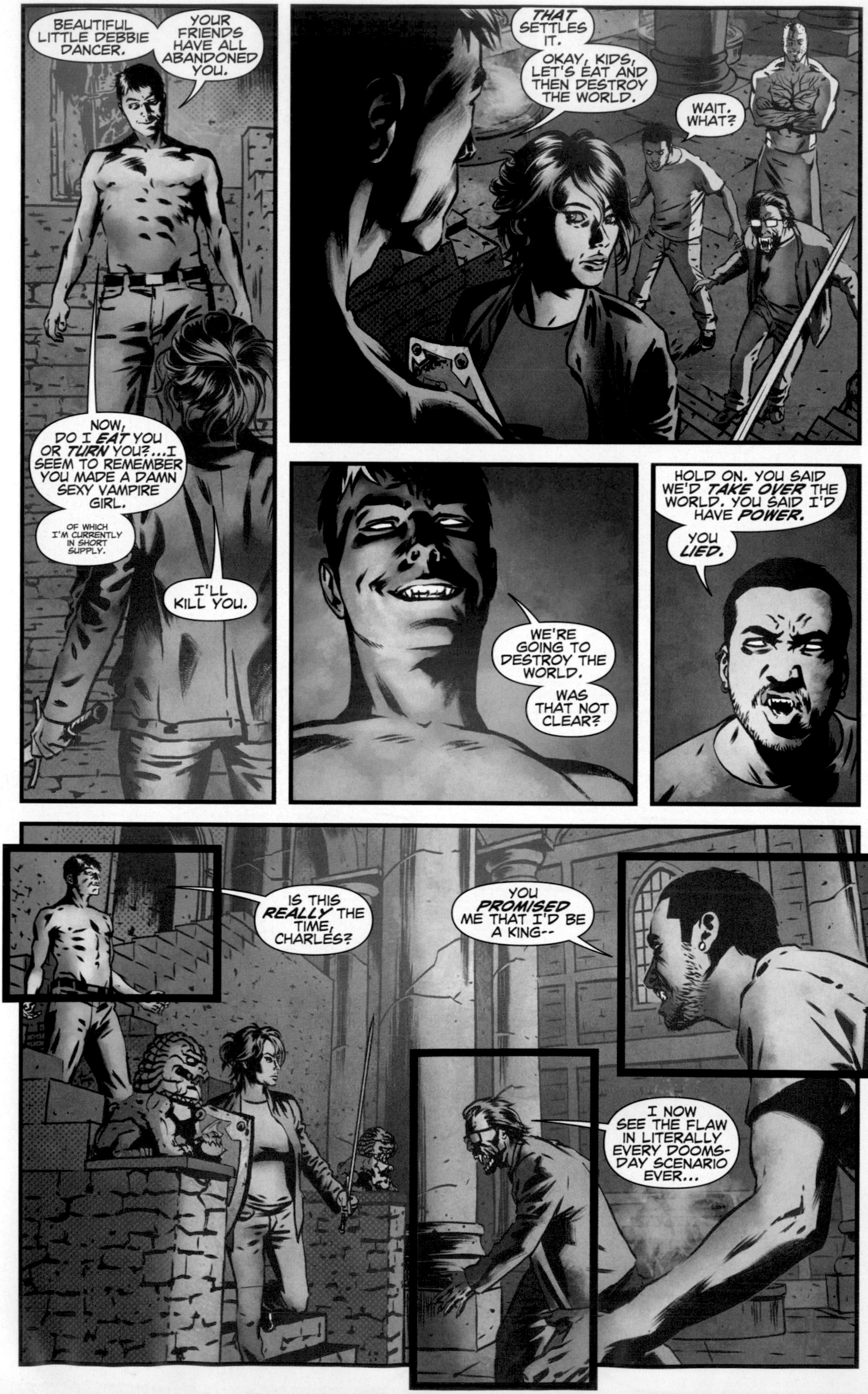
BEAUTIFUL LITTLE DEBBIE DANCER.
YOUR FRIENDS HAVE ALL ABANDONED YOU.
NOW, DO I *EAT* YOU OR *TURN* YOU?...I SEEM TO REMEMBER YOU MADE A DAMN SEXY VAMPIRE GIRL.
OF WHICH I'M CURRENTLY IN SHORT SUPPLY.
I'LL KILL YOU.
THAT SETTLES IT.
OKAY, KIDS, LET'S EAT AND THEN DESTROY THE WORLD.
WAIT. WHAT?
WE'RE GOING TO DESTROY THE WORLD.
WAS THAT NOT CLEAR?
HOLD ON. YOU SAID WE'D *TAKE OVER* THE WORLD. YOU SAID I'D HAVE *POWER.*
YOU *LIED.*
IS THIS *REALLY* THE TIME, CHARLES?
YOU *PROMISED* ME THAT I'D BE A KING--
I NOW SEE THE FLAW IN LITERALLY EVERY DOOMS-DAY SCENARIO EVER...

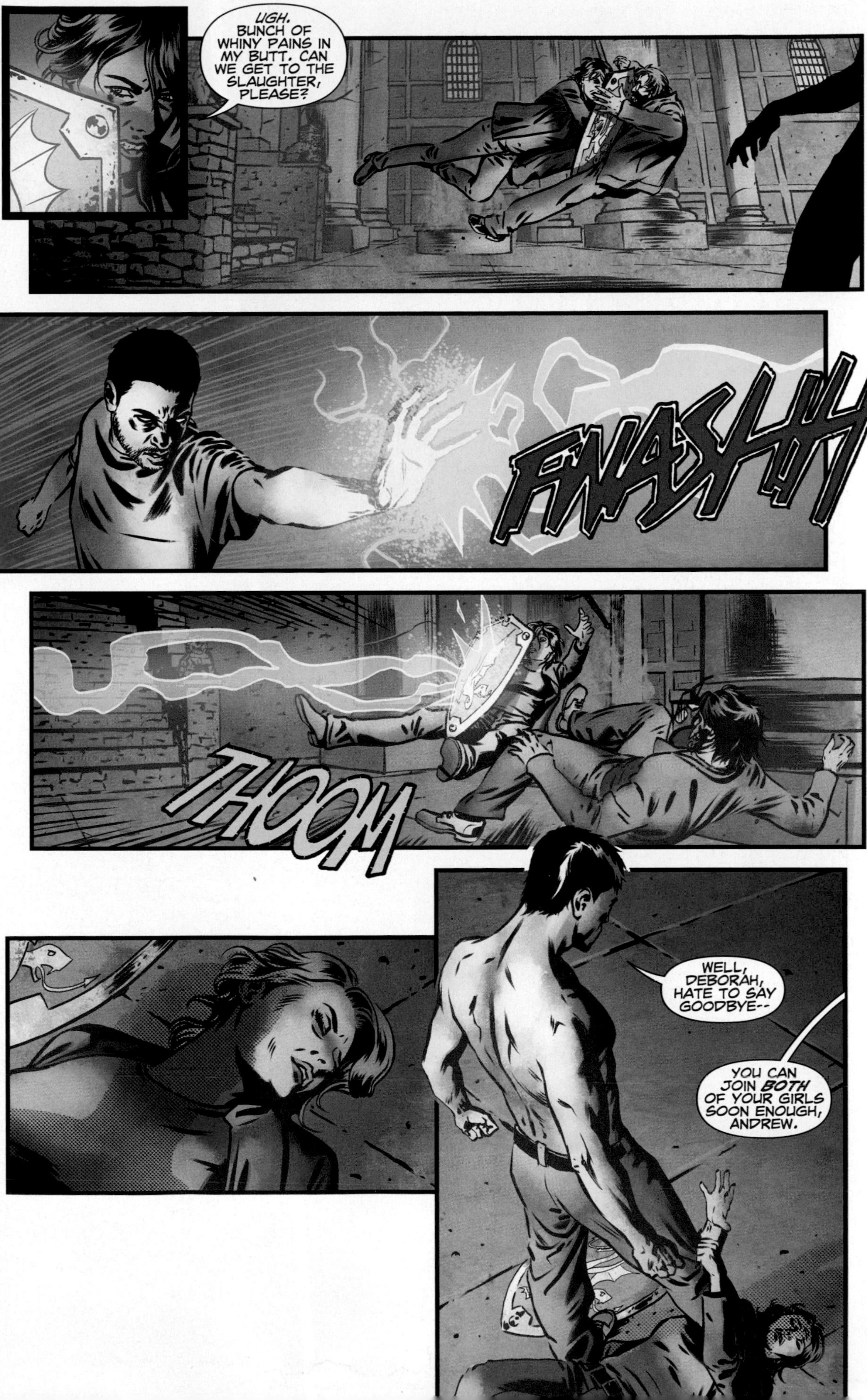
UGH. BUNCH OF WHINY PAINS IN MY BUTT. CAN WE GET TO THE SLAUGHTER, PLEASE?
FNASHH
THOOM
WELL, DEBORAH, HATE TO SAY GOODBYE--
YOU CAN JOIN BOTH OF YOUR GIRLS SOON ENOUGH, ANDREW.

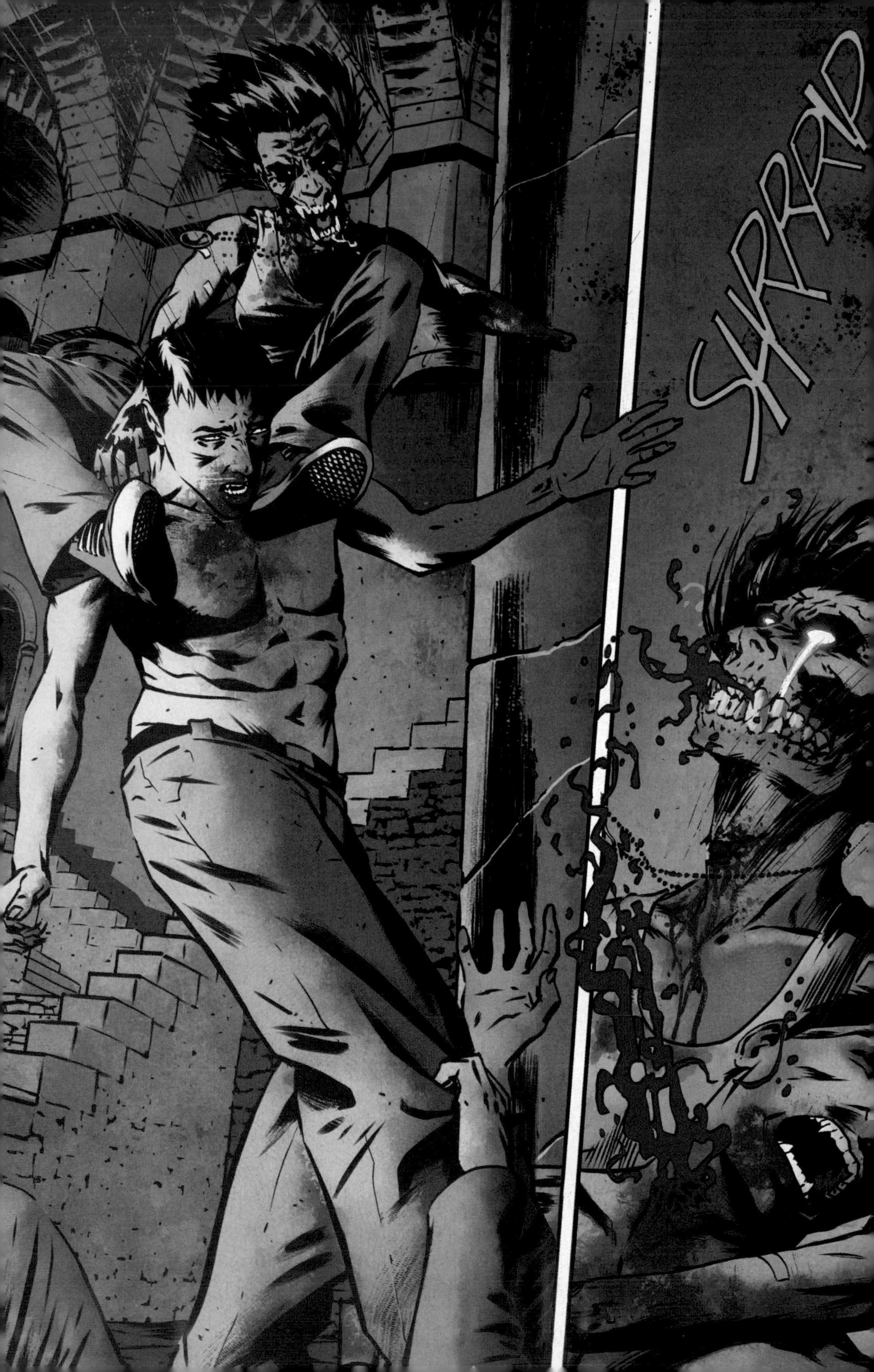
SHRRRD

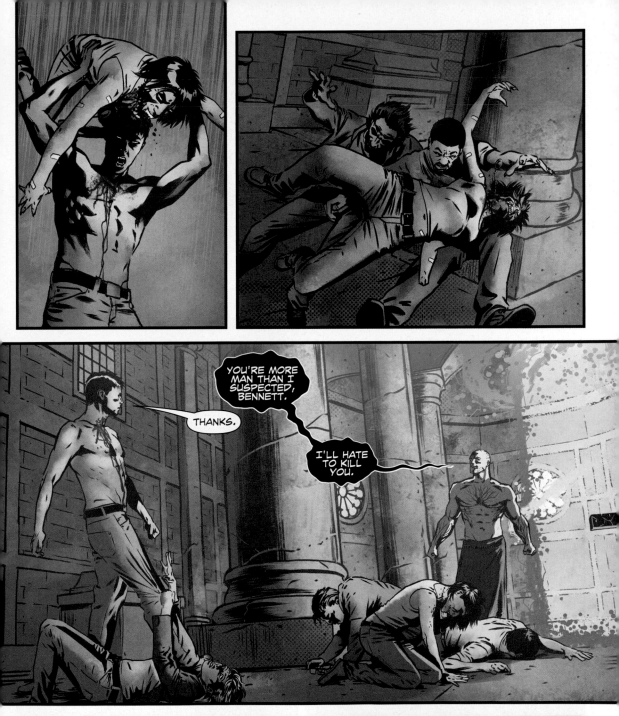

YOU'RE MORE MAN THAN I SUSPECTED, BENNETT.

THANKS.

I'LL HATE TO KILL YOU.

LOOK, CAIN, I'M NOT HAVING A GREAT DAY.

CAN'T WE JUST LET HEAVEN AND HELL COME CRASHING INTO EACH OTHER AND DESTROY THIS WORLD *TOGETHER?*

≣GAASSP≣ OH, GOD.

WHAT *HAPPENED* TO YOU? YOU WERE SO NOBLE, SO REGAL, AND NOW... SO *DARK.*

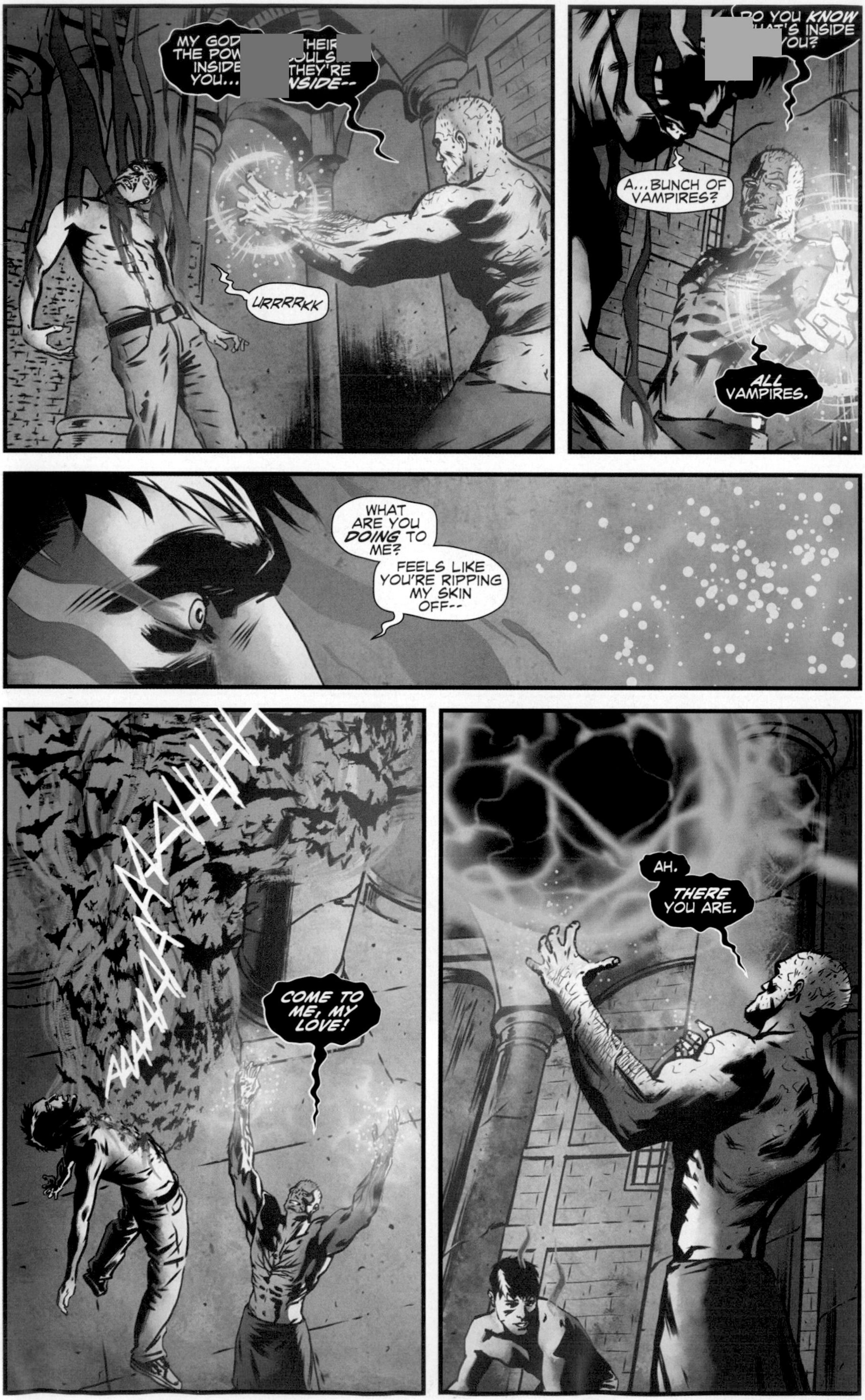

MY GOD THE POW INSIDE YOU... THEIR SOULS THEY'RE INSIDE--
URRRRKK
DO YOU KNOW WHAT'S INSIDE YOU?
A...BUNCH OF VAMPIRES?
ALL VAMPIRES.
WHAT ARE YOU DOING TO ME?
FEELS LIKE YOU'RE RIPPING MY SKIN OFF--
AAAAAAAAHHHH
COME TO ME, MY LOVE!
AH.
THERE YOU ARE.

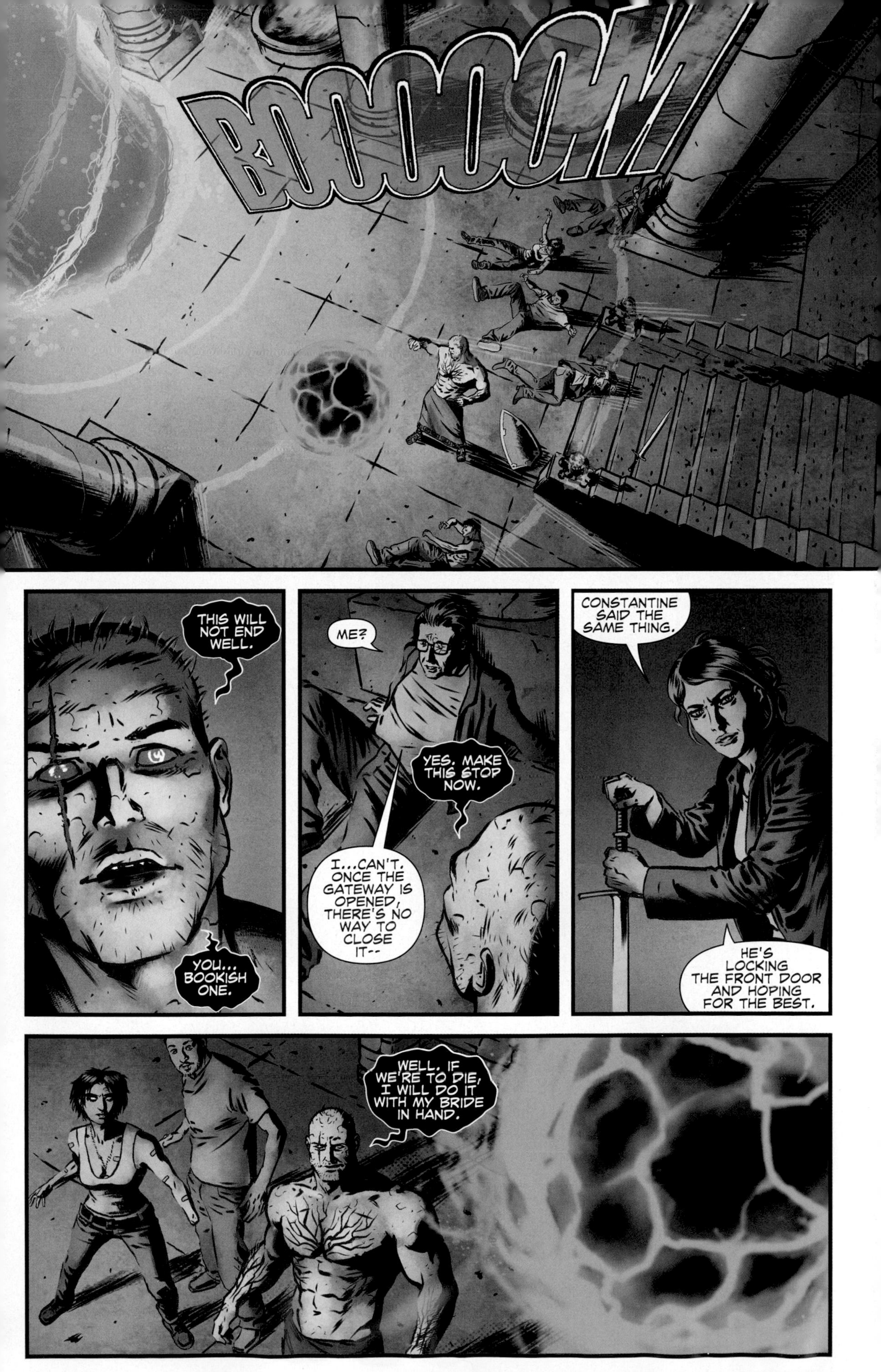
BOOOOOOM!!
THIS WILL NOT END WELL.
YOU... BOOKISH ONE.
ME?
YES. MAKE THIS STOP NOW.
I...CAN'T. ONCE THE GATEWAY IS OPENED, THERE'S NO WAY TO CLOSE IT--
CONSTANTINE SAID THE SAME THING.
HE'S LOCKING THE FRONT DOOR AND HOPING FOR THE BEST.
WELL. IF WE'RE TO DIE, I WILL DO IT WITH MY BRIDE IN HAND.

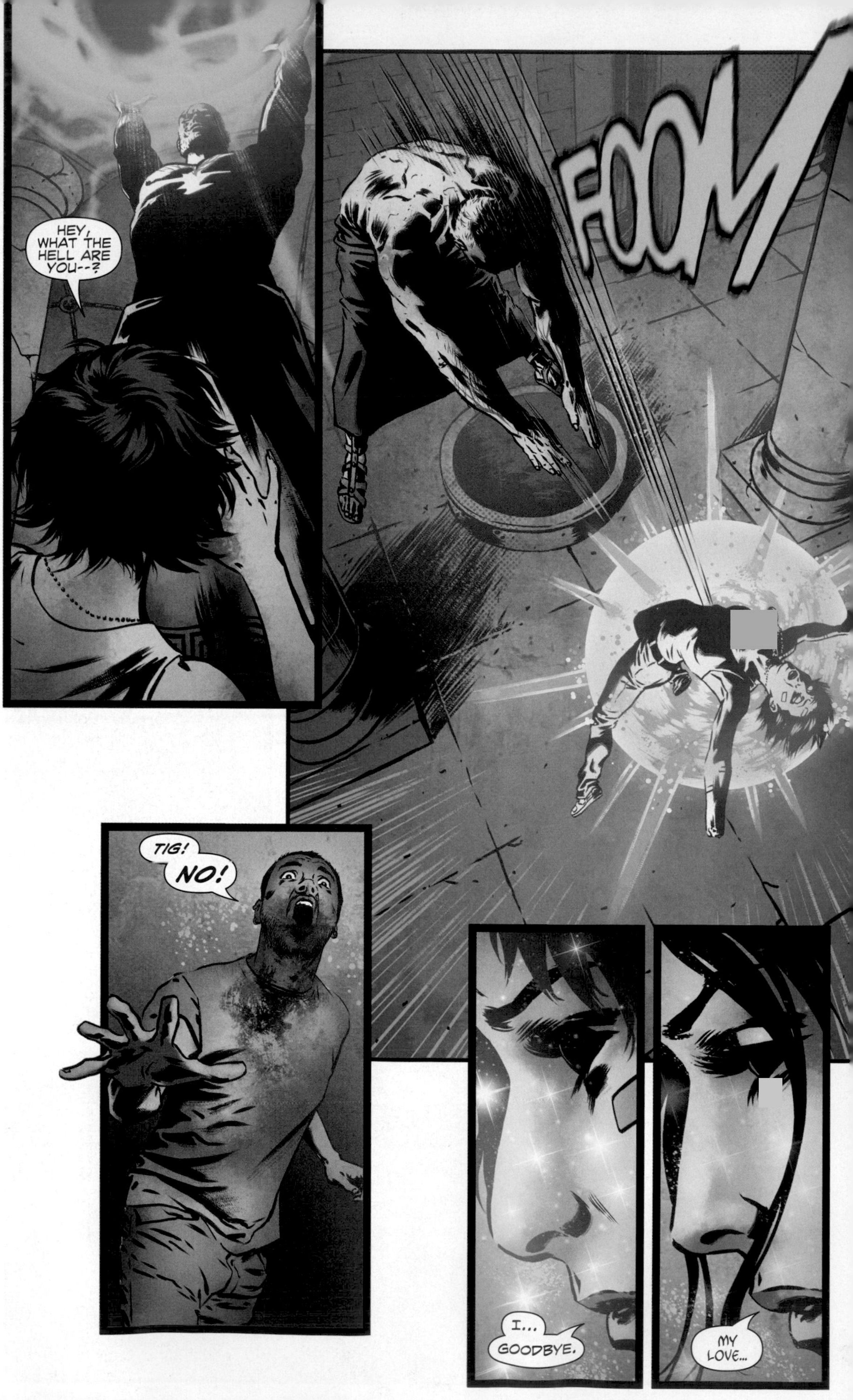
HEY, WHAT THE HELL ARE YOU--?
FOOM
TIG!
NO!
I... GOODBYE.
MY LOVE...

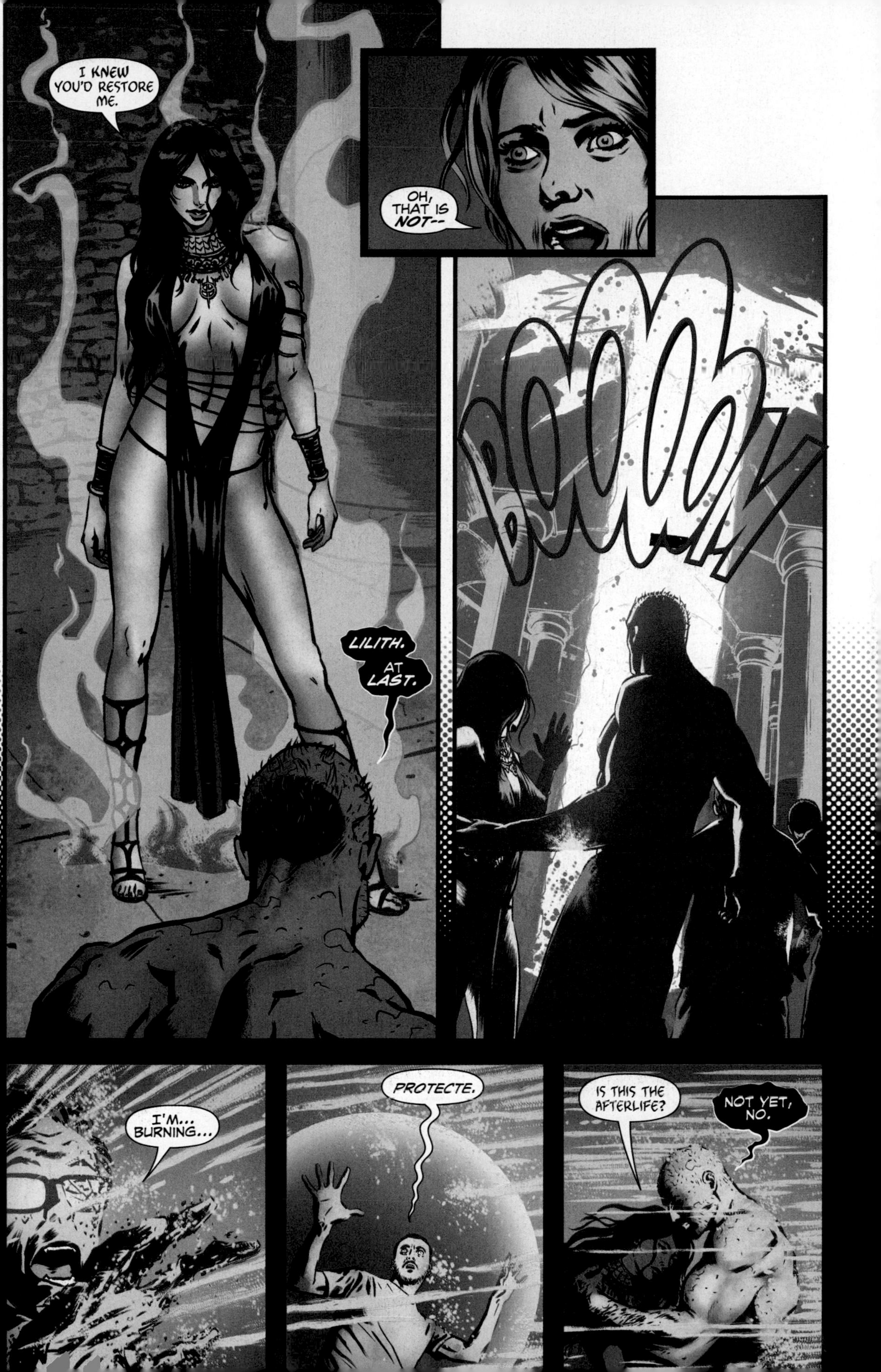
I KNEW YOU'D RESTORE ME.
OH, THAT IS NOT--
BOOOM
LILITH. AT LAST.
I'M... BURNING...
PROTECTE.
IS THIS THE AFTERLIFE?
NOT YET, NO.

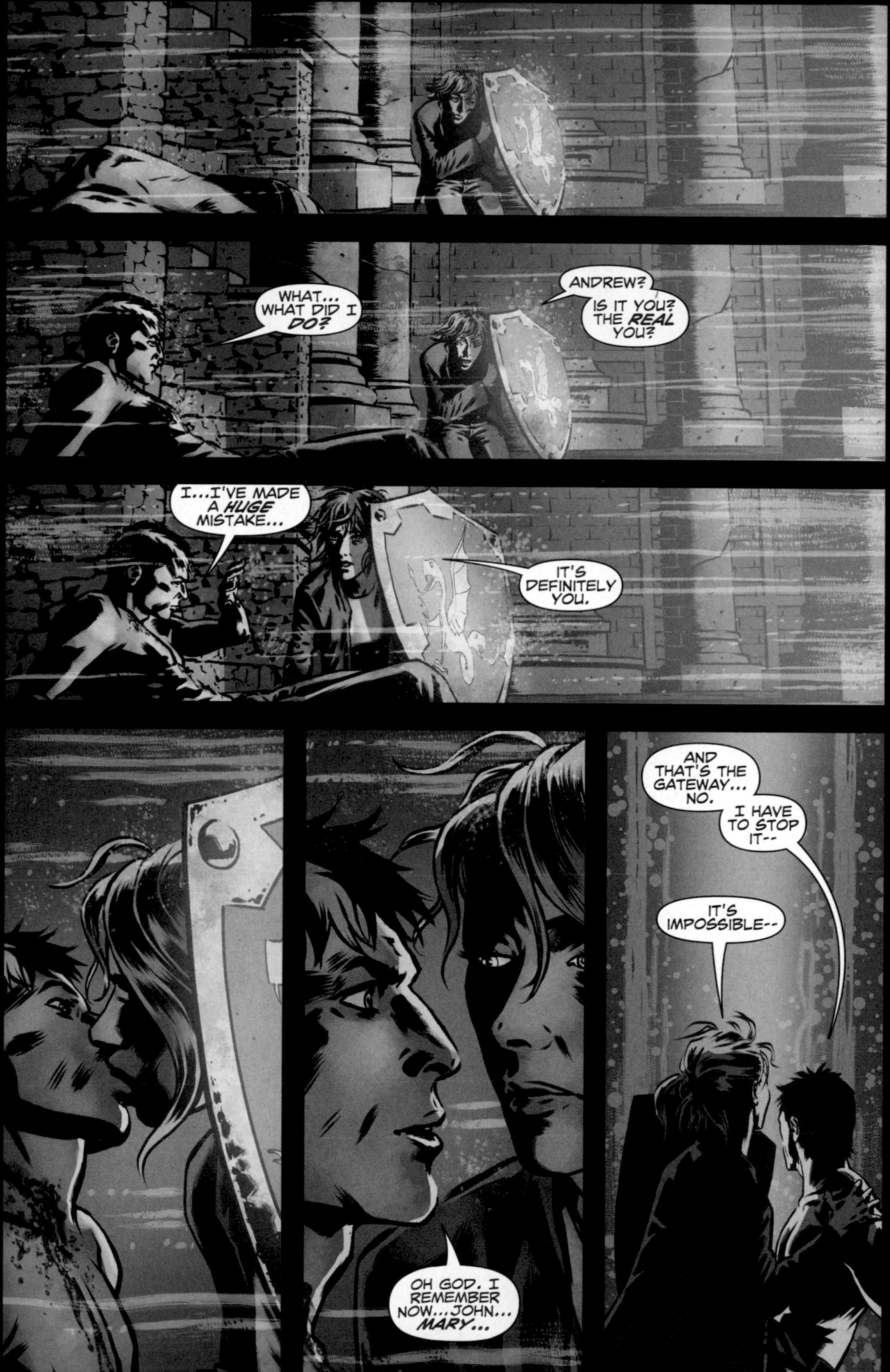
WHAT... WHAT DID I DO?
ANDREW?
IS IT YOU? THE REAL YOU?
I...I'VE MADE A HUGE MISTAKE...
IT'S DEFINITELY YOU.
OH GOD. I REMEMBER NOW...JOHN... MARY...
AND THAT'S THE GATEWAY... NO.
I HAVE TO STOP IT--
IT'S IMPOSSIBLE--

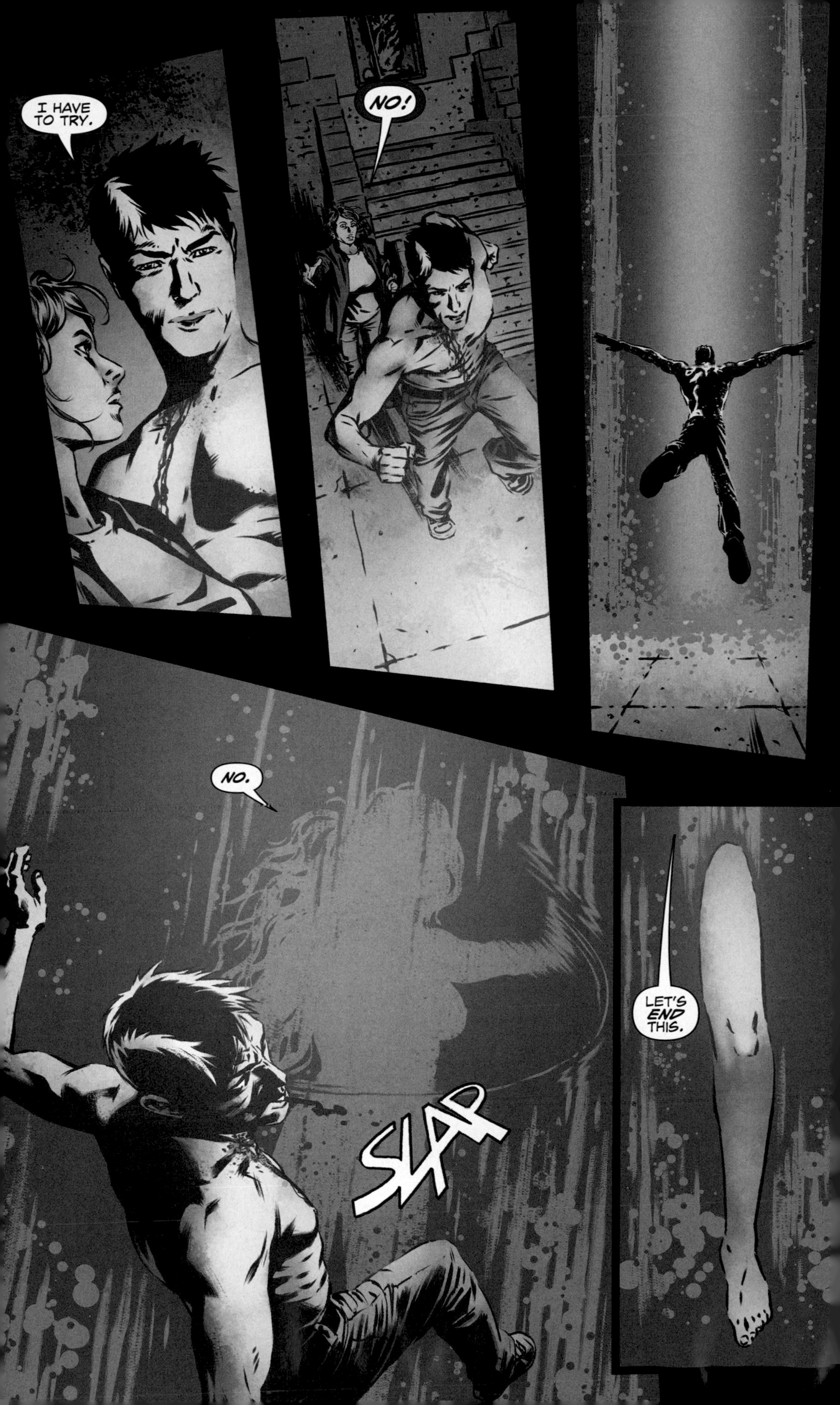
I HAVE TO TRY.
NO!
NO.
SLAP
LET'S END THIS.

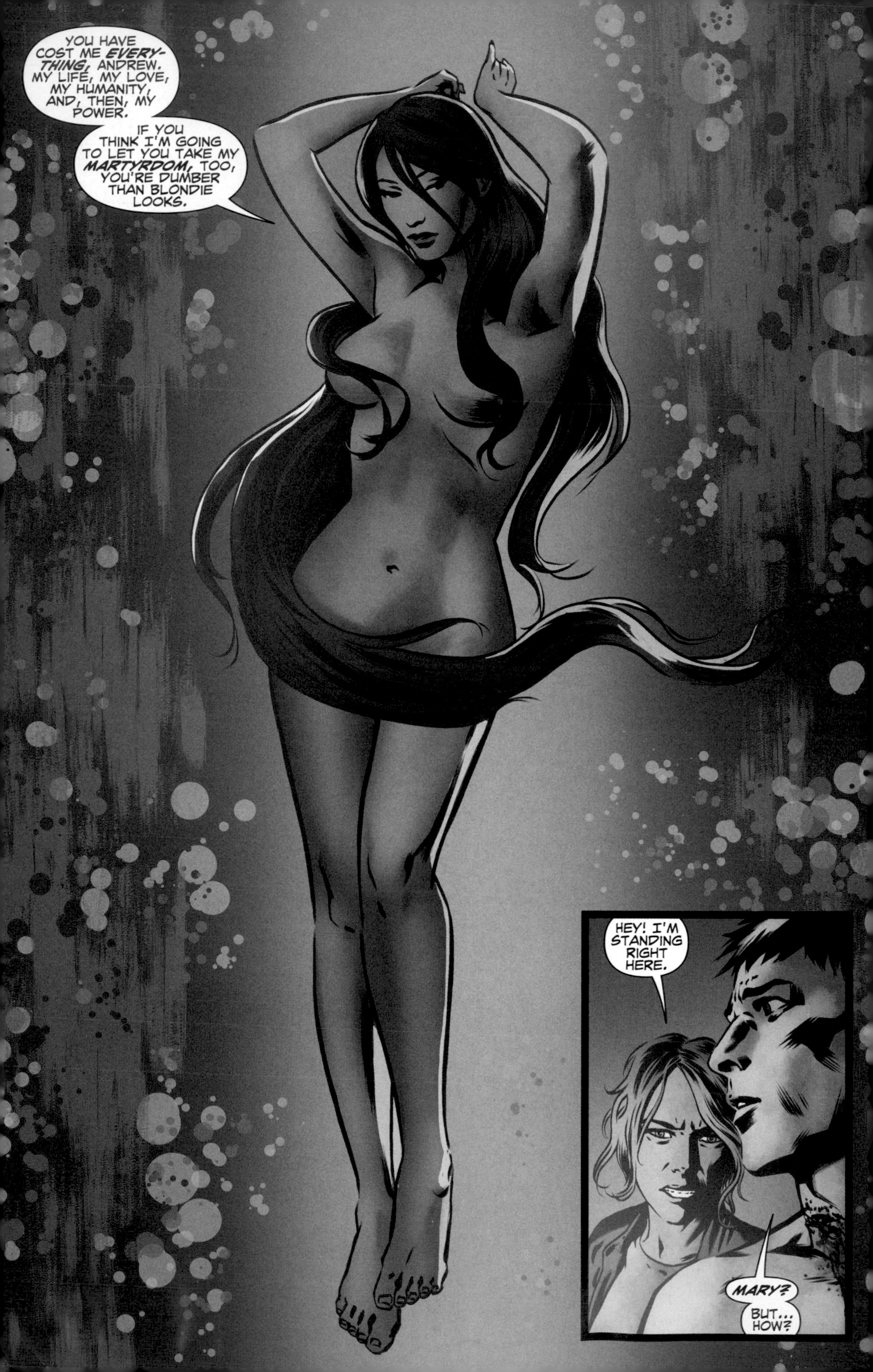
YOU HAVE COST ME EVERY-THING, ANDREW. MY LIFE, MY LOVE, MY HUMANITY, AND, THEN, MY POWER.
IF YOU THINK I'M GOING TO LET YOU TAKE MY MARTYRDOM, TOO, YOU'RE DUMBER THAN BLONDIE LOOKS.
HEY! I'M STANDING RIGHT HERE.
MARY?
BUT... HOW?

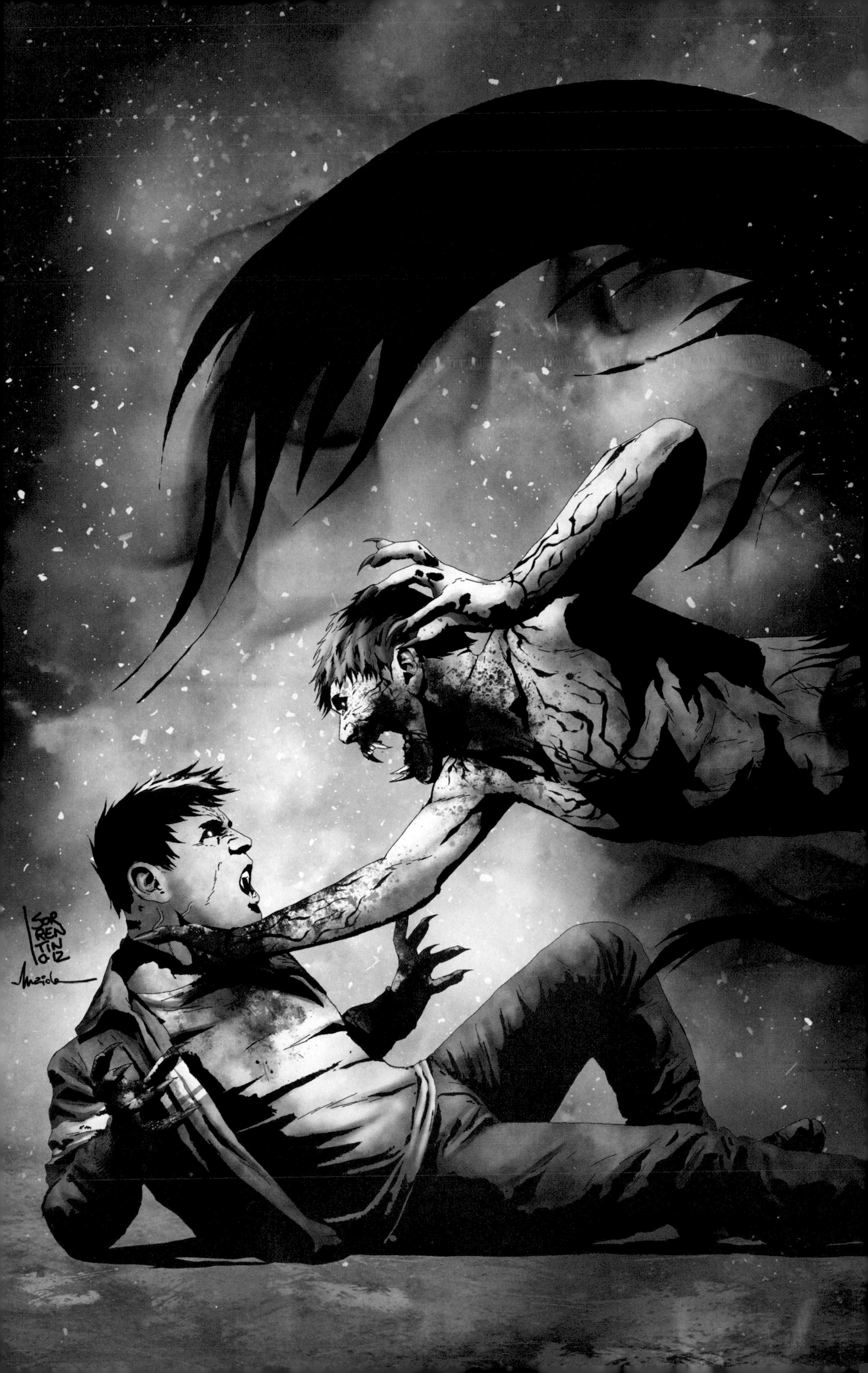
SOR
REN
TIN
O'12

CARIBOU

JOSHUA HALE FIALKOV writer FERNANDO BLANCO & ANDREA SORRENTINO artists cover art by ANDREA SORRENTINO & MARCELO MAIOLC

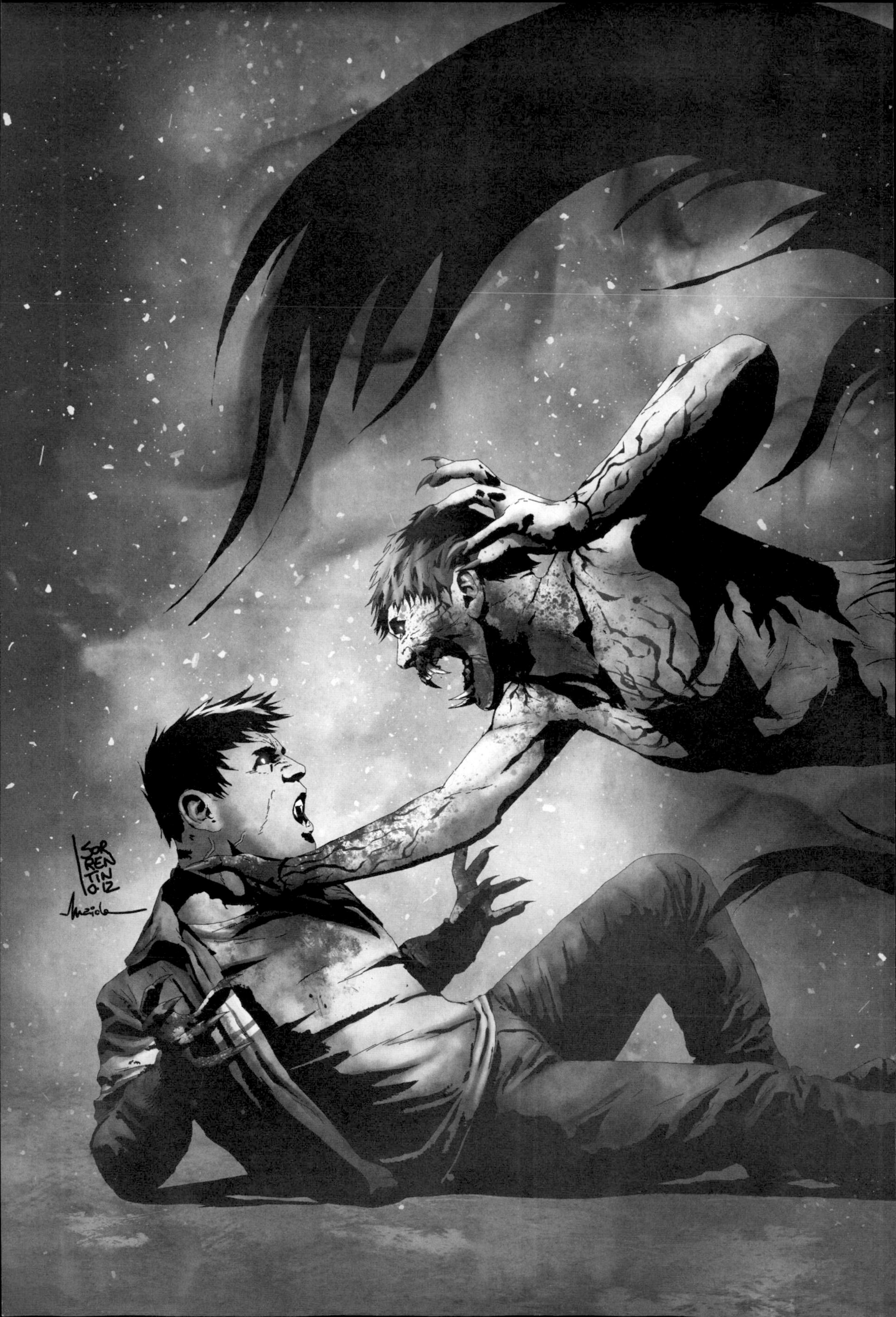
SORRENTINO 012

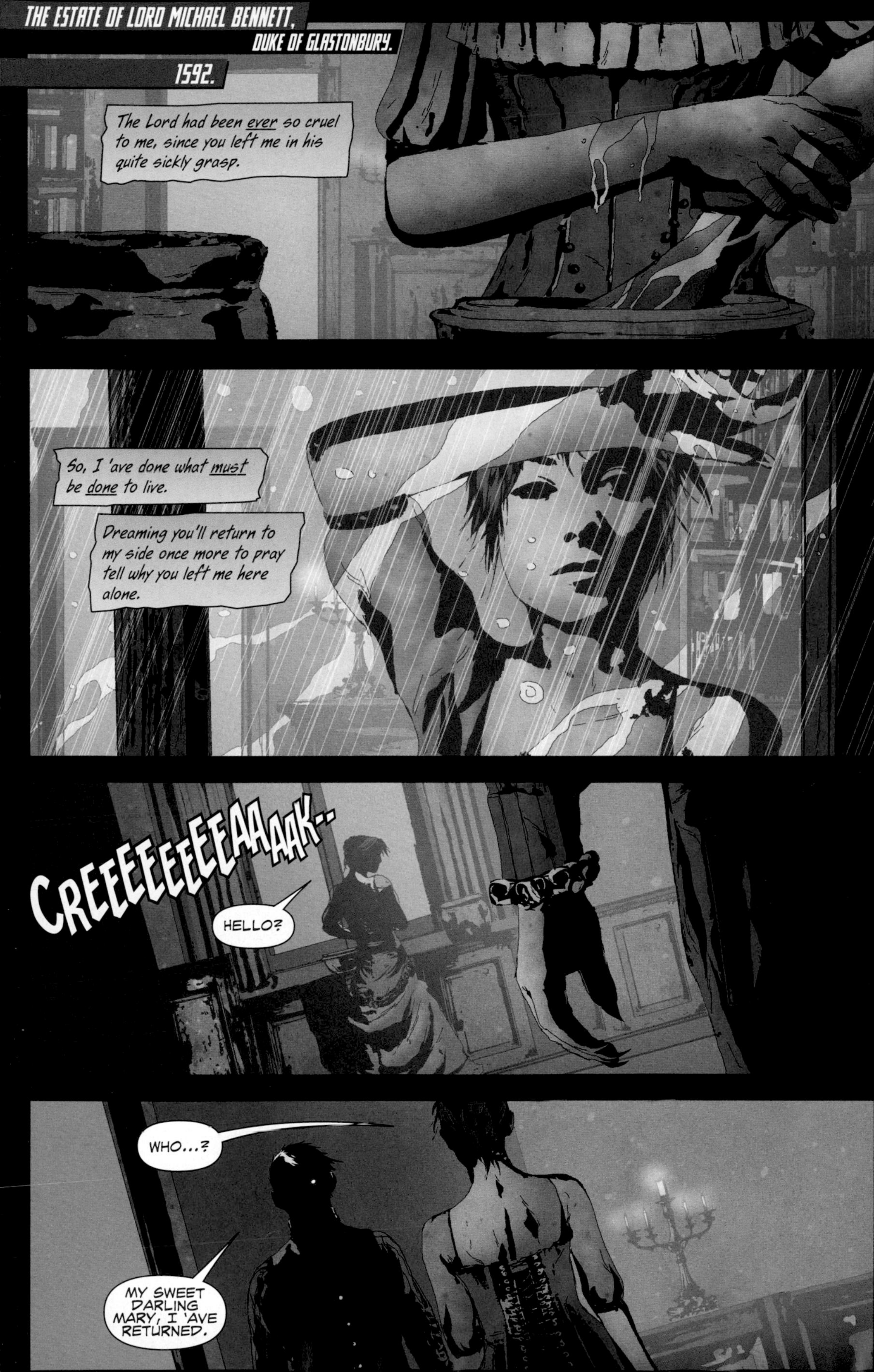
THE ESTATE OF LORD MICHAEL BENNETT,
DUKE OF GLASTONBURY.
1592.
The Lord had been ever so cruel to me, since you left me in his quite sickly grasp.
So, I 'ave done what must be done to live.
Dreaming you'll return to my side once more to pray tell why you left me here alone.
CREEEEEEEEAAAAK..
HELLO?
WHO...?
MY SWEET DARLING MARY, I 'AVE RETURNED.

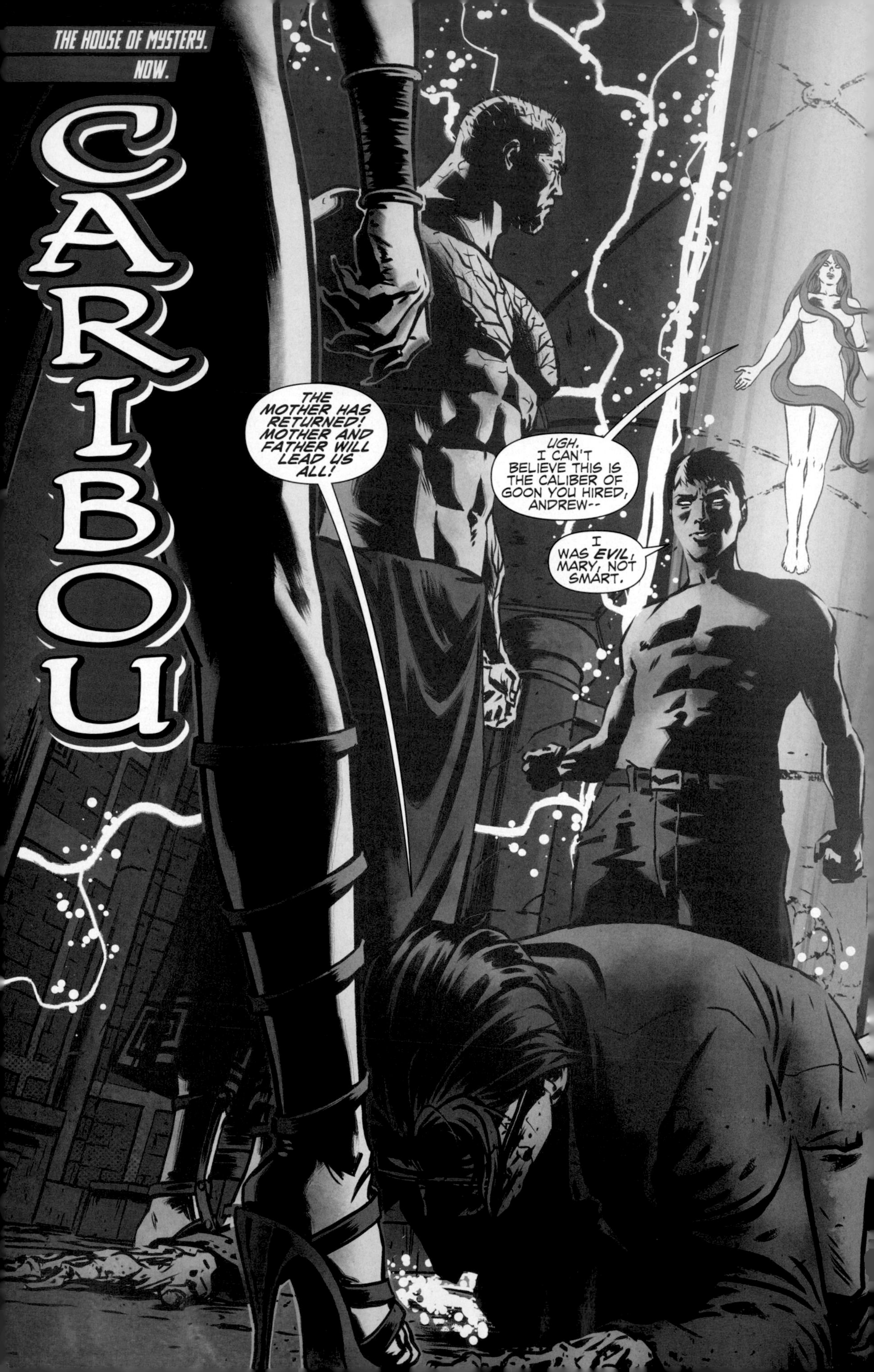
THE HOUSE OF MYSTERY.
NOW.
CARIBOU
THE MOTHER HAS RETURNED! MOTHER AND FATHER WILL LEAD US ALL!
UGH. I CAN'T BELIEVE THIS IS THE CALIBER OF GOON YOU HIRED, ANDREW--
I WAS EVIL, MARY, NOT SMART.

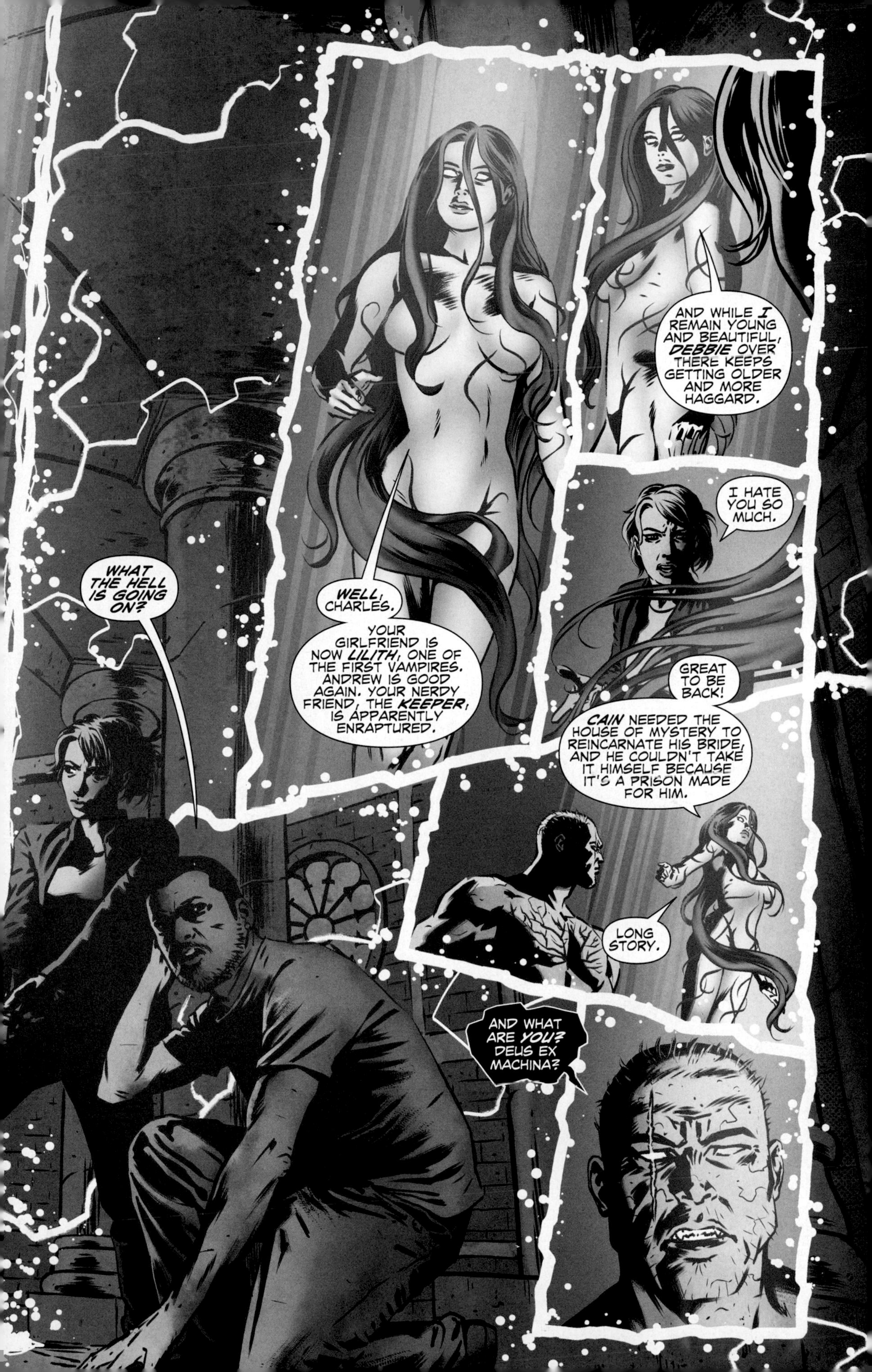
WELL, CHARLES.
YOUR GIRLFRIEND IS NOW LILITH, ONE OF THE FIRST VAMPIRES. ANDREW IS GOOD AGAIN. YOUR NERDY FRIEND, THE KEEPER, IS APPARENTLY ENRAPTURED.
AND WHILE I REMAIN YOUNG AND BEAUTIFUL, DEBBIE OVER THERE KEEPS GETTING OLDER AND MORE HAGGARD.
I HATE YOU SO MUCH.
GREAT TO BE BACK!
CAIN NEEDED THE HOUSE OF MYSTERY TO REINCARNATE HIS BRIDE, AND HE COULDN'T TAKE IT HIMSELF BECAUSE IT'S A PRISON MADE FOR HIM.
WHAT THE HELL IS GOING ON?
LONG STORY.
AND WHAT ARE YOU? DEUS EX MACHINA?

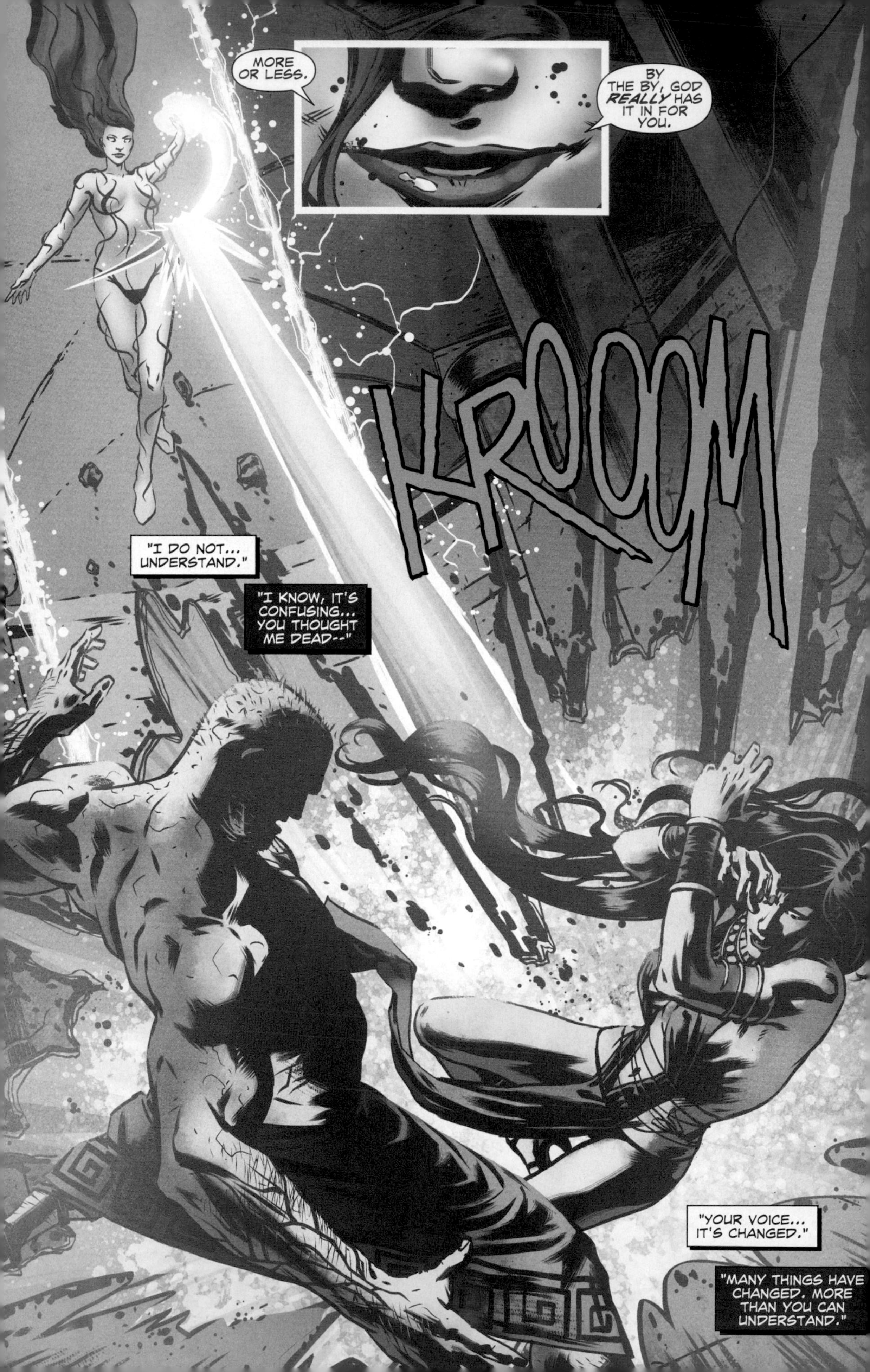
MORE OR LESS.
BY THE BY, GOD REALLY HAS IT IN FOR YOU.
KROOOM
"I DO NOT... UNDERSTAND."
"I KNOW, IT'S CONFUSING... YOU THOUGHT ME DEAD--"
"YOUR VOICE... IT'S CHANGED."
"MANY THINGS HAVE CHANGED. MORE THAN YOU CAN UNDERSTAND."

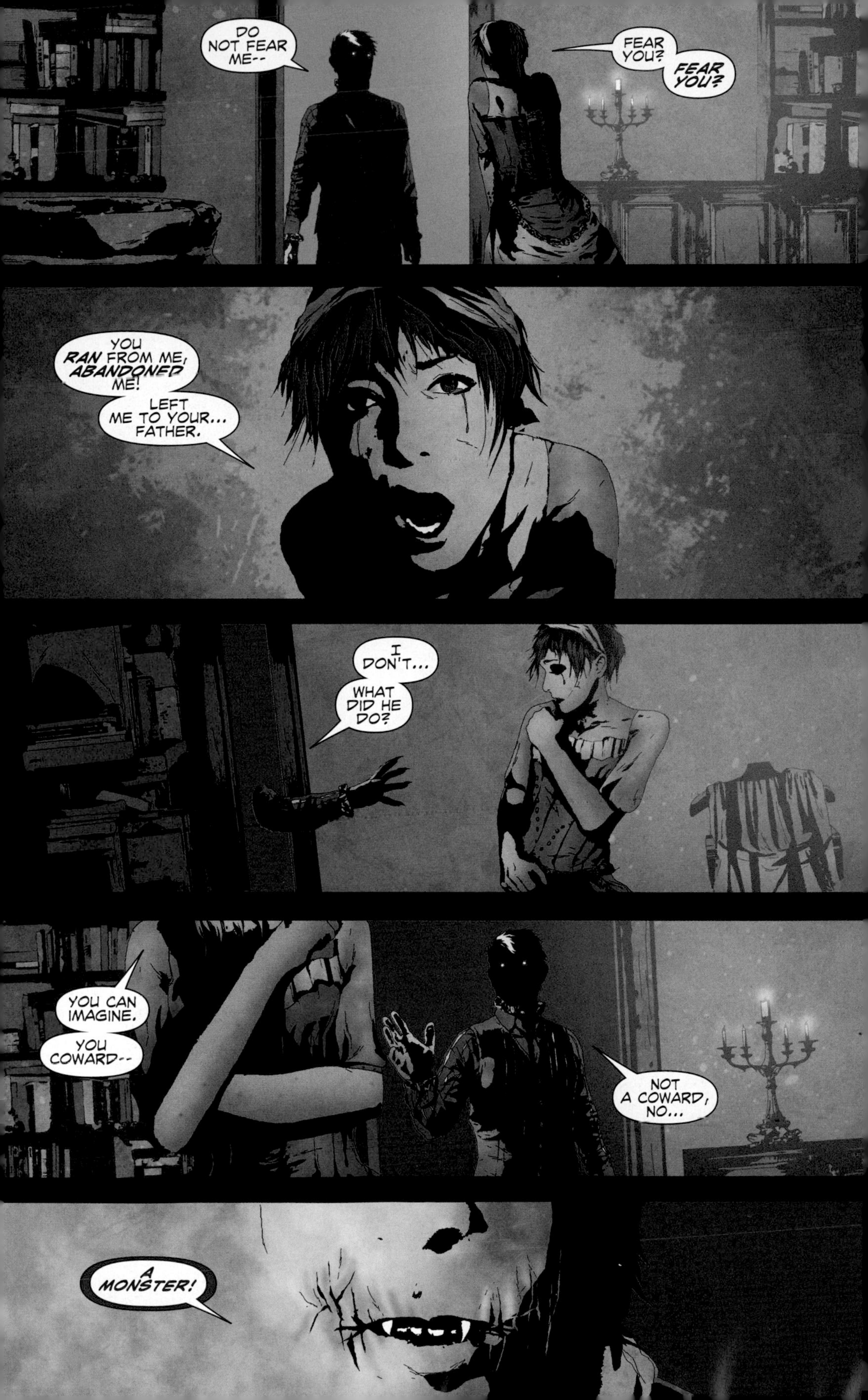

DO NOT FEAR ME--
FEAR YOU? FEAR YOU?
YOU RAN FROM ME, ABANDONED ME!
LEFT ME TO YOUR... FATHER.
I DON'T...
WHAT DID HE DO?
YOU CAN IMAGINE.
YOU COWARD--
NOT A COWARD, NO...
A MONSTER!

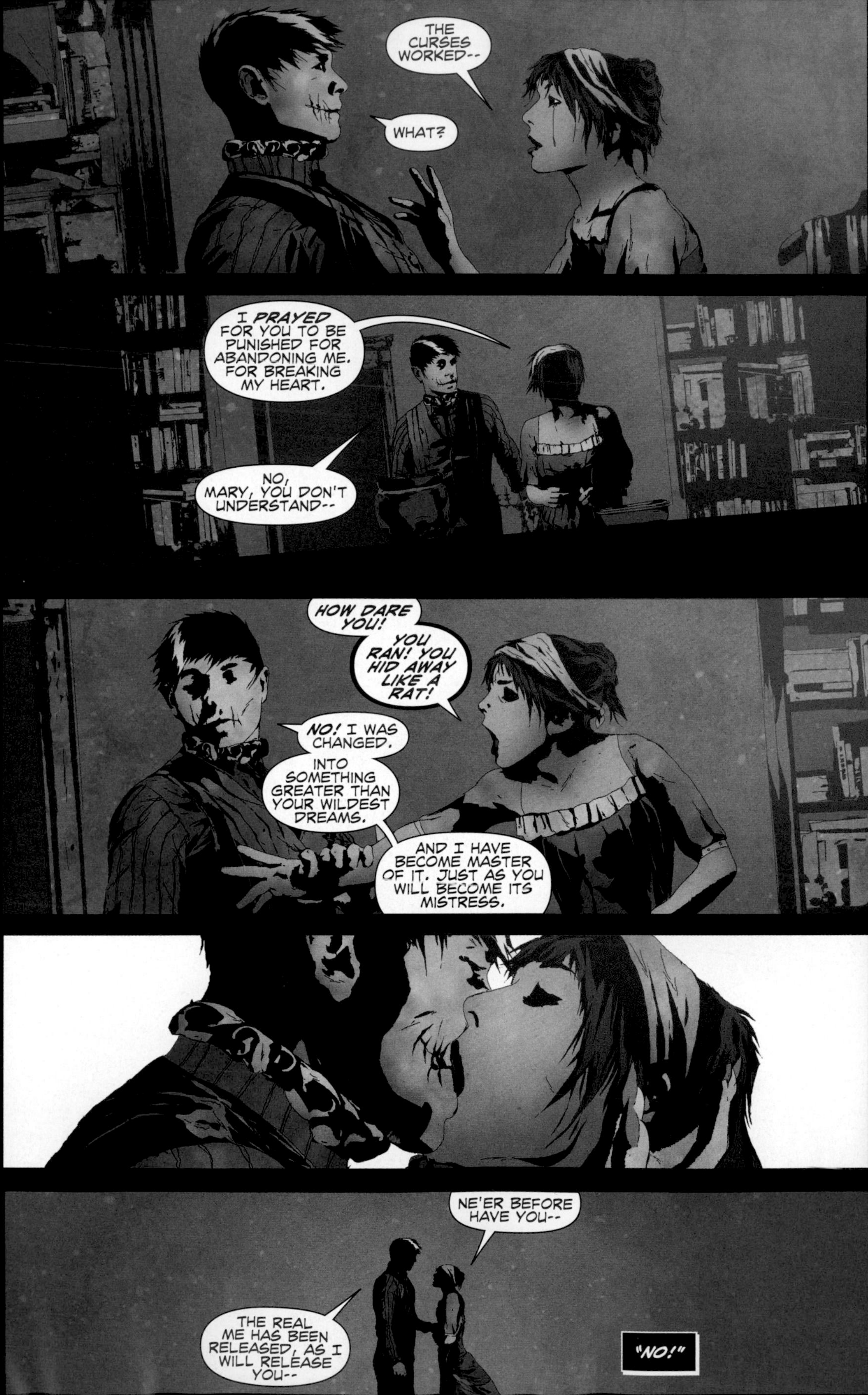

THE CURSES WORKED--
WHAT?
I *PRAYED* FOR YOU TO BE PUNISHED FOR ABANDONING ME. FOR BREAKING MY HEART.
NO, MARY, YOU DON'T UNDERSTAND--
HOW DARE YOU!
YOU RAN! YOU HID AWAY LIKE A RAT!
NO! I WAS CHANGED.
INTO SOMETHING GREATER THAN YOUR WILDEST DREAMS.
AND I HAVE BECOME MASTER OF IT. JUST AS YOU WILL BECOME ITS MISTRESS.
NE'ER BEFORE HAVE YOU--
THE REAL ME HAS BEEN RELEASED, AS I WILL RELEASE YOU--
"NO!"

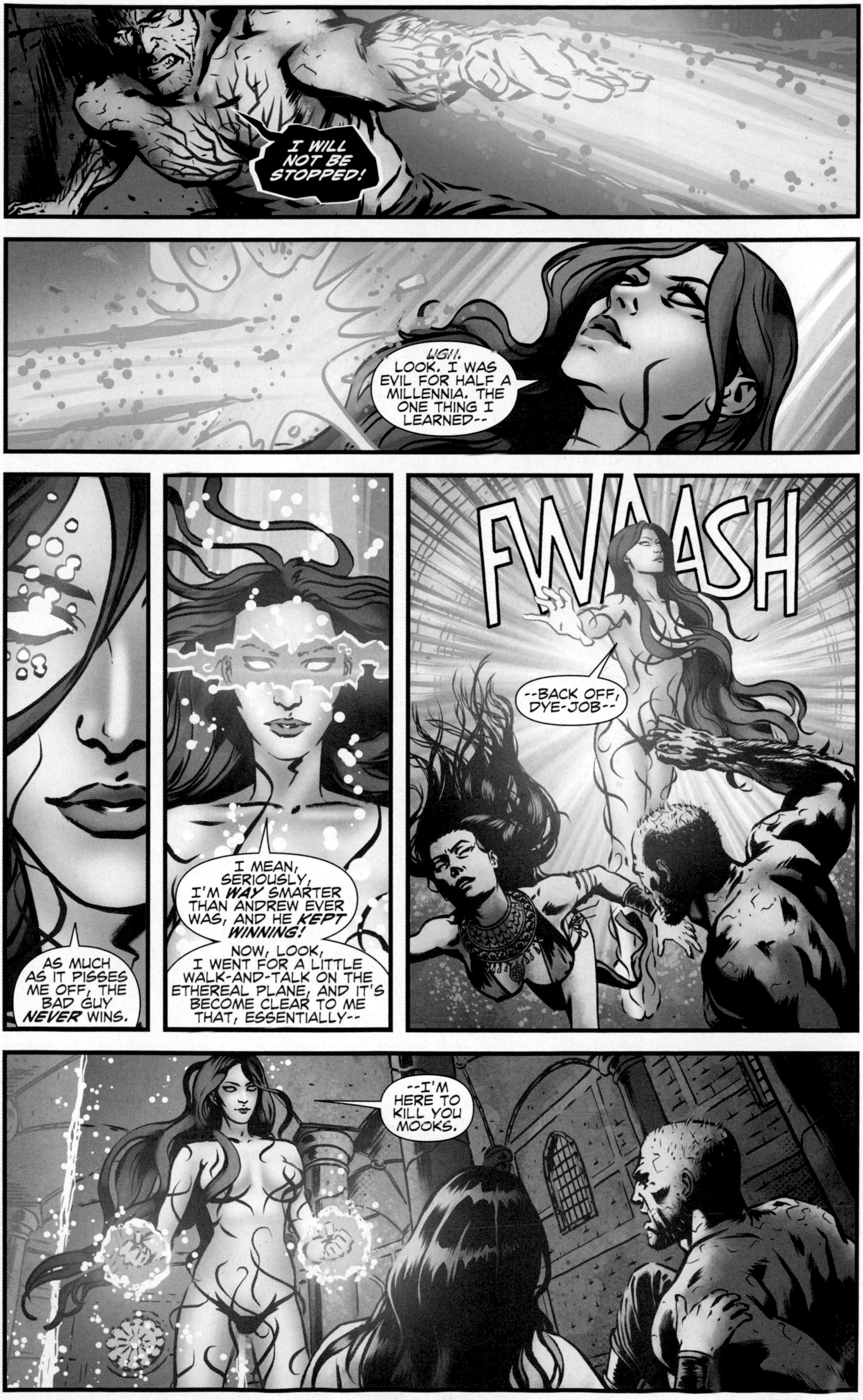
I WILL NOT BE STOPPED!
UGH. LOOK. I WAS EVIL FOR HALF A MILLENNIA. THE ONE THING I LEARNED--
AS MUCH AS IT PISSES ME OFF, THE BAD GUY NEVER WINS.
I MEAN, SERIOUSLY, I'M WAY SMARTER THAN ANDREW EVER WAS, AND HE KEPT WINNING!
NOW, LOOK, I WENT FOR A LITTLE WALK-AND-TALK ON THE ETHEREAL PLANE, AND IT'S BECOME CLEAR TO ME THAT, ESSENTIALLY--
FWAASH
--BACK OFF, DYE-JOB--
--I'M HERE TO KILL YOU MOOKS.

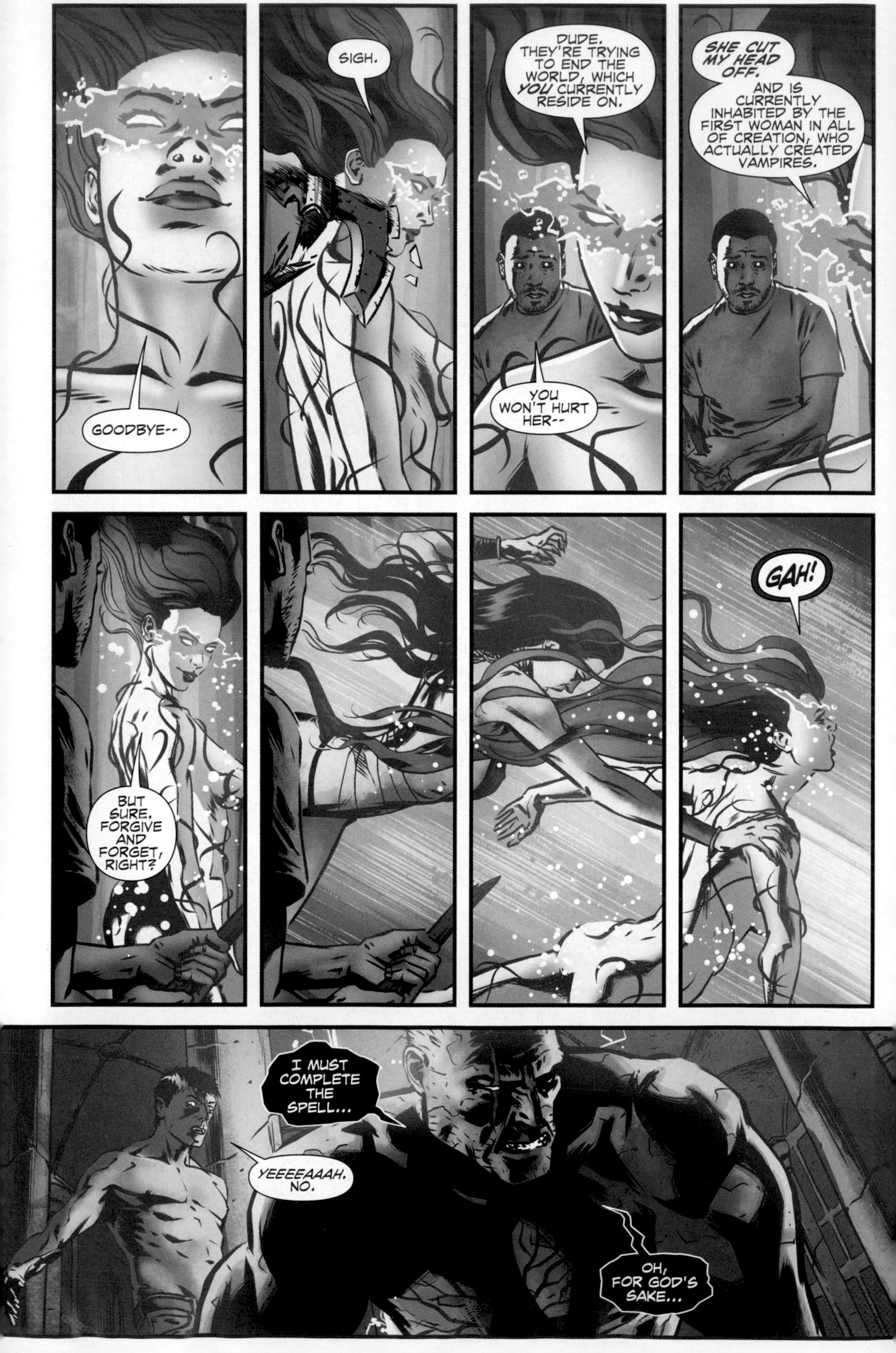
GOODBYE--
SIGH.
DUDE. THEY'RE TRYING TO END THE WORLD, WHICH YOU CURRENTLY RESIDE ON.
YOU WON'T HURT HER--
SHE CUT MY HEAD OFF.
AND IS CURRENTLY INHABITED BY THE FIRST WOMAN IN ALL OF CREATION, WHO ACTUALLY CREATED VAMPIRES.
BUT SURE. FORGIVE AND FORGET, RIGHT?
GAH!
I MUST COMPLETE THE SPELL...
YEEEEAAAH. NO.
OH, FOR GOD'S SAKE...

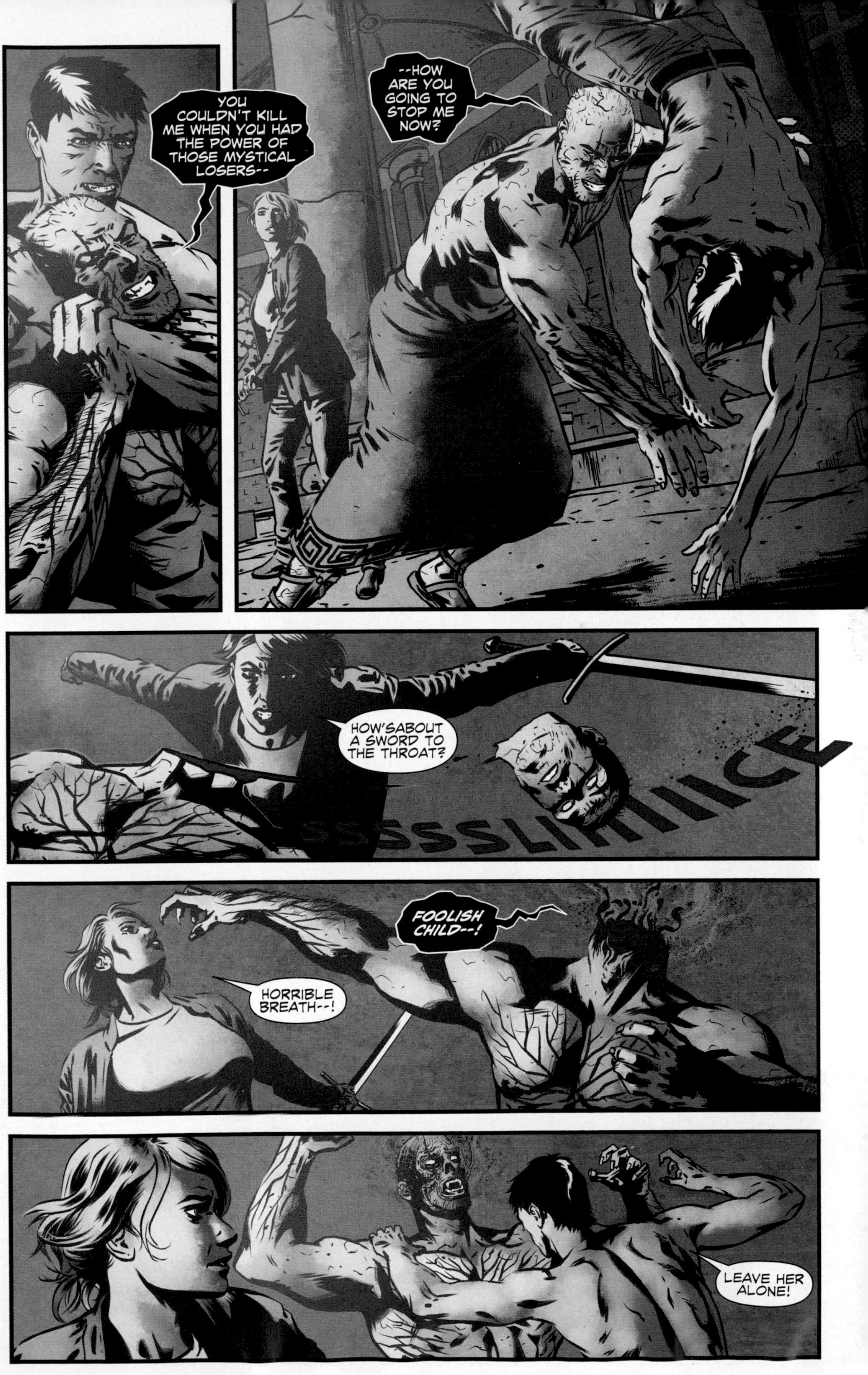
YOU COULDN'T KILL ME WHEN YOU HAD THE POWER OF THOSE MYSTICAL LOSERS--
--HOW ARE YOU GOING TO STOP ME NOW?
HOW'SABOUT A SWORD TO THE THROAT?
SSSSSLIIIIIICE
FOOLISH CHILD--!
HORRIBLE BREATH--!
LEAVE HER ALONE!

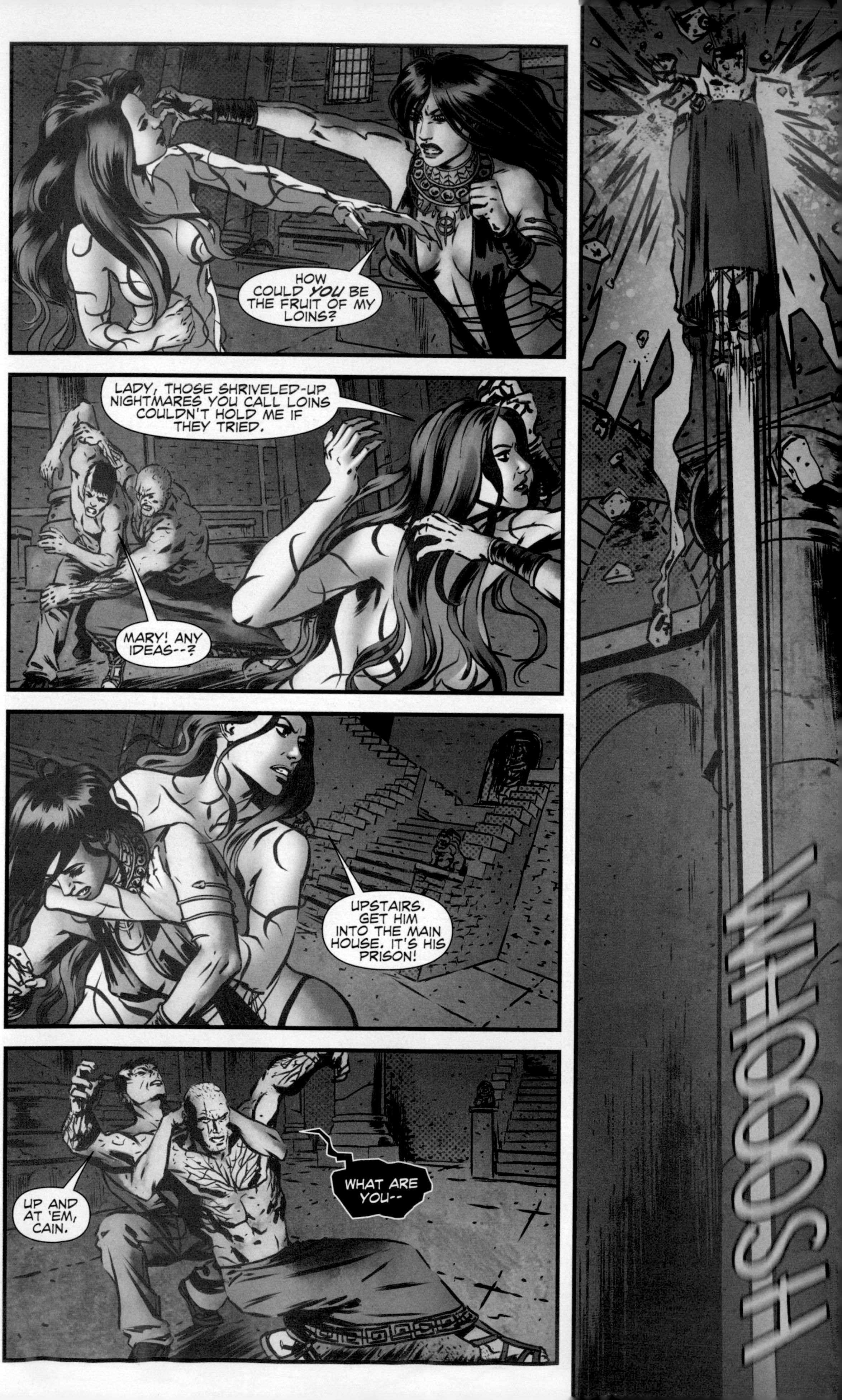
HOW COULD YOU BE THE FRUIT OF MY LOINS?
LADY, THOSE SHRIVELED-UP NIGHTMARES YOU CALL LOINS COULDN'T HOLD ME IF THEY TRIED.
MARY! ANY IDEAS--?
UPSTAIRS. GET HIM INTO THE MAIN HOUSE. IT'S HIS PRISON!
UP AND AT 'EM, CAIN.
WHAT ARE YOU--
WHOOSH

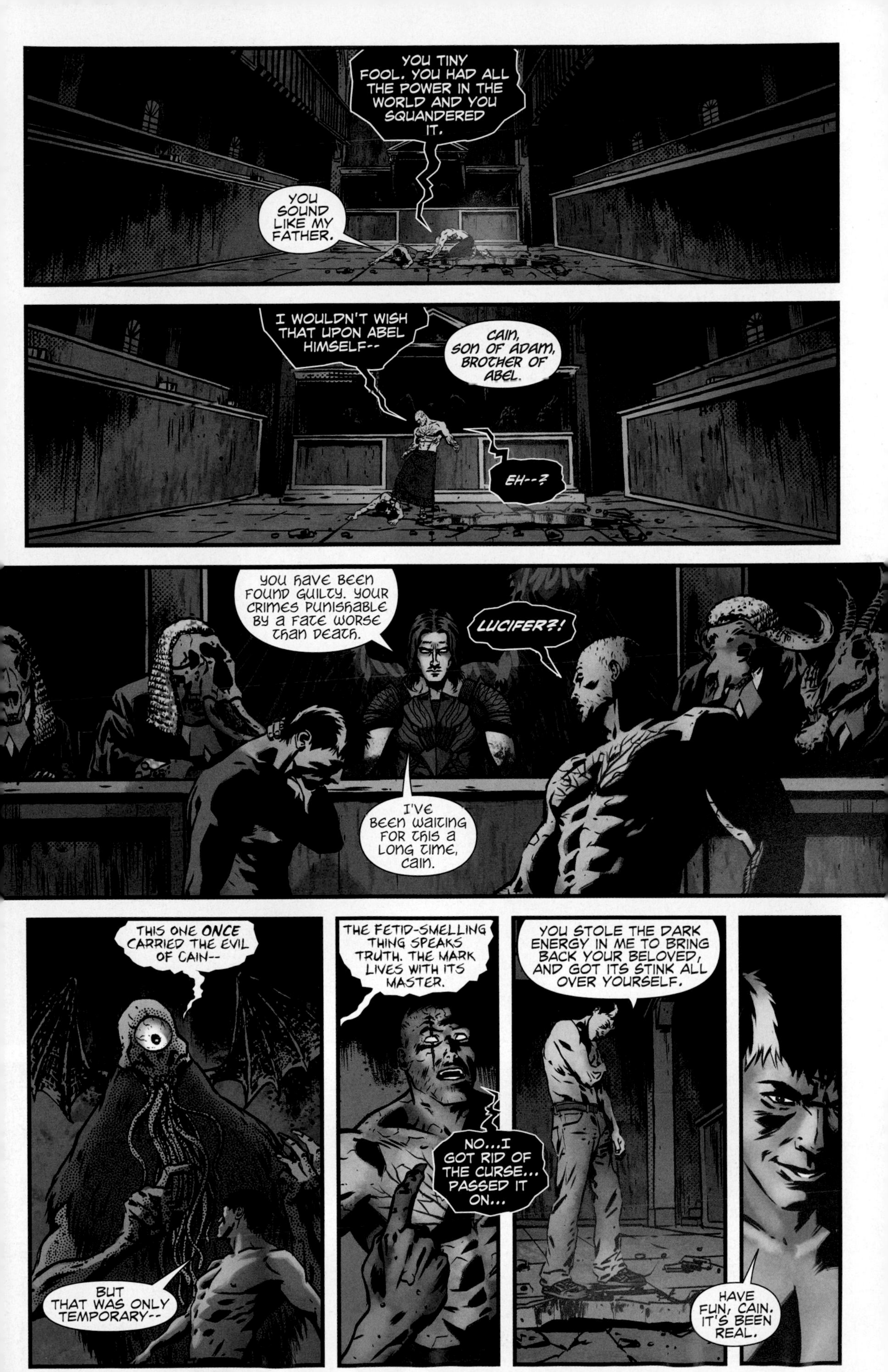
YOU TINY FOOL. YOU HAD ALL THE POWER IN THE WORLD AND YOU SQUANDERED IT.
YOU SOUND LIKE MY FATHER.
I WOULDN'T WISH THAT UPON ABEL HIMSELF--
CAIN, SON OF ADAM, BROTHER OF ABEL.
EH--?
YOU HAVE BEEN FOUND GUILTY. YOUR CRIMES PUNISHABLE BY A FATE WORSE THAN DEATH.
LUCIFER?!
I'VE BEEN WAITING FOR THIS A LONG TIME, CAIN.
THIS ONE ONCE CARRIED THE EVIL OF CAIN--
BUT THAT WAS ONLY TEMPORARY--
THE FETID-SMELLING THING SPEAKS TRUTH. THE MARK LIVES WITH ITS MASTER.
NO...I GOT RID OF THE CURSE... PASSED IT ON...
YOU STOLE THE DARK ENERGY IN ME TO BRING BACK YOUR BELOVED, AND GOT ITS STINK ALL OVER YOURSELF.
HAVE FUN, CAIN. IT'S BEEN REAL.

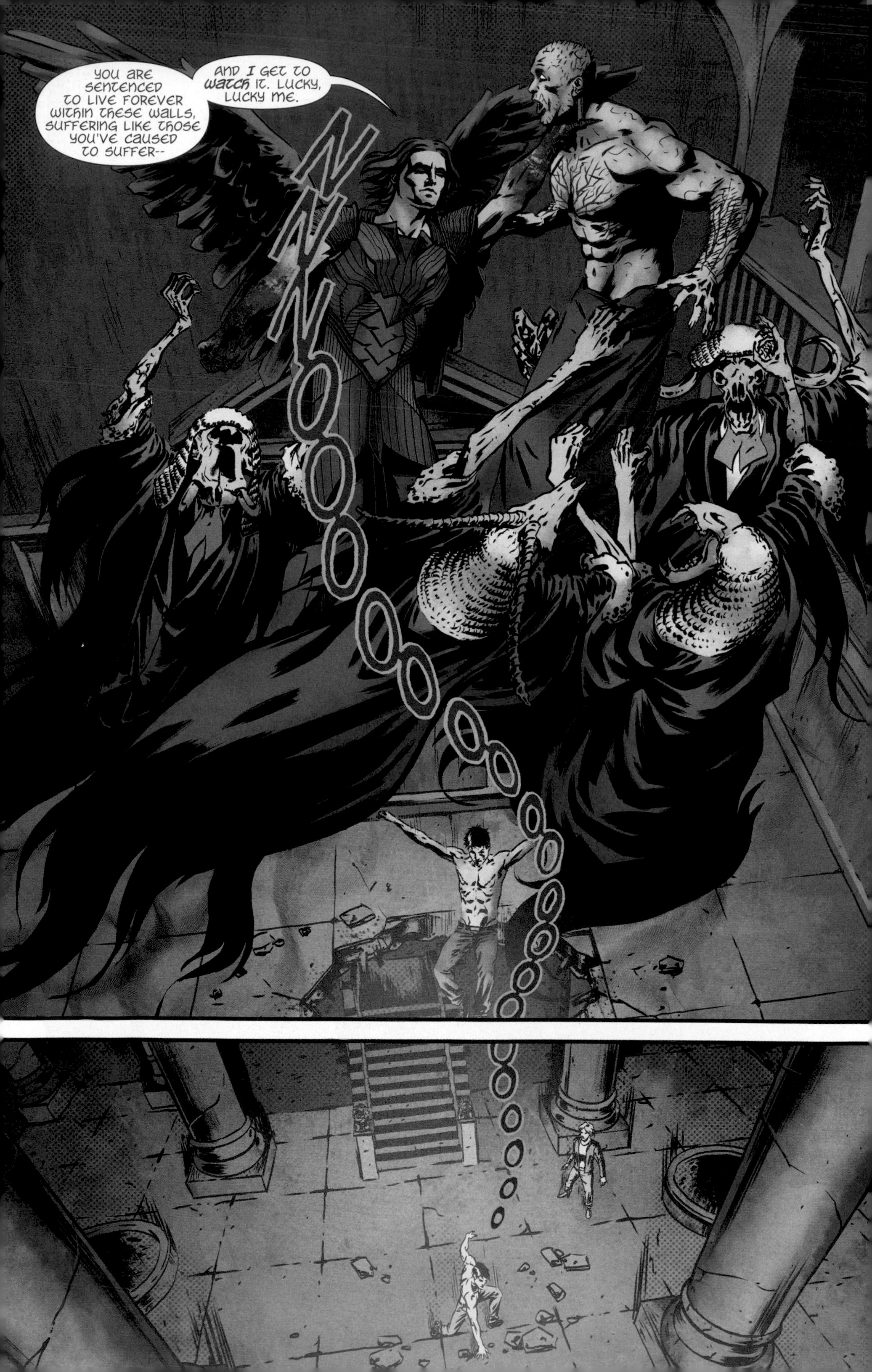
YOU ARE SENTENCED TO LIVE FOREVER WITHIN THESE WALLS, SUFFERING LIKE THOSE YOU'VE CAUSED TO SUFFER--
AND I GET TO WATCH IT. LUCKY, LUCKY ME.
NNNOOOOOOOOOOOOOOOOOOOO

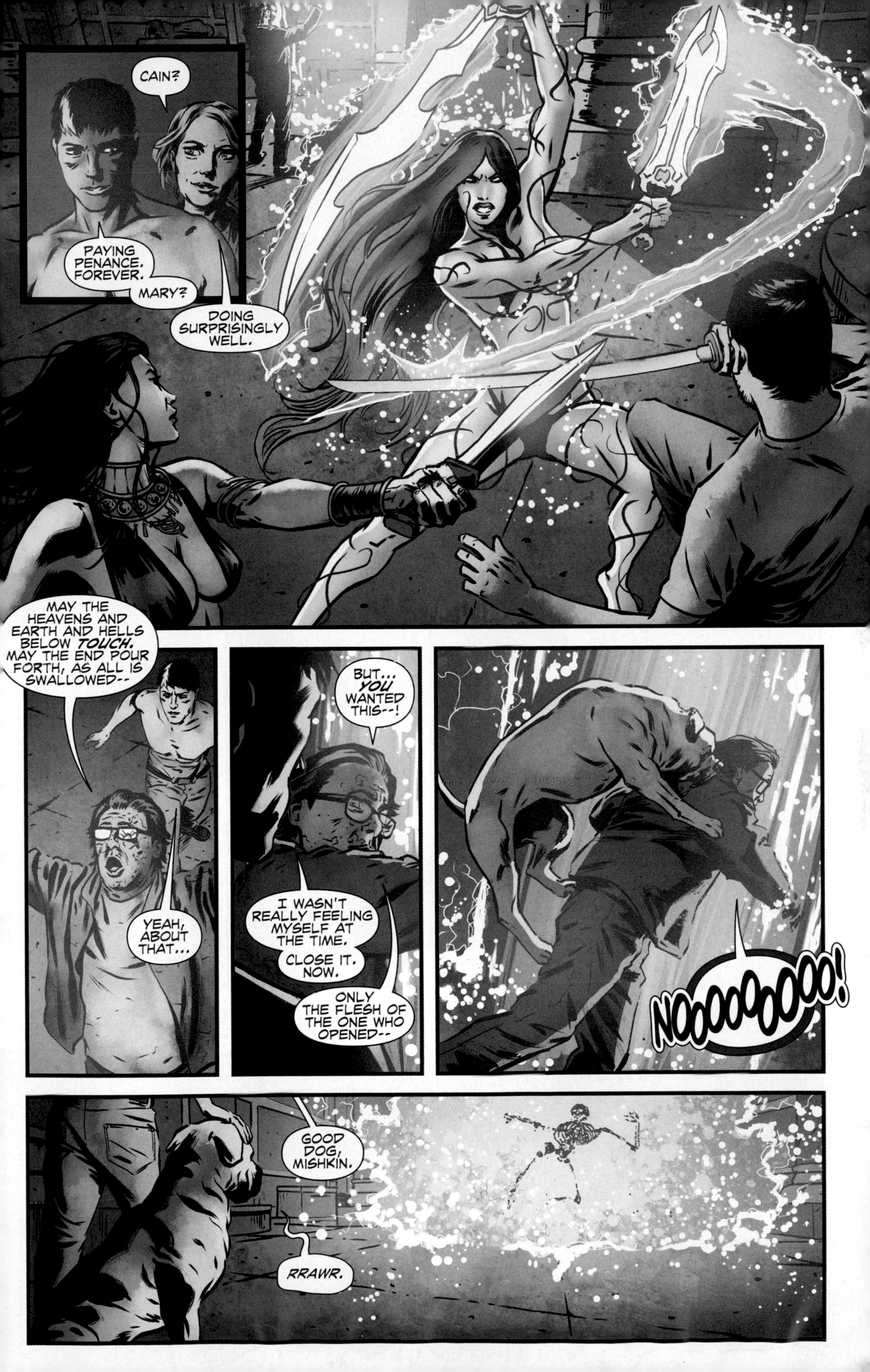
CAIN?
PAYING PENANCE. FOREVER.
MARY?
DOING SURPRISINGLY WELL.
MAY THE HEAVENS AND EARTH AND HELLS BELOW TOUCH. MAY THE END POUR FORTH, AS ALL IS SWALLOWED--
YEAH, ABOUT THAT...
BUT... YOU WANTED THIS--!
I WASN'T REALLY FEELING MYSELF AT THE TIME.
CLOSE IT. NOW.
ONLY THE FLESH OF THE ONE WHO OPENED--
NOOOOOOOOO!
GOOD DOG, MISHKIN.
RRAWR.

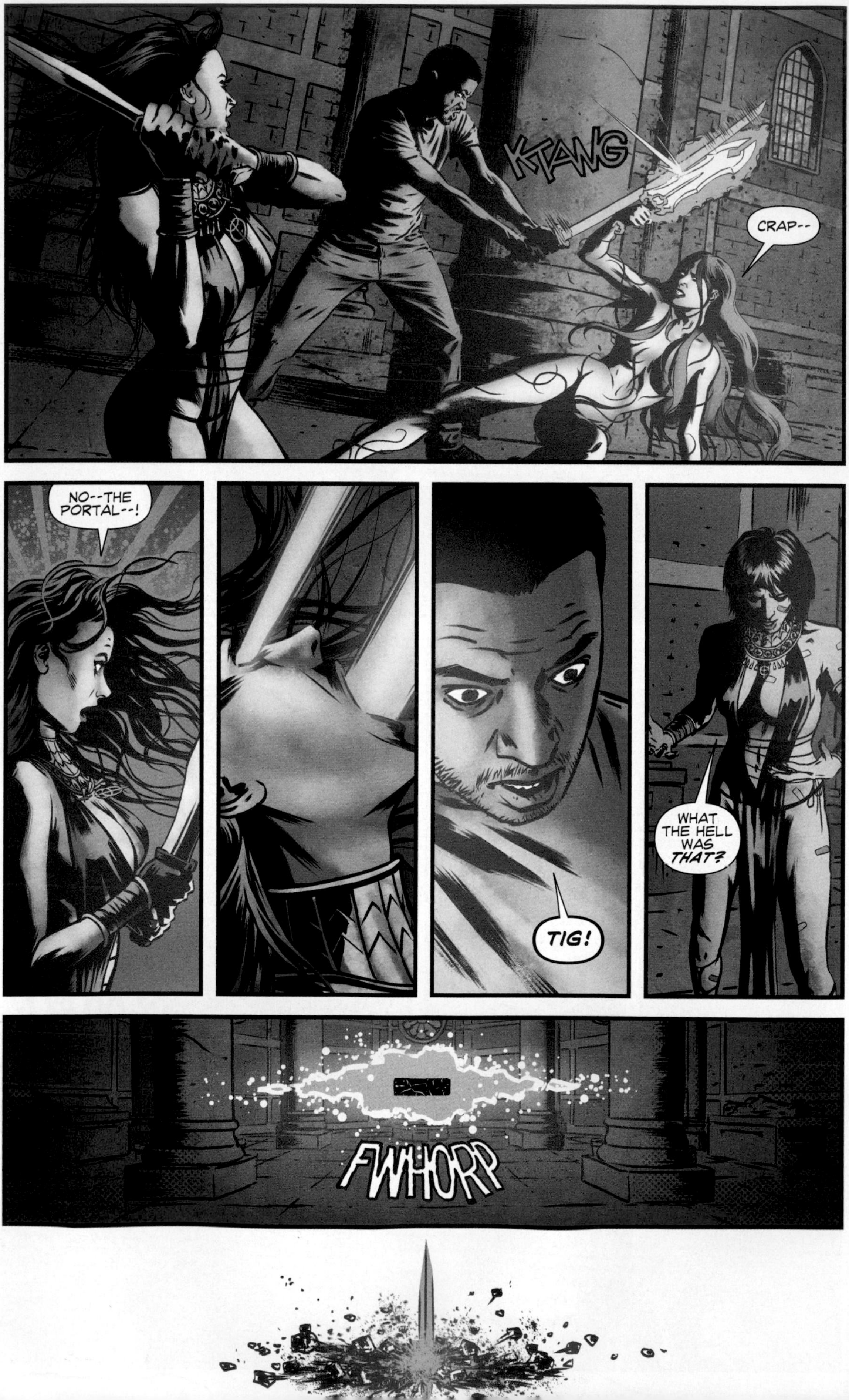
KTANG
CRAP--
NO--THE PORTAL--!
TIG!
WHAT THE HELL WAS THAT?
FWHORP

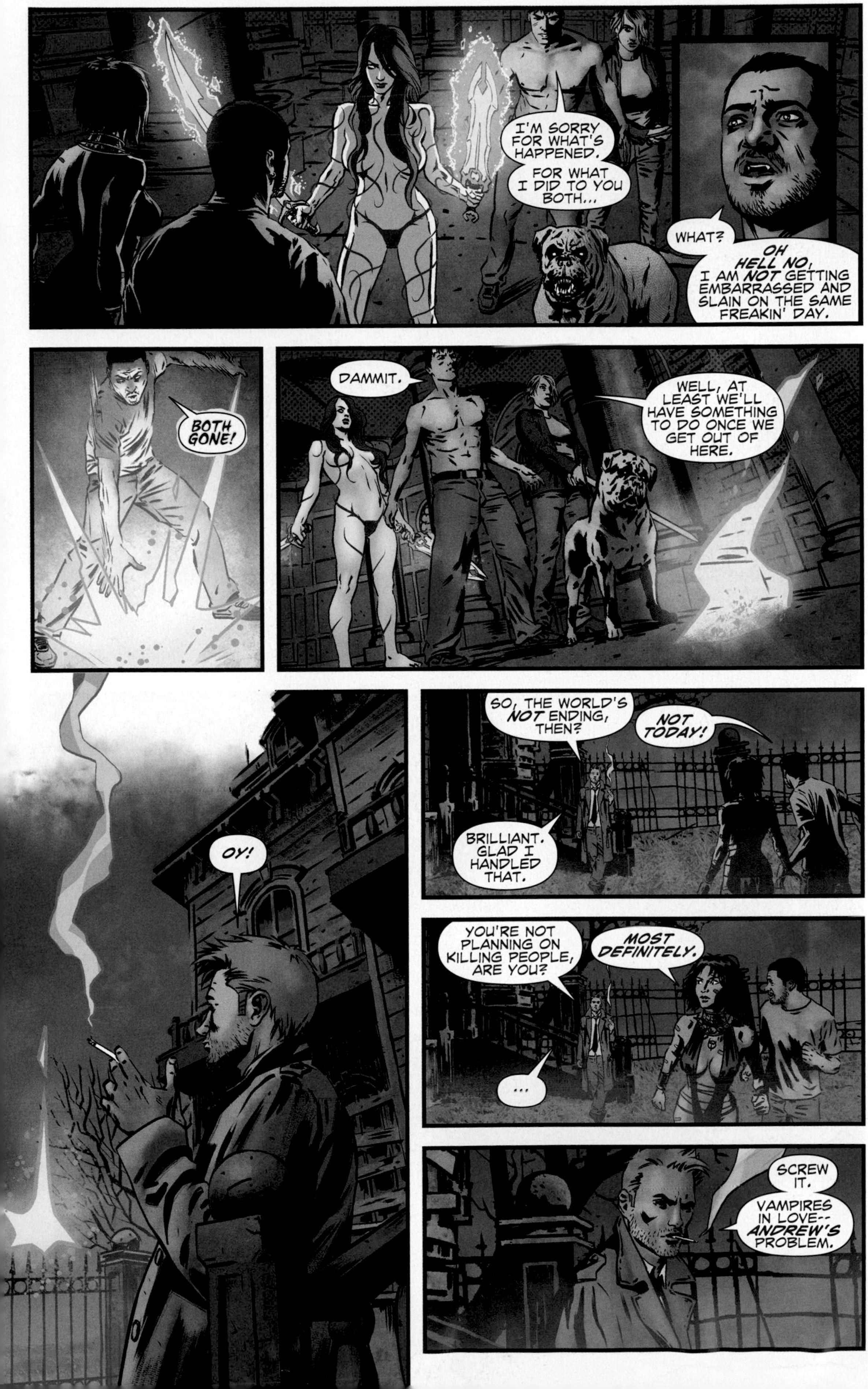
I'M SORRY FOR WHAT'S HAPPENED.
FOR WHAT I DID TO YOU BOTH...
WHAT?
OH HELL NO, I AM NOT GETTING EMBARRASSED AND SLAIN ON THE SAME FREAKIN' DAY.
BOTH GONE!
DAMMIT.
WELL, AT LEAST WE'LL HAVE SOMETHING TO DO ONCE WE GET OUT OF HERE.
OY!
SO, THE WORLD'S NOT ENDING, THEN?
NOT TODAY!
BRILLIANT. GLAD I HANDLED THAT.
YOU'RE NOT PLANNING ON KILLING PEOPLE, ARE YOU?
MOST DEFINITELY.
...
SCREW IT.
VAMPIRES IN LOVE-- ANDREW'S PROBLEM.

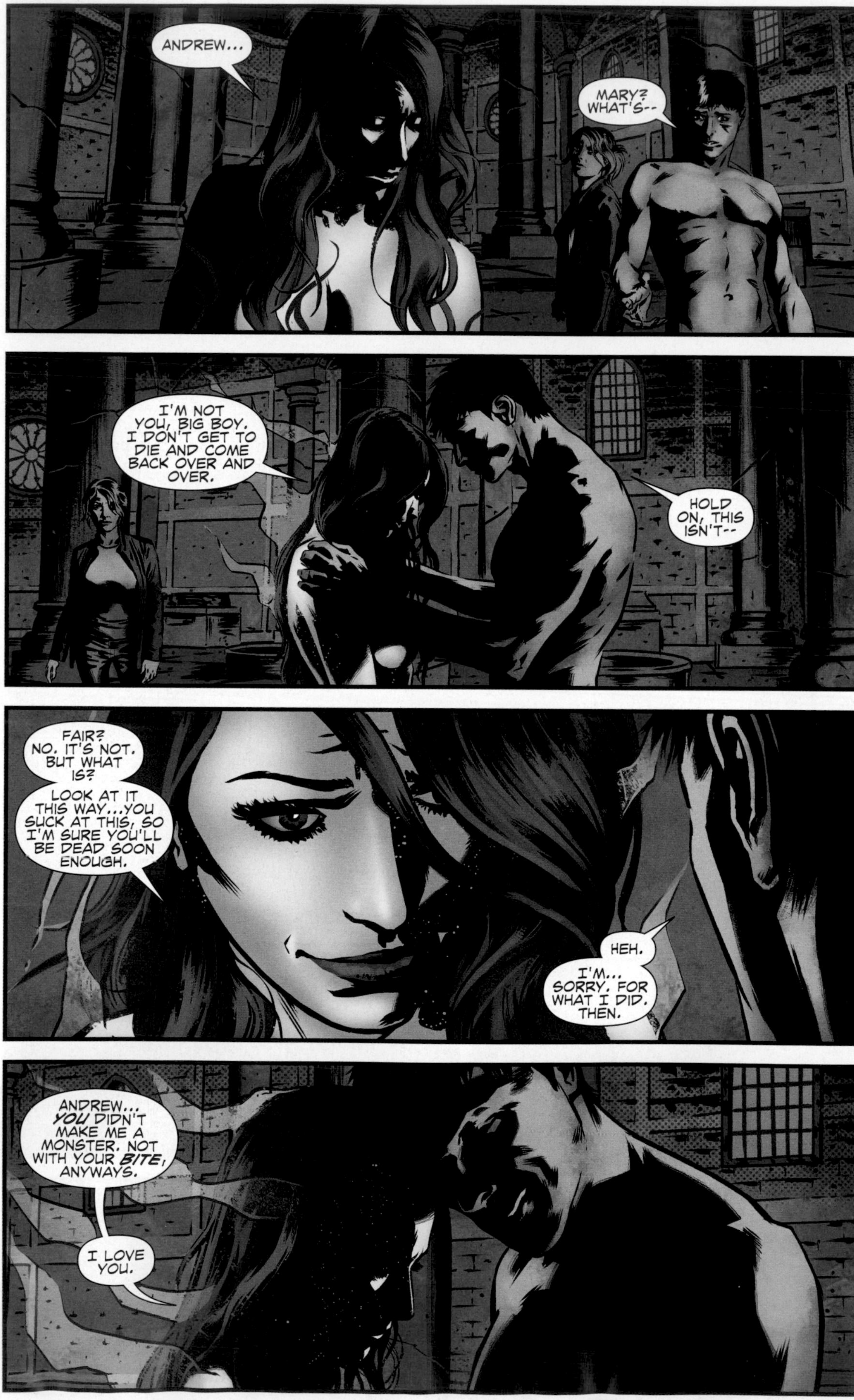
ANDREW...
MARY? WHAT'S--
I'M NOT YOU, BIG BOY. I DON'T GET TO DIE AND COME BACK OVER AND OVER.
HOLD ON, THIS ISN'T--
FAIR? NO. IT'S NOT. BUT WHAT IS?
LOOK AT IT THIS WAY...YOU SUCK AT THIS, SO I'M SURE YOU'LL BE DEAD SOON ENOUGH.
HEH.
I'M... SORRY. FOR WHAT I DID. THEN.
ANDREW... YOU DIDN'T MAKE ME A MONSTER. NOT WITH YOUR BITE, ANYWAYS.
I LOVE YOU.

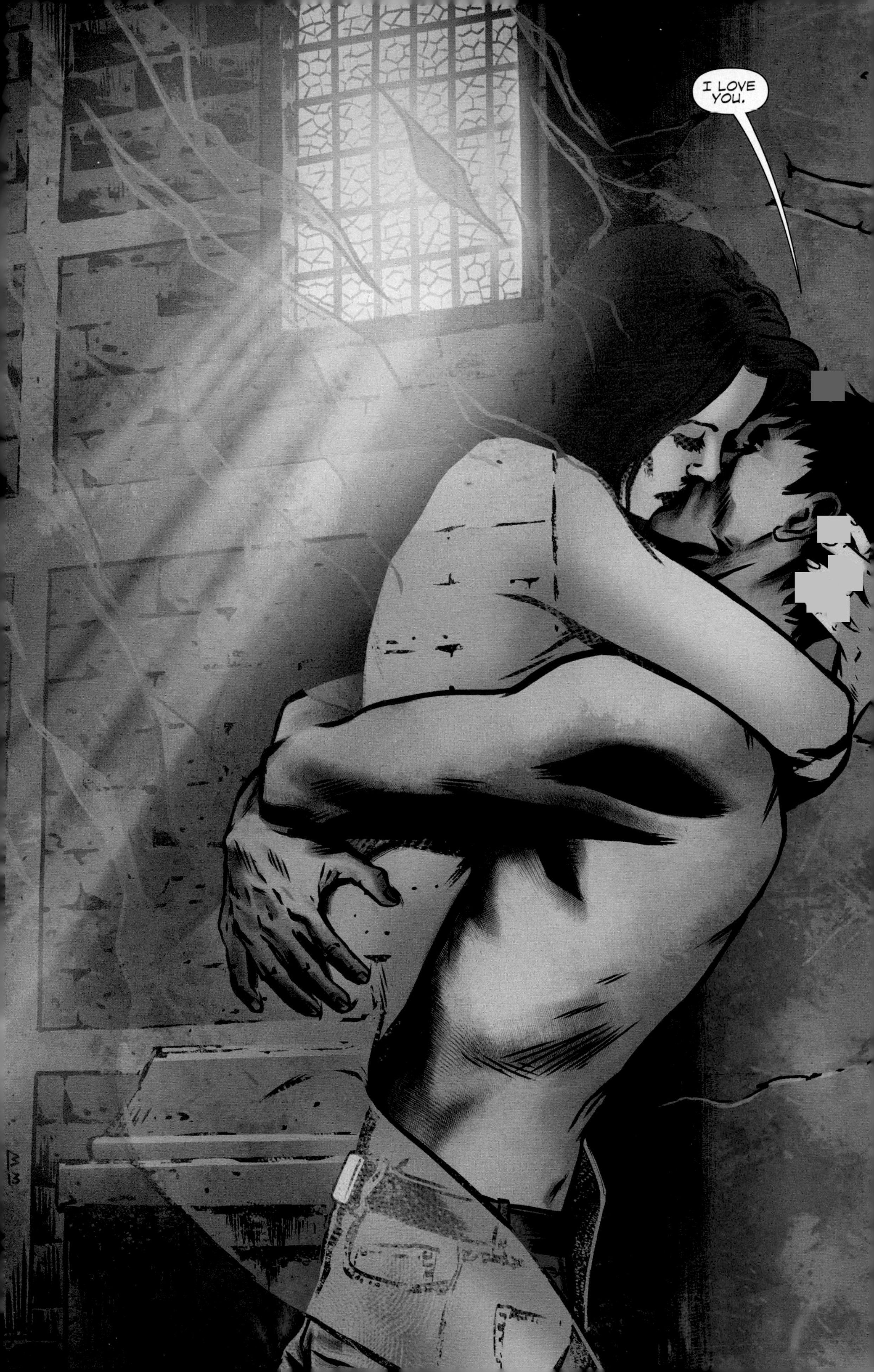
I LOVE YOU.

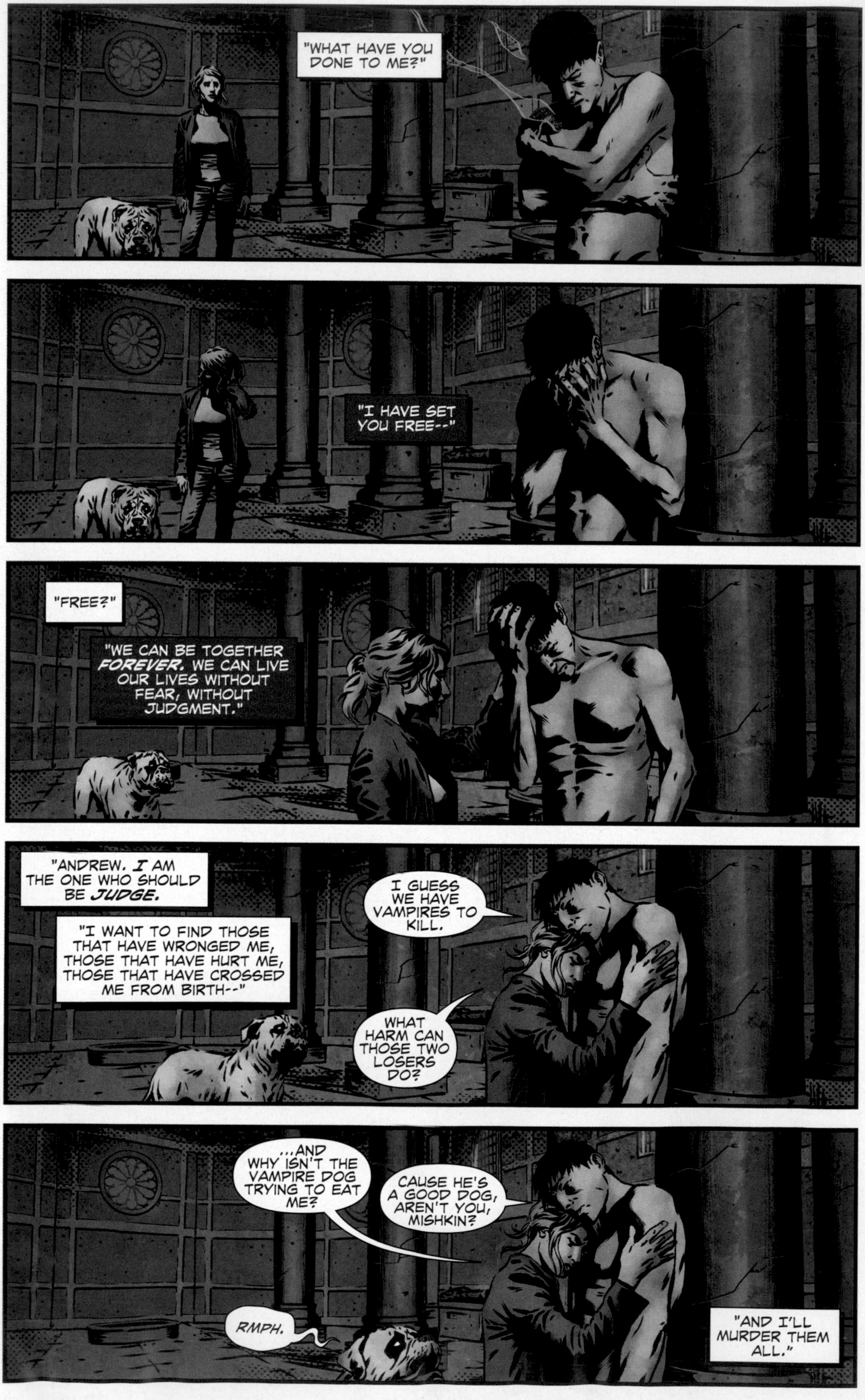
"WHAT HAVE YOU DONE TO ME?"
"I HAVE SET YOU FREE--"
"FREE?"
"WE CAN BE TOGETHER FOREVER. WE CAN LIVE OUR LIVES WITHOUT FEAR, WITHOUT JUDGMENT."
"ANDREW. I AM THE ONE WHO SHOULD BE JUDGE.
"I WANT TO FIND THOSE THAT HAVE WRONGED ME, THOSE THAT HAVE HURT ME, THOSE THAT HAVE CROSSED ME FROM BIRTH--"
I GUESS WE HAVE VAMPIRES TO KILL.
WHAT HARM CAN THOSE TWO LOSERS DO?
...AND WHY ISN'T THE VAMPIRE DOG TRYING TO EAT ME?
CAUSE HE'S A GOOD DOG, AREN'T YOU, MISHKIN?
RMPH.
"AND I'LL MURDER THEM ALL."

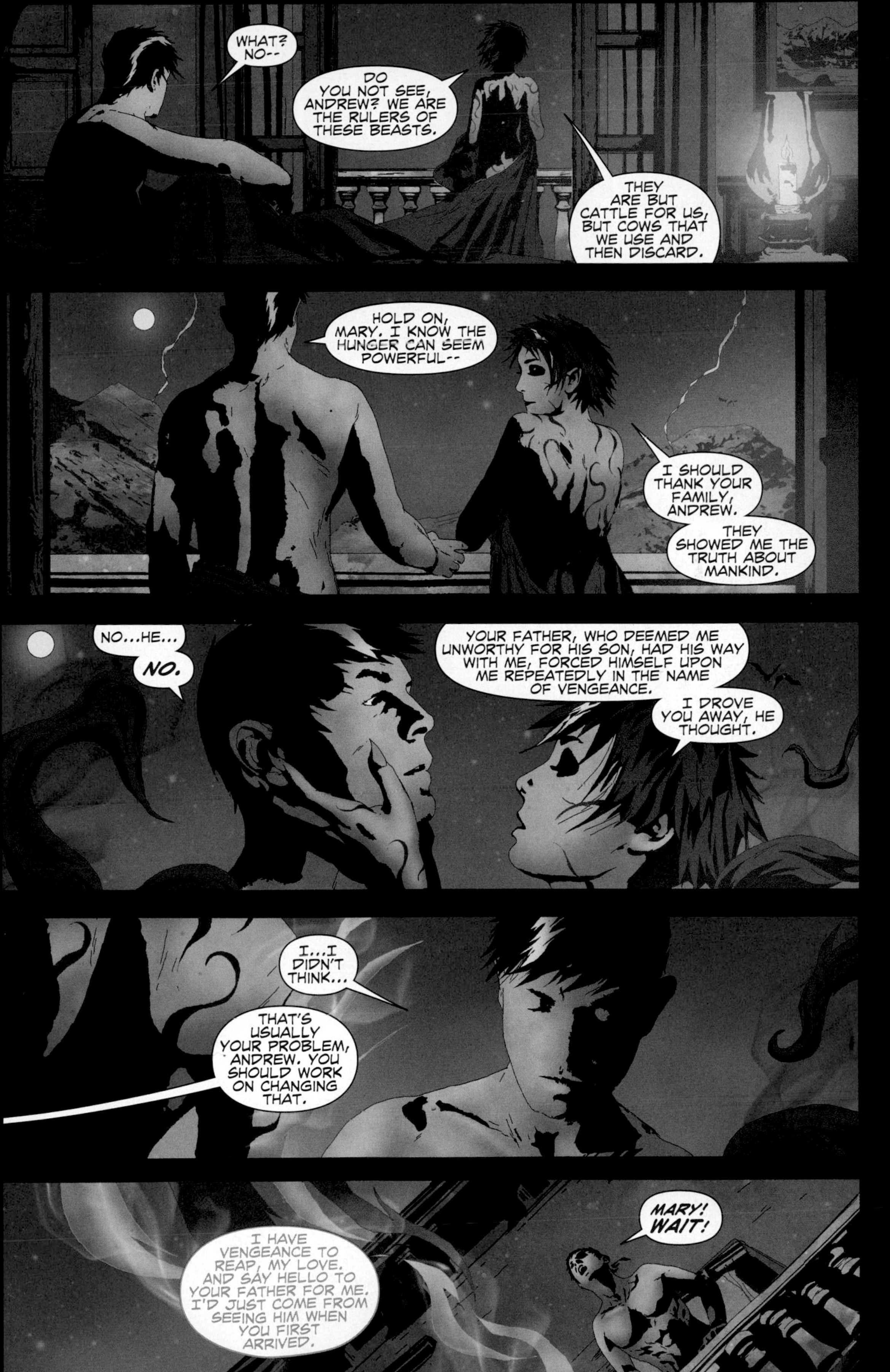
WHAT? NO--
DO YOU NOT SEE, ANDREW? WE ARE THE RULERS OF THESE BEASTS.
THEY ARE BUT CATTLE FOR US, BUT COWS THAT WE USE AND THEN DISCARD.
HOLD ON, MARY. I KNOW THE HUNGER CAN SEEM POWERFUL--
I SHOULD THANK YOUR FAMILY, ANDREW.
THEY SHOWED ME THE TRUTH ABOUT MANKIND.
NO...HE... NO.
YOUR FATHER, WHO DEEMED ME UNWORTHY FOR HIS SON, HAD HIS WAY WITH ME, FORCED HIMSELF UPON ME REPEATEDLY IN THE NAME OF VENGEANCE.
I DROVE YOU AWAY, HE THOUGHT.
I...I DIDN'T THINK...
THAT'S USUALLY YOUR PROBLEM, ANDREW. YOU SHOULD WORK ON CHANGING THAT.
I HAVE VENGEANCE TO REAP, MY LOVE. AND SAY HELLO TO YOUR FATHER FOR ME. I'D JUST COME FROM SEEING HIM WHEN YOU FIRST ARRIVED.
MARY! WAIT!

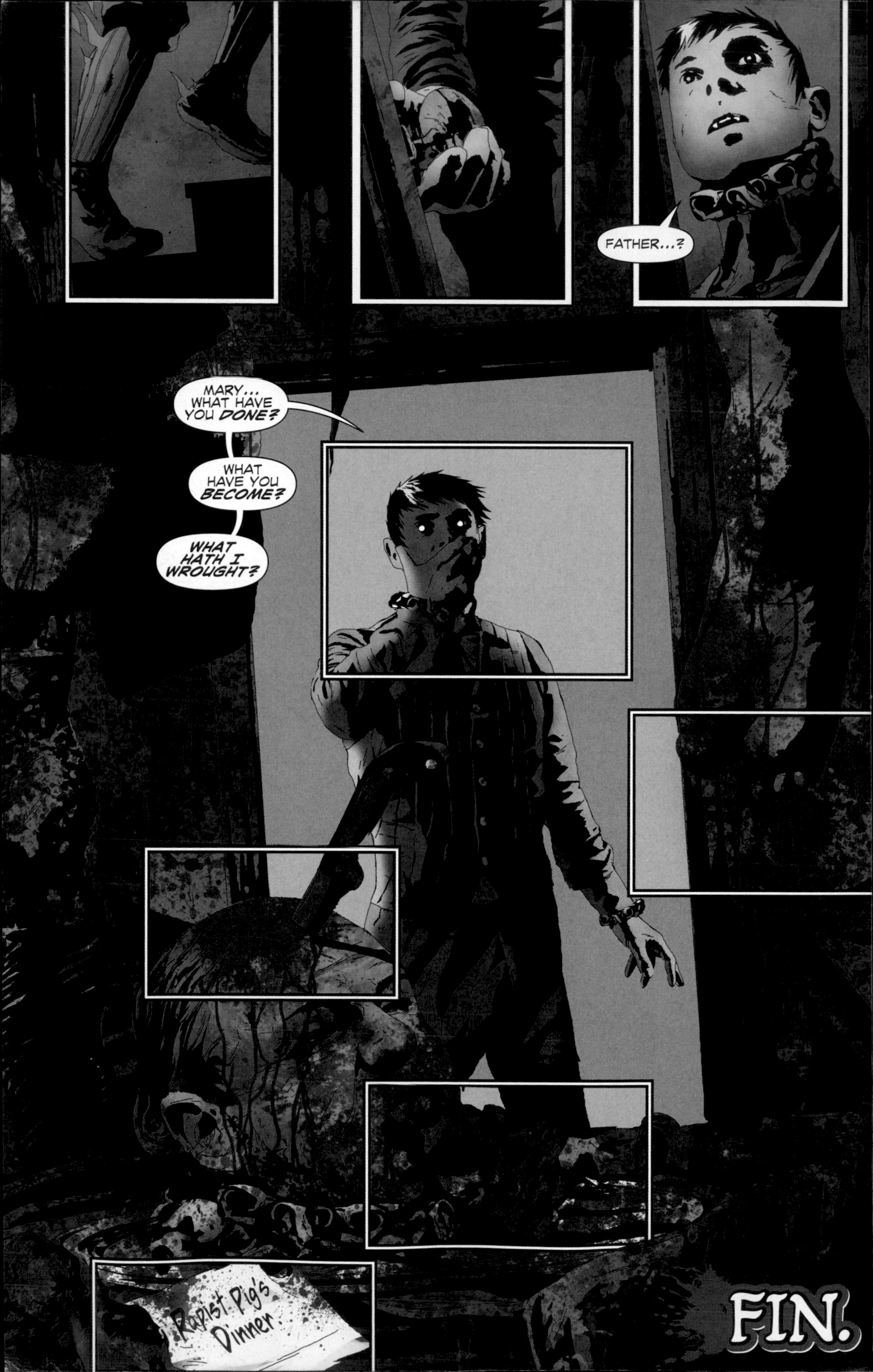
FATHER...?
MARY... WHAT HAVE YOU DONE?
WHAT HAVE YOU BECOME?
WHAT HATH I WROUGHT?
Rapist Pig's Dinner
FIN.

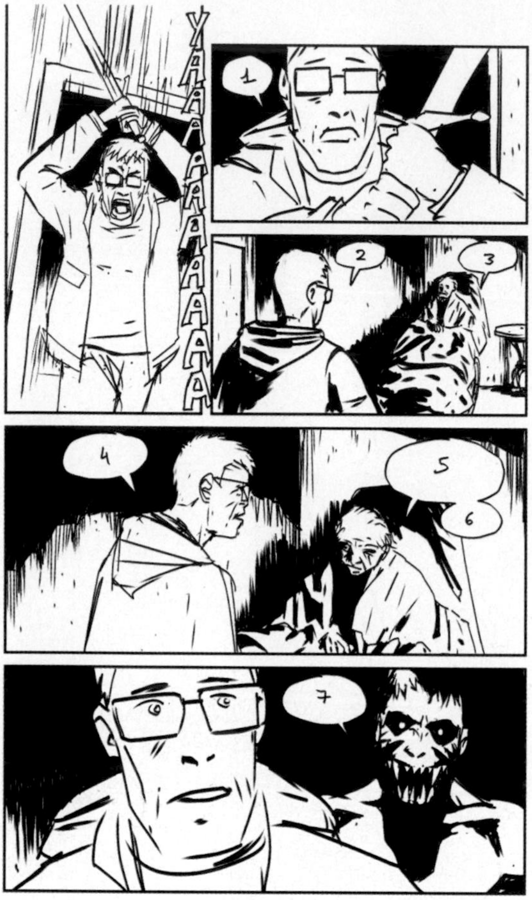
1
2
3
4
5
6
7

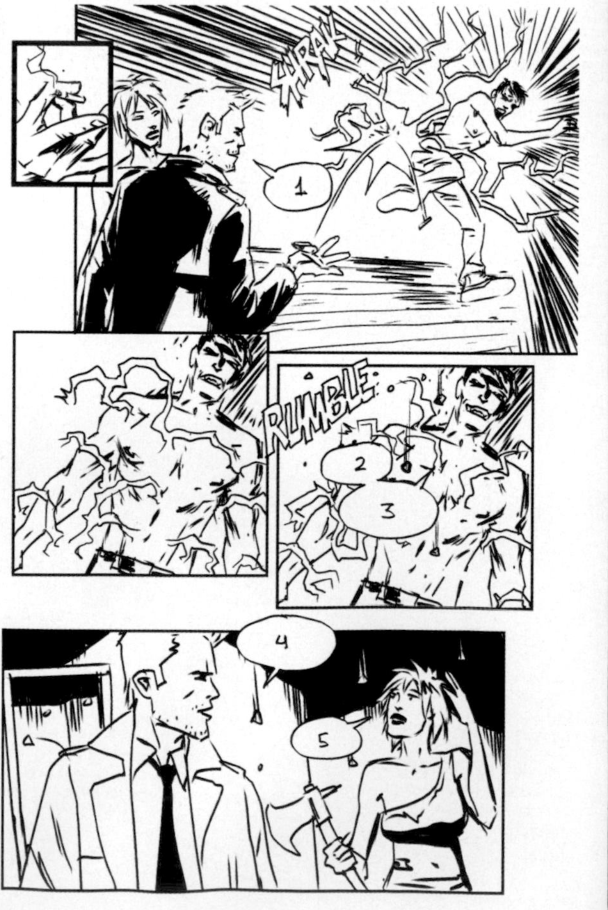
1
RUMBLE
2
3
4
5

Editor's note: Fernando Blanco's initial layout roughs are fully rendered, with many details in place, and sometimes only figures need to be fleshed out. He also considers the balloon placements, which is the sort of detail that will make an editor fall platonically in love with you without fail, every time. —CC

I, VAMPIRE
ISSUE #18 AND #19 LAYOUTS BY FERNANDO BLANCO

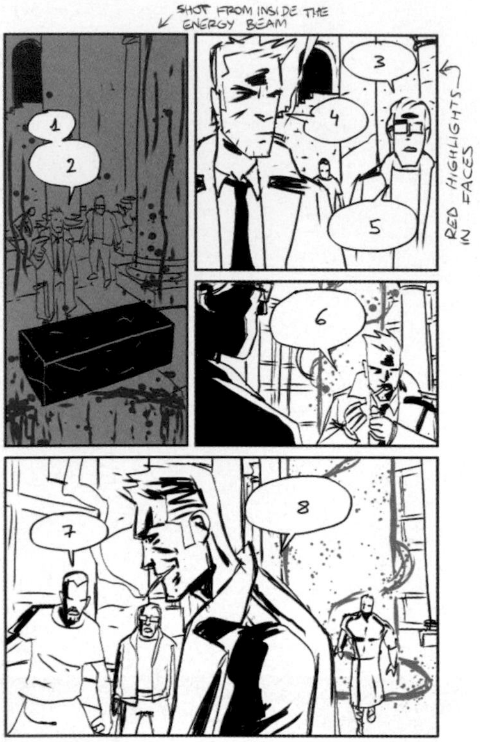
SHOT FROM INSIDE THE ENERGY BEAM
RED HIGHLIGHTS IN FACES

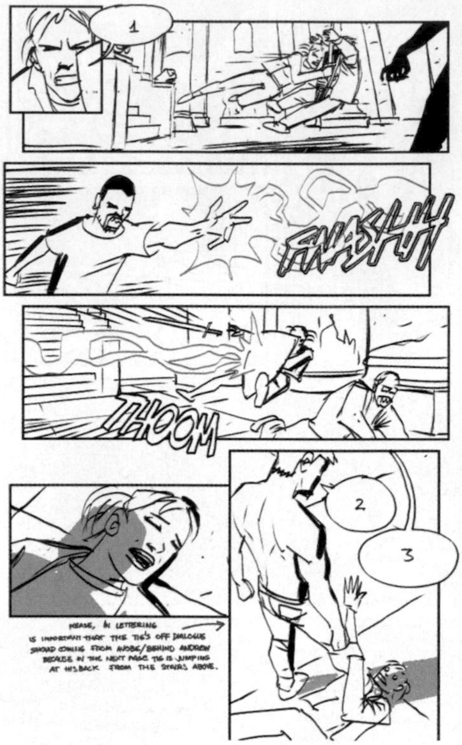
THOOM
PLEASE, IN LETTERING IS IMPORTANT THAT THE TIG'S OFF DIALOGUE SHOULD COMING FROM ABOBE/BEHIND ANDREW BECAUSE IN THE NEXT PAGE TIG IS JUMPING AT HIS BACK FROM THE STAIRS ABOVE.

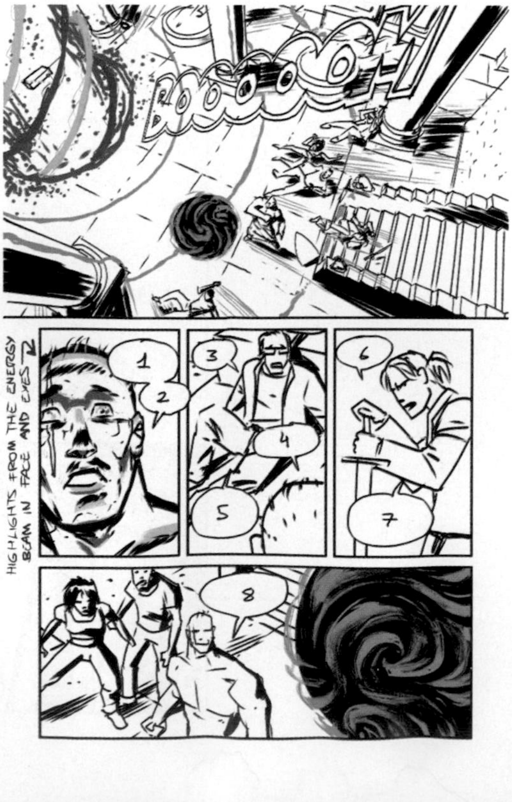
HIGHLIGHTS FROM THE ENERGY BEAM IN FACE AND EYES

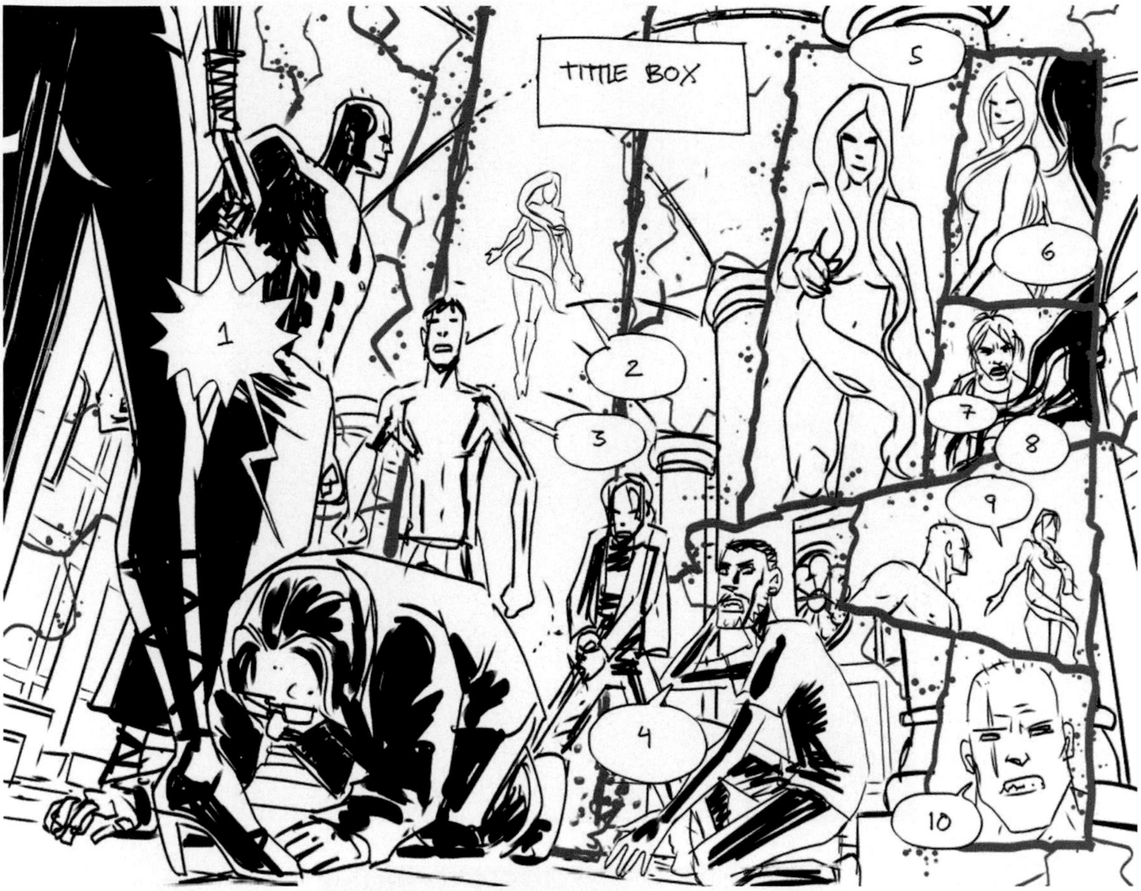
TITTLE BOX
1
2
3
4
5
6
7
8
9
10

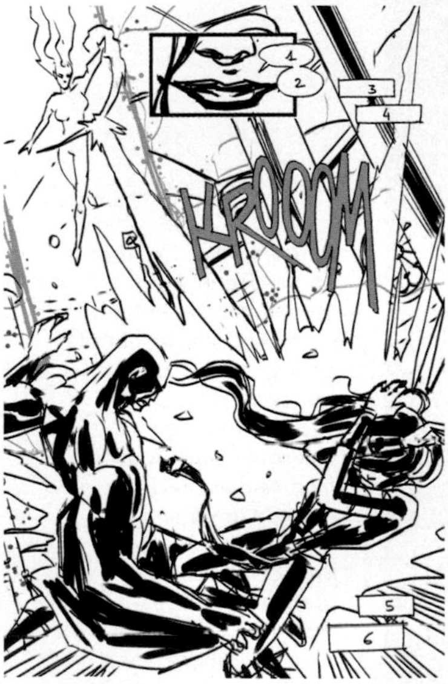
1
2
3
4
KROOOM
5
6

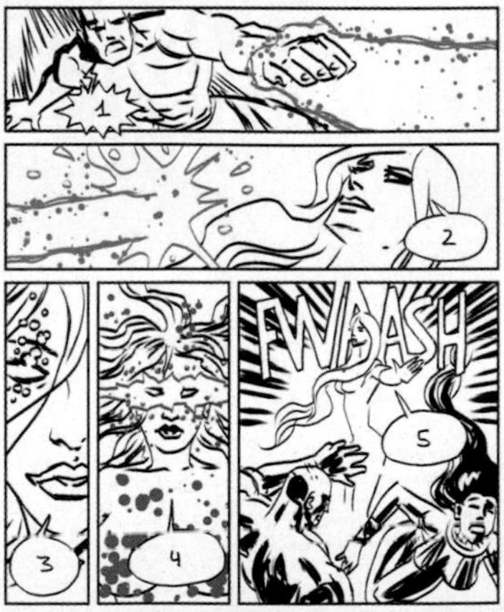
1
2
3
4
FWOOSH
5
6

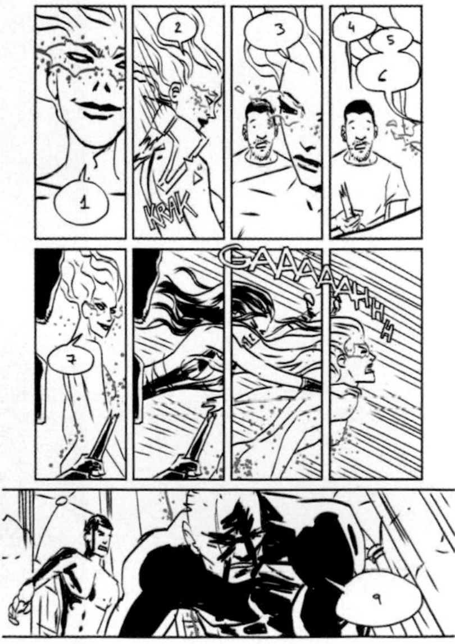
1
2
KRAK
3
4
5
6
GAAAAAHHHH
7
9

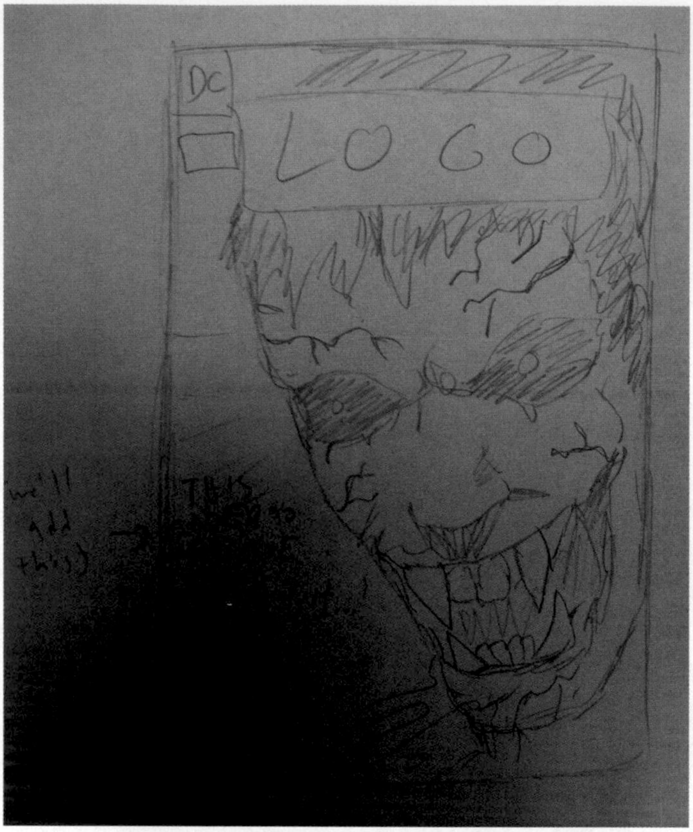

DC
LOGO

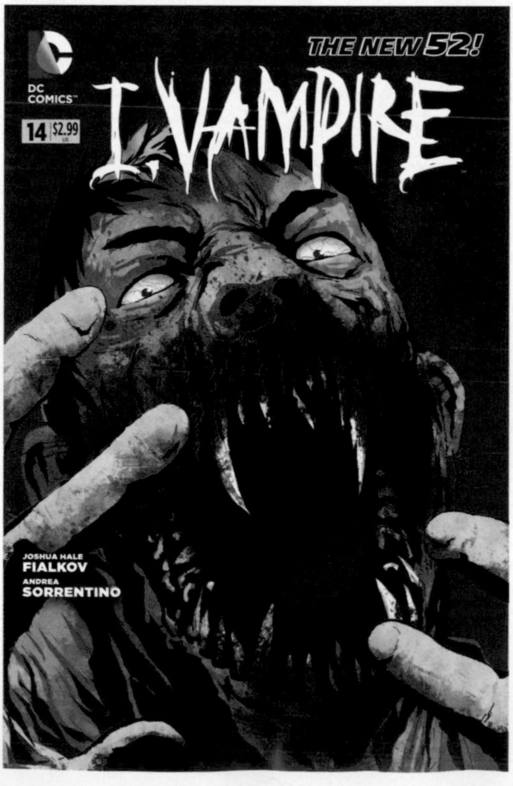

DC COMICS
THE NEW 52!
14 $2.99 US
I, VAMPIRE
JOSHUA HALE FIALKOV
ANDREA SORRENTINO

Editor's note: I whipped up this frankly quite terrible cover sketch to show Andrea the simple concept I had in mind for issue #14's cover, showcasing the awesome Dark Andrew face Andrea had created in issue #12. Predictably, Andrea's final cover was so grotesquely awesome that the corny cover copy seen here wasn't at all necessary. —CC

I, VAMPIRE #15 cover sketches by Guillem March

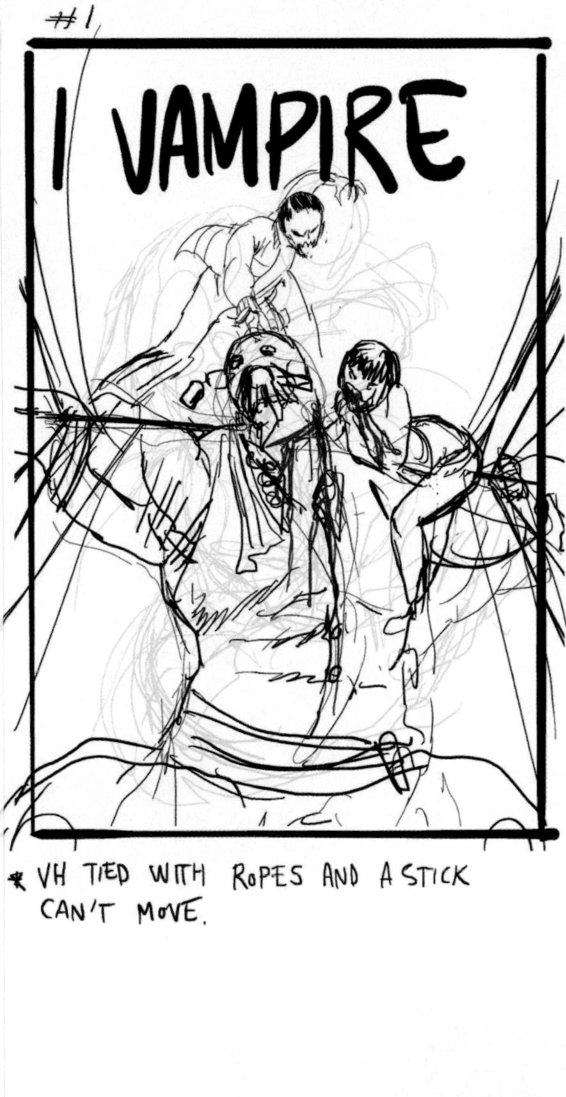
#1
I VAMPIRE

* VH TIED WITH ROPES AND A STICK CAN'T MOVE.

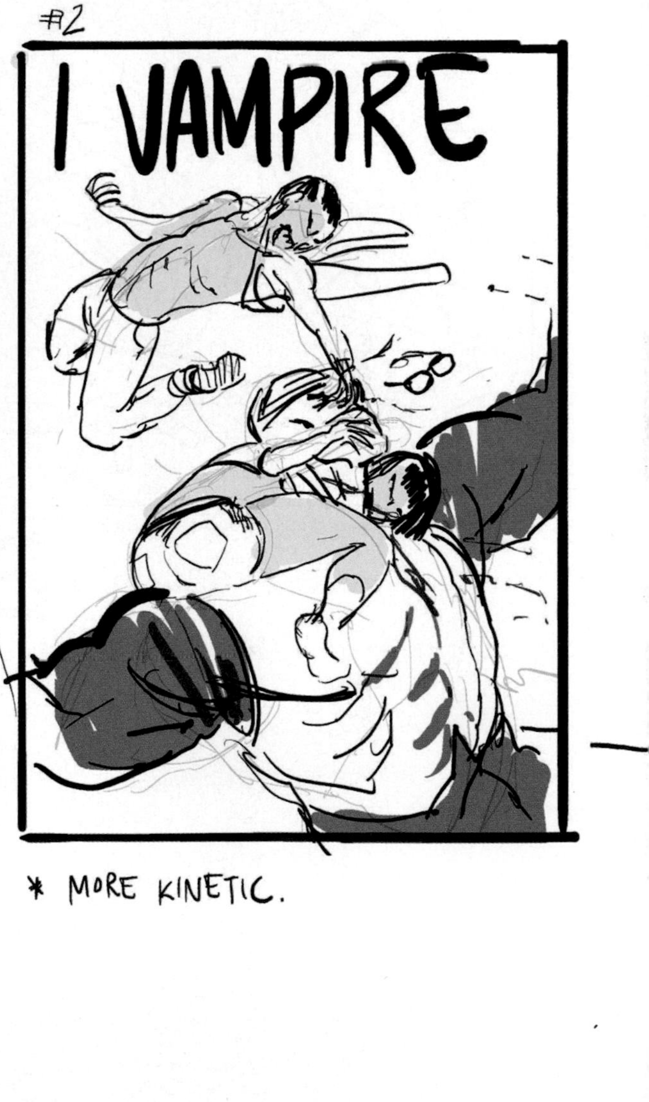
#2
I VAMPIRE

* MORE KINETIC.

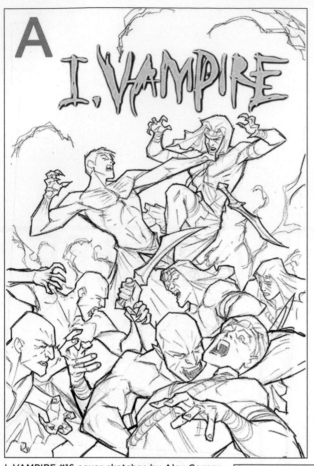

I, VAMPIRE #16 cover sketches by Alex Garner

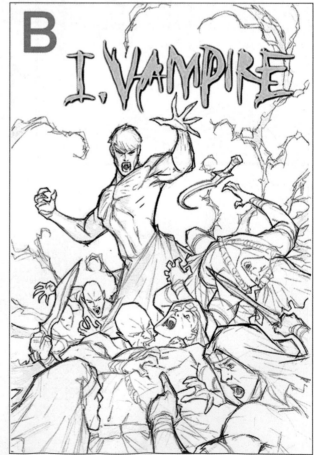

I, VAMPIRE #17
cover sketch and inks
by Andrea Sorrentino

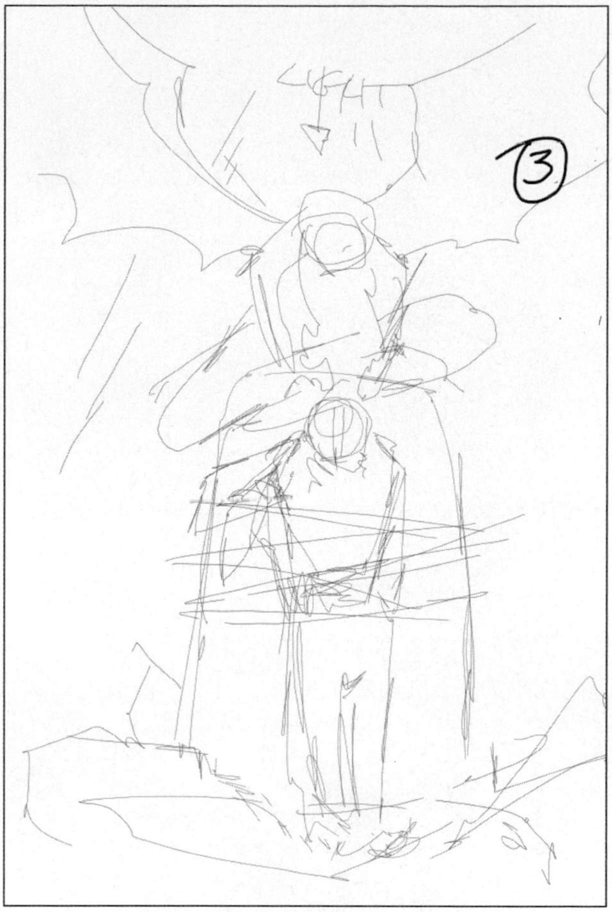
LIGHT
3

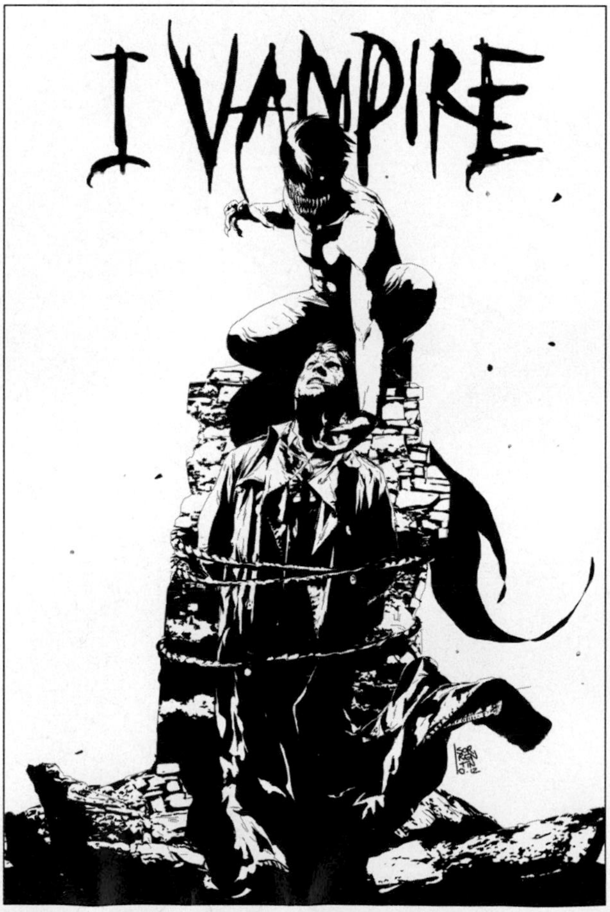
I VAMPIRE

Full I, VAMPIRE #19 cover by Andrea Sorrentino & Marcelo Maiolo

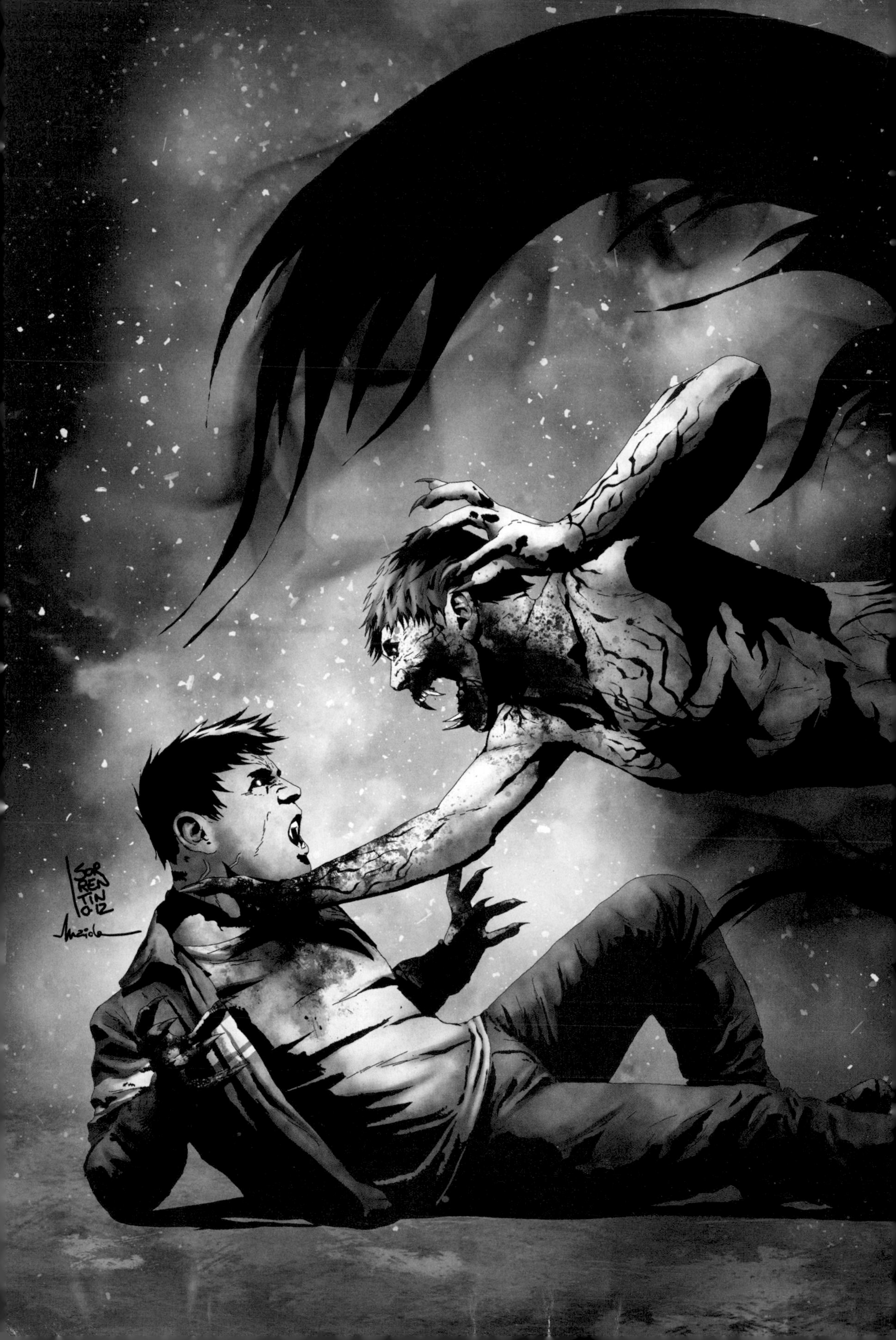
SOR
REN
TIN
O12

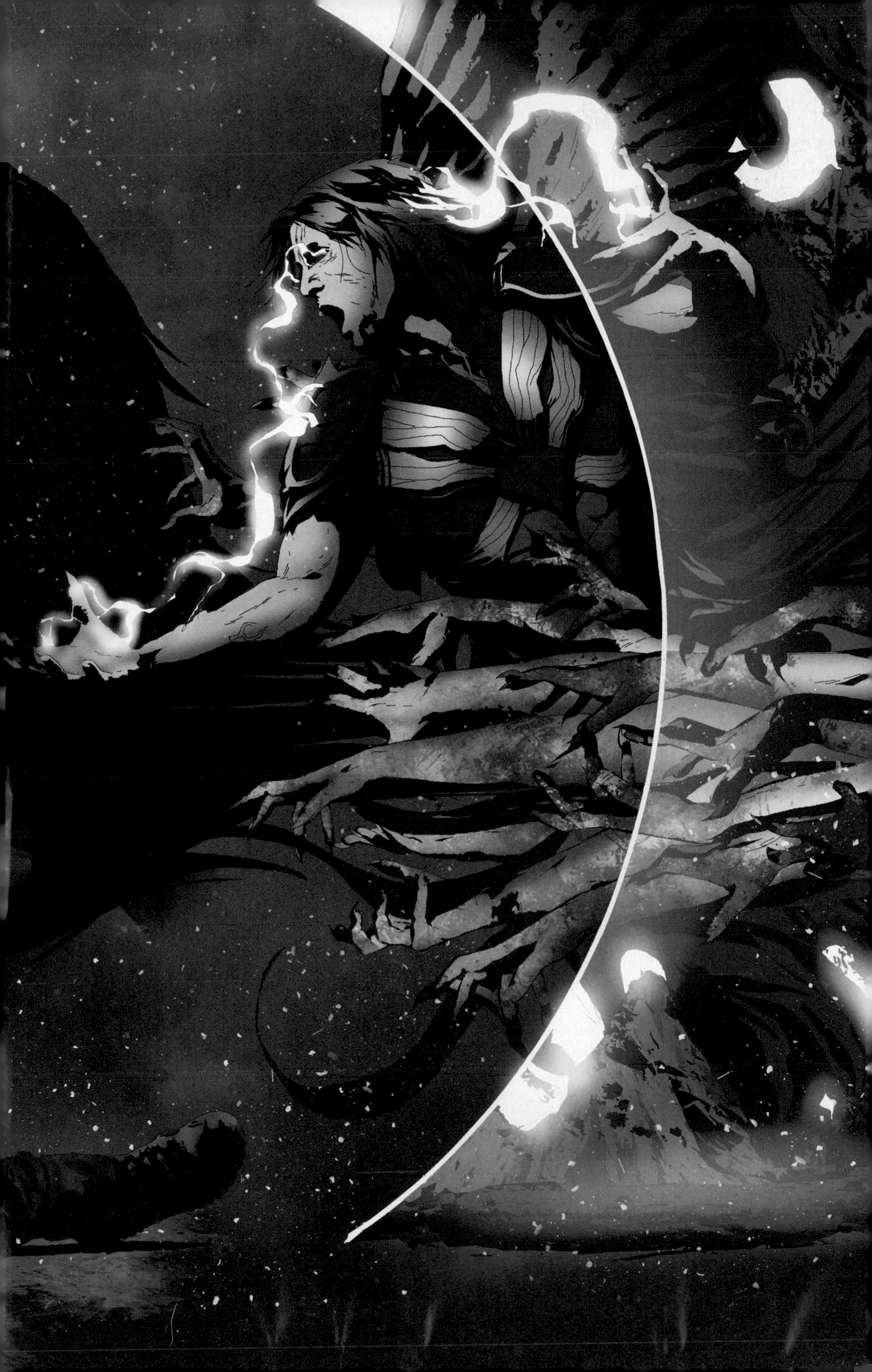

DC COMICS™

"SWAMP THING is a series that you need to be reading, no questions asked."
—IGN

"A thoughtful, well-executed new take on a great character."
—PUBLISHERS WEEKLY

START AT THE BEGINNING!

SWAMP THING VOLUME 1: RAISE THEM BONES

I, VAMPIRE VOLUME 1: TAINTED LOVE

DEMON KNIGHTS VOLUME 1: SEVEN AGAINST THE DARK

DC UNIVERSE PRESENTS VOLUME 1: FEATURING DEADMAN & CHALLENGERS OF THE UNKNOWN

SCOTT **SNYDER**   YANICK **PAQUETTE**   MARCO **RUDY**